BROWN WARRIORS OF THE RAJ
RECRUITMENT AND THE MECHANICS OF COMMAND IN THE SEPOY ARMY, 1859–1913

BROWN WARRIORS OF THE RAJ

RECRUITMENT AND THE MECHANICS OF COMMAND IN THE SEPOY ARMY, 1859–1913

KAUSHIK ROY

MANOHAR
2008

First published 2008

© Kaushik Roy, 2008

ISBN 81-7304-754-5

Published by

Ajay Kumar Jain for
Manohar Publishers & Distributors
4753/23 Ansari Road, Daryaganj
New Delhi 110 002

Typeset at

Digigrafics
New Delhi 110 049

Printed at

Lordson Publishers Pvt. Ltd.
Delhi 110 007

*In
Memory
of
My Father*

Contents

Preface

This book is the modified version of my Ph.D. titled 'The Colonial Indian Army: Recruitment and Command Mechanism, 1859-1913', submitted at the Centre for Historical Studies, School of Social Sciences, Jawaharlal Nehru University at New Delhi in 2000. The origin of this thesis can be traced to my childhood interest in matters military. Before going to sleep, my father would tell me stories about the German *Blitzkrieg* and the Japanese advance in Singapore. I little realized that, from these bedtime stories, I would develop a strong interest which in turn would shape my career.

I learnt the basics of history at Presidency College especially from Prof. R.K. Ray and Prof. S. Chakrobarty. While doing my Ph.D. I went through cycles of depression and frustration. I am indebted to my supervisor for his constant encouragement and his generosity in accepting my idiosyncratic behaviour. I am thankful to the late Professor P.S. Gupta for reading parts of my drafts. And I greatly appreciate the late Professor Dharma Kumar's affectionate help during the early stages of the research.

This thesis would not have been possible without the moral and financial support from my parents and the ICHR Junior Research Fellowship. For the field trip to London, I am grateful to the Charles Wallace Fund. Then my thanks to Dr Saul David for the fruitful discussion on matters military in his picturesque farm house. I also thank Suhrita for forcing me to complete the thesis as quickly as possible, just as the *Fuehrer* pressurized Manstein to finish the Don operation. I also thank the late Professor Ravinder Kumar, one of my external examiners. I am indebted to Professor Hew Strachan. Besides his comments, I also gained a lot of insight from the discussion which I had with him in 2001 at a pub in eastern London. I also thank Professor Dennis Showalter for encouraging me to publish this thesis. And in the end Pratik for advising me to come up with a better title.

KAUSHIK ROY

Abbreviations

Army Committee	*Proceedings of the army in India Committee 1912* (Simla: Central Govt. Press, 1913)
ADG	Adjutant General
BL	British Library
Bull. Hist. Med.	*Bulletin of the History of Medicine*
CJH	*Canadian Journal of History*
Eden Commission	*Report of the special commission appointed by the Governor General in council to inquire into the organization of the Indian Army* (Simla: Govt. Central Printing Office, 1879)
EHR	*English Historical Review*
FD	Foreign Department
GO	General Orders by the Commander-in-Chief
GoI	Government of India
Hamilton Papers	Private papers of George Hamilton
Hancock Report	*Report of Major General H. Hancock on the organization of the Indian Army,* Cd 2516 (London: HMSO, 1859)
HD	Home Department
IESHR	*Indian Economic and Social History Review*
JAS	*Journal of Asian Studies*
JBS	*Journal of British Studies*
JICH	*Journal of Imperial and Commonwealth History*
JMH	*Journal of Military History*
JRAS	*Journal of the Royal Asiatic Society*
JSAHR	*Journal of the Society for Army Historical Research*
JSS	*Journal of Strategic Studies*
JUSII	*Journal of the United Service Institution of India*
Kitchener Papers	Private papers of Lord Kitchener
MAS	*Modern Asian Studies*
MD	Military Department
MDP	Military Department Proceedings
Military despatches of the Secretary of State	Military despatches of the Secretary of State to the Governor-General in Council
M/F	Microfilm
Military letters from Nepal	Military letters from the Resident at Nepal regarding the Gurkha auxiliary expedition at Lucknow, 1857–9

NAI	National Archives of India
Norman Minutes	Military miscellaneous minutes by Major-General H.W. Norman, 1863–76
OIOC	Oriental and India Office Collection
PP (1867)	*Parliamentary papers, Return East India and native troops*, Commons 500 (1867)
Peel Committee	*Report of the commissioners appointed to inquire into the organization of the Indian Army*, Cd 2515 (London: HMSO, 1859)
PWD	Public Works Department
SIH	*Studies in History*
Supplementary Report	*Papers connected with the reorganization of the army in India supplementary to the report of the army commission*, Cd 2541 (London: HMSO, 1859)
WBSA	West Bengal State Archives
4th Battalion	Digest of services of the 4th Battalion 9th Jat Regiment
8th Bombay Infantry	Historical Records of the 8th Regiment Bombay Infantry, 1768–1893
9th Bombay Regiment	Historical Records of the 9th Bombay Regiment
14th Madras Infantry	Digest of services of the 14th Regiment of the Madras Infantry, 1775–1913
28th Bombay Regiment	Lieutenant (Adjutant) Carter, Record Book of 28th Regiment Bombay Infantry, 1846–1913
44th Merwara Infantry	Digest of services of the 44th Merwara Infantry, 1818–1916

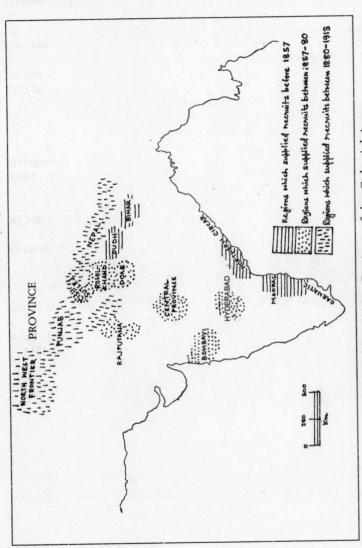

Map 1: Principal Recruiting Regions of the Colonial Army

NORTH WEST FRONTIER PROVINCE

PUNJAB

NEPAL

KUMAON
ROHIL KHAND
OUDH
DOAB
BIHAR

RAJPUTANA

CENTRAL PROVINCE

BOMBAY

HYDERABAD

MADRAS

NORTHERN CIRCAR

CARNATIC

Regions which supplied recruits before 1857

Regions which supplied recruits between 1857-80

Regions which supplied recruits between 1880-1913

0   250   500
Km.

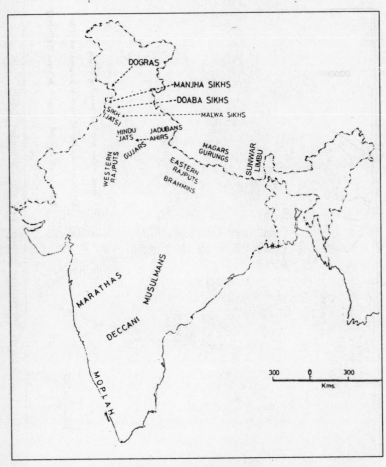

Map 2: Different Groups whom the Handbook Writers wanted
in the Colonial Army

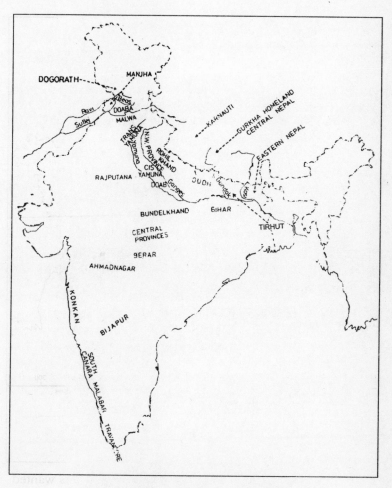

Map 3: Different Regions from where
the Handbook Writers wanted the
Colonial Indian Army to Recruit

Dissecting the Sepoy Army

The considerations which are involved in every question that does or may effect... our Native army are, in my mind, of the highest importance. It cannot too often be repeated, this army is our safety and our danger... we have through the efforts of our Native army, triumphed in wars, and rebellious plots and conspiracies.

John Malcolm[1]

The Sepoy Army or the British led Indian Army or the colonial Indian Army was the pillar of Britain's Indian Empire. Often the fate of the subcontinent was decided in gargantuan battles, like Assaye (1803) and Imphal (1944), conducted by the Sepoy Army. The British controlled Indian Army was an effective combat force as it destroyed all the contemporary military powers within South Asia. Then it functioned as an Imperial Fire Brigade for policing India as well as the non-Indian British overseas possessions, and as an Imperial Reserve during the two World Wars.[2] For the colonized also, the Sepoy Army was vital, as it was one of the largest employers in India and consumed a huge chunk of the government's revenue.[3]

Nevertheless, the Sepoy Army remains marginal in Indian historiography.[4] However, the role of armed forces in the construction of colonialism is not entirely missed out in the British-Imperial historiography. What could be labelled as a 'Technological Determinist' approach, emphasizes the role of military hardware. Daniel Headrick claims that their superior weapons system enabled the Europeans to defeat the Afro-Asians.[5] Modern researchers have, however, shown that there was no significant technological gap as regard the military technology used by the British led armies and the forces of the indigenous powers in the subcontinent. Till the 1850s, the Raj enjoyed no significant technical edge over its opponents. The

Maratha field artillery was technically at the same level with the cannons deployed by the Company.[6] Again, during the First Anglo-Sikh War (1845–6), the Sikhs deployed heavier cannons compared to the artillery possessed by the East India Company's Army.[7] Two historians claim that even in the post-1859 northwest frontier warfare, advanced technology was not of much aid to the Sepoy Army against the tribal guerrillas.[8]

Towards the end of the 1980s, the historiography of African and Asian colonialism have registered a shift away from the technological superiority of the West to cultural and institutional spheres.[9] Different military establishments, despite possessing the same level of technology, had different sorts of military cultures, which in turn generated asymmetric military effectiveness. This is the operative assumption of the 'Strategic Culture' approach. Dirk Kolff asserts that the chief factor was the political culture which in turn shaped the nature of warfare. He seems to make a case that the Asian culture of warfare did not grasp the logic of the Western form of warfare—the quest for decisive battles for complete annihilation of the enemy.[10] This line of argument is pushed forward by Jos Gommans who claims that the Western concept of total military victory was absent among the Asians.[11] This military culture theory is derived from the conceptualization of Victor Davis Hanson.[12] Nevertheless, decisive battles for total destruction of the enemy forces within a confined space and time were practised in India in the pre-British era. The First Battle of Panipat on 21 April 1526 which resulted in the destruction of the 100,000 strong Lodhi Army by Zahir-ud-Din Babur within a single afternoon is a case in point.[13]

To explain the military supremacy of the numerically inferior Sepoy Army, against the indigenous powers, a group of social scientists focus on the symbiotic relationship between the colonial army and the Indian society. Since this perspective assumes that social factors shaped the configuration of the armed forces, this group could be categorized as the 'Societal Determinists'. Seema Alavi and Stephen Peter Rosen argue that the Sepoy Army was able to dominate Indian society by functioning as a vehicle of upward mobility for certain social groups.[14]

That superior managerial expertise, as evident in the cohesive internal structure of the Raj's military establishment, made its army dominant, is the basic premise of a certain group of historians. Because of their preoccupation with the structural aspects of the military forces, this approach is labelled as the 'Organizational' perspective. This methodology points out that the army was a complex bureaucracy with its own ethos, code of conduct and laws, and that it was partly alienated from the social fabric. Hence, social imperatives could not totally explain the inner configuration of the armed forces.[15] A military organization did not operate in a vacuum. Social and cultural factors certainly mediate the functioning of the military bureaucracy. But, the key integers remained the structural apparatus of the military organization. What then were the institutional characteristics of the Raj's army? Geoffrey Parker asserts that the western style armies, which were based on drilled infantry armed with muskets and led by a professional officer cadre, were the products of the Military Revolution in early modern Europe. When imported in the Afro-Asian world, they gave the Europeans supremacy over the Afro-Asian polities.[16]

What Parker's broad survey overlooks is that the metropolitan armies when imported in the Afro-Asian world underwent a mutation due to constant interaction with the 'native' societies. The Sepoy Army, the workhorse of British imperialism, was a hybrid organization which integrated some elements of the Indian social structure and cultural ethos with the Western military organization. Thus, a conceptual framework of Military Synthesis is more applicable. With the aid of Military Synthesis model, the focus in this book will be on the institutional aspects of the Sepoy Army. Who were inducted in the service, and how they were controlled are the two inter-related problematic that are dealt in this monograph.[17] Comparisons with the Sepoy Army's Indian predecessors and the foreign armies are done in order to assess the British Indian military establishment's uniqueness.

The focus of this study is on the second half of the nineteenth century. Scholars generally neglect this period as uneventful and they turn their eyes to the world-shaking events like the 1857 Mutiny or the two World Wars. The bloodbath of 1857 involved massive changes in the social architecture and the organizational format of the army. Later, from 1914 onwards, the Sepoy Army registered massive expansion. So, the period between the 1857

Mutiny and the First World War, which is the time frame of this study, constitutes a sort of historical unity. However, 1857 did not represent a complete break with the past. The implications of my study have bearings for the earlier period also. Section I examines the literature on recruitment. Section II evaluates the problematic of the Sepoy Army's command structure.

I

MILITARY RECRUITMENT AND THE MARTIAL RACE THEORY

What I maintain is that no amount of frontier training will fit the Bombay sepoy to take his place in line against a European enemy, and however much the Government of India may desire to employ the armies of the three presidencies, I feel quite certain that no commander would venture to trust an ordinary Bombay regiment of infantry in the frontline (even though it may have had the advantage of having been stationed in its turn on the Baluchistan frontier), any more than he would a Madras regiment, or a Bengal Hindustani regiment. It is not a question of training, but of race capacity, which includes physique, stamina and military instinct, and these essential qualities the men of southern India do not now possess.

Field Marshal Frederick Roberts[18]

Even after the great rebellion of 1857, the Sepoy Army had to use South Asian manpower, because Britain lacked adequate number of males to garrison the subcontinent. Moreover, the sepoys compared to the British soldiers were three times cheaper and far more effective in the Indian climate.[19] For inducting indigenous manpower, the imperialists fabricated the Martial Race theory. Though scholarly understanding of this ideology has changed with time, the Martial Race paradigm dominates analysis of military recruitment.

For a number of authors, the Martial Race ideology was the principal component of the British policy geared towards the internal consolidation of the colonial order. Some scholars like Nirad C. Chaudhuri, K.M.L. Saxena and Chander S. Sundaram presume that the British deliberately used the Martial Race theory to prevent the growth of nationalism in India, for furthering the imperial hegemony.[20] The perspective of these three scholars could be categorized as the 'Nationalist approach'. Chaudhuri attempts a comparison between the metropolitan and the colonial military establishments. He asserts that the Sepoy Army was used for guarding India against the Indians. So, it could not afford short-service enlistment of all types of Indians, as European armies did with Europeans in Europe. Universal military service was prevented by the Martial Race ideology. For him, this theory was an imperial technique to confine recruitment to certain selected groups. The Martial Race theory also stifled the growth of a pan-Indian nationalism among such groups by emphasizing caste and tribal loyalties.

The next attempt to revive the Nationalist approach is K.M.L. Saxena's monograph.[21] Saxena writes that recruitment was guided by the 'Divide and Rule' principle, as the army's main function after 1857 was internal security. Saxena asserts that the Martial Race ideology was the continuation of the *Divide et Impera* strategy as the various martial groups balanced each other in the war machine. Chander S. Sundaram in two articles shows that in the late-nineteenth century Sepoy Army, a marginal faction was for commissioning Indians as officers. The imperial conviction was that if Indians were to be made officers at all then it would be better to enlist the loyal 'martial' groups rather than the 'seditious babus', i.e. the university educated urban middle class.[22]

Besides the Nationalist approach, we have the Functionalist perspective which argues that the imperatives for ruling India and certain traits of the Indian society gave birth to the Martial Race ideology. The spokesmen of this approach are the historian David Omissi, an ex-Indian Civil Service officer named Philip Mason and the American political scientist Stephen P. Cohen. Cohen's monograph[23] asserts that the Indian Army's recruitment policy was an imperial response towards two components of the indigenous society. These were the militarism of the landed gentry and the rising nationalism of the middle class. The Martial Race theory was a formula for excluding the politically conscious groups. Both Cohen and Mason accept that the intellectual paradigm of the Martial Race ideology was rooted in indigenous society. While Cohen says that the British exaggerated and systematized the mental and physical differences among the different indigenous groups, Mason goes to the other extreme and puts the onus fully on Hindu civilization. He argues that the Martial Race ideologues did not fabricate an imaginary martial-unmartial division among the Indian groups but made use of the Hindu division of labour in which *Kshatriyas* were natural warriors.[24] A similar argument is put forward by Philip Constable. In his framework the imperial ideology of recruitment was modification and accommodation of the closed status *Kshatriya naukri* tradition of pre-colonial India. In accordance with this tradition only selected communities were allowed to carry arms.[25]

About two decades after Mason, Omissi discussed the issue of the social and political basis of recruitment.[26] For Omissi, the recruitment policy was composed of two components: indigenous and imperial. Only those groups responded to the call of arms for whom soldiering offered social and economic advantages. The principal component was the imperial agenda— the search for loyal and brave soldiers, which was shaped by the colonizer's need to sustain the regime by dividing and manipulating different Indian groups. The process of categorization and classification helped the Raj to identify potential allies, who were then drawn into the army.[27] Omissi writes that the theory of the Martial Races as it evolved in the 1880s, appropriated the idea of enlistment of the selected few, thus resulting in Punjabization.

In the 1980s a new tool, that of ethnicity, was introduced by the political sociologist Cynthia H. Enloe, for understanding the Martial Race ideology. For Enloe, the members of an ethnic group believe in common descent and possess a distinct geographical and cultural identity. Enloe and DeWitt C. Ellinwood claim that the recruitment of the ethnically distinct regiments (Sikhs, Gurkhas) by the Raj was the British response to social reality. Ellinwood argues that religion, caste and region fragment Indian society. These fissures also fragment the social complexion of the military forces.[28] There is a lacuna in Enloe and Ellinwood's framework. They have used ethnicity as a catch-all term. Enloe and Ellinwood's portrayal of ethnic politics by the colonial army appear similar to Saxena's 'Divide and Rule' policy. However, on one point they differ from Saxena. Saxena writes that this Divide and Rule strategy had no roots in the Indian society, because indigenous society was not divisive. Rather, imperial politics fragmented it. But, Enloe and Ellinwood argue that the politics of divided communities was the result of the divisiveness inherent in Indian society.

To sum up, the British had different recruitment policies at various moments of time. Saxena's attempt to establish continuity throughout the second half of the nineteenth century is problematic. This book argues that the Martial Race ideology was not the continuation but the opposite of the 'Divide and Rule' strategy. While the 'Divide and Rule' policy aimed to establish a balance between various groups recruited from all over India, the Martial Race ideology aimed at intensive recruitment from particular areas like Nepal and Punjab.[29]

Thus the British had complicated ideologies. But, the brass-stacks of recruitment were something more than the imperial attitudes. Especially when the British cast their nets to draw recruits from beyond their actual line of control, like Nepal, the recruitment policy, argues a group of scholars, involved *realpolitik*. Since this group turns the spot light on the tortuous diplomatic activities of the British policy makers and the Kathmandu government, their approach could be labelled as the 'Diplomacy' perspective. Two scholars, Mary Des Chene, an American, and Purushottam Banskota, a Nepali, explore the linkages between recruitment of the 'martial races' and the Raj's coercive diplomacy. Des Chene in her article shows that recruitment was a continuation of diplomacy by other means.[30] Nepal was an independent state, and enlisting its subjects necessitated diplomatic manoeuverings, which Des Chene and Banskota chart. They write that the Gurkhas became vital to the Raj with the rise of the Martial Race theory in the last decades of the nineteenth century. The Nepali elite used the Gurkhas as bargaining counters to extract the maximum advantage from British India. In return, the Ranas retained their autonomy. Banskota elaborates the impact of Kathmandu's court politics on recruitment. Banskota shows that factionalism pushed the court towards the British.[31]

That long-term impersonal forces like demography also shaped the size and composition of the armies, is the argument of a group of historians who could be classified as 'Demographic Determinists'. Dirk Kolff and F.W. Perry argue that, not the official mind of imperialism or the underlying social and cultural milieu of the subcontinent, but massive manpower resources was the principal historical primer in shaping the contours of the militaries. They claim that due to the enormous human resources of India, the British could afford to be choosy about which groups to recruit and designate them as 'martial'. Kolff writes that if one takes a long *duree* perspective then it is clear that the key factor, which shaped the Sepoy Army's enlistment, was the huge supply of manpower linked with the ecology of the subcontinent.[32] For the manpower problem of the Indian and other Commonwealth armies during the two World Wars, we have Perry's monograph. In his framework the influence of demography is mediated by other factors like the relation between the armies and the polities.[33]

Kolff and Perry open up a new perspective by connecting the growth of the armies with the available demographic resources, making ideology and diplomacy appear secondary. While the chief determinant in Kolff's model is ecology, Perry amalgamates the effects of demography with the nature of polity. However, Perry's methodology is too mechanical. He deals with dry statistics, with such questions as the number of units, and does not take into account the passions and emotions of the recruits.

Imperial and Indigenous perceptions of the 'martial' recruits are the concern of another group of scholars. Since these scholars examine the role of ideas behind the imperial and the colonizers' outlooks as regards the 'warrior' groups, their approach could be termed as the 'History of Ideas' approach. The 'martial' groups, it was believed, possessed masculine qualities like honour, courage, vigour, loyalty, etc. British recruitment of indigenous manpower created stereotypes among the officers about certain groups. The British officers believed that the Gurkhas were warlike. Lionel Caplan argues that the British military literature on the Gurkhas was an attempt by the colonizers to transform the 'inferiors' into cherished docile warriors.[34] Pradeep Barua throws new light on the imperatives behind the Martial Race doctrine.[35] For him, the Western intellectual climate mostly shaped the Martial Race theory. Barua writes that the Martial Race ideology was connected with the growth of Victorian geology, anthropology and eugenics.

The Sepoy Army had an internal value system—the Martial Race ideology, which shaped the army officers' view about the recruits. Richard G. Fox, an anthropologist, shows that this value system spilled into Punjabi society.[36] However, the reach of the Martial Race theory was limited. Michael Hutt shows that Nepali society evolved a separate value system in opposition to the army's recruitment rhetoric.[37] Hutt breaks new ground in constructing the Nepali perception of the Gurkhas from twentieth century Nepali literature. Nepali prose depicts the Gurkhas as drunkards and rogues.

Let us now sum up the contours of historiography on the Martial Race theory. Those who try to link up the Martial Race ideology with British India's recruitment strategy, diplomacy and demography, throw light on the structures and processes involved in acquiring military labourers while the 'History of Ideas' perspective addresses the experiences and perceptions of the recruits. The approaches of the various scholars differ greatly. Cohen and Omissi link up recruitment with the Raj's politics. Barua's work represents a paradigm shift as he fuses the colonial enlistment strategy with the evolution of the Western concept of race. As regards the role of caste system in shaping the Martial Race ideology, we have two opposite interpretations. Kolff argues that the castes were fluid categories and by-products of military service. But Enloe and Ellinwood argue that castes had fixed boundaries and were not colonial constructs. Hence, the caste system was one of the building blocks of the imperial ethnic game. The latter group's argument is more reliable because the British perceived Indian society as divided along caste lines. This is evident from the army's internal documents.[38] Then how alien was the Martial Race ideology? While authors like Mason, Enloe, Ellinwood and Constable argue that the Martial Race theory had an indigenous base, others like Chaudhuri, Saxena and Barua point out that the Martial Race theory was a foreign project on the Indian soil. For Saxena and Chaudhuri, the causative factor behind shaping the imperial discourse lay in the periphery, in the imperial necessity to divide the colonized. But for Barua, the principal imperative behind the British theoretical model was in the metropole: the evolution of pseudo-sciences in the West. Douglas M. Peers rightly comments that the Martial Race theory is a hybrid dogma with both Oriental and Occidental elements.[39] But, this needs to be worked out in greater detail.

Faction fights within the colonial polity influenced the rise and fall of the different recruitment ideologies at various moments of time. But, factional struggles within the army are neglected in the recruitment literature. The victory of a particular faction, by itself a micro phenomenon, occasionally had a macro effect. Ideas emerged over a long period, but when and how a particular organization (in this case the Sepoy Army) accepted the dominant intellectual trend, depended on internal factors such as contests among the various cabals within the war machine and the differing perception of strategic threats. Which communities could be categorized as martial was an issue that rocked the army only with the emergence of Field Marshal Frederick Roberts and his coterie towards the end of nineteenth century. Once they were in power they propagated the Martial Race ideology. But their theory was not a complete break with the past. They absorbed several trends, which had evolved over the first half of the nineteenth century. Chapter 2 addresses this issue. The wider intellectual currents influenced some votaries of the Martial Race theory. This inter-relationship between the military recruitment and the broader intellectual currents is studied in Chapter 3.

Most scholars working on the Sepoy Army in their eagerness to link up recruitment ideology with the prevailing social and intellectual mores of the second half of the nineteenth century, have neglected the presence of a body of ideas which was different from the Martial Race ideology. This ideology was the polar opposite of the Martial Race ideology which Chapter 1 deals with. After the 1857 Mutiny, the opponents of the Martial Race ideology became dominant. They followed what I term as 'Balanced Recruitment Policy'. From the 1880s, the Martial Race ideology again held sway. To maintain chronological clarity, this book will first deal with the corpus of ideas that differed from the Martial Race theory.

II

COMMAND MECHANISM REVISITED

The Native Army would do well as any European army. None of the European governments had any idea of the superior quality of the Native Army we have in India. The Native Army is the nucleus of an excellent powerful force.

General Hugh Rose[40]

Once the recruits joined the imperial military machine, they were conditioned into soldiers. The army not only attracted the personnel, but also retained them and motivated them to fight the imperial wars; and even prevent mutinies. This problematic is termed as the command mechanism.[41] Most of the literature emphasizes the sahib-sepoy interaction. Amiya Barat in her monograph claims that the paralysis of the command structure in the 1850s was due to the qualitative and quantitative decline of the British officers in the regiments of the Bengal Army.[42]

A particular group of scholars view the white officer corps as the fountain of all patronage for the Indian soldiers. Mason and Charles Allen write that the officer-soldier relationship in the Indian Army was a sort of father-son relationship. This was possible because of the inborn leadership quality of the British landed gentry who constituted the officer corps, and their public school training.[43] What Mason and Allen overlook is that most of the British officers of the Sepoy Army came from the urban middle class of Britain.[44]

Cohen interprets the sahib-sepoy relationship as a dependent tie, which was loaded in favour of the sahibs.[45] It seems to be a core-periphery model, in which the British officers constituted the core and the Indian personnel symbolized the periphery. For Cohen, the Indians, in return for a position in the colonial system, gave their obedience to the sahibs. Lorenzo M. Crowell elaborates and modifies Cohen's line of analysis by conceptualizing a sort of colonial professionalism among the white officer corps. The elements of colonial professionalism were caring for the Indian troops' religious and cultural sensibilities, and the officers' command over the vernaculars.[46] By these techniques, the officers acquired the sepoys' affection and loyalty. While Crowell focuses on the early nineteenth century Madras Army, Peers shifts the limelight to the pre-1857 Bengal Army.[47] He asserts that the Bengal Army's British officers lost command over their troops' language and this was a vital factor in the disintegration of the loyalty mechanism in 1857. Even for the early twentieth century, Edwin Latter regards the personal loyalty of the troops towards their officers as the key factor in the functioning of the Sepoy Army.[48]

Another approach, as followed by the American historian Jeffrey Greenhut, assumes that the perceptions and the responses of both the partners—the sahibs and the sepoys—were shaped within the frame of their distinct cultural paradigms. Greenhut writes that the sahibs functioned, not merely as representatives of Victorian paternal liberalism, but as bridges between the subcontinent's ruralites and the Western military system. The officer-soldier relationship was actually an amalgam of horizontal and hierarchical relationships. The British officers believed that their actions would provoke equivalent reactions from the soldiers. But, this was not the case since the Indian peasants who joined the army believed in hierarchical relations; they regarded it as their *dharma* to obey their superiors, the officers, just as they obeyed their natural and social superiors, the zamindars.[49] To conclude, Greenhut over-emphasizes the role of the social and cultural milieu in influencing the officer-soldier interaction. Recently, to explain the Indian soldiers' obedience to the imperial war machine, Omissi has brought in two more additional factors—the personal loyalty of the sepoys and the sowars towards the Commander-in-Chief and the King Emperor.[50]

Significantly, the studies of the British officer cadre of the Sepoy Army by Cohen, Crowell, Peers, Gerald Bryant and Raymond Callahan[51] have led them to conclude that the white officer corps were indeed a professional body with corporate ethos. However, all the scholars in viewing the Sepoy Army's command system in terms of a personalized sahib-sepoy relationship overlook the structural apparatus of control. These historians of the Sepoy Army have failed to emancipate themselves from the discourse of the regimental British officers who served in the Sepoy Army and believed that they themselves constituted the bedrock of command.[52]

The term professionalism in this monograph refers to the military bureaucracy's success in separating its personnel from the traditional mores of the society and motivating them to fight and die for an impersonal cause.[53] Professionalism also refers to military personnel with long-term commitments to soldiering and who drew increasing amount of identity from their warrior profession.[54] To ensure all these, an organizational apparatus was necessary for separating the army from society in order to build new cultures of loyalty which was different from loyalty exercised by tribal and kinship leaders.[55]

While constructing the Sepoy Army, the British introduced a new organizational gamut borrowed from Europe. This organizational infrastructure involved three elements: a welfare bureaucracy, regimental organization and the court martial mechanism. The point to be noted is that the western military organizational format when imported to India experienced continuous intercourse with the colonial scenario, thus giving birth to a hybrid culture of command. For the first time in Indian history, the colonial army offered a welfare package, which included both tangible and non-tangible incentives for purchasing its personnel's loyalty. And many incentives were traditional indeed. Chapter 4 discusses this issue. Further, the British replaced the *mansabdari* organization with the regimental organization. But, this European institution absorbed a corpus of indigenous traits like the caste and clan ethos and mutated into a new entity, which was geared to generate regimental loyalty among the personnel of the colonial war machine. This is the theme of Chapter 5. Some amount of coercion in the form of military laws and the court martial apparatus was also necessary for the proper functioning of the command structure. Chapter 6 shows the imperial perception regarding the role of force in preventing insubordination among the soldiers. The last chapter portrays the actual working of the disciplinary mechanism in keeping the rank and file loyal. Again the scholars of the Sepoy Army neglect the Indian officers who were known as Viceroy's commissioned officers. Chapters 6 and 7 attempts to assign the Indian officers their rightful place within the disciplinary apparatus.

The Sepoy Army was always engaged in combat, either in great battles or in sub-conventional conflicts. The British withdrawal from the east of Suez was partly linked with loss of imperial control over the subcontinent's military force. Here lies the importance of the British led Sepoy Army. A proper understanding of British India would be possible, only when the sepoys and the sowars occupy the centre of the historical canvas. Without them there would have been no colonialism, at least not the one which the Indians experienced. So far as colonial India is concerned, Clio can no more afford to neglect Mars.

NOTES

1. Minute by J. Malcolm, Bombay, 27 Nov. 1830, *Parliamentary Papers* (*PP*) (1867), p. 179.
2. G.J. Bryant, 'Pacification in the Early British Raj, 1775–85', *JICH*, vol. 14, no. 1 (1985), pp. 3–19; Byron Farwell, *Armies of the Raj: From the Great Indian Mutiny to Independence, 1858–1947*, 1989, reprint, London: Viking, 1990, pp. 65–77, 105–19, 191–203, 226–48, 303–17; Lieutenant-General S.L. Menezes, *Fidelity and Honour: The Indian Army from the Seventeenth to the Twenty First Century*, New Delhi: Viking, 1993, pp. 1–80, 144–87, 241–62, 340–71; Lieutenant F.G. Cardew, *A Sketch of the Services of the Native Army to the year 1895*, 1903, reprint, New Delhi: Today and Tomorrow's Printers and Publishers, 1971, pp. 74–5, 109–10, 193–4, 316–17, 378–9, 381–8, 428.
3. Between 1859 and 1913, the share of defence was about 30 to 46 per cent of the government's budget. The Sepoy Army's size during peace exceeded 120,000 and the annual demand of the army was about 20,000 men. T.A. Heathcote, *The Military in British India: The Development of British Land Forces in South Asia: 1600–1947*, Manchester/New York: Manchester University Press, 1995, p. 241; David Omissi, *The Sepoy and the Raj: The Indian Army, 1860–1940*, Basingstoke/London: Macmillan, 1994, p. 78; Lanka Sundaram, *India's Armies and Their Costs: A Century of Unequal Imposts for an Army of Occupation and a Mercenary Army*, Bombay: Avanti Prakashan, 1946, p. 55; *Army Committee*, vol. 1-A, *Minority Report*, pp. 156, 158.
4. For the not so developed state of Indian military historiography see Kaushik Roy, 'Mars in Indian History', *SIH*, vol. 16, no. 2 (2000), pp. 261–75.
5. Daniel R. Headrick, *The Tools of Empire: Technology and European Imperialism in the Nineteenth Century*, New York/Oxford: Oxford University Press, 1981.
6. John Pemble, 'Resources and Techniques in the Second Maratha War', *Historical Journal*, vol. 19 (1976), pp. 375–404; Randolf G.S. Cooper, *The Anglo-Maratha Campaigns and the Contest for India: The Struggle for Control of the South Asian Military Economy*, New Delhi: Foundation Books in association with Cambridge University Press, 2005.
7. Byron Farwell, *Queen Victoria's Little Wars*, 1973, reprint, Hertfordshire: Wordsworth, 1999, pp. 37–50.
8. T.R. Moreman, *The Army in India and the Development of Frontier Warfare: 1849–1947*, Basingstoke/London: Macmillan, 1998; Alan Warren, *Waziristan, The Faqir of Ipi and the Indian Army: The North West Frontier Revolt of 1936–37*, Karachi: Oxford University Press, 2000.
9. Michael Howard, 'Colonial Wars and European Wars', in J.A. de Moor

and H.L. Wesseling, ed., *Imperialism and War: Essays on Colonial Wars in Asia and Africa*, Leiden: E.J. Brill, 1989, p. 221.

10. Dirk H.A. Kolff, 'The End of an *Ancien Regime*: Colonial War in India', in Moor and Wesseling, ed., *Imperialism and War: Essays on Colonial Wars in Asia and Africa*, pp. 22–49.

11. Jos Gommans, 'Indian Warfare and Afghan Innovation during the Eighteenth Century', *SIH*, vol. 11, no. 2 (1995), pp. 261–80.

12. V.D. Hanson asserts that the culture of decisive encounters between the armies first originated with the Greeks and then nurtured by the Romans. This tradition continued in the Middle ages and reached its logical culmination in the industrial era. Hanson, *Warfare and Agriculture in Classical Greece*, 1983, reprint, Berkeley/Los Angeles: University of California Press, 1999, pp. 174–84; Hanson, 'The Ideology of Hoplite Battle, Ancient and Modern', in Hanson, ed., *Hoplites: The Classical Greek Battle Experience*, 1991, reprint, London: Routledge, 1993, pp. 3–11. For a more recent account see Hanson, *Carnage and Culture: Landmark Battles in the Rise of Western Power*, New York: Doubleday, 2001, pp. 1–24.

13. Jadunath Sarkar, *Military History of India*, 1960, reprint, Bombay/New Delhi: Orient Longman, 1970, pp. 49–55. For the decisive battles fought in pre-British India refer to Kaushik Roy, *India's Historic Battles: From Alexander the Great to Kargil*, New Delhi: Permanent Black, 2004.

14. Seema Alavi, *The Sepoys and the Company: Tradition and Transition in Northern India, 1770–1830*, Delhi: Oxford University Press, 1995; Stephen Peter Rosen, *Societies and Military Power: India and Its Armies*, Delhi: Oxford University Press, 1996.

15. Organizational theory demands the autonomy of military institutions and the role of power-politics in shaping military organization's culture. See Theo Farrell, 'Figuring out Fighting Organizations: The New Organizational Analysis in Strategic Studies', *JSS*, vol. 19, no. 1 (1996), pp. 122–33.

16. Geoffrey Parker, *The Military Revolution: Military Innovation and the Rise of the West, 1500–1800*, Cambridge: Cambridge University Press, 1988.

17. My perspective demands a top-down approach. Most of the nineteenth-century sepoys and sowars being illiterate have left us with no written records. The only exception is Subedar Sita Ram memoirs. James Lunt, ed., *From Sepoy to Subedar: Being the Life and Adventures of Sita Ram, a Native Officer of the Bengal Army*, 1873, tr. by Col. Norgate, 1970, reprint, London: Macmillan, 1988. Even its authenticity could be challenged.

18. Roberts to Lansdowne, 16 May 1890 in General Frederick Roberts, *Correspondence with the Viceroy of India* (*The Marquis of Lansdowne*):

26 Nov. 1888–2 April 93, Calcutta: Superintendent of Govt. Printing, 1893, p. 50, Part 5, Indian series, L/MIL/17/5/1615, OIOC.

19. *Peel Committee*, pp. 1, 11. In 1864, the annual cost of maintaining an Indian infantry regiment in India was Rs 183000 and the annual cost of maintaining a British infantry regiment in India came to Rs 609000. To the Secy. to the GoI, MD, Simla, no. 1108, 21 April 1864, Records of Chief Commands, 1865–76, Notes and Minutes by Napier of Magdala, MSS.EUR.F.114, 5 (4), OIOC.

20. Nirad C. Chaudhuri, 'The Martial Races of India', *Modern Review*, vol. XLVIII, no. 1 (1930), pp. 41–51, no. 3 (1930), pp. 295–305, vol. XLIX, no. 1 (1931), pp. 67–79, no. 2 (1931), pp. 215–28; Chaudhuri, 'India and Imperial Defence', vol. XLIX, no. 4 (1931), pp. 386–96.

21. K.M.L. Saxena, *The Military System of India: 1850–1900*, New Delhi: Sterling, 1974.

22. Chandar S. Sundaram, 'Preventing "Idleness": The Maharajah of Cooch Behar's Proposal for Officer Commissions in the British Army for the Sons of Indian Princes and Gentlemen, 1897–98', *South Asia*, vol. 17, no. 1 (1995), pp. 115–30; Sundaram, '"Martial" Indian Aristocrats and the Military System of the Raj: The Imperial Cadet Corps, 1900–14', *JICH*, vol. 25, no. 3 (1997), pp. 415–39.

23. Stephen P. Cohen, *The Indian Army: Its Contribution to the Development of a Nation*, 1971, reprint, Delhi: Oxford University Press, 1991.

24. Philip Mason, *A Matter of Honour: An Account of the Indian Army, Its Officers and Men*, 1974, reprint, Dehradun: EBD Publishers, 1988.

25. Philip Constable, 'The Marginalization of a Dalit Martial Race in Late Nineteenth and Early Twentieth Century Western India', *JAS*, vol. 60, no. 2 (2001), pp. 439–78.

26. Omissi, *Sepoy and the Raj*.

27. David Omissi, '"Martial Races": Ethnicity and Security in Colonial India, 1858–1939', *War & Society*, vol. 9, no. 1(1991), pp. 1–27.

28. Cynthia H. Enloe, 'Ethnicity in the Evolution of Asia's Armed Bureaucracies', and DeWitt C. Ellinwood, 'Ethnicity in a Colonial Asian Army: British Policy, War, and the Indian Army, 1914-18', in Enloe and Ellinwood, ed., *Ethnicity and the Military in Asia*, New Brunswick/London: Transaction Books, 1981, pp. 1-17, 89–144.

29. *Army Committee*, vol. 1-A, *Minority Report*, p. 156; *Supplementary Report*, p. 4, Appendix no. 22.

30. Mary Des Chene, 'Soldiers, Sovereignty and Silences: Gorkhas as Diplomatic Currency', *South Asia Bulletin*, vol. 13, nos. 1–2 (1993), pp. 67–80.

31. Purushottam Banskota, *The Gurkha Connection: A History of the Gurkha Recruitment in the British Indian Army*, New Delhi: Nirala, 1994.

32. Dirk H.A. Kolff, *Naukar, Rajput and Sepoy: The Ethnohistory of the*

Military Labour Market in Hindustan, 1450–1850, Cambridge: Cambridge University Press, 1990.

33. F.W. Perry, *The Commonwealth Armies: Manpower and Organization in Two World Wars*, Manchester: Manchester University Press, 1988.

34. Dewitt C. Ellinwood Jr., *Between Two Worlds: A Rajput Officer in the Indian Army, 1905–21, Based on the Diary of Amar Singh of Jaipur*, Boulder: Hamilton Books, 2005, p. 9. Lionel Caplan, ' "Bravest of the Brave": Representations of "The Gurkha" in British Military Writings', *MAS*, vol. 25, no. 3 (1991), pp. 571–97; Caplan, *Warrior Gentlemen: 'Gurkhas' in the Western Imagination*, Providence/Oxford: Berghahn Books, 1995, pp. 1–25.

35. Pradeep Barua, 'Inventing Race: The British and India's Martial Races', *Historian*, vol. 58, no. 1 (1995), pp. 107–16.

36. Richard G. Fox, *Lions of the Punjab: Culture in the Making*, New Delhi: Low Price Publications, 1990.

37. Michael Hutt, 'A Hero or Traitor? Representations of the Gurkha Soldier in Modern Nepali Literature', *South Asia Research*, vol. 9 (1989), pp. 21–32.

38. The army officers' conception of the caste system can be deduced from Caste returns, no. 4495, ADG's office, Simla, 14 August 1862, ADG's circulars, vol. 2, NAI.

39. Douglas M. Peers, 'Contours of the Garrison State: The Army and the Historiography of Early Nineteenth Century India', in Nancy G. Cassels, ed., *Orientalism, Evangelicalism and the Military Cantonment in Early Nineteenth Century India*, Lewiston/Queenstown: The Edwin Mellen Press, 1991, pp. 116–17.

40. Hugh Rose to John Lawrence, para 6, 14 February, 1864, Correspondence between the Commander-in-Chief and the Viceroy, John Lawrence Collection, MSS.EUR.F.90/59, OIOC.

41. For an exhaustive analysis of the literature on command mechanism see Kaushik Roy, 'The Historiography of the Colonial Indian Army', *SIH*, vol. 12, no. 2 (1996), pp. 255–66.

42. Amiya Barat, *The Bengal Native Infantry: Its Organization and Discipline 1796–1852*, Calcutta: Firma KLM, 1962.

43. Mason, *A Matter of Honour*, Charles Allen, *Soldier Sahibs: The Men who Made the Northwest Frontier*, London: John Murray, 2000.

44. T.A. Heathcote, *The Indian Army: The Garrison of British Imperial India, 1822–1922*, Newton Abbot/London: David & Charles, 1974, pp. 123–4, 141; P.E. Razzell, 'Social Origins of Officers in the Indian and British Home Army: 1758–1962', *The British Journal of Sociology*, vol. 14 (1963), pp. 250–8.

45. Cohen, *Indian Army*, pp. 49–50.

46. Lorenzo M. Crowell, 'Military Professionalism in a Colonial Context: The Madras Army circa 1832', *MAS*, vol. 24, no. 2 (1990), pp. 249–74.

47. Douglas M. Peers, ' "The Habitual Nobility of Being": British Officers and the Social Construction of the Bengal Army in the Early Nineteenth Century', *MAS*, vol. 25, no. 3 (1991), pp. 545–69.

48. Edwin Latter, 'The Indian Army in Mesopotamia, 1914–18', *JSAHR*, vol. LXXII, no. 291 (1994), pp. 160–73.

49. Jeffrey Greenhut, 'The Imperial Reserve: The Indian Corps on the Western Front, 1914–15', *JICH*, vol. 12, no. 1 (1983), pp. 54–73; Greenhut, 'Sahib and Sepoy: An Inquiry into the Relationship between the British Officers and Native Soldiers of the British Indian Army', *Military Affairs*, vol. XLVIII, no. 1 (1984), pp. 15–19.

50. Omissi, *Sepoy and the Raj*, pp. 103–11.

51. G.J. Bryant, 'Officers of the East India Company's Army in the Days of Clive and Hastings', *JICH*, vol. 6 no. 2 (1978), pp. 203–27; Raymond Callahan, *The East India Company and Army Reform: 1783–98*, Cambridge/Massachusetts: Harvard University Press, 1972.

52. The regimental officers' views are discussed in Chapter 6.

53. Jacques Van Doorn writes that detribalization and nationalization of the officer corps represent the genesis of a professional officer cadre. To my mind, at least the first aspect could also be utilized to gauge the nature of professionalism among the privates and the troopers. Doorn, 'Political Change and the Control of the Military: Some General Remarks', in Doorn, ed., *Military Profession and Military Regimes: Commitments and Conflicts*, The Hague/Paris: Mouton, 1969, p. 19.

54. I am influenced by Dennis Showalter's concept of professionalism. See his 'Caste, Skill and Training: The Evolution of Cohesion in European Armies from the Middle Ages to the Sixteenth Century', *JMH*, vol. 57, no. 3 (1993), p. 416.

55. Stanislav Andreski's *Military Organization and Society*, 1954, reprint, Berkeley/California: University of California Press, 1968 has influenced me. See especially p. 34 of Andreski's book.

ONE

An Army from the People

Since the Mutiny of 1857 the prevalent idea has been that we should try to do away with caste as much as possible, and open our ranks to all, whatever their creed may be; that one fights as well as another, and that all should be thrown together in the same regiment.

Major-General Charles Reid[1]

There was a group, which in reaction to the 1857 Mutiny became dominant and chalked out policies that were diametrically opposed to recruitment of selected groups from particular areas. They could be labelled as the 'Egalitarian Recruitment School' or 'Balanced Recruitment School'. This School proposed the broadening of the social and territorial bases of the army. Inspite of the dominance of the spokesmen of the 'martial races' from the last two decades of the nineteenth century, the Egalitarian Recruitment lobby challenged and somewhat modified the operation of the Martial Race ideology.

This chapter focuses on the nuances of the Egalitarian Recruitment lobby's programme. K.M.L. Saxena writes that to destroy nationalism in India, the imperialists after 1857 balanced the Indian soldiers along various caste and religious lines.[2] This is a mechanical interpretation of British policy. To search for national consciousness in the second half of the nineteenth century is an anachronism. After all, the different communities like the Rajputs, and the Sikhs possessed different languages, religions and cultures. So, Cynthia H. Enloe's argument that the ethnic cleavages in Indian society were real is more applicable. While Enloe emphasizes the role of social division in the formulation of the Martial Race ideology,[3] this chapter shows how the Raj systematically structured such differentiation in constructing the 'Balanced Recruitment' formula, which was the core aspect of the Egalitarian Recruitment lobby's ideology. This recruitment strategy was the direct response to the challenge of preventing another mutiny in the Bengal Army, in the immediate aftermath of 1857. This enlistment policy accommodated and accentuated a sophisticated balancing structure by inducting various hetero-geneous groups from a wide area. David Omissi states that the post-1859 Bengal Army's social composition was mixture of accident and a 'Divide and Rule' policy.[4] This view is similar to Philip Mason's interpretation that the post-Mutiny Bengal Army's composition was *ad hoc*.[5] However, this chapter argues that Balanced Recruitment, which was dominant between 1859 to 1880, was the end result of a detailed blueprint that emerged after hectic debates among the imperial elites.

I

BALANCED RECRUITMENT BEFORE 1857

The core of the Balanced Recruitment principle could be traced back to the pre-1857 days. This doctrine denied any linkage between the recruits' martial instincts and their socio-cultural and occupational backgrounds, heredity, diet and climate. This ideology operated both in the Bombay and the Madras armies. There was a lobby in the Madras Army, which pursued what can be termed as an 'Open Door' policy as regards enlistment. The pre-1857 Bengal Army officers, who constituted a lobby that I call the Bengal School, were for recruiting the *Purbiyas* (high caste Hindus like the Brahmins and the Rajputs from Bihar and Awadh). In 1798, Lieutenant-General George Harris, Com-mander-in-Chief of the Madras Army argued that though the south Indians were inferior in size and appearance compared with the so called martial *Purbiyas*, the former were hardy, thrifty and lacked religious prejudices. Thus, the south Indians were better soldiers than the *Purbiyas*. This doctrine also disregarded the criterion of height. Even in the prestigious cavalry regiments, short men were taken. In 1839, the general orders of the Commander-in-Chief of the Madras Army laid down that Indians of all castes were eligible for recruitment. The Tamils of Trichinopoly, the Telugus of the Northern Circars and the Muslims from Karnataka were enlisted to maintain a rough balance.[6]

The Bombay Army maintained a bipolar balance between the Hindustanis (Hindus and Muslims from north India which was also known as Hindustan) and the Konkanis (men from the Konkan region of western Maharashtra). Before the Third Maratha War (1817–18), there were only 4,000 Hindustanis in the Bombay Army. But during the war, extra manpower became necessary and the British were unwilling to recruit the Konkanis as many of their brethren were in the *Peshwa's* Army and had sympathy for the Maratha Confederacy. Hence, the British turned towards the Hindustanis. By 1824, the numbers of Hindustanis had jumped to 7,465 men. Major General John Malcolm warned William Bentinck (Governor General 1828–35), the supporter of the *Purbiyas*, against further increasing the number of the Hindustanis as the balancing game would be upset. Malcolm concluded that the three presidency armies must have different social and regional compositions to prevent any unified combination against the British. Hence, recruitment of the Hindustanis stopped. Thus, in 1830, a bipolar balance existed between 10,015 Konkanis and 12,476 Hindustanis.[7] A tripolar balance also existed in the Punjab Frontier Force. This force came into existence in 1849. Just before the 1857 Mutiny, it had 14,692 Sikhs from central Punjab, 30,188 Muslims from west Punjab and Rohilkhand (western part of present-day Uttar Pradesh) and 7,566 Hindus of mixed castes like Ahirs and the Gujars from the North-West Province (present-day Haryana and Rohilkhand).[8]

In the pre-1857 Madras and Bombay armies, the Egalitarian Recruitment ideology scored a victory because of certain factors. Awadh and Bihar being under the jurisdiction of the Bengal Presidency, the Bengal Army had the first choice in these areas. As a result, it monopolized the 'better' variety of *Purbiya* recruits leaving 'second grade' material for the other regional forces. Some *Purbiyas* who joined the Madras Army deserted because of the high cost of living in the Madras Presidency. The Bombay Army enlisted the *Purbiyas* from Mhow. Most of them joined with the aim of saving some money. After few years service, they deserted. The Punjab Frontier Force was deployed along the northwest frontier. The *Purbiyas* were not willing to serve in a region with harsh climate and far away from their home.[9] All these factors prevented a predominance of the *Purbiyas* in these armies, which in turn saved these forces from the tumult of 1857.

The Egalitarian Recruitment theory existed in the first half of the nineteenth century though, scholars neglect this point. Those who have concentrated on the pre-1857 Indian Army are obsessed with linking the army's recruitment programme with the 1857 Mutiny.[10] They neglect the fact that the Mutiny was no break as far as recruitment in the Bombay and Madras armies and the Punjab Frontier Force was concerned. These forces continued to absorb a motley collection of communities from a wide region, as they had done before 1857. These armies followed this policy till the 1880s. Scholars miss this point because they give the lion's share of attention to the Bengal Army. Eric Stokes implied that the sepoys were peasants in uniform. This encouraged historians to link the army's social composition with the agrarian uprising of 1857. As a result a simplistic picture emerged. The Bengal sepoys were seen to have rebelled because the high caste peasants of Awadh rebelled.[11]

There is a tendency among all scholars who have worked on the pre-1857 Bengal Army, to link the recruitment policy of enlisting high castes with the 1857 uprising. So, they have introduced the notion of inevitability. This approach is consistent with the social scientists' search for long-term structural factors especially as the role of chance is caricatured as the 'Cleopetra's nose' approach to history.[12] However, Clio occasionally plays dice as the course of history frequently show that it is shaped by contingent.[13] If the Bengal Army had rejected its homogeneous recruitment policy in the 1830s in favour of the Balanced Recruitment policy adopted by the other regional forces, then the 'winds of madness', which blew in May 1857 might have been averted.

II

BALANCED RECRUITMENT AFTER 1857

'*Divide et impera*', is the principle I would advocate.
                                        Brigadier General C.H. Brownlow[14]

In the summer of 1857, the Bengal Army disintegrated. About 70,000 soldiers turned their muskets against their white masters and 30,000 troops of dubious loyalty deserted.[15] This catastrophe triggered off a grand debate among the British about how best to construct a polyethnic army for the future. In the Mutiny's aftermath, the imperialist opinions were divided. Some officers were for minimal trusting of the Indian military manpower. At the other end of the spectrum, there was a minority section, which aimed to acquire the trust and confidence of the Indians by increasing the concessions, which were allowed to them. This group, which wanted to accommodate the brown soldiers on favourable terms, can be labelled as the 'Liberal' lobby. But, the majority view was for striking a compromise formula between the two widely divergent viewpoints. The general aim was to reduce over-dependence on two groups from north India: the *Purbiyas* and the Hindustani Muslims (Muslims recruited from the North-West Province).

However, the British could not agree on the quantum of the intake of the other groups. This was because the imperial interpretation of the response of the various Indian communities during 1857 was contradictory. The British policy makers agreed on the utility of the white forces to deter the brown soldiers. Lord Clyde, the Commander-in-Chief of the Indian Army (1857–60) voiced the general opinion, when in 1859 he said 'increased vigilance and maintaining awe of European troops . . . had become essential after 1857'.[16] However, the British faced the same dilemma which the Dutch faced in Indonesia during the nineteenth century. European soldiers were necessary for 'frightening' the colonial soldiers but acquiring an adequate number of white soldiers remained a problem.[17] The British had to decide on the size of the white forces, which they could maintain in India as this influenced the number of Indians they needed to enlist.

George Clerk, a civilian bureaucrat who became Governor of Bombay, argued that the intensity of the 1857 outbreak was directly proportional to the paucity of white soldiers.[18] Pradeep Barua erroneously states that the Peel Committee reached a consensus of deploying one European soldier for three Indian soldiers.[19] Among the British there was much disagreement as evident from Table 1.1 about the proportion of British troops required to hold the Indian troops in check. As regards regional deployment of the British soldiers to balance the Indians, the political and military circles failed to generate a consensus. This

TABLE 1.1: BALANCING SCHEMES PROPOSED BY THE OFFICERS IN 1859

Name of the Person	Ratio of European to Indian Soldiers
Colonel Burlton	1: 5
Captain G.F.S. Browne	1: 4
Lieutenant General George Pollock	1: 4 (excluding artillery which he wanted to be manned completely by the Europeans)
Lievtenant General	1: 3 (including artillery)
George Pollock	Pollock's balancing scheme does not take into account the Irregular forces
George Clerk	1: 4 (including the regular and the irregular sepoy units but excluding police)
George Clerk	1: 3 (including only the regular sepoy units)
Lieutenant-Colonel Thomas Lowth Harington	1: 3 (including only the regular sepoy units)
Major David Baird	1: 1 or if it was not possible then 1: 2.

Source: Peel Committee, pp. 1–3, 30–4, 38–40, 46.

was because the social composition of each of the four regional armies was different. John Lawrence, the Chief Commissioner of Punjab, Brigadier-General Neville Chamberlain and Lieutenant-Colonel Herbert B. Edwardes, officers of the Punjab Frontier Force, constituted a lobby, which could be categorized as the Punjab School. This lobby claimed that the Punjabis were the most martial, Hindustanis were a bit less so, and the Madrassis (south Indians) were the least warlike. So, they demanded one British soldier for every two Sikh or Pathan soldiers, one British soldier for every three Hindustani soldiers, and one European soldier for every four Madrassi soldiers.[20]

In the 1880s, General George Chesney formulated a pan-Indian balancing scheme that was somewhat similar to that of the Punjab School. He wanted the white soldiers' proportion to be highest in the Punjab Frontier Force. In the Punjab Frontier Force, he demanded one European for every 1.5 Indian soldier but for the Madras and Bengal armies, one British was adequate for balancing two Indian soldiers. One can guess the reasoning behind Chesney's scheme. In the 1880s, unlike in 1859, not the Bengal Presidency but the region west of the Sutlej was considered to be strategically most vital. The Punjab Frontier Force at this time was considered as the shock troops of the Indian Army. And, the imperial belief was that the striking power of the army was directly proportional to the number of white soldiers present. Moreover, the Punjab Frontier Force was mostly composed of Punjabis, the most 'martial people' in India. So, to deter them larger number of white soldiers were necessary.[21]

In 1859, for Bengal, Punjab and the North-West Frontier Province, Lieutenant General George Pollock demanded 27,000 Europeans to balance the 60,000 Indians required for policing these areas. Previously, 80,000 Indians were required but Pollock considered this figure as too large to be safe. The upper limit of the European soldiers for these areas was fixed by Clerk. He wanted 60,000 British troops. For the Bengal Presidency, Major David Baird calculated a total of 50,000 Europeans. Captain G.F.S. Browne of 24th Madras Infantry reduced this figure by 10,000. Pollock wanted 12,000 Europeans for balancing 50,000 Indian soldiers stationed in the Bengal Presidency. He claimed 20,000 Europeans for Punjab to balance the 30,000 Indians in the Punjab Frontier Force.[22] Bartle Frere, the Commissioner of Sind demanded 12,500 white troops to balance 37,500 Indians in the Bombay Army.[23]

There was similar disagreement about the number of white soldiers required for holding India as a whole just after 1859. Browne wanted a maximum of 200,000 white troops. The majority opinion, as supported by Baird, Major General H. Hancock of the Bombay Army and Clyde, considered 80,000 as adequate.[24] Even in the 1890s, one of the principal proponents of balancing, Lieutenant M.J. King-Harman of the 2nd Battalion of 4th Gurkha Rifles thought that the 80,000 figure as adequate.[25] After the Mutiny, the government accepted the ratio of one European for two Indian soldiers. The empire deployed 60,000 British soldiers in India. The size of the Indian military manpower stood at 130,000 men.[26] The proportion of roughly one European to two Indians continued in the British Indian Army till 1912, as evident from Table 1.2.

The British policy makers for both racial and pragmatic reasons agreed to keep the European troops as a separate contingent, instead of mixing them up with the Indian soldiers within the regiments. Actually the officers of the 'native' regiments were very possessive of the Indian soldiers they commanded and they were unwilling to share power with the commanders of the British units, who they were sure would dominate, if the Indian

TABLE 1.2: CHANGING PROPORTION OF THE BRITISH AND INDIAN SOLDIERS

Date	Army	British	Indian
1772	Madras Army	1	5.3
	Bombay Army	1	1.4
	Bengal Army	1	6.8
1794	Indian Army (including the irregulars)	1	5
	Indian Army (including only the regular units)	1	5.1
1856	Indian Army	1	6.3
1872	Indian Army	1	2
1879	Indian Army (including irregular units and the Imperial Service Corps)	1	2.5
1882	Indian Army	1	2
1885	Indian Army	1	1.8
1912	Indian Army	1	2.2

Sources: Chesney, *Indian* Polity, pp. 206, 208–9, 211, 215–16, 223–4, 227; Proportion of British to Indian troops, George S. White, para 15, 20, 28 July 1893, 1Q/10, George White Collection, MSS.EUR.F.108/24, OIOC; Note on military expenditure, 1871–2, Calcutta, 1 May 1872, Norman minutes, NAI; *Army Committee*, vol. 1, p. 36.

units were amalgamated with the white units. The British officers of the Indian regiments also advanced other reasons. If the European soldiers were permanently attached with the Indian regiments, the Punjab School warned, then the sepoys would catch the 'vices' of the European privates from close association. Brigadier J. Christie, commander of the Dinapore Division during 1858, claimed that if the European cavalry troopers were mixed with the irregular Indian cavalry units, then the Indians' mobility, which was their chief advantage, would decline as the European troopers would need commissariat stores.[27] Keeping the white troops separate from the colonial soldiers was probably a general trend among those European maritime powers who carved out overseas empires in Afro-Asia. From the seventeenth century, the Dutch also raised troops from the Indonesian archipelago. But, the colonial soldiers were not integrated with the all white units but were organized separately under command of the European officers.[28]

The white troops were outnumbered by the Indian troops. The dominant imperial view as propounded by Clyde was as follows: 'We should never rely upon . . . any of their supposed feelings, but place it altogether out of their power to do serious mischief'.[29] Superior firepower was one of the crucial factors which enabled the numerically inferior British to overwhelm the 1857 rebels.[30] So, one way of deterring the numerically superior Indian soldiers was to deny them sophisticated modern weapons and entry into the scientific branches like the sappers and the miners. This was the policy followed by the Portuguese and the French in maintaining their empires in Africa *vis-à-vis* their black troops. Pollock stressed that this policy would prevent the Indian soldiers from learning the superior tactics of offence and defence. But, this was a double-edged policy. This would undoubtedly raise the Raj's internal security but it would reduce the British Indian Empire's external security. If two thirds of the army (colonial soldiers) were armed with second grade weapons, then it meant that the Indian Army's military efficiency was drastically reduced. Nevertheless, officers like Lieutenant Colonel Wyllie emphasized that the post-Mutiny strategic demand of the Indian Army was to police India. The Sepoy Army were not destined to meet any foreign power but only disarmed Indians and the second grade troops of the Indian princes. So, arming the bulk of the personnel with inferior arms and denying them superior training was practicable.[31]

Lieutenant Colonel Thomas Lowth Harington wanted the Indian sappers and miners to perform unskilled menial jobs like digging trenches, making roads, etc. They were to be denied engineering skill and prevented from entering the laboratories and the arsenals.[32] Hancock was, however, against the exclusion of the Indians from the duties of artificers in the arsenals and laboratories. He feared that if Harington's policy was followed, then many arsenals would have to close down. Hancock agreed to reduce the Indians in the sapper branch from 98 per cent to 87 per cent. To fill this gap, he wanted the raise the European contingent by 11 per cent. For extra security, Hancock added that in the sapper and the miner corps, all the commissioned and non-commissioned officers were to be Europeans.[33]

The British officers concluded that the artillery was the queen of the battlefield. Long ago in 1748, the Directors of the East India Company had forbidden the entry of the Indians in the artillery branch. But, the high cost of maintaining the European gunners in India and the lack of their availability forced the

Company to enlist Indians.[34] But they rebelled in 1857. What was shocking was that the rebels managed their small stock of artillery very well. Harington after analysing the conduct of 1857 Mutiny concluded that the Indians were over-reliant on artillery support. So, if the army had no Indian gunners, he asserted, the Indian infantry and cavalry would never have dreamt of rebellion. The general imperial view was that to prevent any future mutiny, most of the artillery should be concentrated in British hands which in turn would strengthen the deterrence mechanism. Baird and Browne demanded that the Indians should not be allowed to become gunners and not even drivers of the gun carriages. They could only be gun lascars for menial jobs like washing the guns, etc.[35]

Clerk belonged to the Liberal lobby. He linked Egalitarian Recruitment policy in the army with the broader political aspect of imperialism. From the narrow military perspective, he argued, the military officers' programme of excluding the Indians from the scientific branches of warfare was perfectly consistent. But, this was inconsistent, he claimed, with the broader mission of the Raj. The Indians were trained in European literature and science. Their loyalty could only be won by trusting them. This was necessary since India could not be held by brute force alone. If the British were able to win the Indians' confidence by trusting them, said Clerk, they would be able to command zealous service from 'the natives'. For winning the Indians' confidence, he wanted their entry in the higher branches of warfare. In the artillery, he wanted to retain the pre-Mutiny ratio of three Europeans for five Indians. However, in the battle winning six-pounder horse artillery branch, for security reasons Clerk decided to have greater European numerical dominance, i.e. two Europeans for one Indian. With the passage of time, he was ready to devolve the vital task of guarding frontier outposts to the Indian artillery.[36]

Hancock came up with a compromise formula. He demanded British dominance also in the foot and siege artillery. In the artillery, he wanted to cut Indian manpower by 25 per cent and to raise the strength of the European contingent from 41 per cent to 66 per cent. The reduced Indian manpower could be deployed in the unhealthy regions, so as to save white men's lives. During the hot and rainy seasons, small infantry detachments needed artillery support. Hancock wanted such arduous duties to be performed by the Indian artillery. Each Indian artillery battalion was to be composed of six guns and one hundred fifty men (gunners, drivers and lascars).[37]

In the end, Clerk's broad-minded policy was not implemented and Hancock's compromise formula won the day. Before 1857, there were 5,950 Indian gunners, lascars and drivers. In 1859, Hancock wanted their numbers to be reduced to 2,900.[38] Lieutenant-General Robert Napier Commander-in-Chief of the Bombay Army also emphasized that the Europeans must dominate the Indians in the artillery branch in order to balance the numerical dominance of the Indians in the cavalry and infantry. When Bartle Frere demanded reduction in the artillery branch in a minute dated 1865, Napier replied: 'Our artillery service in India has always been required as a counterpoise to superior numbers'. In 1864, there were 2,992 Europeans and only 532 Indians in the artillery of the Bombay Army.[39] Between 1885 and 1893, there existed a shortage of gunners for the coast defence guns. But, General Frederick Roberts (later Field Marshal), the Commander-in-Chief of the Indian Army (1885–93) remembering the proficiency of the rebel Indian gunners during 1857 was against recruiting Indian gunners.[40] By 1912, the Sepoy Army possessed only 3,876 Indian gunners and 4,000 Indian sappers and miners.[41]

Though the size of the Indian artillery remained small, their loyalty was crucial. So, balancing them by recruiting diverse groups became an important plank of the British recruitment policy. Hancock warned that from 1837 onwards, all the Bombay Army's gunners had been *Purbiyas*. Dependence on a particular group from a narrow region was considered to be dangerous. Hancock demanded that the *Purbiyas* be balanced by recruiting men from west India.[42] For the Punjab Frontier Force artillery, the Punjab School recruited three distinct communities from three different regions: Sikhs from the Sutlej area, Punjabi Muslims from west Punjab (present-day Punjab in Pakistan) and Hindustanis from the North-West Province. For the Bengal Army's artillery, they proposed the replacement of the *Purbiyas* (whose preponderance was considered as one of the primary reasons for the 1857 Mutiny) with the Anglo-Indians, low castes and Muslims from the *bazars* and the cantonments at Meerut and

Kanpur. The British were aiming to create a rural-urban divide between the gunners, the infantry and the cavalry as the latter two branches enlisted men from rural backgrounds.[43] The crux of the problem, however, for the British was how to disaggregate the manpower pool of the Indian infantry and the cavalry.

Even though a large number of the sepoys rebelled in 1857, the British could not totally forego Indian manpower. General John Jacob in June 1858 summed up the position by writing: 'We cannot hold India by an army . . . composed of English soldiers, and . . . to attempt to do so must be attended with speedy and utter ruin. . . . England could not supply the number of soldiers . . . required for the purpose of maintaining such an army'.[44] Beside the demographic limitation of Britain, Jacob pointed out the political compulsions of recruiting indigenous troops. He continued:

And . . . it is clear . . . that, if we could command even such a host of Europeans as the grand army with which Napoleon invaded Russia, the attempt to coerce India with such forces would only end in more complete and hopeless failure. The mere brute force of hundreds of thousands of men becomes powerless before that of hundreds of millions of such people as the nations of India. The whole force of the Mogul empire was never able to subdue even one of these nations, the Rajputs.[45]

Even as late as 1893, the British policy makers pointed out that recruitment of the Indians in the Sepoy Army was necessary for co-opting the military elements and to use their military pride for fighting imperial wars.[46]

In the immediate aftermath of the 1857 Mutiny, the questions before the British were, then, which 'nationalities' to recruit, in what proportions and how to organize them. 1857 slowed down the growth of a pan-Indian Army within the colonial context. Clyde voiced the post-Mutiny policy. He asserted: ' . . . the distinct organization I believe to have been a benefit. If we had possessed one army in 1857, instead of four armies, we should have lost India'.[47] Charles Wood (the Secretary of State for India from 1859 to 1866) emphasized territorial balancing. To prevent the growth of wider feelings, which he considered to be the root cause of the 1857 Mutiny, Wood wanted the regiments to enlist from particular districts. He considered this scheme to be more useful than trying to balance various castes within the units. In the aftermath of the 1857 disaster, the imperialists agreed, for political if not for military reasons, to have separate regional armies each with a separate organization and distinct social compositions and territorial bases. Segregation was considered necessary to prevent the growth of sentiment of unity among the colonial soldiers, and to utilize the local armies against each other if necessary.[48] The vexed question, which the policy makers faced, was how to organize enlistment in the regional forces.

The balancing was effected at two levels: among the various regional armies, and among different groups within the regiments. Clerk, an advocate of centralization from the top, pursued the line that the detailed modalities for balancing within each army were too serious a business to be left to the regimental colonels. So, the army headquarter should fix the regulations as regards balancing, which the regimental commanders must follow.[49]

The question then arose as to whether to go for general service corps or local units. Browne demanded that every Indian should be enlisted for general service, which would provide the government maximum flexibility in arranging deployment to suit the balancing principles. To prevent the growth of territorial ties, he was against stationing soldiers in their recruiting grounds. He wanted the Madras Army, which recruited from the Madras Presidency, to garrison the Bengal Presidency and the Bengal Army, which enlisted from its own presidency, to police the Madras Presidency.[50] Deployment of subject peoples away from their recruiting zones, in order to prevent any bonhomie between the civilians and the troops, was a policy followed by the European powers even at home. During the First World War, the Alsatians and the Lorrainers who were recently brought under the German Empire were stationed not in northern France but in eastern Europe.[51]

Harington spearheaded the dissent. He claimed that the imperial policy of recruiting men from a particular area for general service and then deploying them into another corner of India was unworkable. He pointed out that some communities were unwilling to serve in all parts of India. He said that the Sikhs would not serve in Bengal and, when they were posted there, they deserted.[52] Harington actually was making a case for maintaining local irregular corps for particular regions.

Frere pointed out that the characteristic qualities of the

different groups ought to be encouraged and the lack of overall assimilation among the groups within the units would prevent any mutiny from becoming wholesale. As regards the deployment and organization of the different groups in the regiments, the Punjab lobby argued that the general service corps containing all the 'races' and 'tribes' (mixed indiscriminately and eligible for service anywhere) should not be raised. This was because if the inhabitants of different regions and communities remained together for a long time, then they would lose all their distinctions and a corporate sense might develop among them, and then it might take an anti-British colour.[53]

Clerk supported Harington's and the Punjab lobby's proposal. The problem with Browne's scheme of having four distinct territorial zones for the four regional armies (Bombay, Bengal, Madras and the Punjab Frontier Force) was that the different communities were not evenly distributed throughout India. For example, the Muslims were concentrated in some pockets, so if different regiments of a particular army were assigned a region within that army's territorial boundary then there was a high probability of ethnic imbalance, which in turn would neutralize the whole logic of balancing. Clerk gave the example of the Guides Corps of the Punjab Frontier Force. The Guides were assigned to Peshawar Valley (within the region west of the river Sutlej demarcated for the Punjab Frontier Force's recruitment) which had a concentration of Muslims. So, the Guides got mostly Muslims and few Sikhs, as the latter were concentrated in central Punjab (present India's Punjab). Hence, instead of the four regional armies recruiting from four distinct areas, Clerk wanted the recruitment area of all the armies to be the Ganga–Jamuna doab region and west India. The voice of disagreement was from Lieutenant-Colonel E.B. Johnson, the officiating Adjutant General. In 1862, he asserted that some regions like the western half of north India, where the rebellion was intense, should be excluded from the army's enlistment zone.[54]

However, the general opinion was that no area should be totally neglected. Major-General H. Tombs commanding Awadh Division in the mid 1860s was for continued enlistment of the *Purbiyas* in the Bengal Army's infantry because of their good physique as well as for their political co-option.[55] General Hugh Rose, the Commander-in-Chief of the Indian Army from 1860 to

1865, pointed out that for a broad-based balancing, a particular presidency army might recruit part of its manpower from another presidency. He wanted the Bombay Army to balance the Marathas from Maharashtra, its own territory, with the Hindustanis recruited from Hindustan, the Bengal Army's recruiting ground, and the Deccanis, drawn from the Madras Army's enlistment zone. Rose pointed out that if the Bombay Army's recruiting were confined within the Bombay Presidency, then enough communities would not be available for balancing. Further, an adequate number of Marathas would not be available to balance the other communities in the other regional forces.[56] Hancock modified Rose's policy and stated that every presidency army should enlist three-fourths of its personnel from its own presidency and the rest from other presidencies for greater social and territorial heterogeneity. During 1870, the Commander-in-Chief of India adopted Hancock's policy.[57] Hancock's scheme with minor modifications continued till 1878.

Following Hancock's policy, the Bombay Army recruited 29 per cent of its manpower from the Bengal Presidency and the rest from Bombay Presidency in 1879. The Eden Commission in 1879 reintroduced Browne's plan. It wanted the three presidency armies to enlist from their own presidencies.[58] However, the Eden Commission's recommendation was not implemented in toto. In 1888, the Hyderabad Contingent[59] of the Madras Army recruited 75 per cent of the manpower from the region south of the Narmada and Mahanadi (area demarcated for the Madras Army) and the rest, 25 per cent, from Delhi and Punjab (regions demarcated for the Bengal Army and the Punjab Frontier Force). So, a somewhat diluted form of Hancock's policy was being followed. Several officers of the Madras Army like General Protheroe were against any restrictions regarding recruitment. Protheroe was a supporter of general service units. He wanted the Hyderabad Contingent to recruit from all over India.[60]

The next tricky question, which the British had to solve, was how to establish a balance between the four regional armies and especially what to do with the big bad wolf: the Bengal Army. Poilock was also nervous about the 80,000 Punjabis (mostly Sikhs and Punjabi Muslims) in the Punjab Frontier Force and the Bengal Army. So he proposed cuts. In order to maintain four equal sized armies, Clerk wanted to raise the size of the Madras and the

Bombay armies. But, the problem still remained, because Bengal Army had to be very big, as its duty was to police the Bengal Presidency, which was the biggest presidency. Clerk wanted to reduce the size of the Bengal Presidency by transferring areas in central India (Nagpur, Saugor and Bundelkhand), as well as Burma to the Madras Presidency, and Rajputana to the Bombay Presidency. These areas were to be garrisoned by the Madras and the Bombay armies respectively.[61] Hancock in a similar vein added that the Bengal Army, being spread over a wide area in north and central India, could not be supervised efficiently. So, it should be concentrated for proper surveillance, by transferring large chunks of central India to the Madras and the Bombay presidencies. The Bengal Army should only guard the region from Cuttack to Gwalior. This plan, claimed Hancock, had a further advantage. By deploying men from south and west India (who constituted the Madras and the Bombay armies) into large parts of north India, the Hindustanis who had rebelled in 1857 could be kept under check.[62]

The Balanced Recruitment lobby's ideologues pointed out that the domination of the Bengal Army by one group, i.e. the *Purbiyas*, resulted in the catastrophe of 1857. Consequently, their aim was to make this army's composition cosmopolitan. Pollock's policy was to establish a balance within the Bengal Army by enlisting two different groups—Punjabis and Hindustanis.[63] The Punjab School hit upon the idea of balancing the Hindustanis in the Bengal Army with the Sikhs and the Pathans, groups which fed the Punjab Frontier Force. The lobby, which included Frere and Rose, could be termed as the 'Sind School', altered the geographical locales and wanted to balance the *Purbiyas* with the inhabitants drawn from Konkan and Sind. Christie focussed on balancing within the cavalry corps. Over-dependence on either the high caste Hindus or the Muslims of a particular region was equally dangerous for him. He argued that, before the 1857 Mutiny, mostly Hindustani Muslims joined the irregular cavalry units of the Bengal Army, and they had rebelled. He wanted to establish equilibrium by enlisting the Shekawatis from Rajasthan and the Marathas.[64] In 1862, Lieutenant-Colonel H.W. Norman (who later rose to the post of Major-General) argued that the Punjabis (Sikhs and Muslims from Punjab) should not be allowed to exceed 50 per cent of the Bengal Army's strength and the

Muslims from the region around the river Indus (i.e. North-West Frontier Muslims) not to exceed 12.5 per cent of the personnel.[65]

Finally, the Bengal Army's recruiting ground, instead of being limited to only Hindustan, also came to include Punjab and Nepal. Recruitment from the latter two regions went on increasing with the passage of time. In the 1860s, most of the regiments included *Purbiyas*, Hindustani Muslims, Jats, Sikhs and Punjabi Muslims. In 1862, the Bengal Army recruited four infantry regiments from Nepal, another sixteen from Punjab and about twenty-eight infantry units from Haryana and Awadh (present-day central Uttar Pradesh).[66]

The balancing policy worked well in the Madras Army, where three groups from south India, and the other communities enlisted from outside the Madras Presidency, prevented the domination of any single community. This is evident from Table 1.3. Browne in 1859 warned the authorities that the number of Deccani Muslims (i.e. Muslims from south India) ought to be decreased as they constituted four-fifths of the Madras cavalry. Their proportion in the infantry remained one-third, and hence manageable.[67] The dominance of the Deccani Muslims reached a dangerous proportion especially in the four cavalry regiments of the Hyderabad Contingent. In 1875, the Deccani Muslims constituted about 87.5 per cent of the Hyderabad Contingent cavalry.[68] The Resident of Hyderabad in 1876 informed the commanding officers that each cavalry regiment ought to be composed of three squadrons. And one squadron should consist of either Deccani or Rajputana Muslims (Muslims from present day Rajasthan), one squadron from the North-West Frontier Muslims and the third squadron should be raised from the Sikhs. Each infantry regiment of the Hyderabad Contingent was composed of eight companies. The Resident directed that four companies should be composed of North-West Frontier tribes, one company to be raised from the Deccani Muslims, one from the Deccani Hindus and two companies from the Sikhs.[69] In 1892, the Officiating Resident at Hyderabad, T.J.C. Plowden warned the Government of India's Military Department regarding the political dangers of over-relying on the Deccani Muslims in the Hyderabad Contingent's cavalry.[70] Table 1.3 shows that between 1859 and 1894, the size of the Deccani Muslim contingent in the Madras Army was reduced from 58 per cent to 41 per cent. By

1898, the Hyderabad Contingent infantry also recruited Ahirs (middle castes) from Haryana.[71]

In the mid 1870s, the Resident of Hyderabad was pressurized by the Military Department of the Government of India to rely more on the 'martial races' of north India. The Resident counter-argued that instead of relying on the Sikhs, Hindustani Muslims and the Rajputs who were joining the Bengal Army in large numbers, the Hyderabad Contingent should try to balance the Deccani Muslims with the Marathas and other Hindus from central and south India. In the end, Colonel H.K. Burne, Secretary to the Government of India in the Military Department accepted the wisdom of policy of not relying too much on the 'martial races' from Hindustan.[72] The territorial balancing in the Madras Army is shown in Table 1.4. Within the Madras Presidency, four regions supplied recruits, which ensured balancing. And Hindustan played a secondary role in this balancing scheme.

TABLE 1.3: SOCIAL COMPOSITION OF THE MADRAS ARMY, 1859–94

Groups	1859 (%)	1861 (%)	1876 (%)	1878 (%)	1879 (%)	1880 (%)	1894 (%)
Deccani Muslims	58	58	38	36	33.5	37	41
Tamils	10	9.6	16	9	10.5	9	12
Telugus	23	23	28	38	36	36	35
Hindustanis	9	9.4	18	17	20	18	12

Sources: Lieutenant-Colonel Gautam Sharma, *Indian Army through the Ages*, Bombay: Allied, 1979, p. 242; Dodwell, *Sepoy Recruitment*, pp. 47–8; Progs. no. 4584, 20 August 1879, MDP, NAI.

TABLE 1.4: REGIONAL COMPOSITION OF THE MADRAS ARMY, 1878–94

Regions Supplying Recruits	% of Recruits at Different Dates			
	1878	1879	1880	1894
Karnataka	23.6	24.2	24.5	16.7
Trichinopoly	17.7	17.6	17	30.9
Northern Circars	43.4	42.7	43.4	35.1
Mysore and Ceded Districts	11.4	12.1	11.8	11.2
North India	3.9	3.4	3.3	6.1

Source: Dodwell, *Sepoy Recruitment*, pp. X–XIII, 47.

Omissi writes that the objective of British recruitment policy in the 1860s was to divide the Indian Army into four main components, which were recruited from different areas. In the north, he continues, the Hindustanis balanced the Punjabis; and the Bombay and Madras personnel balanced the Bengal Army.[73] But, as this chapter shows no such coherent all-India doctrine actually existed among the proponents of the Egalitarian lobby. The Punjab School filled up the Punjab Frontier Force with the Pathans, Punjabi Muslims and the Sikhs, and wanted the *Purbiyas* in the Bengal Army to be balanced with the Punjabis. The Sind School wanted the Bombay Army to procure manpower from west, central and north India and the Madras Army followed the pre-1857 mixture of enlisting men from south and west India.

Next the Balanced Recruitment lobby turned their attention to the inter-ethnic and intra-ethnic amalgamations among and within the regiments—the basic building block of the Sepoy Army. Each infantry regiment had about 800 to 1,000 men divided into eight to ten companies.[74] In the pre-1857 era, the social, religious and territorial bases of the Bengal Army regiments were very narrow. The infantry regiments were a monopoly of the *Purbiyas*, with a few Ahirs from north India. The cavalry regiments were composed of Muslims from Rohilkhand. In the 1850s the authorities attempted a half-hearted policy of balancing the high caste Hindus in the infantry with the Sikhs. The Bengal units stationed in Punjab were ordered to fill up the vacancies with Sikhs, whose number were to vary between 100 to 200 men per regiment.[75] However, the quantum of Sikh recruitment was inadequate to balance the *Purbiyas*. When the Bengal Army was cut to ribbons in 1857, the British got a free hand to reorganize the regiments on new ethnic lines.

Not unity but diversity became the post-Mutiny imperial maxim. Clyde formulated the new principles in the following words: 'A craving for uniformity has already done much mischief in the native army. What seems to be wanted is not uniformity, but dissimilarity. We should therefore have corps of all races and under different systems.'[76] The general opinion was that all the units should be multi-ethnic. However, discussion on the issue of arrangement of the various ethnic groups within each regiment continued throughout the nineteenth century.

One lobby argued for a general mixture even within the

companies. Wyllie wanted all the 'races' to be distributed promiscuously within the companies, thus resulting in the general mixture of units.[77] Lieutenant-Colonel R.H. Gall of the 14th Kings Light Dragoons wanted different groups from separate areas to be mixed up within the *risalahs* (equivalent to troops) of the irregular cavalry. He was sure that the lack of sympathy among men of dissimilar social and territorial backgrounds would prevent another mutiny.[78]

The case for class company regiments was put forward by Browne. He wanted a regiment to have companies of different groups, but there should not be any mixture within the companies. He was apprehensive that a general mixture would reduce the sense of distinct ethnic identities of the various groups thus disturbing the logic of 'divide and rule'. His model was Colonel Coke's Rifles, which was raised in 1849 with separate Afghan, Pathan and Sikh companies led by Indian officers from the same ethnic groups. Browne asserted that this system would create a competitive spirit among the distinct 'racial' companies, and the Indian officers of the same community would understand their men better.[79] For similar reasons Christie demanded each *risalah* should have a distinct ethnic group drawn from a particular district to prevent Muslim domination in the cavalry regiment.[80] Another votary of the class company system was Lieutenant-Colonel W. Mayhew, Adjutant General of the army. He pointed out the advantages of this system from the perspective of playing off the various Indian communities against each other within a regiment. In 1861 he wrote: 'The advantage of the company composition is, that a fraction of a corps may be tainted, without the other parts being affected; that the rivalry or antagonism of different sects is not rubbed away or weakened by general mixture.'[81] During the sixteenth and the seventeenth centuries in the Spanish Army of Flanders many *tercios* seemed to have operated on a sort of class company system. Each *tercio* had companies formed of various nationalities like Spanish, Walloon, German, Italian and the British.[82]

Major-General S. Cotton, commanding Peshawar Division in 1860 was for class regiments of different religious and caste groups. The class regiments were a modification of the district regiments. The latter enlisted from a certain district. Two examples were the Ludhiana and the Ferozepur regiments.

However, a district regiment might include more than one community. But, this was not the case in class regiments. They recruited a particular group from a particular area. Cotton wanted Sikh regiments, Dogra regiments, Punjabi Muslim regiments and Afridi (Indus tribe) regiments.[83] Class regiments remained a favoured option for Major-General Charles Reid, ex-commandant of the Sirmoor Rifles. In 1867, Reid pointed out the advantages of the class units over class company units in the following manner:

Class companies will never, in my opinion, prevent a combination of the whole corps; but class corps, from the very fact of their being kept distinct, and encouraged to stand aloof, must bring about rivalry and emulation, and we should not hear of one corps of Brahmins and Rajputs combining with a Muslim regiment, or a Sikh corps with a Gurkha. Each keeping up their nationality would prevent combination.[84]

The Punjab School came up with a compromise solution for pleasing the various dissenting factions. The Punjab School argued that some regiments should be homogeneous, i.e. class regiments. The remaining regiments should be heterogeneous; a mixed of class company and general mixed regiments. For the class company regiment the Punjab School proposed the following proportions: four Muslim companies, four Sikh companies and two Rajput companies or five Muslim companies, three Sikh companies, one Hindustani company and one Hill Rajput company[85] or five Sikh companies, three Muslim companies, one Hill Rajput company and one Hindustani company. The basic principle was that in a particular regiment, no group would be allowed to exceed 50 per cent of the personnel strength.[86] In a similar vein, Clerk agreed that the guiding principle should be that no community from a particular locality would be allowed to dominate in a particular regiment. He wanted 50 per cent of the regiments to be of general mixed units and the rest to be class company units.[87] The Bengal Army also had some local regiments like the Assam and the Sylhet regiments. They recruited from the region where they were deployed mainly for policing duties. For heterogeneity, Norman in 1862 advocated that such units should recruit at least one fourth of their personnel from north India.[88]

In the end, the Punjab School's scheme supported by Lieutenant-Colonel E.B. Johnson, officiating Adjutant General of the army won the day, in a somewhat modified form. In 1864, of the nineteen Bengal cavalry regiments, three were class regiments (one was composed of the Hindustani Muslims, another of the Jats and the third was composed of trans-Indus tribes), six were mixed (Sikhs, Jats, Rajputs, Brahmins mixed with the *risalahs*) and rest were class company regiments.[89] Of the fifty Bengal Army infantry regiments, sixteen were class company units, six were class regiments and the rest were mixed regiments.[90] General mixed regiments predominated in the Bombay Army. This was because Lord Napier of Magdala, Commander-in-Chief of the Bombay Army from 1866 till 1869 remained a votary of the general mixed units. In his view the Bombay regiments of mixed races which included Marathas, Hindustani Muslims, Sikhs, Pathans, etc., did well in foreign services.[91]

Brigadier-General Chesney pointed out the deficiencies of the general mixed regiments. In the year after the Second Afghan War (1878–80) ended, Chesney claimed:

In the very interesting and valuable 'Autobiography of a Sepoy', lately published, it is said that the Sikh recruits were looked upon at first with loathing by the Brahmin sepoys, as unclean. But the feeling wore of by degrees, and it did not prevent the great number of the Sikh soldiers in these regiments from taking at least a passive part in the outbreak. So, I am against General Mixture.[92]

In the last decade of the nineteenth century, when the trend was towards class regiments, C.B. Pritchard pointed out the necessity of having class company regiments. In 1893, he wrote to the Commander-in-Chief of the Indian Army: 'I believe that internal disturbances still remain the chief danger to which our rule is liable . . . the risks of the recurrence of internal trouble have been aggravated by the advance of Russia towards our borders'.[93] He was afraid that the class regiments might take the side of either Hindus or Muslims in case of communal riots between these two communities. Pritchard warned that full reliance could not be placed upon class regiments if they were called to act against men of their own race or religion across the frontier. In April 1892 disturbances broke out in Kalat. And the Agent to the Governor General in Baluchistan reported that that he could not rely on the 40th Pathans, 24th and 26th Bombay infantry regiments. These three units were class regiments composed of

Muslims and quartered in Quetta. The warning given by Brigadier-General Chamberlain in 1862 that Muslim class regiments might fraternize with the tribes of the North-West Frontier came true.[94] Pritchard concluded his argument by saying: 'Class regiments are more combat effective against external threats, but from the point of view of internal insurrections, it is dangerous to convert the class company and mixed regiments of the Bombay and the Madras armies into class regiments recruited from upper India'. Hence, wrote Pritchard, the Martial Race ideologues' policy of converting the class company and mixed regiments of the Bombay and the Madras armies into class regiments recruited from the martial races of North-West Frontier was impolitic.[95]

The two most crucial dimensions of ethnic balancing were caste and religion. In the 1890s, with the dominance of the Martial Race theory, argues DeWitt C. Ellinwood, the British initiated socio-religious manipulation of the Indian soldiers, which he terms as ethnic policy.[96] From the following pages it will be clear that disaggregating Indian military manpower on the basis of social and religious identities, and then altering the proportion in the army to suit the imperial needs, was very much a feature of the Sepoy Army's enlistment policy from 1859 onwards.

III

RELIGION AND THE BALANCED RECRUITMENT LOBBY

A fault line appeared among the imperialists as regards their perceptions of the effects of various religions on the temperaments of different communities. The minority group of officers perceived no link between the different faiths of the various social groups and their sense of loyalty. But, the majority opinion was that religion and loyalty were intermixed. Harington represented the first group. He said that there was no intrinsic connection between the religion a group followed and the mentality of its members. So, religious identities should not guide enlistment. He claimed that the 1857 Mutiny did not occur due to any religious factors. Faith was used as a medium to legitimize the grievances, which he identified as non-religious (like the annexation of Awadh, withdrawal of family pension from the families of many soldiers, etc.).[97]

But, the dominant faction linked religion with the recruitment programme, because they believed in the religiosity of some groups. Clerk, one spokesman of this lobby, argued on just the opposite lines of Harington. Clerk claimed that the religious fanaticism of the *Purbiyas* encouraged them to rebel.[98] All the advocates of this lobby agreed that no particular religious groups were to be allowed to dominate the army. Nonetheless, there was much disagreement among them concerning which religious groups were most dependable.

Following the assumption that members of the same religion would be loyal to each other, Browne wanted the Indian Christians for the crucial job of driving the artillery carriages. The perceptions of the British about the performance of the various groups during 1857 influenced their balancing paradigm. To strengthen his case, Browne claimed that the Indian Christians remained loyal in 1857. Toeing this line, Hugh Rose ordered that Indian Christian drummers and bandsmen of those *Purbiya* regiments which were disbanded because of their part in the 1857 Mutiny and those Anglo-Indians who wanted to join the army were to be inducted as soldiers.[99] Rose continued that the Indian Christians had the advantage of knowing the customs and languages of the Indians, so they could function as proper feedback channels. For this reason, Rose also wanted the Indian Christians in the commissariat and military transport.[100] In 1864, Rose wrote to John Lawrence the Governor General, that the lessons of the Mutiny should not be forgotten. The British were able to recruit gunners and sappers from the Eurasians when the Hindus and the Muslims rebelled. He argued that the Eurasians should also be inducted in the cavalry since they fought gallantly in several regiments like the 3rd Bombay Light Cavalry.[101]

The Punjab lobby contended that, if adequate numbers of Indian Christians were not available, then the Karens of Pegu were to be utilized, because they had embraced Christianity. Traditional enmity existed between the Burmese and the Karens. And the Burmese were enemies of the British. For the Raj, the enemy's enemy was a friend. So, the Karens were a favoured group. The Punjab lobby felt that if the Asian Christians were scattered indiscriminately, then they would lose their distinct Christian ethos, and the main purpose of recruiting them would be lost. Thus, they wanted separate Christian regiments, which should also include pastors, to strengthen the ethos of Christianity within the units.[102]

The Eurasians were organized into the East Indian Regiment. But, in 1864, the government decided to demobilize this unit. In February 1864, Lieutenant-Colonel Carey commandant of the Eurasian regiment protested to Colonel Haythorne, Adjutant General of the Army in the following words:

The Regiment has not had a fair trial. I am still of opinion a good and most serviceable corps could be made out of half castes, provided the recruits and men furnished to me were young and tractable like some of my last arrivals, and not broken down and crooked drummers like those enlisted on the first raising of the Regiment and of which some fifty or sixty remains.[103]

Carey's appeal was followed by a letter in March 1864 from Hugh Rose to John Lawrence. Rose reminded Lawrence:

It would be erroneous to disband or discharge veterans who are steadily improving in discipline and organization . . . the native army should be composed of as many diverse elements as possible that would make it difficult in acting in unison against the government. For this very reason, the Native Christian Regiment should be retained . . . . Instead of disbanding the Native Christian Regiment, the experiment should be followed on a bigger scale. The Native Christian Regiments should recruit from the Indian Christians scattered in all parts of India.[104]

One aspect of the imperial plan was that the 'innately disloyal traits' of the high caste Hindus were to be checked by balancing them with an antagonistic religious community, other than the Indian Christians. Browne said that the Brahmins in the Madras Army, unlike their counterpart in the Bengal Army, did not rebel. The secret was that the high caste Hindus of north India in the Madras Army, were balanced by the Deccani Muslims.[105] This scheme was provided as a prescription for the Bengal Army. For some of the imperial elite, Muslims emerged as the most favoured potential candidates. Wyllie wanted to balance the 'treacherous' and 'fanatical' Brahmins with the Muslims. He assured his superiors that pan-Islamism was a myth and the Muslim soldiers of the Sepoy Army would certainly fight other Muslims.[106] At the same time, over-reliance on the Muslims was considered dangerous. In 1876, the Resident of Hyderabad reminded his colleagues that it would be dangerous to have a very large number of 'treacherous' Deccani Muslims in the Madras Army.[107]

Besides the Hindus and the Muslims, the other religious community that attracted much imperial attention was the Sikhs. In 1859, Baird wanted the Sikhs in greater proportion than other religious groups.[108] But, this line of thinking was challenged by some of his colleagues. Browne and Clerk sounded a note of caution. For them, the high caste Hindus who had recently mutinied, was the immediate danger. But, they claimed, the so called 'loyal' Sikhs posed the greatest potential danger. Browne said that favouring them was dangerous, as it would result in over-dependence on them in the long run, just as the British were over-dependent on the goodwill of the *Purbiyas* in the 1850s. He continued that the Sikhs had no intrinsic loyalty to the Raj. They joined the British banner for pay, plunder and hatred for the Hindustanis. Many British officers reported that the Sikhs had told them half-seriously and half-jokingly: 'The time will come when we will settle with you; we hated the Hindustanis and we killed them. The Raj will be yours tomorrow, but who can say whose it will be in another two years?' Browne supplemented this grim warning by saying that he himself had conversed with the Sikhs and their opinion was that, it was just a matter of chance as to who had the upper hand. If any Punjabi chief rebelled, Browne asserted, then the Sikhs would rise in mutiny.[109] Clerk ended the debate by saying that an equal proportion should be maintained among the different religious groups from different areas—Sikhs from central Punjab, the Muslims from west Punjab, and Hindus from north India.[110] Ultimately, Browne and Clerk's suggestions were implemented.

In 1876, the Resident of Hyderabad tried to balance the Deccani Muslims in the Hyderabad Contingent with the Sikhs. He reminded the commandant of this force that when in 1857 the 1st Hyderabad Contingent Cavalry rebelled at Aurangabad, the Sikhs remained loyal. Again, the 3rd Hyderabad Contingent Cavalry did not mutiny because a large number of the sowars were Sikhs. So, the Resident concluded that in future when vacancies occured they ought to be filled with Sikhs.[111] However, the Sikhs never became predominant in the Madras Army. Even in 1892, General Protheroe was against having more than one Sikh squadron in each cavalry regiment of the Hyderabad

Contingent.[112] Despite such opposition, as we will see in the next chapter, under the aegis of the Martial Race ideologues, the share of the Sikhs and the Punjabi Muslims became disproportionate in the Sepoy Army in the last decade of the nineteenth century.

Let us look at balancing of the religious groups at the macro and micro levels. Major-General J. Hope Grant, who commanded the Awadh Field Force during the Mutiny, favoured a bipolar balance within the irregular cavalry regiments. His scheme was that the Pathans of the Indus frontier were to balance the Sikhs within each unit. He was against considering the Muslim community of north-west India as a monolithic entity. He implied that the mentalities of the Muslims varied with regions. The Yusufzai tribe among the trans-Indus Pathans hated the Punjabi Muslims of western Punjab and considered them inferior. So, he was ready to experiment with a tripolar religious balance within each regiment with the Sikhs of central Punjab, the Punjabi Muslims of Jhelum-Chenab area, and the Yusufzai Pathans from the Indus border.[113] Clyde's principle was lack of uniformity. Any uniform plan for organizing the religious groups was dangerous in his eyes. He pointed out that at the macro level, Hindu regiments must balance the Muslim regiments. The Hindu regiments may be mono-caste units or multi-caste units (composed of Brahmins and Rajputs, but organized in separate companies). He was also for mixing up the Hindus and the Muslims within the regiments. The religious elements of a particular unit were to come from a particular district and in some cases also from different areas.[114]

Let us glance at the religious balancing which occurred in reality. In 1883, the 17th Bengal Infantry, a class company regiment, had three Hindustani Muslim companies which were balanced by five Hindu companies (two Brahmin and three Rajput). This was a case of bipolar religious balance. The 22nd Infantry Regiment of the Bengal Army exemplified a tripolar balance. Within it, there were four Sikh companies, one Brahmin company and three Punjabi Muslim companies, balancing each other.[115] The tripolar religious cum territorial balance was exemplified in the 37th Madras Infantry Regiment, which was a microcosm of the other units of the Madras Army. Of the eight companies, five were composed of Hindus enlisted from

Masulipatnam, Madurai and Trichinopoly. The Muslims from Karnataka, Vellore and Hyderabad constituted two companies. And the Indian Christians from Arcot and Kolar constituted one company.[116]

IV

CIVILIZING THE SAVAGES: MARGINAL GROUPS AND THE BALANCED RECRUITMENT LOBBY

To this day, caste and calling are alike hereditary.

Brigadier C.H. Brownlow[117]

Next came the troublesome question of caste. The British accepted caste as one of the principal determinant of Indian society, which could not be ignored in constructing an Indian Army. Frere represented the minority position, when he asserted

Race, caste and tribe should be used in case of a soldier as a matter of identification like his father's name or surname. Any good recruit should be taken. . . . The native soldiers should be treated as men with feelings, passions and prejudices . . . and not as mere machines or animals obeying some invariable instinct of caste or race. . . . Race alone to which we are now trusting will be a most fallacious guide. Not only shall we dismiss many good and useful soldiers and retain many bad and traitorous one, but we shall perpetuate a false and dangerous principle.[118]

This is probably the most open challenge to the Bengal School's preference for the high castes and Field-Marshal Lord Roberts' later dalliance with the martial-unmartial division of the Indian 'races'.

Harry G.W. Smith voiced the dominant imperial opinion in 1859 when he said 'the subject of caste is a matter of utmost importance to the future army of India'.[119] So, the British policy makers spent much ink over the caste question. The imperial policy of using the various castes of India for the policy of 'Divide and Rule' was succinctly put forward by Major-General Charles Reid. In 1867 Reid wrote:

So long as we keep up caste, which is our tower of strength in India, and have men of different religions to deal with, we can, by keeping them separate, and by encouraging the feeling which, happily, already exists, of one standing aloof from other, effect our object, which we do not at present, in my opinion, by throwing all classes together in the same corps.[120]

When the *Pandies* turned their muskets against their masters, the British, while trying to absorb the shock, over-reacted. In a fit of revenge, some officers who operated in Hindustan enlisted the low castes to teach the 'disloyal' high castes a lesson. After the Mutiny, the army became a peacekeeping force and was reduced to half of its pre-1857 size.[121] The British then had to decide whether these low status groups had to be integrated on a regular basis and, if so, up to what extent. From the British officers' discourse, we can reconstruct the varying imperial images about those who were at the lower strata of the ritual hierarchy. The imperial positions on low-caste enlistment were conflicting. One group was for their exclusion. Baird was against the inclusion of the low castes, because in his view the sweepers and the water carriers of Punjab fought badly in 1857. He claimed that the high-caste soldiers should get the real credit because they valiantly led the newly raised low-caste levies during the Mutiny.[122] But, the majority opinion was to recruit the low castes for ending the high-caste monopoly in the army.

The lobby for the inclusion of the low castes witnessed the emergence of two factions who may be categorized as the Gradualists/Moderates and the Radicals. The Gradualists were for the slow and limited inclusion of selected fringe groups. They were cautious in their approach, so as not to threaten existing social reality and they did not want to alienate the high and the middle castes. The Radicals were for the unlimited entry of the marginal groups, and that too in the major branches of the army. They were for quickly changing the Indian social structure through recruitment and service in the armed forces. Their policy could be termed as 'Active Recruitment policy' as opposed to 'Passive Enlistment policy' of the Gradualists.

Lieutenant-Colonel W. Mayhew, the Adjutant General of the post-Mutiny army was an advocate of the Active Recruitment policy. He wanted the army to function as a motor of social change. Mayhew argued that the socially degraded groups, who lacked self-esteem because of their lower position, could and should be improved, by recruiting them and then disciplining them. It was hoped that this scheme would transform their nature. Mayhew accepted that the low castes were 'ignorant' and 'barbaric'; but he held that in the army, as they would interact with the high castes on the basis of equality, their sense of inferiority would disappear. The army's appreciation of merit would implant self-respect among the low castes, and they would try to emulate their betters and get a chance to prove themselves. Mayhew continued that the personal hygiene of the low castes would improve with military discipline. Captain E. Hall, commandant of the Aligarh Levy in 1860 argued in a similar tone that though the Chamars were given to drugs and liquor, once within the army, their habits would change and they would become good soldiers. To cap it all, Charles Wood, the Secretary of State for India wrote from London that low castes had performed well. Wood warned that in the mixed regiments, the low castes would be depressed due to interaction with the high castes. So, for him the solution was to set up low-caste regiments where, with the support of the British officers, all the marginal groups would develop proper self-confidence.[123] Lieutenant-Colonel H. Bruce, chief of Awadh Police and Colonel E. Darvali, commander of the 3rd Bengal European Regiment belonged to the Radical section. In 1860 they supported the enlistment of even the lowest castes like Domes and Pasees from north India.[124]

The Gradualists were against allowing entry to all the low castes. Brigadier F. Wheeler, the spokesman of the Gradualist section of the low caste lobby, divided the low castes into lower and lowest castes. For him, the Jats, Ahirs, Gujars and Lodhs were the lower castes, whom he considered to be disciplined, and hence eligible for enlistment. He believed that though the lowest castes like the Bhungies were loyal they could not command obedience from others. Hence, Wheeler regarded them as ineligible for enlistment.[125] Frere was also against the recruitment of the lowest castes like Maugs and the Mehters, who were hereditary hangmen and sweepers. Similarly, the Punjab lobby was against including the Mazhbi Sikhs (sweepers) and the Mosulles (Muslim sweepers). While they agreed that in theory they ought to rise above casteism, in practice they could not do so because in India caste was a social reality, as the Indians themselves maintained the caste system. If the lowest castes were allowed to join the army, then the British feared that the high and middle castes would avoid the army. And this would jeopardize the balancing game. The Punjab School warned that the high-castes would tolerate to serve with the Shudras (who joined the Punjab Frontier Force), but not with the lowest castes, because the Shudras' position was higher than the lowest castes like the Mehters. Secondly, they feared that the Indian officers from the lowest caste would have no influence over the high-caste privates. The imperialists were convinced that the marginal groups were themselves not ready to challenge the existing social order, even with the sahibs' backing. The Punjab lobby cited an episode in 1857 when a high caste Bengal Army regiment mutinied, the low-caste camp followers and the sweepers followed them.[126]

To challenge the tyranny of the high castes, the Punjab School hit upon the idea of creating some exclusive low-caste regiments. While Wood was for enlisting all sorts of low castes in such regiments, the Punjab School was for inclusion of certain selected low castes in the low-caste units. Gradually, the Punjab School proposed, some mixed regiments ought to be raised, where some high castes would join for the want of employment. Slowly but steadily, some lower castes should also be inducted in these mixed-caste regiments. This would give rise to voluntary association among the castes. However, they cautioned, if lower castes were suddenly forced upon the high castes, the result would be chaos.[127] In 1861, Mayhew wanted the low castes in the class company regiments. He wrote to the Government of India's Military Department: '. . . whilst the low-caste man can keep up his social independence in a company composed of his own caste, he would if the mixture were general, succumb to the overwhelming influence of the Brahmins or high-caste men'.[128]

The Punjab lobby wanted to recruit the lower castes for purely pragmatic reasons. This lobby pointed out that low castes would remain loyal to the British because in the new order they would gain power and status, while if British rule was replaced by a high-caste regime then they would again sink back to their deplorable position. The spokesmen of the Punjab School argued that if commissioned grades were opened to the low castes then they would prove to be more loyal, as this move would inculcate the ambition and the desire for upward mobility among the low castes.[129]

Some elements of the Martial Race paradigm seeped within the Gradualists' framework. The Gradualists linked soldiering capacities with occupations. Wheeler believed that agriculture bred the best warriors. This was similar to the pre-1857 Bengal School and later Martial Race ideologues' assumption that agriculturists were the best soldiers.[130] Wheeler wanted to enlist those low castes that were engaged in agriculture but not those marginal groups who were engaged in occupations hated by the high castes.[131]

Bruce and Hall challenged the connection between fighting capacity and occupation. They argued that sweepers, watermen and even looters could become soldiers. Bruce did not care about the caste Hindus' sensibilities regarding occupations. He said that the Bhungies being hereditary sweepers were hated by the high castes. Military service, he asserted would raise the Bhungies' status in Indian society. Not only for symbolic functions, but also for military reasons, Bruce wanted low castes from diverse professional backgrounds. He wanted the Pasees in the prestigious sapper corps. Their hereditary occupation was mining. Bruce wanted to utilize their specialized professional skill in blowing up fortifications with mines during siege operations.[132]

Similarly, the advocates of Bheel recruitment belonging to the Radical section pointed out the strategic advantages which the Raj would derive by enlisting the tribes who existed outside the domains of Hindu society. John Malcolm and Captain A.H.M. Simcox argued that if the Bheels were not recruited then they would become marauders which in turn would cause a large-scale law and order problem for the British in central India.[133] Lieutenant H.L. Showers felt that the Bheels should first be inducted in the local corps, and if provided further financial incentives, then the Bheels would be willing to serve even in the North-West Frontier.[134] This was a radical policy statement indeed as no other officer came up with the idea of pitting central Indian tribes against the Pathans and the Afghans of the Indus frontier.

The Gradualists, like the Bengal School and the Martial Race ideologues, rejected those groups which did not follow high-caste dietary preferences.[135] Wheeler was against enlisting the Kunjurs (a group which in his classification belonged to the lowest caste) as their staple diet was considered horrendous by the established norms of high-caste society. But Hall and Bruce rejected this connection between 'proper diet' and service in the army.[136] The Martial Race theorists and the Bengal School considered personal hygiene of the recruits as vital.[137] Wheeler argued that Bhungies were dirty, consequently had skin diseases, and so they should be excluded. But, Mayhew and Bruce asserted that military service would reform their habits.[138]

Both the Gradualists and the Radicals agreed that low castes had innate martial qualities but differed on the question of how quickly those qualities could be utilized. The Gradualists, led by Brigadier M.G. Dennis, argued that traditions and customs were social realities, and hence it would be time consuming to transform the current status of the low castes into a higher ascribed status provided by the army. He wanted protracted social engineering before the low castes could function as soldiers. But the Radicals led by Major A.J. Austen, commanding at Nagode, Major-General J.F. Bradford commanding Meerut division, and Bruce argued that the low castes were better soldiers than the high castes.

Dennis argued that since the low castes hated the high castes, the former were more anxious to prove their loyalty and capability in the eyes of the British. Further, he believed that the low castes had more endurance, and were hence capable of laborious tasks. As they had no caste bias, they unlike the Brahmins were willing to work in the entrenchments and fortifications. But, he warned, generations of servitude had created in their minds the conviction that they were inferior to the high castes. This was proved by the fact that despite assurances of support from the British officers, they submitted to the higher castes in the army. Dennis concluded that it would take time, under benevolent British patronage, to convert them into fighting material by enhancing their morale and inducing self-respect.[139]

The Gradualists demanded social engineering, with the aid of imported institutions, to transform the promising raw materials into proper soldiers. Rose pointed out that, like the low castes, other marginal groups like the Bheels and the Gonds were unwilling to join the army because military service meant going away from home. He concluded that these 'savage', 'alcoholic' and 'polygamous' tribes could be converted into soldiers by military training. This could be provided within a quarter of a

century with the aid of the Grenz Regiments utilized by the
Austrian Army to coopt and discipline the frontier tribes. The
Grenz Regiment was both a social and a military institution since
it not only socialized the tribes but also transformed them into
soldiers. Both, the Punjab lobby and Rose accepted that since
the 'aboriginal races' like the Santhals and the Bheels would not
like to serve far away from their home for a long period, their
recruitment could only be gradual. Within the Grenz Regiments,
they would slowly appreciate military service and probably go
to any part of India on duty.[140]

From the opposite end of the spectrum, Austen provided
empirical data to show that even in the immediate context, low
castes had proved to be far better and more loyal than the high-
caste personnel. One Havildar Bindha of Bhalleca caste remained
loyal, when his high-caste colleagues in the 11th Regiment of the
Bengal Army rebelled in 1857. Then Havildar Girwar, a Lodh of
1st Punjab Infantry, performed extremely well in the siege of
Delhi.[141] Bradford stated that from the target firing practice and
drill, it was evident that the low-caste privates performed better
than the high-caste ranks and files. He continued that the low-
caste commissioned and non-commissioned officers were much
better than their high-caste counterparts.[142]

Bruce asserted that the low castes were better soldiers than
the high castes because the latter's ritualized lifestyle impeded
their capabilities as soldiers. They spent one-fourth of the day in
cooking, another one-fourth in rituals, etc. So, the high castes
were effeminate and the middle castes were also influenced by
such customs. Hence, Bruce shot down Darvali's plan of creating
an alliance between the middle castes and the low-caste to tide
over emergencies.[143] Rose and Mayhew rounded off the discussion by saying that recruitment should be guided by egalitarian-
ism. Low castes were to be given an equal opportunity to join the
army, as they too were the Queen's subjects.[144]

What were the actual reasons behind low-caste enlistment?
Stephen P. Cohen, in one of his articles, suggests that during a
crisis, the intake of the low castes increased, and in peacetime
their induction decreased.[145] He does not provide any figures to
back up his claim, but my statistics show that Cohen's model is
correct. In 1858, when the Raj was in a deep crisis, the low
castes constituted 18 per cent of the Sepoy Army. In 1885 their

share was reduced to 8 per cent and it further declined to 1.5 per cent in 1912. The absolute numbers of low castes on those dates were 17,309, then 10,000 and finally 2,000 in 1912.[146] The discussion regarding the marginal groups within the army was intense just when the crisis was over and before the retrenchment begun to occur.

We could hazard a guess about why the low castes failed to gain a substantial foothold in the army, despite having the support of the Commander-in-Chief and the Secretary of State. One reason may be factionalism—the split between the Gradualists and the Radicals within the low-caste lobby. And the second factor was Indian reality. Even in the pre-British armies, the low castes always occupied a fringe position. Dirk Kolff argues that many low status groups gained *Kshatriya* status after joining the pre-colonial armies. What Kolff overlooks is the fact that this sort of upward mobility occurred only in the infantry but never in the elite branch, the cavalry.[147] The absence of the tradition of long-distance *naukri* among the low castes and the tribes also hampered their prospects of recruitment. The Deoli Regiment recruited Meenas (a low caste) from Rajasthan.[148] In 1894, Major-General W. Galbraith, Adjutant General of India informed the Government of India's Military Department that the personnel of the Deoli Regiment were unwilling to serve away from their home.[149] Probably one could also sense a 'high-caste conspiracy' in preventing the entry of the low castes in significant number. The inclusion of the Brahmins and the Rajputs were necessary for balancing the various communities within the army. And the high castes tended to avoid the regiments enlisting low castes because they were unwilling to have any contact with those lower in the *varna* hierarchy. By 1867, the British were having problems in recruiting adequate number of high castes. In Charles Reid's words:

That our service has fallen into disrepute, and that there is a want of confidence in the minds of the very men we would wish to see flocking to our standard. . . . It has been entirely to our own seeking. We have told the high castes that we see no distinction, and that high and low are to be thrown together in the same corps. This is one of the causes of our being unable to recruit Rajputs . . . we have lowered ourselves in their eyes.[150]

Moreover, the high-caste soldiers sneered at the low-caste

officers and socially boycotted them.[151] So, besides imperial conceptions regarding Indian society, the subcontinent's social reality also played a role in shaping recruitment policies of the Sepoy Army.

CONCLUSION

The Balanced Recruitment lobby's broad-based egalitarian policy of accommodating as many communities as possible (even the low castes and the tribals who existed at the fringe of the society), was an attempt to make the military force socially and territorially diverse, and thus give a wide base to the colonial state. The Balanced Recruitment policy despite having strands of 'Divide and Rule', was somewhat uncolonial as the attempt in the long run was to create an army which would be representative of the indigenous society. And this policy had both an indigenous as well as a European base. The Balanced Recruitment lobby's attack on the Martial Race paradigm regarding 'race' shows that not all British officers were 'racist'. Historians miss this point[152] because of their concentration on the private papers of personalities like Roberts and others, who were at the highest echelon of the military bureaucracy.

The propagation of the Egalitarian Recruitment ideology by the Balanced Recruitment lobby somewhat modified the Martial Race ideology itself. The greatest proponent of the Martial Race theory after Roberts, Major G.F. MacMunn accepted, unlike his illustrious predecessor, that many south Indian 'races' were indeed 'martial'.[153] What effect did the Balanced Recruitment lobby have on actual recruitment? Even in 1912, 34 per cent of the recruits came from the 'unmartial races'.[154] Moreover, despite the attempt by the Martial Race theorists to convert all regiments into class regiments, class company regiments continued to exist though in fewer numbers. This by itself was no mean achievement. With the advantage of hindsight one can say that a broad based balancing, as proposed by the ideologues of Balanced Recruitment policy could have saved the Sepoy Army from the chaos and confusion in 1914–15 when selective enlistment, as propounded by the Martial Race ideologues, failed to meet the huge vacancies in the ranks caused by the demands of Total War.

NOTES

1. Inefficient State of the Indian Army and difficulty in recruiting, Major General Charles Reid, Memorandum no. 2, Barrackpur, 25 December 1867, Colonel William Merewether Collection, MSS.EUR.D.625/3, OIOC.

2. Saxena, *The Military System of India*.

3. Cynthia H. Enloe, *Ethnic Soldiers: State Security in Divided Societies*, Harmondsworth, Middlesex: Penguin, 1980, pp. 23–42.

4. Omissi, *Sepoy and the Raj*, pp. 6–10.

5. Mason, *A Matter of Honour*, pp. 317–27.

6. Jac Weller, *Wellington in India*, London: Longman, 1972, pp. 16, 20, 25, 28; H.H. Dodwell, *Sepoy Recruitment in the Old Madras Army*, Calcutta: Superintendent of Govt. Printing, 1922, pp. 15–16, 37–8, 45–6; Lieutenant-Colonel W.J. Wilson, *History of the Madras Army*, vol. 3, Madras: Government Press, 1883, p. 151.

7. Minute by Malcolm, 27 November 1830, *PP* (1867), p. 175.

8. Tan Tai Yong, 'Sepoys and the Colonial State: Punjab and the Military Base of the Indian Army, 1849-1900', in P.S. Gupta and Anirudh Deshpande, ed., *The British Raj and Its Indian Armed Forces: 1857–1939*, New Delhi: Oxford University Press, 2002, p. 11; *Supplementary Report*, p. 4.

9. Dodwell, *Sepoy Recruitment*, pp. 15–16; *Supplementary Report*, p. 46; Minute by Malcolm, *PP* (1867), pp. 175, 177.

10. Kolff, *Naukar, Rajput and Sepoy*, pp. 176–99; Alavi, *The Sepoys and the Company*, pp. 49–92, 292–4; J.W. Hoover, 'The Recruitment of the Bengal Army: Beyond the Myth of the Zamindar's Son', *Indo-British Review*, vol. 21, no. 2 (1996), pp. 144–56.

11. C.A. Bayly, ed., Eric Stokes, *The Peasant Armed: The Indian Revolt of 1857*, Oxford: Oxford University Press, 1986, pp. 51, 66, 100–15.

12. E.H. Carr, *What is History?* , 1961, reprint, Harmondsworth: Penguin, 1986, pp. 87–108.

13. Russell H.S. Stolfi in 'Chance in History: The Russian Winter of 1941–42', *History*, vol. LXV (1980), pp. 214–28 rightly asserts that at times the historical process depends on the random roll of dice.

14. Notes on the Indian Army of Bengal: Its present material and organization as compared with the past, Brigadier-General C.H. Brownlow, September 1875, L/MIL/17/2/468, OIOC.

15. Cohen, *The Indian Army*, p. 35.

16. The quotation is from *Peel Committee*, Appendix no. 58, para 40; Menezes, *Fidelity and Honour*, p. 534.

17. Martin Bossenbroeck, 'The Living Tools of Empire: Recruitment of European Soldiers for the Dutch Colonial Army, 1814–1909', *JICH*, vol. 23, no. 1 (1995), pp. 26–53.

18. Cohen, *Indian Army*, p. 38; *Peel Committee*, pp. 38–9.
19. Pradeep Barua, 'Strategies and Doctrines of Imperial Defence: Britain and India', *JICH*, vol. 25, no. 3 (1997), p. 241.
20. *Supplementary Report*, pp. 8, 14, 30.
21. General George Chesney, *Indian Polity: A View of the System of Administration in India*, 1894, reprint, New Delhi: Metropolitan Books, 1976, p. 249; Memorandum on the visit of the Commander-in-Chief to the trans Indus frontier, para 16, Lieutenant-Colonel H.W. Norman, Secy. to the GoI, Fort William, 14 January 1863, Norman minutes, NAI.
22. *Peel Committee*, pp. 1–3, 30–4, 38–40, 46.
23. *Supplementary Report*, pp. 45, 47–8.
24. *Peel Committee*, pp. 1–3, 30–4, 38–40; *Hancock Report*, pp. 9, 31.
25. Lieutenant-Colonel M.J. King-Harman, 'Second Essay', *JUSII*, vol. 20, no. 86 (1891), p. 170.
26. Menezes, *Fidelity and Honour*, p. 189.
27. *Supplementary Report*, pp. 32, 309. Each irregular cavalry or infantry regiment had four British officers while each regular infantry or cavalry regiment possessed between eight to twelve British officers. Greater latitude was given to Indian tradition and custom regarding dress and discipline in the irregular regiments. Most of the irregulars were local, i.e. used for operation in the area from which they were raised. However, during emergencies, the irregulars were deployed throughout the subcontinent. Chandar S. Sundaram, 'Reviving a "Dead Letter": Military Indianization and the Ideology of Anglo-India, 1885–91', in Gupta and Deshpande, ed., *The British Raj: Its Indian Armed Forces*, p. 88, footnote 59.
28. Jaap de Moor, 'The Recruitment of Indonesian Soldiers for the Dutch Colonial Army, *c*. 1700–1950', in David Killingray and David Omissi, ed., *Guardians of Empire: The Armed Forces of the Colonial Powers c. 1700–1964*, Manchester/New York: Manchester University Press, 1999, p. 55.
29. *Peel Committee*, Appendix 57, para 42.
30. P.J.O. Taylor (General Editor), *A Companion to the Indian Mutiny of 1857*, Delhi: Oxford University Press, 1996, p. 20.
31. V.G. Kiernan, 'Colonial Africa and Its Armies', in Brian Bond and Ian Roy, ed., *War and Society: A Yearbook of Military History*, vol. 2, London: Croom Helm, 1977, pp. 21–2; *Peel Committee*, pp. 5–6, 29. During the second half of the nineteenth century, the total forces commanded by the Indian princes amounted to 93,000 soldiers. Of them about 18,000 were categorized as Imperial Service Troops. They were given some weapons and training by the British officers seconded from the Sepoy Army. The Imperial Service Troops followed the Sepoy Army in campaigns inside and outside India. Boris Mollo, *The Indian Army*, Poole/Dorset: Blandford Press, 1981, p. 103; Brigadier-General

Stuart Beatson, *A History of the Imperial Service Troops of Native States*, Calcutta: Superintendent of Govt. Printing, 1903.

32. *Peel Committee*, pp. 46–7.

33. *Hancock Report*, pp. 21, 26–7.

34. R.C. Butalia, *The Evolution of the Artillery in India: From the Battle of Plassey to the Revolt of 1857*, New Delhi: Allied, 1998, pp. 180–1, 335.

35. *Peel Committee*, pp. 31–2, 39, 47, Appendix 58, para 38.

36. Ibid., pp. 38–9, 46.

37. *Hancock Report*, pp. 18, 21.

38. Ibid., p. 24.

39. Napier's quote is from Minute on inexpediency of the reduction of artillery, 17 August 1867, Notes and Minutes by Napier, 1866–9; From the ADG to the Secy. to the Govt. MD, Bombay, no. 337, 27 February 1864, Records of Chief Commands, 1865–76, Notes and Minutes by Napier of Magdala, MSS.EUR.114, 1©, OIOC.

40. General Frederick Roberts, *Short Report on Important Questions dealt with during the tenure of Commander of the Army in India: 1885–93*, Simla: Govt. Central Printing Office, 1893, p. 13, L/MIL/17/5/1613, OIOC.

41. *Army Committee*, vol. 1-A, *Minority Report*, p. 135.

42. *Hancock Report*, p. 26.

43. *Manual for Bengal and Punjab Cavalry*, 1893, reprint, Delhi: Mayur Publications, 1985, p. 103; *Supplementary Report*, pp. 20–1, 24, 273–5.

44. General John Jacob's letter to Colonel Durand, 7 June 1858, quoted in *Hancock Report*, p. 18.

45. Ibid., p. 19.

46. Minute by C.B. Pritchard, Enclosure no. 2, 1Q/14, para 13, 29 August 1893, George White Collection, MSS.EUR.F.108/24, OIOC.

47. *Peel Committee*, Appendix 58, para 20.

48. Ibid., pp. 8, 28; Charles Wood to the Governor-General, no. 73, 8 February 1861, Military despatches of the Secretary of State, NAI.

49. *Peel Committee*, p. 40.

50. Ibid., p. 35.

51. David Englander, 'Mutinies and Military Morale', in Hew Strachan, ed., *The Oxford Illustrated History of the First World War*, Oxford: Oxford University Press, 1998, p. 194.

52. *Peel Committee*, p. 48.

53. *Supplementary Report*, pp. 14, 57.

54. Ibid., p. 14; *Peel Committee*, pp. 40, 44; ADG's office, Jhansi, no. 7049, 16 December 1862, ADG's circulars, vol. 2, NAI.

55. Notes by Major-General H. Tombs commanding Awadh Division, 21 April 1864, Record of Chief Commands, Notes and Minutes by Napier of Magdala, MSS.EUR.F.114, 5(4).

56. Menezes, *Fidelity and Honour*, p. 534; *Supplementary Report*, p. 71.

57. Minute by the Commander-in-Chief in India on despatch no. 23 from India Office, April 1870, Records of Chief Commands, 1865–76, Correspondence and memoranda on the organization of the Indian Army, Notes and Minutes by Napier, MSS.EUR.F.114, 5 (2).

58. Saxena, *Military System of India*, p. 108; Brian Robson, 'The Eden Commission and the Reform of the Indian Army, 1879-1895', *JSAHR*, vol. LX, no. 241 (1982), pp. 4–13; *The Army in India and Its Evolution*, 1924, reprint, New Delhi: Anmol Publications, 1985, pp. 21–2, 196; *Hancock Report*, p. 27; *Eden Commission*, pp. 77–80.

59. The Hyderabad Contingent was a military force officered by the British. Though nominally under the Nizam, this force functioned as part of the Madras Army. It was used for policing the princely state of Hyderabad but during emergencies it was used for operations all over India. In 1862 its strength was 5,000 infantry and 2,000 cavalry. Copy of a letter from Colonel A. Broome, Chief of the Military Finance Department, Calcutta, no. 225-C, para 1, 10 June 1883, L/MIL/7/14966, OIOC.

60. From T.J.C. Plowden, offg. Resident at Hyderabad, to the Secy. to the GoI, MD, no. 26, 22 February 1892, Military Collection, Hyderabad Contingent Files, L/MIL/7/14966.

61. *Peel Committee*, pp. 3, 39–40, 44.

62. *Hancock Report*, pp. 30–1.

63. *Peel Committee*, p. 8.

64. *Supplementary Report*, pp. 14, 27, 29–31, 45, 50, 308–9.

65. From Lieutenant-Colonel H.W. Norman, Secy. to the GoI, MD, to the offg. ADG of the army, Fort William, no. 729, 25 November 1862, Records of Chief Commands, Correspondence and Memoranda, Notes and Minutes by Napier, MSS.EUR.F.114, 5(2).

66. Lieutenant F.G. Cardew, *A Sketch of the Services of the Bengal Native Army to the Year 1895*, 1903, reprint, New Delhi: Today and Tomorow's Printers and Publishers, 1971, pp. 329–31, 405–9; From Norman, Secy. to the GoI, MD, to the offg. ADG, 25 November 1862, Correspondence and Memoranda, Notes and Minutes by Napier.

67. *Peel Committee*, p. 35.

68. Correspondence between the Resident of Hyderabad and the Brigadier-General commanding Hyderabad Contingent on the subject of improving the organization, para 26, Progs. no. 107, May 1876, L/MIL/7/14966.

69. Ibid.

70. From T.J.C. Plowden, offg. Resident at Hyderabad, to the Secy. to the GoI, MD, no. 26, 22 February 1892, L/MIL/7/14966.

71. Extract of a letter from GoI, para 8, no. 114, 28 July 1898, L/MIL/7/14966.

72. From Colonel R.J. Meade, offg. Resident at Hyderabad, to Colonel H.K.

Burne, Secy. to the GoI, MD, Fort William, from Burne to the Resident at Hyderabad, Progs. nos. 112–13, 19 February & 10 April 1876, L/MIL/ 7/14966.

73. Omissi, *Sepoy and the Raj*, p. 10.

74. For an account of the Indian Army's regimental fabric see John Gaylor, *Sons of John Company: The Indian and Pakistan Armies, 1903–91*, 1992, reprint, New Delhi: Lancer, 1993 and *Army Committee*, vol. 3, p. 950.

75. Barat, *The Bengal Native Infantry*, pp. 120–1; Major G.F. MacMunn, *The Armies of India*, 1911, reprint, New Delhi: Heritage Publishers, 1991, pp. 83–92; *Peel Committee*, Appendix 58, para 3; *Supplementary Report*, pp. 27–8.

76. *Peel Committee*, Appendix 58, para 21.

77. Ibid., p. 27.

78. *Supplementary Report*, p. 273.

79. *Peel Committee*, p. 33; Field Marshal Earl Roberts, *Forty-one Years in India: From Subaltern to Commander-in-Chief*, 1897, reprint, London: Richard Bentley & Son, 1898, p. 68.

80. *Supplementary Report*, p. 309.

81. From Lieutenant-Colonel W. Mayhew, ADG of the army, to the Secy. to the GoI, MD, Calcutta, 19 October 1861, Correspondence and Memoranda, Records of Chief Commands, Notes and Minutes by Napier, MSS.EUR.F.114, 5(3).

82. Geoffrey Parker, *The Army of Flanders and the Spanish Road: 1567–1659, The Logistics of Spanish Victory and Defeat in the Low Countries' Wars*, 1972, reprint, Cambridge: Cambridge University Press, 1995, p. 13.

83. From Major-General S. Cotton, commanding Peshawar Division, to the ADG of the army, Calcutta, no. 723, 26 July 1860, Correspondence and Memoranda, Notes and Minutes by Napier, MSS.EUR.F.114, 5(3).

84. Inefficient state of the Indian Army and difficulty in recruiting, no. 2, 25 December 1867, Merewether Collection.

85. Hill Rajputs were Rajputs recruited from the mountainous Garhwal region (present-day Himachal Pradesh).

86. *Supplementary Report*, pp. 27–8, 30–1; From Lieutenant-Colonel E.B. Johnson, offg. ADG of the army, to the Secy. to the GoI, MD, Simla, 1 May 1862, Correspondence and Memoranda, Notes and Minutes by Napier, MSS.EUR.F.114, 5(3).

87. *Peel Committee*, pp. 40–1.

88. From Norman to the offg. ADG, no. 729, 25 November 1862, Notes and Minutes by Napier.

89. See Appendix I for a detailed social, religious and territorial break up of a class company regiment.

90. Cardew, *Bengal Native Army*, pp. 329–31; Johnson to the Secy. to the GoI, MD, Simla, 1 May 1862, Correspondence and Memoranda, Notes and Minutes by Napier.

91. Replies to questions by a committee of the House of Commons on the substitution of Indian for British troops in the colonies in time of peace, by Lieutenant-General Robert Napier, Commander-in-Chief of Bombay, 8 July 1867, Poona, Notes and Minutes by Napier, MSS.EUR.F.114, 1©.

92. Office Notes, Indian Army Commission, Constitution of the Bengal Army, by Brigadier George Chesney, 9 February 1881, L/MIL/17/2/469, OIOC. Chesney was speaking of the memoirs of the Bengal Army's Subedar Sita Ram. Sita Ram, a high-caste from Awadh fought in the Sikh Wars and remained loyal to the British during the 1857 Mutiny. His autobiography was published in the second half of the nineteenth century.

93. Minute by Pritchard, para 1, 1Q/14, George White Collection, MSS EUR F. 108/24 OIOC.

94. Johnson to the Secy. to the GoI, MD, Peshawar, no. 724, 29 January 1862, Correspondence and Memoranda, Notes and Minutes by Napier.

95. Minute by Pritchard, para 13, George White Collection.

96. DeWitt C. Ellinwood, 'Ethnicity in a Colonial Asian Army, in Ellinwood and Cynthea H. Enloe, eds., *Ethnicity and the Military in Asia*, New Brunswick/London: Transaction Books, 1981, pp. 89–144.

97. *Peel Committee*, p. 50.

98. Ibid., p. 38.

99. Ibid., p. 32; ADG's office, Calcutta, no. 2470/A, 24 June 1861, ADG's circulars, vol. 1.

100. *Supplementary Report*, p. 72.

101. Hugh Rose to John Lawrence, 28 April 1864, John Lawrence Collection, 1864–7, MSS.EUR.F. 90/59, OIOC.

102. Constance M. Wilson, 'Burmese-Karen Warfare, 1840–50: A Thai View', in Ellinwood and Enloe, eds., *Ethnicity and the Military*, pp. 18–51; *Supplementary Report*, p. 27.

103. Extract from a letter from Lieutenant-Colonel Carey, commanding East Indian Regiment to Colonel Haythorne, ADG of the army, 19 February 1864, John Lawrence Collection.

104. Hugh Rose to Lawrence, Letter no. 3, 9 March 1864, John Lawrence Collection.

105. *Peel Committee*, p. 35.

106. Ibid., p. 27.

107. Correspondence between the Resident and the Brigadier-General, Progs. no. 107, May 1876, L/MIL/7/14966.

108. *Peel Committee*, p. 30.

109. Ibid., p. 34. The quotation is from the same page.

110. Ibid., p. 39.
111. Correspondence between the Resident and the Brigadier-General, Progs. no. 107, May 1876, L/MIL/7/14966.
112. From Plowden to the Secy. to the GoI, no. 26, 22 February 1892, L/MIL/7/14966.
113. *Supplementary Report*, pp. 274–5.
114. *Peel Committee*, Appendix 58, para 4, 8, 14.
115. Cardew, *Bengal Native Army*, pp. 406–7.
116. Captain E.K. Molesworth, 'Indian Army Castes: Madrassis', *JUSII*, vol. XLII, no. 190 (1913), pp. 57–70; Lieutenant-Colonel F.W. Tyrrell, 'The Races of the Madras Army', *JUSII*, no. 48 (1881), pp. 11–21.
117. Notes on the Indian Army, September 1875, L/MIL/17/2/468.
118. *Supplementary Report*, p. 65.
119. *Peel Committee*, p. 8.
120. Inefficient state of the Indian Army and difficulty in recruiting, Memorandum no. 2, by Charles Reid, Barrackpur, 25 December 1867, Merewether Collection.
121. Chesney, *Indian Polity*, p. 224.
122. *Peel Committee*, p. 32.
123. Mayhew to the Secy. to the GoI, Calcutta, Progs. no. 547, 29 September 1860, Captain E. Hall, commanding Aligarh Levy, to Major of Brigade, Saugor dist., Kishengarh, Progs. no. 7, 6 February 1860, MDP, October 1860, NAI; Wood to the Governor-General, London, no. 73, 8 February 1861, Military despatches of the Secretary of State.
124. Lieutenant-Colonel H. Bruce, Chief of Awadh Police to the ADG, Lucknow; Colonel E. Darvali, 3rd European Regiment, commanding at Fategarh, to Major G.S. Young, offg. Deputy Asst. ADG, Kanpur, Progs. nos. 549, 777, 9 January and 1 February 1860, MDP, October 1860.
125. Brigadier F. Wheeler, commanding Saugor dist., to the offg. Asst. ADG, Simla, Progs. no. 548, 16 February 1860, MDP, October 1860.
126. *Supplementary Report*, pp. 29, 71.
127. Ibid., p. 29.
128. From Mayhew to the Secy. to the GoI, MD, no. 722, Correspondence and Memoranda, Notes and Minutes by Napier.
129. *Supplementary Report*, p. 22.
130. MacMunn, *The Armies*, pp. 130–1; Kolff, *Naukar, Rajput and Sepoy*, pp. 193–9; Barat, *Bengal Army*, pp. 126, 150; Alavi, *Sepoys and the Company*, pp. 35–9, 42–5, 51.
131. Progs. no. 548, MDP, October 1860.
132. Progs. nos. 7, 549, MDP, October 1860.
133. Major-General John Malcolm, *A Memoir of Central India Including Malwa and Adjoining Provinces with the History and Copious Illustration of the Country*, vol. 1, 1880, reprint, New Delhi: Sagar

Publications, 1970, pp. 519–22, 526; A.H.M. Simcox, *Memoir of Khandesh Bhil Corps, 1825–91*, Bombay: Thacker & Spink, 1912, pp. I–II, 17.

134. Lieutenant H.L. Showers, 'The Meywar Bheel Corps', *JUSII*, vol. 20, no. 85 (1891), pp. 87–95. Local units were irregular regiments. They enlisted marginal groups from a particular locality and were used for policing that very area. Captain J.P. Stockley, 'Local Corps in India and Their Military Value', *JUSII*, vol. XLII, no. 191 (1913), pp. 179–83.

135. Alavi, *Sepoys and the Company*, pp. 76–7, 79; Lieutenant-General W.H. Goodenough and Lieutenant-Colonel J.C. Dalton, *The Army Book of the British Empire: A Record of the Development and Present Composition of the Military Forces and Their Duties during Peace and* War, London: HMSO, 1893, pp. 445, 448.

136. Progs. nos. 7, 548–9, MDP, October 1860.

137. Heathcote, *The Military in British India*, p. 121; Major A.H. Bingley, *History, Caste and Culture of Jats and Gujars*, 1899, reprint, New Delhi: ESS Publications, 1978, p. 101; *Peel Committee*, pp. 7–8.

138. Progs. nos. 547–9, MDP, October 1860.

139. Brigadier M.G. Dennis, commanding at Allahabad, to the Asst. ADG, Kanpur, Progs. no. 551, 1 February 1860, MDP, October 1860.

140. *Supplementary Report*, pp. 27, 71–2.

141. Major A.J. Austen, commanding at Nagode, to Captain C. Harris, commanding the Bijnore Levy, Progs. no. 547, 1 February 1860, MDP, October 1860.

142. Major-General J.F. Bradford, commanding Meerut, to the ADG, Meerut, Progs. no. 552, MDP, October 1860.

143. Progs. nos. 549–50, MDP, October 1860.

144. Progs. no. 547, MDP, October 1860.

145. Stephen P. Cohen, 'The Untouchable Soldier: Caste, Politics and the Indian Army', *JAS*, vol. 28, no. 3 (1969), pp. 453–68.

146. *Army Commission*, vol. 1-A, *Minority Report*, vol. 1-A, of *Army Commission is Minority Report*, p. 156; *Peel Committee*, Appendix no. 22, September 1858.

147. Kolff, *Naukar, Rajput and Sepoy*, pp. 157, 196; Jagadish Narayan Sarkar, *The Art of War in Medieval India*, New Delhi: Munshiram Manoharlal, 1984, pp. 57–61, 94–104; S. Inayat Ali Zaidi, 'Ordinary Kachawaha Troopers Serving the Mughal Empire: Composition and Structure of the Contingents of the Kachawaha Nobles', *SIH*, vol. 2, no. 1 (1980), pp. 57–68.

148. Edmund Candler, *The Sepoy*, London: John Murray, 1919, pp. 188–9.

149. From Major-General W. Galbraith, ADG in India to the GoI, MD, Enclosure no. 26, 17 August, 1894, Annual confidential reports on the regiments, L/MIL/7/17008, OIOC.

150. Inefficient state of the Indian Army and difficulty in recruiting, by Charles Reid, 25 December 1867, Merewether Collection.
151. Vivien Ashima Kaul, 'Sepoys Links with Society: A Study of the Bengal Army, 1858–95', in Gupta and Deshpande, eds., *Indian Armed Forces*, New Delhi: Oxford University Press, 2002, p. 161.
152. The historians like Peter Robb and S. Bayly while emphasizing the racial strands of the Martial Race ideologues' thinking, miss the counter-discourse of the opposite camp. Peter Robb, 'Introduction: South Asia and the Concept of Race', and Susan Bayly, 'Caste and "Race" in the Colonial Ethnography of India', in Robb, ed., *The Concept of Race in South Asia*, Delhi: Oxford University Press, 1995, pp. 1–76, 165–218.
153. MacMunn, *The Armies*, pp. 169–72.
154. *Army Committee*, vol. 1-A, *Minority Report*, p. 156.

TWO

The Evolution of the Martial Race Theory

The Hindustanis are not as good in hill fighting as the Gurkhas, Dogras and the Pathans. . . . The Madrassis are not effective in the warm damp climate of Burma nor in the dry cold of Afghanistan. If they cannot fight the half-armed Burman and Kachin dacoits, how could they fight the Afghans or Europeans in the North-West Frontier. . . . Some people fear that the reduction of the Madras Army would destroy the principle of balancing the Indian races. . . . The British force in India is now in greatly larger proportion to the Native than it used to be; the artillery is nearly all in British hands . . . hence we can discard the old policy of balancing.

General George White[1]

The manpower demand that gripped the Sepoy Army during the First World War[2] was partly the result of selective recruitment demanded by the Martial Race ideology. Compared to the vast demographic resources of India, the army's demand for manpower before 1913 was limited. The population of India during the second half of the nineteenth century was 236 million. The annual demand of the Sepoy Army was somewhat less than 20,000.[3] This allowed the British to decide which groups to enlist and on what basis. The varying imperial perceptions about loyalty and courage of the different groups shaped recruitment.

I

BENGAL SCHOOL AS THE PRECURSOR OF THE MARTIAL RACE IDEOLOGY

Heather streets writes that the Martial Race ideology was an imperial strategy to counter rising nationalism among the Irish and Indians both in the metropole and periphery of the British

Empire. This chapter will concern itself with the Martial Race ideology at the periphery of the Empire. Scholars like Stephen P. Cohen argue that the Martial Race ideology which held that only particular groups like the Sikhs, the Gurkhas and the Pathans had the right qualities to produce soldiers, moulded the army's recruitment pattern from the late nineteenth century onwards. The Martial Race doctrine was viewed as a monolithic, un-changing and coherent ideology, which suddenly flowered in the 1880s.[4] However, some historians argue that the core of Martial Race ideology demanded that tall and fair men from north of river Narmada were warriors and this idea was prevalent even before 1857 especially in the Bengal Army.[5] But, these scholars do not develop this point. James W. Hoover writes that the historians' assumption of the Bengal Army being filled with high-caste zamindars' sons from *Purab* is erroneous because numerically the Brahmin and Rajput zamindars of that area were inadequate for that purpose.[6] Hoover has misunderstood the meaning of the term *Purab*. This term denoted the region from Delhi up to Bihar and not merely southern Awadh as Hoover assumes. Actually the Bengal Army recruited Brahmins and Rajputs from small peasant families and also the *Gwalahs* (a middle caste whose hereditary profession was herding and milking cows) from Bihar and Awadh. Moreover large numbers of north Indian Muslims joined the cavalry of the Bengal Army.[7] Just before the 1857 Mutiny, ten regiments of Bengal Light Cavalry were dominated by the Purbiyas. But, the eighteen regiments of Bengal Irregular Cavalry recruited Muslims from the Delhi region and Rohilkhand.[8]

The Bengal School assumed that good warriors came from the families of enterprising agriculturists who cultivated their own lands. Yeomen farmers were believed to be healthy, hard working and sturdy. Robert Orme, one of the historians of the Company, first propounded this view. High castes were regarded as famous for their orderly conduct and loyalty to their salt givers. Low castes and urban occupational groups such as city artisans were rejected, as they lacked the qualifications demanded by the Bengal School. Brahmins and Rajputs from Bihar and Awadh were mostly enlisted. They were preferred because they were tall, ate wheat and came from families owning some land. The British officers described the *Purbiyas* as zamindars or yeomen peasants. All the recruits to the Bengal Army had to be 5'7" tall.[9] William Bentinck (the Governor-General or Viceroy of British India, 1832–5) asserted that the north Indian high castes due to their better stature were bolder and more martial than the Madrassis.[10]

Similar to the Bengal School, a lobby existed in the pre-1857 Madras Army, which could be labelled as the Selective Enlistment School. This group believed that martial spirit was the monopoly of certain groups. This idea was expressed in the military regulations of 1765, which confined recruitment to the Rajputs and the Muslims. This lobby further believed that only those Rajputs and the Muslims engaged in certain occupations possessed soldiering instincts. Hence, weavers were declared unfit for soldiering. Members of this School also stressed on the physical features of the recruits. In 1795, Colonel John Floyd declared that good recruits could not be obtained from the deep south, since this region produced men of small size, under the prescribed minimum height of 5'5". The conviction was that with the passage of time, the south Indians were deteriorating in size and looks, hence they could not become proper soldiers any more.[11] This belief also seeped into the ideology of the civilian elites. Echoing Bentinck, H.T. Prinsep, a civilian bureaucrat in 1835 claimed that the men from the southern peninsula of India were deficient in bodily strength and mental energy and those men should be replaced by the *Purbiyas* who, because of their larger stature, were equal to the British soldier.[12] The *Purbiyas* were much sought after because of their superior physique and 'handsome' looks. In their absence, Telugus were recruited as they somewhat resembled the former. Tamils were not liked because to the British they looked like 'brute beasts'. The Indian Christians were regarded as dirty and alcoholic, and thus were looked down upon. However, this trend remained marginal in the Madras Army which had a dominant 'Open Door' policy of recruitment.[13]

The Bengal School and the Selective Enlistment School both used the same indices for judging the recruits and reached the same conclusions. They held that a warlike spirit was confined to certain groups of particular areas. They liked to recruit a particular group from a particular region because they were convinced that heavy recruitment from a narrow area created military habits and ambitions and the inhabitants then begun to despise a peaceful life. Such people were then easily motivated to fight.[14] The chief assumptions of these two camps were similar to the Martial Race ideology, which appeared in full bloom and percolated in the four regional armies (the Madras Army, the Bombay Army, the Bengal Army and the Punjab Frontier Force) when Roberts became the Commander-in-Chief of the Indian Army in 1885.[15] Roberts and his followers, namely, Major G.F. MacMunn (a prolific writer who later rose to the rank of Lieutenant-General), Colonel L.W. Shakespear (the commandant of the 2nd Gurkha Rifles just before the First World War) and two Royal Artillery officers, Lieutenant-General W.H. Goodenough and Lieutenant-Colonel J.C. Dalton, added some more criteria like climate and frontier. But, the basic paradigm remained same. Only the groups and the regions approved of changed with time. For example, the Sikhs and Muslims of Punjab replaced the *Purbiyas* of north India as 'martial races' towards the end of the nineteenth century.

II

ELEMENTS OF THE MARTIAL RACE THEORY

I have never served against Russian soldiers; but unless history has greatly exaggerated their fighting powers, they ought to prove more than a match for our Indian troops, except perhaps the very best, such as Gurkhas and really good Sikhs.

Field Marshal Frederick Roberts[16]

All the ideologues of the Martial Race camp made a division between the Orient and the Occident. Roberts argued that in the Occident anyone could become a soldier, but in the Orient, due to its peculiar historical and ecological conditions, only some groups were suited for soldiering. He felt that people living in the north-west of India, such as the Sikhs, Dogras and the Pathans, were martial.[17] In a similar tone MacMunn declared: 'In Europe, as we know, every able bodied man, given food and arms, is a fighting man of some sort, in the East . . . certainly in India, this is not so'.[18] MacMunn claimed that in the Orient only a few groups, could bear arms because the other communities lacked physical courage. He linked this up with the theory of the Aryan invasion. According to him, the Aryans invaded India, defeated the Dravidians, and occupied their lands. The Aryan descendants became the yeomen peasants and landowners of central and northern India. The landless labourers who migrated to the towns were the defeated Dravidians. The land owning and the cultivating groups, who were supposed to have descended from the Aryans, were categorized as martial. These Aryans prevented the defeated groups from bearing arms; as a result the non-Aryans lost their martial traditions. MacMunn warned his fellow officers that in India, for the foregoing reasons, the French practice of *levee en masse* or the British practice by which the rich pay and the poor fight was inapplicable.[19]

The Muslims and the Rajputs of Punjab were categorized as martial by MacMunn because they were regarded as descendants of the Central Asian Aryans, who occupied the land by driving out the original inhabitants. The 'martial Aryans' never indulged in trade, commerce and artisanal activities, or in pursuits, which MacMunn said required brains. He labelled the groups following such occupations, especially business communities such as the Khatris and the educated Bengalis, as non-martial.[20] Actually, MacMunn followed in the footsteps of his illustrious predecessor Roberts who in a confidential memorandum dated 1895 asserted that military characteristics of the Indians were inversely proportional to their educational qualifications.[21] Goodenough and Dalton also highlighted the linkage between agriculture and the warrior ethos. The Jats were fine agriculturists, so they were regarded as fine fighting material.[22]

Certain cultural and physical attributes were ascribed to the 'martial races'. For Roberts, Goodenough and Dalton, the martial communities were well built, smart, fair and handsome. The Martial Race ideologues assumed that wheat and meat eating people were warriors. Hence, the rice eating Madrassis were dubbed as unwarlike. The Martial Race lobby assumed that the wheat and meat eating Sikhs and the Pathans with excellent physiques were culturally conditioned for warfare.[23] Roberts argued that they loved fighting and the excitement of war. The Bengal School and the Martial Race lobby's emphasis on the dietary criteria was somewhat similar to a tradition that existed in Europe. From the late Middle Ages, the military theorists of West Europe accepted the linkage between diet and military prowess. They believed that eating boar made perfect soldiers.[24] Like the Bengal School, the Martial Race enthusiasts also preferred tall men of about 5'7".[25] In 1888, Roberts commented: 'The 35th Sikhs is a newly raised regiment and promises to be a very fine corps. Average height of the men is 5'9"'.[26]

The role religion played in generating 'martialness' among the recruits was another facet of the Martial Race doctrine. MacMunn pointed out that the warlike instinct of the Sikhs was due to the militant faith of Guru Govind Singh and those Jats who accepted Sikhism became warriors due to the Calvinistic effect of the Gurus' teachings.[27] However, long before MacMunn, a Scottish officer of the Bengal School, W.L. McGregor, who fought in the First Anglo-Sikh Wars (1845–6) claimed that the martial religion— Sikhism, transformed its followers into warriors.[28] Even before McGregor, Lieutenant-Colonel Malcolm in 1812 pointed out that Sikhism generated civic militarism. Unlike Hindu mythologies, Guru Govind, argued Malcolm, emphasized courage and honour among his followers.[29]

The Martial Race ideologues tried to distinguish among various 'martial' groups. MacMunn tried to differentiate between the various 'martial' communities on the basis of their regional locations, physical and mental attributes, languages, social and cultural characteristics and religious sensibilities. MacMunn differentiated the Sikhs of central Punjab with long hair and curled beards from the Pathans who had a 'Jewish' appearance. Further, he believed that the Sikhs were slow witted but doggedly courageous, while the Pathans were characterized by their irresponsible manners.[30]

Roberts believed that climate and region influenced the biological and sociological attributes of the inhabitants. He asserted that in the hot climate of India, even erstwhile warlike races rotted. Cold temperate regions produced better warriors than the hot tropics. As north-west India was colder than south and west India, Roberts felt that most of the martial races were located in that corner. Roberts also tried to introduce a connection between the existence of a frontier, mountainous region and the presence of martial traits. He wrote that a live frontier in the hilly region—one with warlike enemies present on the other side—kept alive the martial aptitudes, while long periods of peace, prosperity and security resulted in racial degeneration.[31] In 1882, he wrote: 'It is a remarkable fact that a Maratha can hardly be found in the ranks of any army in India; this race which was so much dreaded hundred years ago is now entirely given up to civil pursuits'.[32] In the same year Roberts asserted: 'The fact is that the Madras sepoy has never encountered a formidable enemy, and nearly 100 years of peace have almost quenched any martial spirit there may have been in him'.[33] The correlation between peace and genesis of unwarlike spirit was already in the air even before the advent of Roberts. E.A.B. Travers, Deputy Adjutant General of the Madras Army who later rose to the post of Assistant Adjutant General, in 1875 informed the Horse Guards in the following terms: 'It has been said that generations of peace destroy all martial spirit in the Asiatic.'[34] The presence of an open frontier, constant warfare was common in north-west India. Hence, claimed Roberts, the Sikhs and the Pathans retained their martial attributes.[35] This theoretical tradition of linking soldiering capabilities with physical geography could be traced back to the Classical Greek tradition. The Greeks following Herodotus divided Europe and Asia into Occident and Orient. Moreover the Greeks depicted most of the people inhabiting Asia as slothful, cowardly with passive temperament owing to agricultural prosperity and the hot climate of Asia. In contrast, believed the Greeks, the cold weather of Europe and the not so fertile soil bred endurance, courage and active manly spirit.[36]

The spokesmen of the Martial Race ideology used history to justify their views. Roberts claimed:

I have been reading lately the history of the Madras army, and I cannot find any occasion on which its fighting qualities were ever severely tried. . . . But a study of the campaigns and battles which took place in the latter half of the eighteenth century proves conclusively that the brunt of fighting was always borne by the Europeans and that the casualties amongst the native troops were never very serious.[37]

Roberts did not provide any figures to support his contention. A glance at the combat casualties suffered by the Madras regiments that fought against Mysore and the Marathas, goes against Roberts' verdict. In the action before Bangalore against Tipu Sultan's army of Mysore on March 1791 and at the Battle of

Assaye (1803) against the Marathas, the Madras units suffered considerable losses.[38] Probably Roberts' plan was to delegitimize the Madrassis and to replace them with the communities from north-west India.

Why did the proponents of Martial Race ideology consider the Sikhs, Pathans and the Gurkhas to be martial *vis-à-vis* the Madrassis? The medical opinion and military reality of colonial India somewhat supported Roberts' contention that the highlands supplied healthy recruits. The lacklustre performance of the Company's Indian troops in the Terai during the Nepal War (1814–15), in the swampy jungles during the First Burma War (1824–6) and in the hot plains of Punjab during the two Sikh Wars (1845–6, 1848–9) on the one hand, and the gallant resistance by the Gurkhas and the Sikhs against the Company's forces on the other hand, convinced the British officers about the combat capabilities of the two latter groups. What the British forgot was that the two war-winning cards of the Company's Army—the horse artillery and the heavy cavalry were not of much use in the hilly terrain of Nepal and the North-West Frontier. Again, the Company's Indian soldiers were not trained in jungle warfare in which the Burmese excelled, and the white officer corps was to be blamed for this deficiency. The sepoys' line tactics, which were well suited to combat in the plains, proved useless in the hills. In mountain warfare skirmishing was vital and the Pathans and the Gurkhas were masters of this craft because of their acquaintance with the terrain from childhood. These two groups were physically and psychologically adapted to cold and rain at a high altitude. During the Anglo-Sikh Wars, the Company utilized some Gurkhas. Observing their actions, Sergeant John Pearman, an Irishman, who was in the Company's force, described the Gurkhas as 'a fearless brave mountainous race' and was for increasing their intake. General Charles Napier (Commander-in-Chief of the Indian Army, 1849–50) and Brian Hodgson perceived the Gurkha as the highlander soldier. Hence, they demanded enlistment of the Gurkhas.[39] The military scenario in the last decades of the nineteenth century strengthened Roberts' position that the North-West Frontier bred warriors. Continuous 'butcher and bolt' expeditions against the frontier tribesmen were going on along that region and for the Indus tribals and the Punjabi soldiers of the Punjab Frontier Force guarding the frontier, this region provided realistic training in hill warfare. Deployment along the frontier was helpful for combat simulation and was much more effective than the parade ground training given to the Madras and most of the Bombay soldiers who were rarely deployed along the frontier.[40]

In 1928, Lieutenant-Colonel W.C. Ross of the Indian Medical Service and then Director of Public Health in Bihar, stated that due to hookworms, the people inhabiting the plains of India, especially the region around Bihar and Orissa, had become weak.[41] Following upon this, the army avoided these two provinces.

C. Enloe asserts that the political dependability of the recruits was the chief criterion of the Martial Race ideology.[42] From the above discussion it is clear that Enloe's view is a bit mechanical. She neglects the religious and cultural elements of the military reality, which went into the making of this complex theory. Further Roberts, the father figure of the Martial Race ideology, argued that combat efficiency was more vital than the political reliability of the groups joining the army. Roberts claimed that some groups like the Pathans were martial but not necessarily loyal; while some like the Sikhs were both loyal and had warrior traits. He was for limited enlistment of the quasi-loyal martial groups like the Pathans. But, he was never for the induction of the groups, which he considered loyal, but unwarlike, for example the Madrassis.[43] And MacMunn never raised the question of political reliability of the recruits.[44]

The Martial Race doctrine was a complex alloy of different elements. One element was the Bengal School's recruitment doctrine. The other strand was introduced towards the end of the nineteenth century by Roberts' caucus. The linkage between martial qualities and the social and occupational backgrounds was present in the Bengal School's enlistment doctrine. This line was pursued vigorously by the Martial Race ideologues. The physical and dietary criteria of the Bengal School were also retained by the high priests of the Martial Race camp. The well built agricultural races remained the best soldiers. It is intriguing why there was this preference for the small farmers.

In general India was an agrarian economy with most people living in the countryside. The army found that many people from an agricultural background were undernourished. So, the army preferred the landowning peasants, who at least did not suffer from the adverse effects of malnutrition. The imperial belief was that the urban people were seditious and the cities were storehouses of diseases because of backward sanitary conditions. The officers were convinced that the cities with their filthy *bazars* and the temptations they offered to the 'natives' resulted in venereal diseases. Further, the terrorists from secret societies, argued the British officials, had links with the urban dwellers. For instance the 16th Jat Regiment, when deployed at Kanpur in 1904, came under the influence of the Arya Samaj and the army discharged many soldiers.[45] Hence, the army looked down upon occupations, which involved going to the cities and which they conceived required brains. They were probably afraid that the inclusion of too many politically educated people might result in the disintegration of British authority. Roberts himself wanted politically inert rural people in the army.[46] In 1882, Roberts informed H. Hensman, the sub-editor of the *Pioneer* that he disliked the Madras recruits because they were mostly educated line boys.[47]

The Bengal School and its lineal descendant the Martial Race lobby's obsession that farmers make the best soldiers could be traced back to European politico-military thought. In contemporary Europe also there was a general belief that the peasants possessed good physiques and, being simpler, were much more malleable compared to the urban underemployed. In the British Army the usual orthodoxy was that urban recruits were less fit than the rural recruits.[48] Niccolo Machiavelli (1469–1527) put the following words in the mouth of Fabrizio who was questioned by Cosimo whether it is better to draw soldiers from the rural areas or the towns:

All authors who have written upon this subject agree that it is better to take them from rural areas, because such men are accustomed to bearing up under hardships and fatigues, enduring all sorts of weather, handling a spade, digging ditches, carrying heavy burdens—these men are, generally speaking, more temperate and incorrupt than others. . . . I would advise . . . the infantry from rural areas.[49]

However, Roberts' emphasis on ecology was a factor, which was absent in the discourse of the Bengal School. Thus the Martial Race ideologues modified, elaborated and revived the Bengal School's image of model soldiers.

III

CONTRADICTIONS WITHIN THE MARTIAL RACE IDEOLOGY

Under the superficial unity, which the Martial Race ideology displayed, there existed several fault lines. David Arnold rightly asserts that the Martial Race ideology was a bundle of contradictory ideas but he does not develop this point.[50] All the scholars have treated this ideology as somewhat frozen in time. Hence, they have missed out the changes, which the Martial Race theory underwent with time.

In the 1890s Roberts, Goodenough and Dalton emphasized the outward appearance, i.e. height and physical features, of the martial groups. In 1911, MacMunn challenged this linkage between physical attributes and soldiering. He had written: 'It is absurd that the great, merry, powerful Kashmiri should have not an ounce of physical courage in his constitution, but it is so. Nor are appearances of any use as a criterion. Some of the manliest looking people in India are in this respect the most despicable'.[51] The Bengal School and some members of its lineal descendant, the Martial Race lobby were obsessed with height. During 1882, when Roberts was Commander-in-Chief of the Madras Army, he complained to Field-Marshal, the Duke of Cambridge: 'The physique of the men is, no doubt, very inferior to that in regiments raised in the more northern parts of India'.[52] It is to be noted that the British Army was also obsessed with height. Only after suffering horrendous casualties in late 1914, for getting replacements quickly and in large numbers, was the height requirement lowered from 5'8" to 5'3".[53] In the Sepoy Army, Colonel Shakespear challenged the criteria of height for inducting his favourites, the short Gurkhas.[54]

The use or rather misuse of history by the theorists constitutes another issue. Both Roberts and MacMunn used history to justify their views but in different ways. Roberts used history negatively: to delegitimize some groups such as the Madrassis and the *Purbiyas*, by pointing out that they lacked martial traditions. MacMunn on the other hand used history positively: to prove that some communities had brilliant fighting records and hence they were warlike. The Jats, in his eyes, appeared to be warlike because they fought very well against General Gerald Lake's besieging army during the siege of Bharatpur fort in 1805.[55]

Generally all the theorists agreed that the martial groups in India were, at their best, the equals of the British soldiers. Before 1857, Hugh Gough, the British general who fought the *Khalsa* Army during the two Sikhs Wars, glorified the Gurkhas and thus set the stage for MacMunn and Shakespear to admire them. Gough's view was that the Gurkhas could be compared with the elite British infantry, the grenadiers. But, Shakespear in 1912 claimed that the Gurkhas were better than the British soldiers.[56] This was indeed a revolutionary statement as for the first and the last time, a British officer openly admitted an Indian 'martial' group's superiority over white men.

While Roberts established a link between religion and disloyalty and applied it in the case of trans-frontier Pathans, MacMunn argued that for the Sikhs, religion functioned as a force multiplier. Thus religion appeared as an important component in the corpus of ideas associated with Roberts' camp. Hence, Cohen's argument that the Martial Race supporters underplayed the religious aspect of the martial groups[57] is untenable.

The Martial Race ideologues attempted to classify and categorize the different 'military races' of the subcontinent. For such an elaborate programme, their analytical categories and the basis of their disaggregation remained ever fluctuating, which in the end produced a confusing picture. Douglas Peers argues that before the 1830s the British used the category caste, for analysing the composition of the army but gradual disillusionment with the Bengal Army's performance forced them to introduce a new analytical category, race.[58] In his monograph, Peers writes that caste was a tool for man management in the hands of the British officers. They assumed that each caste had its own characteristics, but there was some disagreement among the officers on those fundamental attributes. However, in the later nineteenth century, this categorization became more systematic.[59] Omissi writes that the term 'martial races' was used consistently till the early twentieth century when it gave way to martial classes.[60] Actually the terms race, caste and class were used arbitrarily between 1859 and 1913 and there was disagreement about the particular characteristics of these terms.

In his autobiography Roberts used the terms race, caste and class interchangeably while referring to the Sikhs and the Gurkhas.[61] In his correspondence during 1878 he described these two groups as classes but in 1882 he described them as hardier races.[62] MacMunn also used these categories indiscriminately. He described the Pathans as a race that was divided into many tribes, which in turn were further subdivided into clans. But, for him the Pathans were also a class.[63]

IV

A CRITIQUE OF THE 'RACIAL DECLINE' OF THE MADRAS ARMY

The Madras Army has degenerated due to old officers and absence of active service.

Brigadier George Chesney[64]

By the end of the nineteenth century, the Martial Race theorists argued that due to the 'racial decline' of the Madrassis, the Madras Army was getting ineffective. In 1882, Roberts, the father figure of the Martial Race ideology, linked the degeneration of the south Indian recruits with long period of peace and ecology (the hot climate and absence of a frontier in the south).[65] His formula was to reduce the Madras Army's size and to replace the Madrassis with the 'martial races' from north-west India. Roberts underestimated the internal security threat and overestimated the danger of external threat. He claimed that the real danger was a Russian sponsored Afghan invasion, which could only be countered with the 'martial races'. With the development of communications, he stressed that the troops could be transported quickly to meet any local internal threat and was against maintaining a balance between the four regional armies.[66]

Many officers both inside and outside the Madras Army, who were supporters of the Balanced Recruitment lobby, opposed the Martial Race ideologue's plan tooth and nail. The opponents of the Martial Race theory argued that the recruitment should not be restrictive, because to revert to over-dependence on a few groups from a narrow region was impolitic. Moreover, to deny entry to various south Indian communities in the army on climatic and racial grounds, they claimed, was faulty. They pointed out that the decline of the Madras Army was due to managerial and certain structural reasons such as administrative inefficiency, rather than for racial reasons.

Even before Roberts articulated the racial decline of the Madrassis, this notion was quite widespread. The Secretary of State for India attempted to dispel this notion and in a letter to the Government of India dated 2 March 1871, he wrote:

I don't think that the Madrassi races are inferior than the northern races or periods of peace have made Madrassis soft. On the contrary, civilized races are the most capable of military discipline. Physical degeneracy may indeed render a race incapable of being good soldiers; but I have had no evidence that such is the condition of races inhabiting the Presidency of Madras. The Madras and the Bombay armies should be retained as a counterpart to the Bengal Army.[67]

In 1881, Brigadier George Chesney asserted: 'Not racial characteristics but drill and discipline makes an efficient officer.'[68] Lieutenant F.G. Cardew who between 1890 and 1901 served in the Duke of Cambridge's Own 10th Bengal Lancers challenged the Martial Race theorists' assumption that the *Pax Britannica* had reduced the warlike spirit of the Madrassis by inducing their youth to lay aside the sword for the ploughshare.[69] Lieutenant Colonel M.J. King-Harman wrote in 1891 in the service press: 'There is no conducive proof that the much maligned "*Pax Britannica*" has in any way reduced the warlike spirit of these warlike races which have hitherto been enlisted in our Indian Army'.[70]

Another officer, Major E.G. Barrow pointed out the basic fallacy of the Martial Race paradigm by denying the bipolar Oriental-Occidental divide. In 1891, he commented:

It is doubtful if we are fully justified in saying that the 'Pax Britannica' has wholly destroyed the warlike spirit of the peoples who have most profited by it, and though the ploughshare may offer to many greater attractions than the sword, it by no means proves that the former warlike spirit of the people has been deadened thereby, any more than we can assert that the industrial activity of England has destroyed the stubborn tenacity which distinguished the soldier who fought under Marlborough or Wellington.[71]

Captain E.K. Molesworth of the Royal Engineers, by comparing Oriental with the Occidental military history, attempted to challenge the Martial Race paradigm. In 1913, he wrote: 'Long peace need not make a man inefficient for war any more than twenty campaigns could make a soldier of the Frederick the Great's mule'.[72]

Lieutenant R.M. Rainey, commander of the 12th Burma Regiment Madras Infantry in 1891, blamed the erroneous British policy and not the south Indian society, for the Madras Army's ills. Any army will fare badly if suddenly brought out of the cupboard and thrown into battle. It was the Raj's fault, he claimed, in not allowing the Madras Army to participate in the controlled warfare of the North-West Frontier and for not allowing full participation in the Second Afghan War (1878–80). The result was that the Madras Army's British officers and the men had lost military skill.[73]

Rainey argued that the Madras regiments lacked fighting spirit, not because of the recruits, but due to the general mixture of the various 'nationalities' within the regiments, which prevented the growth of a regimental *esprit de corps*. The Tamils, Telugus, and the Deccani Muslims were mixed together within the companies. As these groups had different cultures (customs, languages, etc.), group loyalty could not be constructed from this motley collection. In the regiments, different groups spoke in different languages; and the British officers were not linguists. This created confusion while commanding the various south Indian communities on the battlefields. Rainey claimed that in the Bengal Army, if the Jats, Gujars and the Hindustani Muslims were mixed together within the companies, then there would be only confusion and anarchy resulting in militarily ineffectiveness of these regiments. In a sense Rainey was right, because the trend was towards class regiments. Between 1864 and 1883, mixed regiments were replaced by class regiments in the Bengal Army. Rainey's solution was that the Madras Army should also go for class regiments (Tamil regiments, Telugu regiments, etc.) or if that was not possible, then at least for class company regiments. This, he claimed, would create a regimental ethos, which in turn would give rise to a healthy inter-regimental rivalry, thus raising the army's military effectiveness. These middle ranking officers were aware of military developments in the wider world. From the early eighteenth century onwards, the Prussian Army adopted the canton system, which linked the different regiments with specific localities. Rainey proposed that the Madras Army should also experiment in establishing territorial loyalty through a similar scheme, so that every regiment would recruit from a particular locality, just like the Prussian Army.[74]

Major-General H.W. Norman, the Military Member of the Viceroy's Council (1870–7) pointed out the ageing of the personnel led to the rotting of the Madras Army. He claimed that the Madras Army was not combat worthy because it had the largest number of old men. Norman assumed that the soldiers had a shelf life of fifteen years, after which they became useless. Table 2.1 prepared, from the data supplied by Norman, shows that the Madras Army had the highest number of aged personnel, while the Punjab Frontier Force, generally regarded as the most effective militarily[75] had the lowest percentage of long-service personnel.

Norman tried to grapple with the question of why the Madras Army, unlike the Punjab Frontier Force and the Bengal Army, kept so may old men in its ranks. His view was that Punjab and the western part of north India being agriculturally prosperous, jobs were available. Recent researches support Norman's contention. Most of the soldiers who joined the Punjab Frontier Force and the Bengal Army were younger sons of small farmers from Punjab and western part of Hindustan. During famines, they joined the army and after a short period of service, they went back to their villages and became agriculturists.[76] The death of the elder brothers also encouraged such soldiers to seek voluntary discharge.[77] Rainey rightly concluded that the Madrassi

TABLE 2.1: SOLDIERS WHO TOOK PENSIONS AT DIFFERENT PERIODS OF SERVICE (1870–5)

	After 15 years of Service	After 16–20 years of Service	After 21–5 years of Service	After 26–30 years of Service	After 31–40 years of Service	Above 40 years of service
Bengal Army	40.5%	21%	20%	12%	6%	0.5%
Punjab Frontier Force	35%	40%	22%	2%	1%	
Bombay Army	10%	35%	25%	19%	10%	1%
Madras Army	8%	28%	20.5%	18%	20%	5.5%

Source: Minute on the organization of the Indian Army, Ch. 5, Pension system, para 18, Norman minutes, NAI.

soldiers were far poorer. Further, living conditions were costly in the Madras Presidency. While the Madrassi soldiers had to support their relations, the relatives of the troops from north and north-west India partly supported the soldiers in financial terms.[78] So, for the Punjabis, military service was a strategy to tide over temporary agrarian disasters[79] while for the Madrassis, army service was a long-term solution for unemployment. Further, the call of clan feeling and the attraction of tribal freedom encouraged the tribesman of the Punjab Frontier Force to take early discharge. Voluntary discharges were more or less absent in the Madras Army.[80] Another reason for the relative greyness of the Madras Army was that its soldiers remained loyal during 1857. The middle-aged soldiers of the 1850s were all old men by the 1870s. On the other hand, as the Bengal Army rebelled, the reorganized army in 1859 was able to recruit young men. And due to a quick turnover (a high rate of discharge), the Bengal Army had few long service *jawans*. The Punjab Frontier Force, being newly enlarged, had no long-service soldiers. Thus in the 1870s, the Madras Army compared to the Bengal Army and the Punjab Frontier Force had two and half times more soldiers with thirty to forty years of service behind them.[81]

The Balanced Recruitment lobby also tried to counter the Martial Race lobby's charge that the unwillingness of the Madrassis to join in the cavalry and the high sickness rate of the south Indians while serving in Burma were proof enough regarding the decline of the Madras Army. Cardew opposed the notion, prevalent among the military circles that the Madras Cavalry (composed of the Deccani Muslims) had degenerated. About 11,000 Muslims from Karnataka and Mysore were in the Madras cavalry in the 1890s. Their families had supplied recruits for generations. He asserted that there were many instances of personal bravery among the Madras sowars. The Madras Cavalry was allowed to operate only in the Burmese jungles and it was unfair, argued Cardew, to expect any cavalry to perform well in swampy jungle tracts.[82] Lieutenant-Colonel F.W. Tyrrell, commandant of the 37th Grenadier Madras Infantry Regiment, pointed out in 1881 that the Deccani Muslims, who constituted one-third of the Madras Army, were declining, not for racial but for other reasons. Due to the influence of Islam they lacked the desire to acquire Western education. As the army in the post-

1859 era was to some extent geared towards enlisting English educated soldiers, these Muslims were at a disadvantage *vis-à-vis* the other groups. The decline in the prosperity of the Muslims in peninsular India began with the collapse of Tipu's Mysore. With the army job market collapsing with the slow reduction of the Madras Army from the 1880s, and government favouring the men from north-west India, the south Indians were in dire straits.[83] Again, the unwillingness of the Deccani Muslims to join the Madras Cavalry in large number was not due to the extinction of 'martial' spirit in them but due to economic problems. Most of the Madras Cavalry regiments were irregular or *silladari* units. In such units the recruits had to pay for their horses while joining the army. The price of a horse was about Rs. 600. In addition the sowar had to pay a large contribution every month to the regimental *chunda fund*. When the sowar lost his horse in action then the *chunda fund* offered him some compensation for buying a new horse. By 1891, it was clear to the British officers of the Madras Army that most of the recruits lacked adequate cash for buying horses.[84] The high rate of sickness and invaliding among the Madrassi sepoys garrisoning Burma, was not due to their racial decline but, argued Major-General Blake in a letter to Frederick Haines in 1872, for the fact that the Madras sepoys starved themselves to support their families.[85]

Rainey, Chesney and Norman concluded that for continuation of the divide and rule policy, the Madras Army should not only be maintained, but rejuvenated. They wanted the old troops to be deployed in the veteran corps, destined not for the field but for garrison duties. The real problem, they claimed, was in getting effective British officers. They were not willing to join the Madras Army because it lacked of career prospects, as the army was never used in field duties. Further, the regiments were being broken up and the Madras Army's British officers were discriminated against the British officers from the Punjab Frontier Force and the Bengal Army. As early as 1875, Norman claimed that the crying defect of the Madras Army was its old and inefficient white officers and the solution lay in infusing new blood by inducting young British officers. Even Field-Marshal Kitchener (Commander-in-Chief of the Indian Army from 1902–9) and a follower of the Martial Race ideology accepted that no efficient British officer was willing to join the Madras Army.[86]

V

ASCENDANCY OF THE MARTIAL RACE LOBBY: 1880–1913

Geo-strategic considerations, technology, political factors and personalities interacted constantly to influence the rise and fall of the Martial Race doctrine and its precursor, the Bengal School at various moments of time. Before 1857, the colonial armies were used against the indigenous powers of the subcontinent. The strategic threat centres for the Company shifted to north India in the early nineteenth century. This aided the expansion of the Bengal Army. As the zone of operation was nearest to it, it saved time and transportation costs to deploy the Bengal Army. The continuous success of the Bengal Army also resulted in the acceptance of its recruitment ideology. Since south India was already pacified, and after the first decade of the nineteenth century no big war occurred in that region, the Madras Army did not experience any large-scale operations. This resulted in the decline of its status.[87] Hence, the Bengal School remained dominant and its star continued to rise till the fatal Sunday of 1857 when the *Pandies* (high-caste soldiers of the Bengal Army) turned their muskets against their white masters.

Several factors ensured the decline of the Bengal School. By 1856, the size of the Sepoy Army, including the regulars and the irregulars was 250,000 men and out of them about 120,000 personnel came from north India.[88] The Bengal School's policy of depending on the *Purbiyas* was proved wrong by a series of incidents, which started on 10 May 1857 and finally culminated in the Bengal Army's ruin. Most of the *Purbiyas* rebelled during the 1857 Mutiny. Other factors also downgraded them in the eyes of the military establishment. From 1860 onwards, successive Secretaries of State demanded that the Indian units should be deployed along the imperial outposts in Afro-Asia for policing duties. Charles Wood was one Secretary of State who demanded the Indian units for overseas duties[89] The *Purbiyas*, due to their rituals and customs, were unwilling to cross the *Kalapani*, whereas the Sikhs and the Gurkhas had no such problems. In fact the introduction of the General Enlistment Act in 1856, which stated that soldiers were liable to serve anywhere, provoked the *Purbiyas* to rebel.[90]

By the 1880s the situation again turned in favour of the Martial Race spokesmen. With the passage of time, the memory of the 1857 Mutiny receded and in the official mind the external threat replaced the internal threat. Technology also aided the rise of the Martial Race lobby. The military authorities were confident that they would be able to crush an uprising of the Indian soldiers quickly and easily due to the improved nature of communications and possession of superior breech loading arms by the British. With the development of the telegraph, railways, and fast steamers, the authorities felt confident of quickly concentrating military forces to crush internal uprisings. The network of telegraph lines, argued the military officials of the Raj, would enable the army headquarter to watch every possible sign of a combination against the British and to issue orders to the officers in charge of the local commands. Instantaneous orders from the army headquarter would enable the men on the spot to concentrate forces at the probable threat centres. Further, the Suez Canal route would allow the Raj quicker deployment of white troops from Britain in case of any emergency.[91] In 1893, General George White (Commander-in-Chief of the Indian Army from 1893 to 1898) articulated the reasons behind the shifting strategic paradigm. He contrasted the firepower superiority of the white troops *vis-à-vis* the Indians in the last decade of the nineteenth century with the situation in 1857. He claimed:

In 1857 the country had not been disarmed. The population possessed vast quantities of firearms with ammunition, which in range and accuracy were but little inferior to those in the hands of our troops. However the Arms Act changed all these. . . . A few Mountain Artillery batteries are in the hands of the Indian soldiers. But they are of small caliber and immobile. Hence they can't meet Horse and Foot artillery of the Europeans. . . . We not only have a larger force of artillerymen but also improved guns.[92]

So, the Martial Race lobby thought that the policy of maintaining four different armies recruited from all over India could be done away with. The external threats were of two types: raids by the frontier tribes, and fear of a Russian sponsored Afghan expedition. The Sepoy Army was geared to launch repeated expeditions against the tribes along the North-West Frontier of India. Delhi became a pawn in the 'Great Game' between London and St. Petersburg. The Russian conquest of Turkestan and the construction of Trans-Caspian railway stoked imperial anxiety that about 95,000 Russian troops could actually descend through the mountain passes along north-west India. The military establishment calculated that to retreat inside India before the advancing invaders would cause an uprising of the Indians, especially among the Muslims. So, the generals decided to maintain an advance frontier line in Afghanistan till reinforcements from Britain could arrive. The sepoys recruited from Hindustan and south India were unwilling to serve away from their homes for long periods. This necessitated that most of the recruits needed to be raised from the area around the operational zone, which meant north-west India. Moreover, if the regiments' recruiting grounds were far away from their area of deployment, then it would be time consuming to supply manpower to replace the casualties.[93] Transporting such recruits to the operational theatre would also be costly and might cause logistical logjam.

The aversion among the Madrassis to serve in Burma and in the North-West Frontier, because of the climate and high cost of rice, reduced their prestige in the army's eyes. Burma experienced high rainfall and the unacclimatized Madrassis and the *Purbiyas* fell ill in large numbers. Moreover, the Madras troops' families normally lived with them. The Madrassis were unwilling to leave their families in south India and perform garrison duty in Burma. The army realized that transporting the families of the troops along with the regiments to their area of deployment was very costly. For all these reasons, the army headquarter was against using the Madrassis during the Lushai expedition in 1871.[94] The Martial Race lobby characterized the unwillingness of these communities to serve in the North-East Frontier as evidence of their lack of martial spirit. George White, a follower of Roberts' Martial Race dogma in 1893 asserted:

In Burma I found the Madrassi a spiritless soldier and much given to malingering. He would starve himself, often even selling his ration when issued in kind, not only from penuriousness and want of proper pride in his physique, but with the deliberate purpose of rendering himself unfit for service, and being in consequence invalided back to Madras. Of the eight Madras Infantry regiments stationed in Burma, 1,203 men invalided to Madras.[95]

The intrigues and charisma of Roberts also aided in the victory of the Martial Race lobby. Roberts contacted formally and informally many influential military personalities both inside and outside India. Brigadier-General Charles George Arbuthnot was a field commander in Afghanistan during the Second Afghan War. He was assured by Roberts of the 'cowardliness' of the Madrassis. Roberts also got in touch with the powerful military bureaucrats. He informed the Adjutant General of India in 1878 about the 'unmartial'character of the Bombay Army and the presence of the 'warlike races' around the north-western corner of India. In 1890, George Chesney, the Military Member of Viceroy's Council and a supporter of Balanced Recruitment policy, was told about the combatworthiness of the Punjabis from Roberts. An influential figure Major-General Martin Dillon, the Assistant Military Secretary responsible for India, to the Commander-in-Chief of the British Army, the Duke of Cambridge in London, was told about the 'fearless' Gurkhas by Roberts. In 1879, Dillon was requested by Roberts to present the latter's view in front of the Duke, the most powerful military man in the British Empire.[96]

Roberts' painted a sort of 'enemy at the gates' picture for accelerating the induction of the 'martial races'. As an expert 'man on the spot' Roberts visualized that the Russian hordes along with their Central Asian allies were bent on invading India and consequently informed the metropolitan military figures about the uselessness of the 'soft' Madrassi soldiers in such a contest. In a letter dated 16 June 1882, Roberts in no uncertain term told Dillon:

It is no use our trying to persuade ourselves that the whole of the Indian Army is capable of meeting an enemy from Central Asia or Europe; they are not, and nothing will ever make them. It is not a question of efficiency, but of courage and physique; in these two essential qualities the sepoys of lower India are wanting. No amount of instruction will make up for these shortcomings, and it would be extremely dangerous for us to calculate upon possessing an army which would most assuredly fail us in the hour of danger. . . . You can show this letter to the Duke of Cambridge.[97]

Two years later, Roberts himself took the pen to portray the degenerating condition of the Madras and the Bombay 'races' in contrast to the martial aptitudes of the north-western 'races' before the Duke of Cambridge. From Bangalore, Roberts in a letter dated 9 July 1884, wrote to the high priest of the British Army: 'The ordinary sepoy would do exceedingly well for the work for which he was originally raised, and may be depended upon against Burmese, Chinese, Abyssians and such like, but I sincerely hope when the time comes for us to meet a Russian Army in the field, then our own force will consist mainly of Europeans, Gurkhas, and the best kind of Sikhs and Dogras'.[98] But, the Duke of Cambridge was an arch conservative. He was a member of the Peel Commission which was set up just after the 1857 Mutiny. The Peel Commission agreed on recruitment of a wide variety of communities from all over India and argued for the retention of the Bombay and the Madras armies for maintaining a balance with the communities recruited from north-west India. Feeling frustrated, Roberts in a letter dated 9 May 1886 complained to Lord Dufferin, the Viceroy in the following words: 'The Duke of Cambridge will, I fear, be somewhat troublesome in the matter of the Madras Army, for as you will see from the enclosed letter, he is a warm supporter of the Madrassis'.[99]

Roberts also contacted many powerful politicians both inside and outside the subcontinent. During the Second Afghan War, Roberts wrote to the Viceroy about the excellent performance of the Gurkhas against the Kurram tribes. Later, as the war was drawing to a close, he warned the Viceroy about H.W. Norman, the Military Member of the Viceroy's Council and General Donald Stewart (the Commander-in-Chief of the Indian Army from 1881 to 1885). Ironically Norman and Roberts campaigned together during the 1857 Mutiny and became best friends. But, with the passage of time they became sworn enemies. Norman was for limited induction of the Punjabis but Roberts was for total Punjabization of the army. As neither Norman nor Stewart shared Roberts' rosy views about the 'martial' groups, he regarded them as enemies.[100] On 5 April 1882, Roberts from Ootacamund wrote to Ashley Eden in Calcutta: 'There never was a man whose training rendered him less fitted for a military adviser than Norman, and yet he has been able to delay or prevent every reform required in the Indian Army'.[101] In 1887, Roberts blandly informed Lord Dufferin (the Viceroy from 1884 to 1888): 'I confess I do not believe in the fighting qualities of the Madras sepoys'.[102]

In 1885, Roberts' heard a rumour that the Liberals promised Norman, his archenemy, the post of Commander-in-Chief of India.[103] So, Roberts also privately contacted the influential

Conservative M.P. Lord Randolph Churchill, and informed him about the 'disastrous' performance of the Madrassis in Burma. In one of his despatches, Roberts urged Churchill to accept the post of Secretary of State of India, in the case of a Conservative victory in Britain. Only then, he claimed, would it be possible to fill the Madras and the Bombay armies with the Sikhs and the Gurkhas.[104] Roberts also pointed out to Viscount Cranbrook the necessity of replacing these 'non-martial' Indian soldiers. In a private letter dated 30 June 1882, Roberts wrote to him:

So long as the Indian Army had to fight against men of much the same stamp and caliber as themselves, they were fairly dependable, and on some occasions distinguished themselves, but when they came into contact with the Sikhs, it was quite apparent that they were over-matched, and that they were unable to cope with the hardier races of the north. Now, we cannot disguise from ourselves the fact that, if our Indian soldiers are ever again to be engaged in a war, the possibility, indeed the probability, is that they will have to meet very different foes from those which they have hitherto encountered.[105]

Roberts also tried to win over the influential non-military figures in Britain regarding his scheme of replacing the 'non-martial races' with the 'martial races'. He corresponded with Fitzjames Stephen, the Justice of the High Court at London. Roberts told him in 1884:

I strongly urged the reduction of the Indian Army, which took place two years ago, in order that we might get rid of some of the many regiments I knew could not be trusted in the field against a western enemy. I felt that the time was drawing near when we should require an army mainly composed of the best fighting classes, and that there would be less difficulty in getting the necessary increased agreed to, if some reduction were previously made.[106]

Very few people dared to challenge Roberts, the most distinguished field commander of the day. But some hit back. When Roberts informed Stewart about the utter incapacity of the Bombay and the Madras soldiers to take part in overseas operations or to fight in Central Asia, the latter disagreed. Stewart did not believe that the people of the Bombay and the Madras presidencies, which supplied the bulk of personnel of these two regional armies, were morally or mentally inferior compared to the so-called warlike races of north-west India. Stewart pointed out that many officers were biased against the Hindustanis and were averse to recruiting them. General Frederick Haines, the Commander-in-Chief of the Indian Army from 1876 to 1881, backed Stewart's views.[107] Between 1881 to 1885 when Roberts was Commander-in-Chief of the Madras Army, Brigadier-General Faunce was the Deputy Adjutant General in Madras. Despite pressure from General White and Roberts, Faunce refused to agree that the Madrassi soldiers were worthless. Then Roberts wrote to the Viceroy Lord Lansdowne in 1889 that Faunce had not seen active service, so his views should not be taken seriously.[108]

Roberts' voluminous correspondence filled with venom against the 'non-martial races' in the end bore fruit. He won over important figures in the War Office at London. Major-General Charles Brownlow, Assistant Military Secretary in the War Office, agreed with Roberts that the positive views of Lord Hardinge and Haines about the operational capabilities of the Bombay and the Madras armies amounted to nonsense. Brownlow seconded Roberts' view on demobilizing the Hindustanis and the Deccanis. Powerful civilians such as Dufferin supported Roberts.[109]

The Martial Race lobby knew that the distance between victory and defeat was marginal indeed. When Roberts was the Commander-in-Chief of the Madras Army, there was a chance that he might be appointed as the Adjutant General in Britain (he was interested in that post) and the post of the Commander-in-Chief in India would go to Lord Wolseley. But, the latter was not appointed because London feared that Wolseley being a 'hawk', immediately after coming to India would start a war with the 'Bear'. The Queen and the Duke of Cambridge wanted to appoint the Duke of Connaught as Commander-in-Chief of the Indian Army, but Salisbury's Cabinet opposed this proposal.[110] Ultimately, the coveted post of the Commander-in-Chief of the Indian Army went to Bobs *Bahadur*.

Roberts was also lucky because when he moved to the centre stage of the Indian Army, the opponents of Punjabization were on their way out. In March 1868, William Mansfield, the Commander-in-Chief of the Indian Army was against including the Dogras. But this community in later nineteenth century turned out to be a favoured 'martial race'. Stewart thoroughly opposed reduction in the recruitment of the Hindustani Muslims in the cavalry and was against the dominance of the Sikhs in the infantry. G.F. Hamilton, the Secretary of State, pointed out that had Stewart been in the office for a little longer, then the rise of the Martial Race lobby would have been checked if not blocked completely.[111]

After Roberts' departure from India, the crusade against the Madrassi soldiers was continued by Roberts' successor General George White. Following in Roberts' footsteps, White contacted metropolitan military figures in the attempt to replace the south Indians with the groups from north-west India. White, like Roberts informed the Duke of Cambridge about the 'non-martial' Madras Army. In July 1893, White wrote: 'The Madras officers are irresponsible in resisting the elimination of Madras sepoys. The seven battalions of Madras Infantry regiment should recruit the "warlike races" from Nepal and northern India. The Madras sepoys are unsuitable for frontier fighting in Burma'.[112] Since the Madras officers opposed the scheme of the Martial Race theorists, the latter group perceived the former as obstacles in their path of reform. George White claimed in 1893: 'It is difficult to get reliable reports from the officials of the Madras Army as they were biased in favour of their men and anxious to steer clear of the opprobium of defaming their own service. I got the most reliable information about the different races of the Native soldiers from the political officers and officers of the British Army'.[113]

The appointment of Field Marshal Kitchener as Commander-in-Chief of the Indian Army and Lord Curzon as Viceroy (1899–1905) settled the issue. Whatever might be the difference between the duo, they never disagreed on the issue of the 'martial races'. Both were admirers of Roberts' views as regards the 'martial races', and this is evident from their correspondence. Both wanted to replace the Madrassis with the Gurkhas. Even E.R.E. Ellis, the Military Member of Viceroy's Council and a bitter opponent of Kitchener as regards reorganization of the Indian Army's high command, agreed on the issue of the 'martial races'. In a minute dated 1905, Ellis agreed that the Bombay, Madrassi and the Hindustani regiments of the Bengal Army ought to be replaced with better fighting classes from north-west India. The Martial Race lobby took great pains to keep its opponents out from the corridors of power. Hamilton conspired to keep

Mansfield Clarke out of the post of Military Member of the Viceroy's Council because the latter belonged to the Madras Army. Hamilton feared that Clarke might obstruct the reduction of the Madras Army.[114] The chance factor also aided the rise of the Martial Race lobby. If tortuous British military politics led to the appointment of Wolseley, then instead of Roberts' caucus, the 'Wolseley ring' would probably have ruled the Indian Army and its history might have been different.

The victory of Roberts' group was reflected in the actual social and regional composition of the Indian Army. Table 2.2 shows that in 1885 the social and geographical basis of the army was broad: the groups from north, south and north-west India joined in more or less equal proportions. But, between 1885 and 1912, the share of the Hindustani Muslims, *Purbiyas* and the Deccanis declined drastically. In the same period the proportion of the 'martial' groups, Sikhs, Garhwalis and the Gurkhas, increased proportionately. By 1912, the 'martial' groups from the north-west became as dominant as the *Purbiyas* were just before the 1857 Mutiny. Interestingly the share of the *Purbiyas* in 1857, and Roberts' favourite martial groups (Sikhs and the frontier Muslims) in 1912 was same—44 per cent. The share of the low castes' declined from 6.5 per cent to 1.5 per cent.[115] In the long run there was a decline in the ritual status of the groups that entered the Sepoy Army in the last two decades of the nineteenth century.[116]

Since Roberts was a farsighted soldier, he probably understood the dangers posed by Punjabization in the long run. Hence, his schizophrenic attempts to ascribe martial status to some frontier tribes along the India-Burma border. In 1889, he ordered Brigadier-General Stedman, Inspector General of Police in Burma to assess the fitness of the 'races' inhabiting Indo-Burma border.[117] The Martial Race lobby continued Roberts' search for 'martial races' along the eastern frontier of India. Following this cue, in 1893, the Adjutant General in India, Major-General W. Galbraith pointed to the Secretary to the Government of India's Military Department that troops were required for guarding Burma. And the Madrassis were hopeless in this regard. His policy was to recruit hillmen from Assam. He wrote: 'This unit [10th Madras Infantry Regiment] was composed half of Gurkhas, half of Assamis hillmen [*Jarwahs*]. Though we had looked down

TABLE 2.2: SOCIAL AND REGIONAL COMPOSITION OF THE INDIAN ARMY

Regions	Groups	1857 (%)	1885 (%)	1912 (%)
North-West Frontier Province and Punjab	Pathans, Punjabi Muslims and Sikhs	10	25 (4.5+6.5+14)	44 (7.5+16+20.5)
Himachal Pradesh and Nepal	Gurkhas, Garhwalis and Dogras	2.5	8 (5+3+0)	17.5 (11.5+5+1)
Haryana and Uttar Pradesh	Jats, Ahirs, Gujars, other middle-ranking Hindus and Low Castes	6.5	14	10
Western Uttar Pradesh and Haryana	Hindustani Muslims	18	17	6
North India (Bihar and Uttar Pradesh)	*Purbiyas* (Brahmins and Rajputs)	44	11 (5+6*)	9 (2+7*)
Maharashtra South India	Marathas Madrassis (Tamils, Telugus and Deccani Muslims)	4 15 (8+7)	6 19 (12+7)	3 10.5 (5+5.5)

*Including Rajputs from Rajasthan.

Sources: Gaylor, *Sons of John Company*, pp. 174, 219-35; Chesney, *Indian Polity*, pp. 215–16, 221, 264–5, 267; Cardew, *Bengal Native Army*, pp. 456–9; *Peel Committee*, Appendix nos. 17 & 22; *Army Committee*, vol. 1-A, *Minority Report*, p. 156.

upon the Assamis hillmen, they were doing very well. We must have had a special report on them to increase their supply'.[118] In 1904, Roberts urged Kitchener to enlist the 'martial' tribes inhabiting the Indo-Burma border. Kitchener agreed to Roberts' proposal of using the Burmese frontier tribes as general purpose troops. But, their unwillingness to join in large numbers, even in the local corps, wrecked Roberts' scheme.[119]

The Deccani Muslims from Hyderabad could have functioned as a counterpoise to the 'races' from north-west India. But in Roberts' view: 'Hyderabad is the refuse of all discontented Muslims in India'. The Hindustani Muslims could have been a counterweight to the Sikhs, but anxious officers felt that pan-Islamism might hamper the loyalty of the Muslim soldiers. Some officers believed that it was necessary to reduce the enlistment of the Muslims further, because if the Middle East politician Arabi Pasha declared a *jihad* against the British, then the Muslim sepoys of the Raj might turn their loaded rifles against the British.[120] Roberts himself was anxious regarding the strength of pan-Islamic feeling among the Muslims. In 1883, he claimed 'a strong religious feeling existed amongst some of the Muslim sepoys in our Indian regiments, which made them very averse to fighting against the *Amir* of Afghanistan'.[121]

The fear that the Muslims, though 'martial', were disloyal spread like an epidemic within the higher echelons. Hamilton in 1897 warned Lord Elgin (Viceroy of India) not to use the 'disloyal Muslims' in the North-Western Frontier. For this reason, Hamilton did not want any Muslim soldiers in the Chitral Expeditionary Force. In the end, Roberts became desperate. He understood where his own doctrine was leading his much loved Sepoy Army. His attempt to balance the 'martial' groups was in complete ruins. Like a drowning man clutching to a straw, he turned to his one time enemy Chesney, to enquire about the possibility of using the 'martial' Zulus to balance the Punjabis.[122]

Roberts' successor George White also understood the danger of concentration of the 'martial races' in the Bengal Army. So, he was for a division of this army and playing off the various 'martial races' against each other. In 1893 he commented:

It is open to argument whether classing together in one army corps Sikhs, Pathans and Punjabi Muslims, our very best fighting material, is the happiest device. . . . The danger ahead of us calling for counterpoise is from the northern fighting races . . . I would prefer devoting money to making the segregation of those northern races very defined, the one from the other. The Northern Army [Bengal Army] is dangerous as it has become too big. The Sikhs and the Punjabi Muslims should be made into one army, while the Pathans and the Afghans recruited from west of Indus into another army. Thus we would be able to revive the old antagonism between the Punjabis and the Afghans.[123]

The point to be noted is that White's scheme of dividing the Bengal Army was different from the scheme proposed by Chesney in the 1880s. While Chesney a member of the Balanced Recruitment lobby wanted the north Indians in the Bengal Army to balance the Punjabis and the trans-Indus personnel, White was for the Punjabis to balance the trans-Indus personnel. Since the Bombay Army's soldiers were not willing to serve in Baluchistan, so, under Roberts' scheme, the North-West Frontier personnel replaced the Bombay sepoys. Instead of depending too much on these so-called martial communities, White wanted to use the Baluchis in the Bombay Army but found out that they were not interested in joining in significant numbers to act as a counterpoise to the Punjabis.[124]

The Sikhs, Pathans, and the Punjabi Muslims from north-west India supplied the bulk of the army's recruits under the Martial Race game plan. As evident from Table 2.2, their share between 1885 and 1912 due to the policy of the Martial Race lobby jumped from 25 per cent to 44 per cent. In 1885, when Roberts' ring had just taken over, the army drew only 19.5 per cent of its personnel from Punjab, but by 1912 this proportion rose to 36.5 per cent. Around 1912, the army drew about 61.5 per cent of its manpower from central Nepal, Punjab and the North-West Frontier Province. In 1912, at the eleventh hour when the army committee met, they realized that the Martial Race doctrine was indeed faulty because the army had become over-dependent on a few groups from a narrow region. The *Akali* disturbances further unnerved them. The officers realized that the Sikhs had become 'swollen-headed', and demanded reduction in the entry of the Punjabis.[125] By then it was too late, as the Great War was coming.

Some long-term factors also aided the induction of the *Purbiyas* before 1857 and the Sikhs after 1880 respectively. The Sepoy Army was generally deployed at the borders of the British-Indian Empire, and after conquering the frontier enemies, slow induction of the ex-enemies started. After the lapse of a certain period, the volume of recruitment of the ex-enemies rose. The frontier then advanced again, new frontier groups became favourites, and the old frontier groups were then sidelined. This was partly the product of cooption. After conquering the frontier enemies, the British officers also developed a healthy respect for these groups. The officers recognized their soldierlike qualities and created a literature about their martial activities, which generated interest about these groups and accelerated their enlistment in the military establishment. This process operated throughout the nineteenth century.

In the last half of the eighteenth century, the Bengal Army was deployed along the frontiers of Awadh. The heavy enlistment of the *Purbiyas* in the Maratha regular infantry, and the tough fight put up by these units made the British interested in enlisting them. And as the Awadh Nawab's army was reduced, the *Purbiyas* from the Nawab's force were coopted in the Company's Army. This partly explains the rise of the Bengal School. Between 1790 and 1830, the Bengal Army recruited the *Purbiyas* in large numbers. Later, in the 1840s, as the British frontier expanded to the Terai and to Punjab, the tough fight which the Gurkhas and the Sikhs gave, heightened the admiration of the British for these communities. The British officers produced prolific literature on them. The Gurkha and the Sikh recruits started trickling in, partly to absorb the disbanded *Khalsa* Army and the Nepal Army's ex-soldiers. Some Sikh units were raised after the Sikh Wars. But, due to lethargy and institutional inertia, the *Purbiya* dominance continued for some years. After 1857, as the disloyalty of the *Purbiyas* became apparent, the recruitment of the Sikhs and the Gurkhas increased slightly, but became massive from the last two decades of the nineteenth century, as the army was deployed along the North-West Frontier.[126]

The strategic factor also aided Punjabization of the Sepoy Army. Strategy from the last two decades of the nineteenth century demanded that the most potent threat might come along the North-West Frontier. The Punjabis and the trans-Indus Pathans were willing to join the army in bulk because not only the zone of operation was near their homeland but also for the fact that they were used to the climate and terrain of the zone of operation. If the Raj faced a serious threat along its eastern border then the Punjabis and the Pathans would have been unwilling to join the army. This is because they hated serving in the damp climate and marshy terrain of east India. And *atta* which was the staple diet of the Punjabis was not easily available in the North-East Frontier. When they were fed rice either they fell ill or got demoralized.[127] The Punjabis performed badly when the Sepoy Army's units were deployed in campaigns along the eastern theatre. In a letter dated 13 December 1886 and written to Dufferin, Roberts admitted: 'The 26th Punjab Infantry, which formed the main part of the expedition into the Shan hills [along Indo-Burma border] last May, have suffered more than any other Indian regiment in Burma: 102 men have died, and a great many have been invalided.'[128] So, for conducting campaigns in this region, the Raj depended on the Gurkhas and military police battalions that recruited from the inhabitants of this area. One could as well say that if the eastern frontier had become the principal strategic area for the Raj then instead of Punjabization, history would have witnessed Bengalization (recruitment from Bengal Presidency, i.e. from areas like Assam, Manipur, etc.) of the Indian Army.

CONCLUSION

The propagandists of the Martial Race lobby conceived that the subcontinent was composed of various groups and tried to judge their martial capacities with the help of several criteria. The policy of the Martial Race spokesmen was to establish a special collaborative relationship with only some groups from definite areas. So, their doctrine emphasized that soldierlike traits were the monopoly of only certain groups. The strategy of the Martial Race lobby was risky because it tried to fill most of the army with a particular group and if that specially favoured group rebelled, then all was lost. Before 1857, the *Purbiyas* from north India dominated the army and when the British tried to reduce their dominance, the result was the 1857 Mutiny. The Raj, unlike the Bourbons, learnt nothing but forgot everything. Towards the end of the nineteenth century, the Raj's army again became over-dependent on a narrow area—Punjab. The Martial Race ideology, focusing on a few groups, could supply only limited manpower to the army. Hence, this ideology was adequate as long as the Indian Army was engaged in 'small colonial wars' in which the regiments suffered small combat losses. But, when the Sepoy Army was used in the First World War, it suffered huge manpower losses.[129] At that critical juncture, the Martial Race ideology temporarily retreated to oblivion.

NOTES

1. Fitness of the Madras sepoy for service in Burma, 26 June 1893, 1Q/7, George White Collection, MSS.EUR.F.108/24, OIOC.
2. Perry, *The Commonwealth Armies*, pp. 82–91.

3. Leela and Pravin Visaria, 'Population: 1757-1947', in Dharma Kumar, ed., *The Cambridge Economic History of India: c.1757 - c.1970*, vol. 2, 1982, reprint, New Delhi: Orient Longman in association with Cambridge University Press, 1991, p. 487; Norman Minutes, Minute on the organization of the Army of India, 1875, Ch. 5, Pension system para 6, NAI.

4. Heather Streets, *Martial Races*, Manchester: Manchester University Press, 2004, p. l. Cohen, *The Indian Army*, pp. 32–56.

5. Mason, *A Matter of Honour*, pp. 20–4, 344–61; Omissi, *The Sepoy and the Raj*, pp. 1–45; Douglas M. Peers, *Between Mars and Mammon: Colonial Armies and the Garrison State in India, 1819–35*, London: I.B. Tauris, 1995, p. 88.

6. Hoover, 'The Recruitment of the Bengal Army', pp. 144–56.

7. Barat, *The Bengal Native Infantry*, pp. 119–24, 150, 196, 211; Cardew, *Bengal Native Army*, pp. 54–57; *Supplementary Report*, p. 27.

8. Saul David, *The Indian Mutiny: 1857*, London: Viking, 2002, p. 25.

9. Barat, *Bengal Native Infantry*, pp. 120–6, 129; Saxena, *The Military System of India*, p. 13; Alavi, *The Sepoys and the Company*, p. 77; Major George F. MacMunn, *Vignettes from Indian War*, 1901, reprint, New Delhi: Low Price Publications, 1993, pp. 133, 141; Cardew, *Bengal Native Army*, p. 54; Lunt, ed., *From Sepoy to Subedar*, pp. 3–4; Durgadas Bandopadhyay, *Amar Jivancharit* (Bengali), 1924, reprint, Calcutta: Ananya Prakashan, 1985, pp. 12, 16, 51, 57; *Supplementary Report*, pp. 27, 308, 310.

10. Bentinck's minute on corporal punishment, 16 February 1835, Bentinck's minute on military policy, 13 March 1835 in C.H. Philips, ed., *The Correspondence of Lord William Cavendish Bentinck, Governor General of India: 1832-35*, vol. 2, Oxford: Oxford University Press, 1977, pp. 1429, 1431–2, 1445–6, 1451.

11. Dodwell, *Sepoy Recruitment*, pp. 14, 33–6.

12. Minute by Prinsep, 9 June 1835, *PP* (1867), pp. 165–6.

13. Tyrrell, 'The Races of the Madras Army', pp. 11, 18, 20.

14. *The Armies of the Native States of India*, reprinted from *The Times*, London, 1884, p. 23.

15. Menezes, *Fidelity and Honour*, p. 534.

16. Roberts to Randolph Churchill, 20 June 1884, in General Frederick Roberts, *Correspondence with England while Commander-in-Chief in Madras: 1881–85*, Simla: Govt. Central Printing Office, 1890, p. 191, Part 2, Indian Series, L/MIL/17/5/1615, OIOC.

17. Field Marshal Roberts, *Forty-one Years in India: From Subaltern to Commander-in-Chief*, 1897, reprint, London: Richard Bentley & Son, 1898, pp. 499, 530, 532–4; Brian Robson, ed., *Roberts in India: The Military Papers of Field-Marshal Lord Roberts, 1876–93*, Stroud: Alan Sutton, 1993, pp. 256–8, 263–6.

18. MacMunn, *The Armies of India*, p. 129.
19. MacMunn, *The Armies of India*, Ibid., pp. 129–31; Idem., 'The Martial Races of India', *Army Review*, vol. 1, no. 2 (1911), reprinted in *The Panjab: Past and Present*, vol. 4, no. 1 (1970), pp. 73–5.
20. MacMunn, *The Armies of India*, pp. 129–32, 140–5, 155–6, 162–4; Idem., 'Martial Races', pp. 73, 76, 81–2.
21. Roberts, *Short Report on Important Questions*, pp. 86–7.
22. Goodenough and Dalton, *The Army Book*, p. 446.
23. Goodenough and Dalton, *The Army Book*, pp. 445, 448, 467; Roberts, *Forty-one Years*, p. 530.
24. Clifford J. Rogers, 'The Military Revolutions of the Hundred Years War', in idem. ed., *The Military Revolution Debate: Readings on the Military Transformation of Early Modern Europe*, Colorado/Boulder: Westview Press, 1995, pp. 78–80.
25. Robson, ed., *Roberts in India*, p. 266; Inspection Report of the Madras Army for 1874–5, Records of Chief Commands, Notes and Minutes by Napier of Magdala, MSS.EUR.F.114, 5 (4), OIOC.
26. Roberts to the Duke of Cambridge, 8 April 1888, in General Frederick Roberts, *Correspondence with England while Commander-in-Chief in India: 1888-89*, Calcutta: Superintendent of Govt. Printing, 1890, p. 49, Part 8, L/MIL/17/5/1615/8, OIOC.
27. MacMunn, *The Armies*, pp. 133–9; Idem., 'Martial Races', pp. 75-6.
28. W.L. McGregor, *The History of the Sikhs*, vol. 1, 1846, reprint, Allahabad: R.S. Publishing House, 1979, pp. 51, 54, 84–5, 88, 96, 165.
29. Lieutenant-Colonel Malcolm, *Sketch of the Sikhs*, 1812, reprint, New Delhi: Asian Educational Services, 1986, pp. 189–90.
30. MacMunn, *The Armies*, pp. 133–40, 145–54; 'Martial Races', pp. 75–80.
31. Roberts, *Forty-one Years*, pp. 499, 530, 532, 534; Robson, ed., *Roberts in India*, p. 264.
32. Roberts, *Correspondence with England while Commander-in-Chief in Madras*, p. 44.
33. Robson, ed., *Roberts in India*, p. 264.
34. Confidential memorandum on the organization of the Indian Armies, E.A.B. Travers, 12 April 1875, Records of Chief Commands, Notes and Minutes by Napier, MSS.EUR.F.114, 5 (3).
35. Robson, ed., *Roberts in India*, pp. 257–8, 265–6; Roberts, *Forty-one Years*, pp. 499, 532.
36. Edith Hall, 'Asia Unmanned: Images of Victory in Classical Athens', in John Rich and Graham Shipley, ed., *War and Society in the Greek World*, 1993, reprint, London/New York: Routledge, 1995, pp. 123-5.
37. Robson, ed., *Roberts in India*, pp. 263–4.
38. Lieutenant-Colonel W.J. Wilson, *Historical Record of the Fourth Prince of Wales' Own Regiment Madras Light Cavalry*, Madras: Govt. Press, 1877, Appendix A and B, pp. 89–90.
39. John Pemble, *The Invasion of Nepal: John Company at War*, Oxford:

Clarendon Press, 1971, pp. 134–339; George Bruce, *The Burma Wars: 1824–86*, London: Hart-Davis, MacGibbon, 1973; Clive Dewey, 'Racism and Realism: The Theory of Martial Castes', unpublished paper, University of Leicester; Colonel W.G. Hamilton, 'Ochterlony's Campaign in the Simla Hills', *JUSII*, no. 187 (1912), pp. 137–56, 'Ochterlony's Campaign in the Simla Hills-Some Further Notes on', *JUSII*, vol. XLI, no. 189 (1912), pp. 455–8; Colonel L.W. Shakespear, 'The War with Nepal: Operations in Sirmoor', *JUSII*, vol. XLII, no. 193 (1913), pp. 369–79; Lieutenant-Colonel H.M. Sinclair, 'The First Sikh War, 1845-46', *JUSII*, vol. 28, no. 134 (1899), pp. 1–24; Cardew, *Bengal Native Army*, pp. 146, 148, 150, 210; Captain Eden Vansittart, *The Gurkhas*, 1890, reprint, New Delhi: Ariana, 1980, pp. 34–5, 40–1; Marquess of Anglesey, ed., *Seargeant Pearman's Memoirs*, London: Jonathan Cape, 1968, p. 54.

40. From Colonel John A.M. Macdonald, Secy. to Govt., Bombay MD, to Colonel H.K. Burne, MD, Simla, Progs. no. 721, 28 October 1878, MDP, March 1879, NAI.

41. *Royal Commission on Agriculture in India: Evidence taken in Bihar and Orissa*, vol. 13, Calcutta, 1928, pp. 335–49.

42. Enloe, *Ethnic Soldiers*, pp. 23–49.

43. Roberts, *Forty-one Years*, pp. 349, 352; Robson, ed., *Roberts in India*, pp. 34–6, 40–5, 196, 263–6, 317, 392–4.

44. MacMunn, *The Armies of India*, pp. 129-72; Idem., 'The Martial Races', pp. 261–71.

45. *Army Committee*, vol. 3, pp. 647, 677; Proceedings of a special committee assembled at Allahabad by order of Brigadier Fordyce on 10 July to take into consideration and report upon the revision of the cantonment, Progs. no. 12, MDP, October 1860.

46. Roberts, *Correspondence with England while Commander-in-Chief in Madras*, pp. 64–5.

47. General Frederick Roberts, *Correspondence with India while Commander-in-Chief in Madras: 1881–85*, Simla: Govt. Central Printing Office, 1890, p. 50, Part 3, Indian series, L/MIL/17/5/1615, OIOC. Line boys were sons of soldiers born and brought up within the regimental lines.

48. V.G. Kiernan, 'Conscription and Society in Europe before the War of 1914–18', in M.R.D. Foot, ed., *War and Society; Historical Essays in Honour and Memory of J.R. Western, 1928–71*, London: Paul Elek, 1973, p. 144; Strachan, *Wellington's Legacy: The Reform of the British Army, 1830–54*, Manchester: Manchester University Press, 1984, p. 53.

49. Niccolo Machiavelli, *The Art of War*, 1965, reprint, tr. by Ellis Farneworth with an Introduction by Neal Wood, New York: Da Capo Press, 1990, p. 27. At times Machiavelli agrees that training could offset lack of innate martial abilities up to a certain extent. See p. 25, footnote 21.

50. David Arnold, ' "Criminal Tribes" and "Martial Races": Crime and Social

Control in Colonial India', unpublished postgraduate seminar paper, CCSH/84/5, Institute of Commonwealth Studies, University of London.

51. MacMunn, *The Armies of India*, p. 130.
52. Roberts, *Correspondence with England while Commander-in-Chief in Madras*, p. 1.
53. Holger H. Herwig, *The First World War: Germany and Austria-Hungary, 1914–18*, London: Arnold, 1997, p. 119.
54. Colonel L.W. Shakespear, *History of the 2nd King Edward's Own Goorkha Rifles (The Sirmoor Rifles)*, vol. 1, Aldershot: Gale and Polden, 1912, pp. 29, 37.
55. MacMunn, *The Armies of India*, pp. 159–60.
56. Shakespear, Sirmoor Rifles, pp. 29, 37.
57. Cohen, *Indian Army*, p. 49.
58. Peers, ' "The Habitual Nobility of Being" ', pp. 545–6.
59. Dougls M. Peers, *Mars and Mammon*, p. 3.
60. Omissi, *Sepoy and the Raj*, p. 43.
61. Roberts, *Forty-one Years*, pp. 534, 540.
62. Robson, ed., *Roberts in India*, pp. 34–6, 256–9.
63. MacMunn, *The Armies of India*, pp. 145-54.
64. Office Notes, Constitution of the Bengal Army, by George Chesney 9 February 1881, L/MIL/17/2/469, OIOC.
65. Robson, ed., *Roberts in India*, p. 264.
66. Roberts, *Forty-one Years*, pp. 499, 530, 532–4.
67. From the Secretary of State for India, to the Governor General of India, London, no. 72, 2 March 1871, Records of Chief Commands, Notes and Minutes by Napier.
68. Office notes, Constitution of the Bengal Army, by George Chesney, 1881, L/MIL/17/2/469.
69. Lieutenant F.G. Cardew, 'Our Recruiting Grounds of the Future for the Indian Army', *JUSII*, vol. 20, no. 86 (1891), p. 131.
70. King-Harman, 'Second Essay', p. 157.
71. Major E.G. Barrow, 'Third Essay', *JUSII*, vol. 20, no. 86 (1891), pp. 173-4.
72. Molesworth, 'Indian Army Castes', *JUSII*, vol. XLII, no. 190 (1913), p. 57.
73. Lieutenant R.M. Rainey, 'The Madras Army', *JUSII*, vol. 20, no. 85 (1891), p. 79.
74. Hew Strachan, *European Armies and the Conduct of War*, 1983, reprint, London: Routledge, 1993, p. 57; Cardew, *Bengal Native Army*, pp. 329–31, 405–7; Rainey, 'Madras Army', pp. 81, 85.
75. Cardew, *Bengal Native Army*, p. 410.
76. Ian Talbot, 'British rule in Punjab, 1849–1947', *JICH*, vol. 20, no. 2 (1991), pp. 210–13; Minute on the organization of the army, Ch. 2, Conditions of the Bengal Army, para 63, 65–6, 11 October 1875, Norman minutes.

77. Bingley, *Jats and Gujars*, pp. 97–8.
78. Rainey, 'Madras Army', pp. 80–1.
79. The Sikhs like the *Purbiyas* joined the army as part of their multi-dimensional strategy to tide over temporary agrarian downswings. Kolff, *Naukar, Rajput and Sepoy*, pp. 1–31, 193–9; Fox, *Lions of the Punjab*, pp. 43–5.
80. Minute on the organization of the army, Ch. 5, Pension system, Discharges without pension, para 10, Ch. 2, para 63, 66, Ch. 3, Madras Army, para 38, Norman Minutes.
81. Minute on the organization of the army, Ch. 5, para 15, 19, Norman Minutes.
82. Cardew, 'Recruiting Grounds', pp. 146–7.
83. Tyrrell, 'Races of the Madras Army', pp. 12–18.
84. From Captain J.W.B. Meade commanding 3rd Lancers Hyderabad Contingent, to the Asst. ADG Hyderabad Contingent, Boloraum, no. 392, 22 August 1891, L/MIL/7/14966, OIOC.
85. Extract from a letter by Major-General Blake commanding at Burma to F. Haines, 20 July 1872, Records of Chief Commands, 1865–76, Notes and Minutes by Napier.
86. Rainey, 'Madras Army', p. 86; Chesney, *Indian Polity*, pp. 233–4, Kitchener to Roberts, Simla, Q/6, Q/10, 12 March 1903, 10 May 1903, Kitchener papers, Reel no. 2, M/F, NAI; Extract from general observation from confidential report on the inspection of Indian regiments, H.W. Norman, 23 June 1875, Records of Chief Commands, Notes and Minutes by Napier.
87. Menezes, *Fidelity and Honour*, pp. 5–80, 145, 147, 150; V. Longer, *Red Coats to Olive Green: A History of the Indian Army, 1600–1974*, New Delhi: Allied, 1974, pp. 14–54; Mason, *A Matter of Honour*, pp. 29–34, 75–110; Cardew, *Bengal Native Army*, pp. 128–36; *Supplementary Report*, p. 45.
88. Chesney, *Indian Polity*, pp. 221, 224, 236, 239.
89. From Charles Wood to the Governor General, no. 58, para 2, no. 1159, February 1860, Military despatches of the Secretary of State, vol. 1, part 1, 1860, NAI.
90. Longer, *Red Coats to Olive Green*, p. 78.
91. Proportion of British to Indian Troops in India, para 24, 25, 28 July 1893, 1Q/10, George White Collection.
92. Proportion of British to Indian troops, para 28, 30, George White Collection.
93. M.E. Yapp, 'British Perceptions of the Russian Threat to India', *MAS*, vol. 21, no. 4 (1987), pp. 662–3; Pierce G. Fredericks, *The Sepoy and the Cossacks* (London: W.H. Allen, 1972); Cardew, *Bengal Native Army*, pp. 345–75, 380–1, 412–25; Roberts, *Forty-one Years*, pp. 231–4, 499, 503, 505, 530–5; Robson, ed., *Roberts in India*, pp. 207, 349–

50, 352–3; St. John Brodrick, Secretary of State, to Kitchener, 25 April 1904, Lord Curzon, Viceroy of India, to Kitchener, 21 August 1900, Roberts to Kitchener, 27 March 1903, 13 April 1904, Kitchener papers, Reel no. 2, M/F.

94. *Eden Commission,* pp. 82–3.
95. Fitness of the Madras sepoy for service in Burma, 22 June 1893, 1Q/7, George White Collection.
96. Cardew, *Bengal Native Army,* pp. 349, 364, 369; Roberts to Arbuthnot, 6 April 1889, Roberts to the Adjutant General in India, 16 December 1878, 24 December 1878, 30 July 1880, 18 September 1880, Roberts to Dillon, 7 February 1879, Roberts to Chesney, 4 December 1890 in Robson, ed., *Roberts in India,* pp. 40–5, 64, 68, 205–6, 220–2, 392–3.
97. Roberts, *Correspondence with England while Commander-in-Chief in Madras,* pp. 25–6.
98. Ibid., p. 197.
99. General Frederick Roberts, *Correspondence with the Viceroy of India (The Marquis of Dufferin and Ava): 1885–8,* Calcutta: Superintendent of Govt. Printing, 1890, p. 8, Part 4, L/MIL/17/5/1615, OIOC.
100. Menezes, *Fidelity and Honour,* p. 534; Roberts to Viceroy, 14 December 1878, 31 March 1880, in Robson, ed., *Roberts in India,* pp. 38–9, 181–2; Memorandum on the subject of our policy with Central Asia, 5 October 1867, Memorandum on the occupation of Herat, 7 June 1875, Norman minutes.
101. Roberts, *Correspondence with India while Commander-in-Chief in Madras,* p. 32.
102. Roberts to Dufferin, Simla, 2 August 1887, in General Frederick Roberts, *Correspondence with the Viceroy of India: 1885–8,* p. 61.
103. Roberts, *Correspondence with India while Commander-in-Chief in Madras,* p. 185.
104. Roberts to Churchill, Private, 15 April 1885, 1 February 1886 in Robson, ed., *Roberts in India,* 317, 338–41.
105. Roberts, *Correspondence with England while Commander-in-Chief in Madras,* p. 30.
106. Roberts to Fitzjames Stephen, Private, 14 June 1884, in Roberts, *Correspondence with England while Commander-in-Chief in Madras,* p. 188.
107. Menezes, *Fidelity and Honour,* p. 534; Roberts to Stewart, 3 June 1882, Stewart to Roberts, 6 July and 3 August 1882 in Robson, ed., *Roberts in India,* pp. 256–9, 260–1, 263–7.
108. Roberts to the Viceroy, 21 February 1889 in General Frederick Roberts, *Correspondence with the Viceroy of India (The Marquis of Lansdowne).*
109. Roberts, *Forty-one Years,* p. 532; Charles Brownlow to Roberts, 20 June 1884 in Robson, ed., *Roberts in India,* p. 297.
110. Adrian Preston, 'Wolseley, The Khartoum Relief Expedition and the

Defence of India', *JICH*, vol. 6, no. 3 (1978), pp. 254–80; Brownlow to Roberts, Napier to Roberts, 9 July 1885, 31 July 1885 in Robson, ed., *Roberts in India*, pp. 234, 326, 447.

111. Memorandum on the system of promotion to the commissioned grades of the Indian Army of Bengal, Appendix M, Lieutenant-Colonel H. Brooke, Asst. ADG, 21 October 1874, Records of Chief Commands, Notes and Minutes by Napier of Magdala, MSS.EUR.F.114, 5(3); Hamilton to Curzon, 1 March 1900, 11 October 1900, Hamilton papers, Reel no. 1, M/F, NAI.

112. George White to the Duke of Cambridge, Simla, 11 July 1893, Book no. 3, I.B/13, George White Collection, MSS.EUR.F.108/18.

113. Fitness of the Madras sepoy for service in Burma, para 7, 8, 22 June 1893, 1Q/7, George White Collection.

114. Hamilton to Curzon, 1 March 1900, 11 October 1900, Hamilton papers, Reel no. 1; Kitchener to Brodrick, 3 December 1901, 12 March 1903, Kitchener papers, Reel no. 1; Memorandum on the Indian System of Military Administration, 24 January 1905, 1T/22, George White Collection, MSS.EUR.F.108/87&88.

115. *Army Committee*, vol. 1-A, *Minority Report*, p. 156.

116. Unlike the *Purbiyas*, Roberts' martial communities were middle ranking in the ritual hierarchy or the *varna* system. But, they were certainly not low castes. So, the sociologist A. Bopegamage's assertion that the Martial Race lobby favoured the high castes is erroneous. A. Bopegamage, 'Caste, Class and the Indian Military: A Study of the Social Origins of Indian Army Personnel', in Jacques Van Doorn, ed., *Military Profession and Military Regimes: Commitments and Conflicts*, The Hague/Paris: Mouton, 1969, p. 145.

117. Roberts to the Viceroy, 16 February 1889 in Roberts, *Correspondence with the Viceroy of India (The Marquis of Lansdowne)*, p. 3.

118. From Major General W. Galbraith, ADG in India, to the Secy. to the GoI, MD, Simla, 4 August 1893, Enclosure no. 4, Annual confidential reports on the regiments, L/MIL/7/17007, OIOC.

119. Kitchener to Roberts, 4 December 1904, 6 June 1904, Kitchener papers, Reel no. 2.

120. Robson, ed., *Roberts in India*, pp. 64–8, 266–7, 350–1; Roberts, *Correspondence with England while Commander-in-Chief in Madras*, p. 44.

121. Roberts to General Shadwell, London, 8 October 1883, in Roberts, *Correspondence with England while Commander-in-Chief in Madras*, p. 115.

122. Roberts to Chesney, 4 December 1890 in Robson, ed., *Roberts in India*, p. 404; Hamilton to Elgin, 10 October 1895, Hamilton papers, Reel no. 2.

123. Dividing the Bengal Army into two parts, 7 March 1893, 1Q/3, George White Collection, MSS.EUR.F.108/24.

124. Memorandum by Major General Geo S. White, no. 3, 7 March 1893, 1Q/3, George White Collection, MSS.EUR.F.108/24.

125. *Army Committee*, vol. 1-A, *Minority report*, pp. 156–8.

126. H.G. Keene, *Hindustan under Free Lances: 1770–1820, Sketches of Military Adventure in Hindustan during the period immediately preceding British Occupation*, London: 1907, p. 128; Lewis Ferdinand Smith, *A Sketch of the Rise, Progress and Termination of the Regular Corps Formed and Commanded by Europeans in the Service of Native Princes of India with Details of the Principal Events and Actions of the late Maratha War*, Calcutta: J. Greenway Harkaru Press, 1805; McGregor, *History of the Sikhs*, vol. 2, pp. 30, 46–8, 50–1, 63, 72, 77–8, 83–5, 88–9, 135, 139, 165–6, 262, 265–7; Cardew, *Bengal Native Army*, pp. 222, 225, 241, 259, 291–4, 302–3, 329–31, 408–10, 431; MacMunn, *The Armies of India*, pp. 174–86.

127. Kaul, 'Sepoys' Links with Society', p. 133.

128. General Frederic Roberts, *Correspondence with the Viceroy of India: 1885–88*, p. 40.

129. For the horrendous manpower losses suffered by the Sepoy Army in France between 1914–15, see Gordon Corrigan, *Sepoys in the Trenches: The Indian Corps on the Western Front, 1914–15*, Staplehurst: Spellmount, 1999, pp. 125–45, 248–9.

THREE

The Martial Race Theory and the Handbook Programme: 1890–1913

The last two decades before the First World War was the high water mark for the Martial Race ideologues. India appeared to them as a complex mosaic of tribes and castes with varying degrees of loyalty and differing soldiering capabilities. Hence, a sort of anthropological survey was initiated in late-nineteenth century by the army high command. In accordance with the orders of the Martial Race lobby, a group of British officers carried out the project of disaggregation and categorization of the colonial subjects, for the effective utilization of manpower. The information which these officers compiled was later published in the form of Handbooks from 1890 onwards. The Handbook project could be categorized as a sort of Orientalist discourse since its aim was knowing the Orientals and the motive force for knowing the 'other' was that knowledge aids in the consolidation of imperial rule.[1] The result was strengthening of 'martial communities' which in Benedict Anderson's terminology were partially imagined cultural artifacts.[2] The Handbook authors modified the Martial Race ideology. The Handbooks not only influenced the army's recruitment pattern but they also throw light on the complex ideological structures of British India.

I

THE BACKGROUND

Frederick Roberts, the Commander-in-Chief of the Indian Army from 1885 to 1893, was the principal proponent of the Martial

Race theory. Kitchener, the Commander-in-Chief of the Indian Army from 1902 to 1909, carried Roberts' policy to its logical conclusion. It was, under Roberts and Kitchener that the hunt for the 'martial races' began.[3] Roberts and Kitchener ordered a group of British officers to study the food habits, religion, customs and social norms of various groups in order to find out which of them were most suitable for induction in the army. Their aim was probably to reshape the Martial Race ideology in the wake of the challenge posed by the Balanced/Egalitarian/Anti-Martial Race Recruitment lobby. As Edward Said has pointed out, Orientalism as a mode of discourse was characterized by supporting institutions like colonial bureaucracies.[4] In the case of the Handbook project, the Sepoy Army supported and encouraged the whole project of understanding the 'other'.

However, even before the production of the Handbooks, many army officers undertook ethnological studies of various groups in an attempt to aid the army's recruitment programme. Their papers appeared in the Indian Army's professional journal—the *Journal of the United Service Institution of India*—and some also wrote books. One Lieutenant-Colonel Malcolm who visited Punjab in 1805 wrote an ethnographic compendium on the Sikhs. In this monograph published in 1812, he emphasized the 'martial' nature of Sikhism.[5] Lieutenant E.G. Barrow, who happened to be the Deputy Assistant Adjutant General of the Indian Army in the 1880s, attempted an ethnological survey of the Afridi tribe inhabiting Tirah. He divided the Afridis into eight clans, whose total number of fighting males according to his calculation were about 22,500. Barrow found that each clan inhabited a particular area. For example the Aka Khel clan of the Afridis inhabited the Warran valley. He visualized that the British policy of annexation would result in beneficial social changes for the Afridis. Once Tirah was conquered, then, he commented, 'this great clan of robbers would in time, like the Pathans of the Derajat and Yusufzai, settle down into peaceful cultivators and herdsmen or enlist into the army'.[6]

Another such ethnological enquiry was conducted by Captain W.H.F. Basevi of the 6th Burma Battalion. His subjects were the Panthyas, the Muslims of Yunnan. In 1889, Roberts was considering enlistment of the Panthyas for garrisoning Burma. In response, Basevi further developed the linkages between demography and recruitment. He calculated that there were 5,000,000 Panthyas, who could easily supply ten regiments. He further clarified an ecological perspective. Basevi asserted that the physical geography of Yunnan was such that the inhabitants had to be excellent marchers and inured to exposure, both in cold and rain. So, they were well suited to the stress and strain of soldiering. Like the Martial Race theorists, he made a connection between food habits and warlike capacity. The Panthyas, being meat eaters, were regarded as proper fighters.[7]

Captain A. Apthorpe of the 90th Punjabis conducted an ethnological study on the Kachins who inhabited the mountainous tract of north Burma. Apthorpe, Basevi and Barrow accepted Roberts' assumption that warrior races were generally available along the mountainous tracts of the frontier. Further, Apthorpe followed the Martial Race theorists' tendency to link up occupation with war-making capacity. Being agriculturists, the Kachins were regarded as excellent material for the army.[8] Though Basevi and Apthorpe shared many of the assumptions of the Martial Race spokesmen, unlike the latter group, they extended their search away from north-west India to other parts of the subcontinent, and the Handbooks emerged against such a background.

The Raj's civilian officers attached with the military also undertook similar surveys. The underlying conviction was that some groups were more tuned to warfare. So the use of ethnohistory, to find the racial origin of the potential recruits was common. Surgeon Major H.W. Bellew, the Sanitary Commissioner of Punjab in 1880, tried to argue from linguistic, physiognomy and historical evidences that the Afghans were racially linked with the 'martial' Israelites.[9] He was also attached on special political duty at Kabul just after the Second Afghan War and wrote a monograph titled *The Races of Afghanistan*. In the Preface, he says: 'For, to know the history, interests, and aspirations of a people, is half the battle gained in converting them to loyal, contented and peaceable subjects, to willing participators and active protectors of the welfare of the Empire towards which, from position and self-interest, they naturally gravitate.'[10]

II

THE HANDBOOKS

The authors at the Handbooks were commissioned officers. They were neither senior military commanders nor desk staff officers who sat miles away at the headquarter. They were recruiting officers, hence in continuous interaction with Indian society. P. Holland Pryor (who wrote on the Moplahs) was a Major and Eden Vansittart (who focused on the Gurkhas) was a Captain. For his path breaking effort in charting out the ethnology and ethnography of the Gurkhas, Vansittart was promoted to Major and later to Lieutenant-Colonel. While Vansittart was attached to the 2nd Battalion of the 5th Gurkha Rifles, he prepared an ethnological compendium on the Gurkhas.[11]

These books were written by the officers as part of their professional duty, under orders from the Intelligence Department of the Quarter Master General. The aim of these books was to guide future recruiting officers. Vansittart dedicated his book, which came out in 1890, to Roberts, with the latter's permission. Vansittart's third edition which came out in 1906 was dedicated to Kitchener. Major A.H. Bingley initiated his survey of the Jats, Gujars and the Ahirs on the orders of the Government of India. These books aimed at the creation and consolidation of knowledge about Indian society, in order to decide whom to recruit, on what basis, and how to raise the quality of the personnel.[12]

Kate Teltscher while analysing European and British writing on India between the seventeenth and the nineteenth centuries writes that the authors shared certain assumptions, strategies and imageries.[13] This trait could be applied in case of the Handbook writers. The format of all the Handbooks was more or less similar. Each author studied one, two or at best three groups. Vansittart was concerned with the Gurkhas, Major R.M. Betham with the Marathas and the south Indian Muslims, and Bingley with the Jats, Gujars and the Ahirs.[14] Each book was about two hundred pages long and dealt with broadly five themes: the geographical distribution of the groups, their religion, their customs, their history till their confrontation with the British, and finally the recruiting procedures that needed to be followed. These books were thus partly descriptive and partly prescriptive.

Each book was updated in the light of new information. Vansittart originally published his treatise on the Gurkhas in 1890. He updated it twice, in 1896 and in 1906. In his later editions his source base became wider. In his 1896 edition, unlike in his earlier work, Vansittart used Doctor Wright's *History of Nepal* published in 1877 and C.A. Bendall's *Journey in Nepal* which came out in 1886. Further, in this edition, Vansittart studied two new groups of eastern Nepal, the Newars and the Kirantis, in an attempt to widen the recruiting base.[15] This reflected the development of British-Indian empire's feedback apparatus with time.

Most of the books concentrated on particular groups coming from a particular region. Bingley, while collecting data on the Sikhs, put emphasis on areas of central Punjab like Manjha and Malwa.[16] None of these books were all-India studies, the only exception being P.D. Bonarjee's book. Bonarjee was a Bengali 'intellectual' employed in the military department in clerical capacity. The Raj's civilian officers, including British officers like Bellew and Indians like Bonarjee, conducted ethnological studies at the behest of the army. Interestingly, in Bonarjee's conception, the Santhals and the Bheels were also 'martial races'. Further, unlike Roberts, Bonarjee believed that 'martial' groups could also be found in south India. The Tamils and the Malayalis appeared to be 'martial' to Bonarjee. This probably was a tactic to accommodate some of the views of the Balanced Recruitment lobby. Almost all the Handbook authors had a bias towards men from north India, and only Bonarjee and Betham were free from it.[17]

There was constant intercourse between the army's ethnographers and the colonial anthropologists.[18] H.H. Risley, the initiator of ethnography in India, influenced the conceptual framework of the Handbook writers. The methodological assumptions of his work *Tribes and Castes of Bengal*, published in 1891, influenced Vansittart's analytical matrix. Risley even wrote the introduction of Vansittart's 1896 edition. Risley pointed out that the ethnographic programme had two aspects: recording the various social and cultural usages of the different groups and a comparative analysis of human anatomy. Victorian anthropologists like Risley believed that different races had separate physiological and moral qualities. The growth of anthropometry in Western Europe during the eighteenth and the nineteenth centuries influenced colonial India's physical anthropologists. They were influenced by the anthropometric classification system of Paul Broca, the French ethnological expert. Risley accepted skull measurement as a technique of ethnic categorization. According to him, the basis of distinction among the different indigenous groups was the difference in physiognomy and bone structure. Risley claimed that the width of the head was related to racial origin. The data on the width of the heads of various groups were measured through the cephalic index. This showed the relation of the maximum breadth of the head to its maximum length, the latter being taken as 100. The higher the cephalic index, claimed Risley, more the Mongolian blood. The cephalic index of the Limbus was 84.3 while that of the Murmis was 78.5. So, the Limbus were regarded as more Mongolian than the Murmis. Vansittart considered the Mongolians to be good warriors. Thus, for recruitment, he favoured the Limbus rather than the Murmis. For Risley, people with thin noses also belonged to higher racial categories. To measure the length and breadth of the noses, the nasomalar index was used. This tool was first introduced by the anthropologist Oldfield Thomas for measuring the projections or depressions at the base of the noses of different people in relation to the outer edge of the orbit of the noses. Longer and thinner noses gave a higher nasomalar index. Risley argued that higher the nasomalar index, the superior the race. The nasomalar index of the Newars was 110.2 and that of the Pathans was 117.1. So, the Pathans were more favoured than the Newars for recruitment in the Sepoy Army.[19]

Baron Cuvier of Switzerland, and the German scholar S.T. Von Soemmering, felt that they had established a linkage between cranial cavity and intelligence. And these figures influenced the nineteenth century British intellectuals analysing India. Bingley, while observing the Jats, accepted the view of Dr Brereton, author of the *Rajputana Gazetteer*, that the crania of the Jats were elongated and lower than the crania of the Brahmins. The Brahmins, therefore, had more intelligence, and were thus less suited for soldiering than the 'obtuse' Jats. Like Roberts', the Handbook authors accepted the cliche that clever persons could not be transformed into proper soldiers.[20]

However, the Handbook writers also neglected many strands of anthropological thought. The late Victorian belief was that people with Mongolian features—broad cheekbones and scanty beards and moustaches—were generally criminals. But, Vansittart openly declared that such physical features existed among the Gurkhas and they were not only martial but also loyal.[21] Denzil Ibbetson linked physique with racial theory. After comparing the facial features of the Rajputs and the Jats, he claimed that both groups had originated from the same racial stock. Bingley disagreed, claiming that ethnically the Rajputs were Scythians while the Jats were Aryans, but later, the Rajputs absorbed the Aryan culture.[22]

The Victorians also believed that certain climatic zones resulted in racial degeneration.[23] James Wise and E.T. Dalton collected anthropometric data on the various castes and tribes inhabiting the different ecological zones in India which the Handbook authors used. The assumption of the Martial Race ideologues was that only tall and fair skinned men from colder mountainous regions were genetically suited to become fighters. The nineteenth century ethnologists like James Forbes, who argued that the inferior races had darker complexions, probably shaped Roberts' views. Forbes also claimed that south India's hot climate resulted in the degeneration of the races inhabiting that region. Roberts was probably influenced by the Company's theoretician Robert Orme, whose ideas were in turn shaped by the Enlightenment theorists like Montesquieu. The latter assumed a linkage between degeneration of physical strength and temperament of the inhabitants of tropical regions.[24]

One representative of the Egalitarian Recruitment lobby, Lieutenant R.M. Rainey of the Madras Army challenged this linkage between climate, martial aptitudes, physical appearance and especially skin pigmentation. Rainey argued that the short and black Tamils were better soldiers than tall, 'smart' and 'better looking' men from cold, north-west India.[25] The Handbook authors appropriated this critique as well within their framework. Bingley had written that the submontane Himalayan tracts did not produce proper warriors. Further, he said that though central Punjab became very hot during summer, that region still nurtured the warrior Sikhs. The Handbook writers wanted the enlistment of varied groups—from tall, fair-skinned, thin-nosed Brahmins, to the short, dark-skinned tribals. Betham even argued that the shorter south Indian Marathas were better warriors than the taller races hailing from colder north India. The Handbook writers did not regard height as a reliable criterion for recruitment. All men between 5'2" to 5'9" were considered eligible for recruitment. Among the Gurkhas, the members from the Khas tribe were on the average 5'8" tall and the Gurungs were between 5'2" to 5'6" in height, and yet, the latter were favoured. According to Betham and Pryor, the Deccanis were short and dark, with thick lips and high cheekbones. Yet, they considered them better warriors than the north Indians with blue eyes and red lips. Also, valour and stamina were not always equated with good physique. Bingley and Nicholls accepted that the north Indian Brahmins were shorter than the Afghans. But that did not mean, claimed these officers, that the former group was less courageous. Betham concluded that the popularity of the Pathans and the Punjabi Muslims was because of their superficial qualities: they were showy and dressed picturesquely. The groups like the Marathas, on the other hand, were quiet by nature and lacked swagger. So, according to Betham, their military qualities remained un-recognized.[26]

Evangelists like Reverend William Ward of the Serampore Mission used the category 'race' very loosely. The Handbook authors, like the Martial Race spokesmen followed this trend. For Ward, both the Brahmin caste, as well as other Hindu castes, appeared as a race. Such terminological and conceptual confusions were common among the Handbook writers. For Bingley and Nicholls, the Brahmins were simultaneously a race, a tribe and a caste. In Pryor's eyes, the Moplahs were low-caste Hindus who were also tribals. After conversion, he claimed, they became a race. So besides biological origins, customs also determined the British concept of race. Bingley held that due to social factors, the Rajputs constituted a distinct ethnic group vis-à-vis the Jats. Occasionally, religion became the chief deter-minant. According to Bingley, Sikhism made Sikh Jats a different race from the Hindu Jats, though from the biological perspective both these groups were similar. At times race had a residential connotation. In 1890, Vansittart termed the four tribes (Magars, Limbus, Rais and Gurungs) as the Gurkha race because they inhabited a particular tract of central Nepal. However, such labels were flexible. As the British demand for the Gurkhas increased, in 1896 Vansittart included the Newars into the Gurkha category.[27]

Besides observing the bone structure and the skin colour, the military ethnographers also considered other methodological strands of the colonial anthropologists: observation of the behavioural patterns and the social mores of the various groups. The Handbook authors utilized both Indian and British sources to acquire knowledge about the customs of the various indigenous communities. Among the latter, both unofficial and official sources were used. *Census Reports*, especially those of 1881 and 1891, were used for analysing the demographic patterns. For general information on habitats, the *Gazetteers* were consulted. It seems that the Raj undertook the project of census surveys and the *Gazetteer* writing programme to satisfy the army's hunger for knowing the colonized. The Handbook writers calculated the male population of probable group of recruits in different districts, which were then subdivided into smaller administrative divisions like the *tehsils* and the *taluks*. This shows that the imperialists had travelled a long way from the position of the *Supplementary Committee* of 1859, when the military elites failed to demarcate the various recruiting regions clearly. The improvement of grass-root level knowledge of the colonial state in the last decades of the nineteenth century was proved clearly by Vansittart's ability to calculate the number of villages in Nepal which had the potential of supplying recruits.[28]

For precise information about the socio-cultural activities of various 'martial' groups, the histories by the colonial historians like Lane Poole and Lepel Griffin came handy. These sources can be categorized as ethnohistories, as the European observers noted down the food habits, dress, marriage customs, etc., of the various groups they encountered. The Europeans wrote similar accounts when they first came into contact with the tribes of the New World in the sixteenth century. Such ethnohistories constituted the building blocks of the army's ethnological programme in India, and were used by Handbook writers to trace the histories of concerned groups. Those communities which had displayed 'martial' proclivities, were deemed warlike enough to be inducted into the army. The underlying assumption was that those who had displayed martial qualities in the past still retained these virtues. In accordance with the Victorian intellectual currents, the army officers were firm believers in heredity. The perspective of the British historians who operated in colonial India was communal. They argued that the Islamic invasions during the medieval age created disorders in Indian society. The Handbook authors accepted the view that Islamic religious intolerance turned the peaceful Hindu cultivators like the Jats and the Marathas into warriors. Bingley accepted Lane Poole's portrait of Aurangzeb as a villain, whose policies were blamed for causing the alienation of the loyal and martial Rajputs. Bingley compared Aurangzeb's erroneous policy with the Raj's 'foolish' pre-1857 policy that forced these warriors to rebel.[29]

Since the focus of the Handbook authors was on the groups inhabiting particular regions, they also consulted regional histories. While compiling data on the Rajputs of Rajputana, Bingley depended on Tod's *Annals of Rajasthan*. The Raj's civilian officers wrote most of these histories. D. Wright, a doctor, wrote the *History of Nepal* in 1877 and Vansittart used it for portraying the glorious past of the 'martial' Gurkhas. So, collaboration between the army and the Raj's civilian apparatus, for gathering data on the Orient, was a characteristic of the last decade of the nineteenth century. The army probably did not like to depend totally upon the civilians. To reduce this dependence, and to increase the army's information about the various indigenous communities, the military in the first decade of the twentieth century ordered its officers like Lieutenant F.G. Cardew to start writing histories of British India.[30]

Though European writings were more readily accessible, the writers of the Handbooks did not depend only on Occidental sources to understand the Orient. Vansittart used Sarat Chandra Das' account of his journey to Lhasa and central Tibet, published in 1901, for information about the tribes of eastern Nepal. Both, Hindu and Muslim authors were utilized. The project of translation of various vernacular works received a strong impetus from the army's demand to know more about India. *Tahafat ul Mujahidin* was translated by Rowlandson and used by Pryor. To understand the religious mentality of the 'martial races' like the Sikhs, Bingley depended both on the European writer Newall's *Notes on the Hindu Religion*, as well as on an indigenous work like the *Adi Granth*, which was translated by Trump. From the latter, he concluded that Sikhism was a martial religion, and hence its followers were also martial.[31]

The Handbook writers also spoke to the Indian soldiers for gathering information about Indian society. The data they acquired was thus filtered through the minds of the colonized. Havildar Purandhoj Limbu of the 2nd Battalion of the 9th Gurkha Rifles aided Vansittart in classifying the tribes and clans of eastern Nepal. Jemadar Assaram of the 2nd Battalion of the 1st Gurkhas also collected ethnographic data for Vansittart. Besides the Indian officers, the Indian privates also supplied information, which in turn was cross-checked with the information contained in the books written by the Europeans. In 1889, three recruits asserted before Vansittart that they belonged to the Jail clan of the Magar tribe. Information about this clan was absent in the books written by the British.[32]

The Handbook authors also made use of the folk tradition and local proverbs which provided both positive and negative images about various communities. One proverb which was quoted by Bingley, was as follows:

The dog and cat, Ranghars and Gujar,
If it were not for these four, you might
sleep with your doors open.[33]

Such legends might have created a negative image about the Gujars in the imperial mind. The imperialists came to accept them as dacoits and as a result their recruitment suffered. Among the women of the Jangwara clan of the Jats, this couplet was common: 'Below is earth, above is Ram, Between the two, fights Dhopu Ram'. Bingley used this couplet to infer that the Jats were soldiers by tradition. He also accepted the interpretation common in Indian society that Jats were 'thick-headed fools'. However, this fitted well with the assumption of the Martial Race lobby, that proper soldiers should not be intellectually strong.[34] Occasionally the author of the Handbooks accepted indigenous myths and legends about the biological origin of the various groups. Bingley was conscious about the legend that the Jats were descendants of the Jadu Rajputs. Bingley noted that the legends portrayed a view which was different from the view propounded by the European scholars, that the Jats were related to the Scythians.[35]

The Handbook authors believed that Indian society was changing, both from internally generated changes, and the influence of British administration. Bingley had written that the Jats moved into central Punjab about 800 years ago and accepted Sikhism later. This, according to him, was an example of indigenous social dynamics. The officers also viewed the British administration as changing the occupation and culture of a group. After 1857, claimed Bingley, the Meerut canal irrigation transformed the Gujars from cattle raiders into 'peaceful' agriculturists.[36] This belief, that British rule could transform various communities into proper soldier-like material, was consistent with the assumption of military officers turned ethnologists like Barrow, who functioned before the Handbook project. They were probably trying to absorb the Balanced Recruitment lobby's scheme of social engineering.

Warwick Anderson has shown that the dominant scientific belief in the nineteenth century West was that some races, due to their sanitary practices and food habits, developed physiological immunity to certain sorts of diseases. Their sanitation practices were shaped by cultural norms which were determined by race and physical geography.[37] The Handbook authors accepted this as 'scientific'. Some Handbook writers, like the Martial Race ideologues, established a connection between the physical features of the terrain, on the one hand, and the value system, work ethic, occupation and combat capacities of the inhabitants, on the other. Captain R.W. Falcon, who was a recruiting officer in the 4th Sikh Infantry in the last decade of the nineteenth century, specialized on the Punjabis. He believed that the physical surroundings influenced the cultural make-up of the inhabitants. He pointed out that the characteristics of the Sikhs—hardiness, boldness, independence of spirit, etc.— which made them good warriors, were shaped not only by their race and religion, but also the regions that bred them. He continued that hereditary traits interacted with terrain and climate. Moreover, qualities like bravery and obedience varied with region.[38] The Sikhs being a martial community for the British, the imperial assumption was that all the Sikhs ought to be willing to join the Sepoy Army. But, many British officers found that the Sikhs from the agriculturally prosperous area of the Jullundhur doab preferred farming rather than following the arduous career of soldiering. In 1876, Lieutenant-General Charles Reid acidly commented that most Punjabis were more interested in cultivating their fields than soldiering. Most Sikh recruits came from the agrarian deficit area of river Beas and the region around Tarntarn.[39] The officers tried to explain this contradiction between reality and ideology through an amalgam of ecological and cultural factors.

According to Bingley, a damp riverine climate produced unmartial inhabitants, because the presence of fertile plains and river valleys resulted in bumper crops without effort. Thus the people became easygoing, indolent, and their physique declined. The Handbook writers were convinced that endurance acquired through manual labour was an essential quality of soldiering. In ecological zones like unirrigated plains and hilly regions, the inhabitants were forced to work hard to get frugal meals. So they became inured to hardship, and hence were good material for the army. Bingley warned that the Sikhs inhabiting the fertile doab region of Punjab, known as Doaba Sikhs, were inferior than the Malwa Sikhs who were from the comparatively infertile cis-Sutlej area. The Malwa Sikhs, by their sheer labour, had transformed the unirrigated central Punjab into a prosperous area. They had thus acquired endurance which was necessary for being good troops. Hence, he recommended the enlistment of the Malwa Sikhs. Vansittart and Bingley were for recruitment of the tillers. Bingley noted that the Jats of the Bikaner desert below Ferozepur tilled the lands of the Rajput zamindars and had the qualities of patience and endurance, the necessary components for being warriors. Bingley argued that the small peasants, unlike the rich farmers, were industrious and disciplined. As prosperous peasants like the Jats of northern Rajputana were not interested in joining the colonial war machine, Bingley dubbed them as unmartial.[40] That prosperous countries breed soft people is a classical assumption. Herodotus writes: 'Soft countries gave birth to soft men—there was no region which produced very delightful fruits, and at the same time men of a warlike spirit'.[41]

Some Handbook authors were against recruiting from the economic deficit zones. In Vansittart's view, the Terai ecology did not produce enough food for the proper development of muscles and bones of the inhabitants. So, he was against enlisting groups like the Tharus inhabiting that region.[42] Swampy regions were also considered unhealthy. Bingley believed that the Jats who inhabited the drier parts of Punjab were healthier than those Jats who came from the damp areas of the western Gangetic doab. Pryor was for the enlistment of the Moplahs living far away from the coast because they were considered healthier than those Moplahs inhabiting the coast. Pryor claimed that due to the scarcity of water in the coastal area of Malabar, diseases like dropsy and dysentery were very common.[43]

The nineteenth century West believed that eating meat was necessary for good health, and equated vegetarianism with weakness. Bingley and Nicholls said that only those Brahmins, who ate fowl and goats, were to be recruited. The Raghubansis, a subgroup of the Rajputs, though being small farmers, were not enlisted because they were vegetarian.[44]

Another strand of contemporary medical thinking, which influenced the officers, was that many 'races' degenerated due to unsanitary practices and immoral conduct. Many Handbook authors emphasized the personal hygiene and morality of the members of the groups concerned. As far as these aspects were concerned, Bingley and Nicholls concluded that the north-Indian Brahmins were a model race. The officers emphasized that the recruits should enjoy stable family lives, be free from debauchery and dress decently. The British were afraid that extra-marital sex on part of the warrior groups might result in association with the inferior races and lead to the loss of the pure genetic attributes carrying martial qualities. Betham pointed out that the Deccani Muslims had the habit of going to prostitutes, and so they frequently suffered from venereal diseases. This factor somewhat obstructed the recruitment of the Deccani Muslims, because the military saw the devastating effects of venereal diseases on their European troops in India. In general, the Handbook writers felt that those groups which engaged in outdoor sports had well developed limbs, which aided them in battle. The officers, therefore, were encouraged to popularize hockey and *kabbadi* among the groups which supplied military manpower.[45]

The Handbook authors linked occupational backgrounds with cultural traits. They believed that particular sorts of profession gave birth to particular types of mentalities. Most of the writers accepted that the agriculturists constituted the best martial material. This belief was common among the Martial Race ideologues too. However, unlike the Martial Race spokesmen, the Handbook writers like the Balanced Egalitarian Recruitment lobby were willing to recruit men from non-agrarian backgrounds to fill the gap between demand and supply. The Newars and the Khambus were landowners and cultivators of Nepal, but as they were not interested in soldiering, Vansittart had to look towards communities practicing other occupations, like the Limbus who were hunters. Martial qualities were believed to be inherited and socially derived. Vansittart believed that the Limbus, being hunters for generations, were acquainted with forests and would prove to be excellent light infantry for fighting in hilly forest terrain.[46]

The Handbook authors wanted the recruits to be as simple as children. The cultivating groups were favoured because the level of education was very low among them. The Jats were one of the most favoured 'martial' groups. Within that community, only the village headmen were literate. The members of the Raibdar clan of the Jat community were considered famous for their stupidity and they were intensively enlisted. Among the Moplahs, another potential 'martial race', only one in 1,000 could sign their names. The British probably understood that it was more difficult to control men with education. Bingley and Nicholls were against those Brahmins who were literate, because they feared that they would indulge in intrigues, which would adversely affect the army's discipline, so only those Brahmins who were illiterate and practiced agriculture were inducted. The Aroras of Punjab who were generally contractors and traders were not enlisted as their occupation was considered to be brain-taxing.[47]

Prosperous professions were dubbed non-military by the Handbook authors, probably because men following such occupations were not interested in joining the military. The members of Agrai tribe in Nepal worked in the mines and were affluent, so Vansittart considered them as unmartial. The Handbook authors were unwilling to recruit from those professions which were looked down by the Indians. After all, the army was the principal coercive apparatus of the Raj. And if the armed personnel lacked prestige in the colonial society, then indirectly the Raj's prestige would also suffer. Probably for this reason those

Deccani Muslims who were shoemakers or dyers, and were looked down upon in Indian society, were not recruited in the army.[48] This was an instance of Indian value system shaping imperial policy.

Like the Martial Race theorists, the writers of the Handbooks were against enlistment from the cities. Bingley was against inducting men from the urban centres like Mathura and Agra believing that the city populace had degenerated through urban jobs. The officers tried to justify this fact, by arguing that urban dwellers' instincts were non-martial. Secondly, officers like Betham felt that the urban populace was disease ridden from unhygenic sanitary conditions in cities. Contemporary medical science, under the influence of the 'Germ Theory', accepted that the urban populace was in general diseased. From the end of the nineteenth century onwards, the British military establishment in the United Kingdom was also convinced that the peasant recruits were hardier than those from the industrial cities.[49] All these strands of ideas influenced the British military elites in India.

Influenced by the theories of race and to satisfy the quantitative demands of the army, the Handbook authors strongly emphasized the linkages between the demographic distribution of communities, occupation, and the prospect of their recruitment. For instance from the Brahmins of north India, Bingley and Nicholls were for enlistment of only the Gaur Brahmins. Among them, only the Kanaujiyas and Saraswat clans were allowed to join the army, because they practised agriculture. Their recruiting ground was demarcated as the area around Jamuna, Pilibhit, Chambal and Mathura.[50]

R.W. Falcon pointed out that the Sikhs were to be recruited only from those districts of Punjab where they constituted a majority. He warned that those Sikhs who were a minority in certain districts were racially rotten. This was because they were actually immigrants who had married unmartial groups after settling down, and hence, to be shunned in the army. The officers were obsessed with the idea of purity of blood. Falcon pointed out that Sikhs were in the majority in Tarntarn *tehsil* in Amritsar, from where they ought to be recruited and not from the Sharakpur *tehsil* in Lahore district where Sikhs were a minority.[51] As Punjab was the most important recruiting ground for the Raj

Bingley amassed demographic data on that region. He calculated that the land of the five rivers supported 1,000,000 Jat Sikhs, 1,000,000 Brahmins and 1,500,000 Rajputs. Of the latter two groups, only 7,600 and 20,000 had accepted Sikhism. Then there were 447,000 Khatris but only 52,000 among them were Sikhs. As the Brahmin, Rajput and the Khatri Sikhs were minorities in Punjab and the Jat Sikhs were majority, in accordance with Falcon's dictum, only the Jat Sikhs were enlisted. To aid the regiments in recruiting, the male population of each district was calculated. Bingley advocated Patiala and Ferozepur as recruiting grounds since these two regions were most densely populated with Sikhs. The former, Calculated Bingley, had 250,000 male Sikhs in 1891.[52]

III

EFFECTS

Let us assess the impact of the discourse by the Handbook authors on the Sepoy Army's recruitment policy. The Handbook authors made the Martial Race theory more complex. And the Handbook authors' concept of race continued to influence the British officers even during the First World War. Lieutenant-Colonel J.M. Wikeley, an officer of the 17th Cavalry, who could be taken as a representative of the British officer corps, stated in 1915: '. . . there are many types of race, distinguished from one another by their moral and physical characteristics'.[53] Roberts was not particularly preoccupied with the connection between 'warrior' instinct and dietary norms. After Bingley and Nicholls propounded this linkage, Goodenough and Dalton also came to accept it and considered the Jats martial, since they ate wheat and meat.[54] In Roberts' paradigm, which evolved in the 1880s, the Jats were not regarded as a martial group. But following, Bingley's monograph on the Jats, Roberts' supporters like Goodenough and Dalton then approved of their recruitment, but only from north-west India. Betham upheld the cause of the Marathas inhabiting the area south of the Vindhyas and the Deccani Muslims. MacMunn, an early-twentieth century votary of the Martial Race theory accepted the Jats and the Marathas as martial communities.[55] In 1919, Edmund Candler, while writing an ethnographical account of the various Indian communities who served in the Sepoy Army during the First World War admitted:

The Maratha sepoy is certainly no swashbuckler. To look at him, with his dark skin and irregular features, you would not take him for a member of a military caste. No one cares less for appearance; and his native dress—the big, flat pagri, dhoti and large loose shoes of the Deccan and Konkan—do not lend themselves to smartness. . . . What the Maratha and the Deccani Muslims have done may be expected from—has, indeed, been paralleled by—other hardened stocks.[56]

In the first decade of the twentieth century the imperialists attempted to balance the various Hindu and Muslim groups within the regiments. It seems that this was the effect of the communal interpretation of Indian history by Handbook authors, which like an oil slick spread outwards, from the officers authoring the Handbooks to the army in general.

Now let us look at the numbers game. The Madrassis who were dubbed unmartial were discharged and the favourite 'martial' races from north-west India filled their place. During the preparation of confidential report on the Madras Army, the Commander-in-Chief in 1893 considered the soldiers of the 9th and 32nd Madras Infantry Regiments as militarily useless 'parade ground soldiers'.[57] In 1902, the 7th, 9th, and the 14th Madras Infantry regiments were ordered to recruit two different religious communities from the north-west—the Punjabi Muslims and the Sikhs. Only the Jat Sikhs who were engaged in agriculture were enlisted,[58] probably in accordance with the dictum of Falcon and Bingley. The General Order issued from the Adjutant General's office in accordance with the Handbooks even pointed out the districts from which the 'martial' communities were to be recruited. The order stated that the Jats were to be enlisted from Hoshiarpur, Kangra, Nurpur, Palampur (present-day Himachal Pradesh) and Gurdaspur districts of East Punjab.[59] During the same year, 2nd, 6th and 24th Madras Infantry Regiments were ordered to recruit two Sikh and two Rajput companies for each of the concerned regiments. The Adjutant General emphasized that Jat Sikhs from Malwa and Rajputs from north and east Rajputana were to be recruited.[60] In 1903, the 16th, 22nd and 27th Madras Infantry Regiments were ordered to enlist two companies of Jats and two companies of Sikhs for each of the regiments respectively.[61] Bingley did not favour the north-Indian

Rajputs much and probably for this reason, in the beginning of the twentieth century, the axe fell on them. The 12th Bengal Infantry Regiment was ordered to replace its Rajput personnel from north India with Hindu Jats and Lobana Sikhs. Similarly, the 12th Bengal Pioneers Regiment was ordered to recruit Jats and Sikhs. Despite Roberts' opposition to the entry of the Deccani Muslims, the Hyderabad Contingent's cavalry recruited them, because Betham spearheaded their cause. However, the 1st, 2nd and 4th Lancers of the Hyderabad Contingent were ordered to recruit one squadron of Sikhs and one squadron of Jats for each of the regiments.[62] In 1903, the 2nd Lancers of the Hyderabad Contingent was ordered to recruit one squadron of Rajputs from Rajasthan and one squadron of Jats from Bulandshahr district.[63]

From Table 3.1 it is evident that as the imperial demand for the Gurkhas increased, along with the Magars and the Gurungs, the eastern tribes from Nepal were also inducted in larger numbers. The share of the tribes of eastern Nepal in the overall Gurkha contingent absorbed from Nepal increased with time. In 1890–91, their share was only 12.5 per cent, and in 1892–3 it rose to 30.1 per cent. By 1895, the share of eastern Nepali tribes jumped to 44.1 per cent.[64] One must remember that Vansittart in the later editions of his book also included the tribes from eastern Nepal within his construct of the Gurkhas. In 1902, the 8th Gurkha Rifles was formed from the Gurkhas of eastern Nepal. Moreover, the 10th Gurkha Rifles also recruited substantial portion of its manpower from the eastern part of Nepal.[65]

Besides the regular regiments, the irregular units also had to face the blast of the Handbook programme. In the first half of the nineteenth century, the Raj set up the Assam Rifles for guarding the North-East Frontier of British India. The Assam Rifles recruited tribes like the Shans, Nagas and other locals. In the first decade of the twentieth century, three-fourth of each battalion was ordered to be filled up with the Gurkhas from eastern Nepal.[66]

All these had their effects at the macro level. The groups favoured by the Handbook writers increased their share significantly. For instance, the Jats were virtually absent in the army in the 1880s, but after Bingley sponsored their cause, they numbered 9,670 men in 1913.[67] And Column 6 of Table 3.1 shows the increasing volume of Gurkha recruitment. So the Handbook

TABLE 3.1: VOLUME CUM REGIONAL RECRUITMENT OF THE GURKHAS

Year	Central Magars	Nepal Gurungs	Total Numbers Enlisted from Central Nepal	Total Numbers of Sunwars, Limbus and Rais Recruited from Eastern Nepal	Grand Total
1884–5			657		657
1886–7			1082		1082
1887–8			1025		1025
1888–9	622	226	848	24	872
1889–90	725	264	989	18	1007
1890–1	1064	433	1497	392	1889
1891–2	926	371	1297	489	1786
1892–3	613	353	966	766	1732
1893–4	485	287	772	959	1731
1894–5	498	247	745	1121	1866

Sources: Banskota. *The Gurkha Connection*, pp. 86–7, 121; Vansittart, *Gurkhas*, Appendix III, p. 99.

Note. Blank spaces denote unavailability of data.

authors were able to introduce significant policy shifts in the recruitment programme.

CONCLUSION

The Handbook authors were highly influenced by contemporary Western intellectual trends. Yet the construction of the discourse on the Orient was not a one way process. The folk traditions of the subcontinent, along with its Indian agents also, played their parts in the construction of this hegemonic discourse. Thus, the Sepoy Army and the indigenous society played a dialectical game in the creation of stereotypes about the various warrior groups. Mark Harrison argues that findings in the colonies strengthened the racial biological thinking in the metropole.[68] There existed continuous dialectics between the Sepoy Army's ethnographic project and Victorian era's eugenics, medical geography, phrenology and anthropometry. All these probably further strengthened the imperial pseudo-sciences.

Though the military played a vital role in ruling India, historians have neglected the army's images about the Indian society. As is evident from this chapter, the army's thought process had many shades which could not be accommodated within the three-tier ideological structure of the Raj as chalked out by Eric Stokes.[69] The Handbook project was not a part of Liberal, Evangelical or Utilitarian strand of thought. Edward Said has opened our eyes to the imperial construction of Orientalism. But, as far as India is concerned, the scholars miss out the army's contribution in the creation of this discourse and the various complexities of military Orientalism. Lionel Caplan has pointed out that the imperial discourse on the Gurkhas constituted a different sort of Orientalism from that constructed by Said or Ronald Inden.[70] From the Handbooks, we have seen that the imperial theorization on the other 'martial' groups like the Sikhs and the Jats differed significantly from their discourse on the Gurkhas or the Marathas and the army's view of the Orient was not a generalized, oversimplified one.

The aim of the military's ethnographic discourse was in a way different from that carried out by the colonial government. The latter project laid emphasis on the groups whom the colonial government wanted to make powerless by categorizing them as criminal tribes, low castes, etc.[71] But, the army's discourse focused on those who were considered socially powerful, and hence ought to be recruited in the army. However, in the long run, the British programme to chalk out the racial landscape of the subcontinent proved to be a hindrance. The military establishment needed to interpret the social and demographic data in order to operate in an alien landscape. The Handbook authors were small men lost in the vast Indian society. Their procedure was self-defeating because the logic behind their categorization of the inhabitants of South Asia was that each group had a distinct mind-set and inner qualities which they were predisposed to exhibit. Though a faulty logic, all their achievements did not go in vain. The corpus of knowledge about the Indians at the colonial state's disposal registered a quantum jump, but the very selectivity about enlistment which the Handbook authors displayed proved to be a great weakness. The army became dependent on only a few communities hailing from a very narrow tract of India. Alarm bells were ringing in 1913 over the issue of over-dependence on the Punjabis.

NOTES

1. For the concept of Orientalism refer to Edward W. Said, *Orientalism: Western Conceptions of the Orient*, 1978, reprint, New Delhi: Penguin, 2001, pp. 31–2.
2. Benedict Anderson, *Imagined Communities: Reflections on the Origin and Spread of Nationalism*, 1983, reprint, London, New York: Verso, 1987, pp. 13, 15.
3. Menezes, *Fidelity and Honour*, pp. 286–305; Robson, ed., *Roberts in India*, pp. 256–9.
4. Said, *Orientalism*, p. 2.
5. Malcolm, *Sketch of the Sikhs*.
6. Lieutenant E.G. Barrow, 'Tirah and the Afridi Question', *JUSII*, no. 49 (1881), pp. 172–81. The quotation is from p. 173.
7. Goodenough and Dalton, *The Army Book*, p. 445; Captain W.H.F. Basevi, 'A Proposal to Enlist the Panthyas', *JUSII*, vol. 31, no. 147 (1902), pp. 166–9; Roberts, *Correspondence with the Viceroy of India (The Marquis of Lansdowne)*, p. 3, Part 5.
8. Captain A. Apthorpe, 'The Kachins and Others: A New Recruiting Area', *JUSII*, vol. XLI, no. 186 (1912), pp. 53–9; Robson, ed., *Roberts in India*, pp. 262–6.
9. H.W. Bellew, 'A New Afghan Question', *JUSII*, vol. 47 (1881), pp. 49–97.
10. H.W. Bellew, *The Races of Afghanistan being a Brief Account of the Principal Nations inhabiting that country*, 1880, reprint, New Delhi: Asian Educational Services, 2004, p. 6.
11. Major P. Holland Pryor, *Class Handbook on the Indian Army: Mapillas or Moplahs*, Calcutta: Superintendent of Govt. Printing, 1904; Vansittart, *The Gurkhas*.
12. Vansittart, *Gurkhas*; Idem., *Handbooks for the Indian Army: The Gurkhas*, Calcutta: Office of the Superintendent Govt. Printing, 1906, (henceforth *Handbook*); Major A.H. Bingley, *Caste Handbook for the Indian Army: Jats, Gujars and Ahirs*, Calcutta: Superintendent of Govt. Printing, 1904.
13. Kate Teltscher, *India Inscribed: European and British Writing on India, 1600–1800*, Delhi: Oxford University Press, 1995, p. 3.
14. Bingley, *Jats, Gujars and Ahirs*; Major R.M. Betham, *Handbook for the Indian Army: Marathas and Dekhani Musulmans*, Calcutta: Superintendent of Govt. Printing, 1908.
15. Vansittart, *Gurkhas*; Captain Eden Vansittart, *Notes on Nepal*, 1896, reprint, New Delhi: Asian Educational Services, 1992, pp. III, 119–89.
16. Major A.H. Bingley, *Handbook for the Indian Army: Sikhs*, 1899, reprint, Chandigarh: Department of Languages, 1970, pp. 39–107.
17. P.D. Bonarjee, *A Handbook of the Fighting Races of India*, Calcutta:

Thacker & Spink, 1899; Betham, *Marathas and Dekhani Musulmans*, Roberts, *Forty-one Years in India*, pp. 499, 532–4, 540.

18. Mary Des Chene in 'Military Ethnology in British India', *South Asia Research*, vol. 19, no. 2 (1999), p. 126, writes that the Handbook authors were not interested in the methodologies propounded by the colonial anthropologists.

19. Susan Bayly, 'Caste and "Race", in the Colonial Ethnography of India', in Peter Robb, ed., *The Concept of Race in South Asia*, Delhi, Oxford University Press, pp. 170–2; Vansittart, *Notes*, pp. I–X; MacMunn, *The Armies of India*, pp. 145–54.

20. Crispin Bates, 'Race, Caste and Tribe in Central India: The Early Origins of Indian Anthropometry', in Robb, ed., *Race in South Asia*, pp. 219–34; Bingley, *Jats and Gujars*, p. III; Major A.H. Bingley and Captain A. Nicholls, *Caste Handbook for the Indian Army: Brahmins*, Simla: Govt. Central Printing Office, 1897, p. 43.

21. Rachel J. Tolen, 'Colonizing and Transforming the Criminal Tribesmen: The Salvation Army in India', *American Ethnologist*, vol. 18, no. 1 (1991), pp. 106–25; Vansittart, *Gurkhas*, p. 49.

22. Bingley, *Sikhs*, p. 2.

23. Warwick Anderson, 'Disease, Race and Empire', *Bull. Hist. Med.*, vol. 70, no. 1 (1996), pp. 62–7.

24. Bayly, 'Colonial Ethnography', in Robb, ed., *Race in South Asia*, pp. 173–3; Sinharaja Tammita Delgoda, '"Nabob, Historian and Orientalist", Robert Orme: The Life and Career of an East India Company Servant (1728–1801)', *JRAS*, vol. 2 (1992), p. 365.

25. Rainey, 'The Madras Army', pp. 79–86.

26. Longer, *Red Coats to Olive Green*, p. 128; Farwell, *Armies of the Raj*, p. 181; Bingley, *Sikhs*, p. 144; Bingley, *Jats and Gujars*, pp. III, 32; Bingley, *Class Handbooks for the Indian Army: Dogras*, Simla: Govt. Central Printing Office, 1899, p. 19; Roberts, *Forty-one Years*, pp. 499, 530, 532, 534; Vansittart, *Gurkhas*, p. 74; Vansittart, *Notes*, p. 99; Betham, *Marathas and Dekhani Musulmans*, pp. 76, 115; Bingley and Nicholls, *Brahmins*, pp. 43, 52.

27. Bayly, 'Colonial Ethnography', pp. 176–8; Bingley and Nicholls, *Brahmins*, pp. 11, 43; Pryor, *Moplahs*, Preface, p. 17; Bingley, *Sikhs*, pp. 2, 18, 50–4; Bingley, *Jats and Gujars*, p. 31; Bingley, *Handbook on Rajputs*, 1899, reprint, New Delhi: Asian Educational Services, 1986, p. 28; Vansittart, *Notes*, pp. 119–21.

28. Vansittart, *Handbooks,* Appendix C, p. 28; Bingley, *Sikhs*, Appendix A, pp. I–VI, 41–58; *Supplementary Report*, p. 27.

29. Jonathan Haas and Winifred Creamer, 'Warfare among the Pueblos: Myth, History, and Ethnography', *Ethnohistory*, vol. 44, no. 2 (1997), pp. 240–9; Bingley, *Rajputs*, pp. 12–16; Vansittart, *Notes*, p. III.

30. Vansittart, *Notes*, pp. III, 1; Bingley, *Rajputs*, Sources; Cardew, *Bengal Native Army*.

31. Vansittart, *Notes*, pp. I, III; Pryor, *Moplahs*, List of some authorities; Bingley, *Sikhs*, Authorities consulted in the preparation of this work, pp. 71–105.
32. Vansittart, *Gurkhas*, p. 61; Vansittart, *Notes*, pp. I, III.
33. Bingley, *Jats and Gujars*, p. 38.
34. Ibid., p. 43. The couplet is from pp. 18–19; MacMunn, *The Armies of India*, p. 136.
35. Bingley, *Jats and Gujars*, pp. 9–12, 38, 92.
36. Ibid., pp. 46, 48; Bingley, *Sikhs*, p. 15.
37. Warwick Anderson, 'Immunities of Empire: Race, Disease, and the New Tropical Medicine, 1900–20', *Bull. Hist. Med.*, vol. 70, no. 1 (1996), pp. 94–118.
38. Roberts, *Forty-one Years*, pp. 499, 530, 532, 534; Captain R.W. Falcon, *Handbook on Sikhs for the use of Regimental Officers*, Allahabad: Pioneer Press, 1896, pp. 61, 65, 68. The view that physical culture shaped the soldiers' mentality is common among a group of modern historians. One British historian, R. Overy assumes that the Russian soldiers were capable of accepting an enormous amount of stress and strain because the climate and the terrain in which they grew up were harsh. Richard Overy, *Russia's War*, 1997, reprint, London: 1998, p. XVII.
39. Memorandum by Norman on the distribution of the armies in India, para 19, 26 September 1872, Notes of a tour by Norman, November 1871, Norman minutes, NAI; Memorandum on the Indian Army, Inefficient state of the army laid before the Duke of Cambridge, p. 5, 1 July 1876, Colonel William Merewether Collection, MSS.EUR.D.625/3©, OIOC.
40. Bingley, *Sikhs*, pp. 5, 11, 14–15, 30, 39, 45–6; Bingley, *Jats and Gujars*, pp. 14, 28, 42, 97–8; Vansittart, *Gurkhas*, pp. 82, 91.
41. Herodotus, *The Persian Wars*, tr. by George Rawlinson, New York: The Modern Library, 1942, p. 714.
42. Vansittart, *Notes*, pp. 59–60, 116–17.
43. Bingley, *Jats and Gujars*, p. 32; Pryor, *Moplahs*, pp. 16–17.
44. Mark Finlay, 'Quackery and Cookery: Justus Von Liebeg's Extract of Meat and the Theory of Nutrition in the Victorian Age', *Bull. Hist. Med.*, vol. 66 (1992), pp. 404–11; Bingley, *Rajputs*, p. 115; Bingley and Nicholls, *Brahmins*, p. 14.
45. Mark Harrison, *Public Health in British India: Anglo-Indian Preventive Medicine, 1859–1914*, Cambridge: Cambridge University Press, 1994, pp. 36–49, 60–98; Betham, *Marathas and Dekhani Musulmans*, pp. 48, 78, 113; Bingley, *Jats and Gujars*, pp. 170–1; Vansittart, *Gurkhas*, p. 49.
46. Longer, *Red Coats to Olive Green*, p. 128; Bingley, *Jats and Gujars*, p. 38; Bingley, *Sikhs*, pp. 57–8; Vansittart, *Gurkhas*, pp. 6, 39–41, 64–6.
47. Bingley, *Sikhs*, pp. 53–6; Bingley, *Jats and Gujars*, pp. 43, 93, Bingley and Nicholls, *Brahmins*, p. 21; Pryor, *Moplahs*, p. 52.

48. Betham, *Marathas and Dekhani Musulmans*, pp. 117–19; Bingley, *Sikhs*, pp. 53–8; Vansittart, *Gurkhas*, pp. 69, 86, 91.

49. Nancy Tomes, 'The Private Side of Public Health: Sanitary Science, Domestic Hygiene, and the Germ Theory, 1870–1900', *Bull. Hist. Med.*, vol. 64, no. 4 (1990), pp. 509–12; Matthew Handley,' "Help Us to Secure a Strong, Healthy, Prosperous and Peaceful Britain": The Social Arguments of the Campaign for Compulsory Military Service in Britain, 1899–1914', *CJH*, vol. 25, no. 2 (1995), pp. 262–79; Longer, *Red Coats to Olive Green*, p. 128; Bingley, *Rajputs*, Appendix B, p. 29; Betham, *Marathas and Dekhani Musulmans*, pp. 156–67.

50. Bingley and Nicholls, *Brahmins*, pp. 22–9, 30–1, 35.

51. Falcon, *Handbook on Sikhs*, pp. 61, 69.

52. Bingley, *Sikhs*, Appendix A, pp. I–II, VI, 41, 49, 53.

53. J.M. Wikeley, *Punjabi Musalmans*, 1915, reprint, New Delhi: Manohar, 1991, p. 2.

54. Goodenough and Dalton, *The Army Book*, pp. 448, 467.

55. MacMunn, *The Armies of India*, pp. 159–62, 165–8.

56. Edmund Candler, *The Sepoy* (London: John Murray, 1919), pp. 111–13.

57. Annual confidential reports on the regiments, 1893, L/MIL/7/17008, OIOC.

58. *Army Committee*, vol. 3, pp. 895–96; GO, no. 828, Organization–Indian Army, Army HQ, Simla, 12 September 1902, NAI.

59. GO, no. 828, 12 September 1902, p. 542.

60. GO, no. 294, 11 April 1902.

61. GO, no. 261, 27 March 1903.

62. Bingley, *Rajputs*, Appendix A and B, p. 29; GO, nos. 79, 236, 30 January 1903, 27 March 1903.

63. GO, Army HQ, Simla, no. 260, 27 March 1903, p. 214.

64. Vansittart, *Notes*, pp. 7–8. See also Table 3.1.

65. GO, no. 293, 12 April 1902.

66. Colonel L.W. Shakespear, *History of the Assam Rifles*, 1929, reprint, Gauhati: United Publishers, 1980, pp. 5–7, 57.

67. *Army Committee*, vol. 1–A, *Minority Report*, p. 156.

68. Mark Harrison, ' "The Tender Frame of Man": Disease, Climate, and Racial Difference in India and the West Indies, 1760–1860', *Bull. Hist. Med.*, vol. 70, no. 1 (1996), p. 93.

69. Eric Stokes, *The English Utilitarians and India*, 1959, reprint, Delhi: Oxford University Press, 1982.

70. Caplan, ' "Bravest of the Brave" ', pp. 571–97.

71. Rashmi Pant, 'The Cognitive Status of Caste in Colonial Ethnography: A Review of Some Literature on the North West Provinces and Oudh', *IESHR*, vol. 24, no. 2 (1987), p. 161.

FOUR

The Welfare Mechanism and the Generation of Loyalty

It is dangerous to pamper as to starve a mercenary.

Brigadier-General C.H. Brownlow[1]

Once the personnel were recruited they had to be retained within the military machine and made to fight the imperial wars. The imperialists attempted to purchase loyalty by offering a welfare package to the soldiers. This package included a series of incentives which probably created impersonal bonds of loyalty between the troops and the army's high command. Thus an impersonal loyalty structure replaced the pre-British personal loyalty of the soldiers to their clan and tribal chiefs.[2]

In pre-British India, the *jagirdars* were responsible for raising military contingents in exchange for the assignment of land revenue by the monarchs. Since, the *jagirdars* enlisted and maintained the troops, the soldiers were loyal to them. In the Rajput Army, the *jagirs* were more or less hereditary. When the *jagirdars* died, then their sons served in the force and enjoyed the revenue assignments, even if they were incompetent.[3] This hereditary principle implied the absence of professionalism. Due to the absence of a permanent bureaucracy, the welfare schemes for the soldiers remained *ad hoc,* and the *jagirdars* lined their pockets. The lack of cohesiveness of these forces was because the distribution of rewards in such armies remained chaotic. Pay and pension remained in arrears. Medical facilities and the commissariats were non-existent. Promotions were based on nepotism. To avert defeat, Mahadji Sindia and Ranjit Singh tried to Europeanize their armies by bureaucratizing the distribution of incentives to the soldiers. They tried to eliminate the *jagirdars* and bring the armies under their direct administration so that the soldiers would be loyal to the state. But, their reforms were too few and too late.[4]

While constructing the Sepoy Army, the British depended on two sources: the professional military forces of Europe and indigenous military traditions. One of the chief instruments, which enabled the British to craft a new type of army, was the systematic supply of incentives to the soldiers. The British imported some of the incentives that were offered to the Western standing armies. The professional armies, which emerged in the West from 1700 onwards, had regular wages, graduated wage scales, uniforms, and a hierarchy of ranks. The state took over from the private contractors the responsibilities of feeding, clothing and equipping the military personnel. This established the concept of contract between the impersonal armed forces and the military labourers, which replaced the feudal concept of hereditary service among the landlords and the retainers. As the troops shifted their loyalty from the intermediary warlords to the polities, the armies from quasi-private enterprises became public institutions.[5]

A similar mutation occurred in the Sepoy Army of India. A Dutch scholar has rightly said that European colonialism to a large extent depended on local cooperation.[6] The incentive package offered to the sepoys and the sowars was a crucial component for garnering support of the local military labourers in support of the Raj. However, the colonial setting modified some of the incentives which were provided to the troops. Since, the British could not utilize national sentiment of Indian soldiers, it became very important to supply them with monetary and non-monetary incentives, at the right time and right place, and in adequate quantities. So, the colonial army created an administrative machinery to provide various types of rewards to the soldiers. The bureaucratic mechanism geared towards supplying items for the troops' welfare, is referred here as the 'welfare mechanism'. The welfare bureaucracy was flexible, and responded to the soldiers' grievances. Probably by caring for its personnel, the army integrated the troops and prevented desertions, mutinies and treacheries that were endemic in the pre-colonial militias.

Some historians have attempted to study the interface between welfare measures and command. C. Jones shows that the *Ancien Regime* was able to attract volunteers and boost their morale in combat by providing health care, accommodation, etc. J.A. Lynn writes that when the soldiers had no sympathy with the cause for which they fought, it was necessary to buy their obedience with pay and food. His observation is all the more applicable to the Sepoy Army, as the sepoys were volunteers with no sentimental attachment to the imperial cause. L.M. Crowell describes the incentives offered in the pre-1857 Madras Army, but does not link it with the soldiers' loyalty. Tan Tai Yong shows the welfare measures (land grants in the Canal Colonies) introduced in Punjab after World War I to prevent disturbances among the ex-soldiers and to strengthen the loyalty of the serving troops.[7] The interconnection of welfare measures and loyalty in the post-1857 Sepoy Army is yet to be analysed thoroughly.[8] The European empires in Africa were won primarily with the aid of locally recruited indigenous armies officered by the Europeans. The African soldiers also received uniforms and training in drill during the second half of the nineteenth century. The *tirailleurs senegalais* fought for the French in Sudan. They were mercenaries who served the French for plunder and especially for the prospect of getting slaves including female captives.[9] In contrast, as this chapter will show that the incentive structure which kept the sepoys and sowars going was more complex, bureaucratic and at times more modern.

Five aspects of the welfare package offered by the imperialists to the soldiers are studied in this chapter. Section I shows the varied types of tangible goods and non-tangible incentives supplied to the soldiers. Section II portrays the disciplinary aspects of the welfare measures. The next section points out the linkages between the military-financial interests of the Raj and the welfare bureaucracy.[10] The fourth section charts the varied facets of the bureaucratic machinery oriented towards the soldiers' benefits, and the last section focuses on the imperial response to popular grievances.

I

WELFARE PACKAGE FOR THE SEPOYS AND THE SOWARS

Service hitherto in that Army [Sepoy Army] has been very popular. . . .
The behaviour of the Indian soldiers under all the trials of the Afghan

War [Second Afghan War] and their habitual gallantry in action, are ample proof of their loyalty and devotion.

Lord Hartington[11]

The British assumption was that valour and faithfulness could be encouraged by distributing rewards among the troops. So, they provided a series of benefits which were absent in the pre-British Indian militaries. The incentive scheme evolved from the late eighteenth century onwards, and underwent modifications and expansion in the aftermath of the 1857 Mutiny. Greater rewards were reaped by the units destined for the battle zones and overseas service as those activities involved greater stress and strain, physical hardship and long separation from families.

Tangible benefits can be classified into monetary and non-monetary incentives. The most important monetary benefits were wages. The Sepoy Army, from the late-eighteenth century onwards, paid the soldiers regularly in cash, because the British assumed that such continuity and regularity gave the troops a sense of loyalty. In other words, the soldiers' sense of security tied them to the army. Paying salaries punctually in cash was an important innovation introduced by the British in the subcontinent. Even in the nineteenth century, Nepal, trying to model her troops on the West, paid them by granting land. Many months of arrears of pay were common in the *Khalsa* Army, and caused successive mutinies. Extra money was allotted to the colonial soldiers for encouraging overseas service. In 1859, when the 1st Sikh Cavalry went to Aden, the sowars' pay was increased by one-third.[12]

One group of historians, which includes Clive Dewey, David Omissi, R.G. Fox and Rajit Mazumder, argues that the soldiers' pay was so high that they were able to save a lot from their wages. They sent their savings home, and these remittances reinvigorated the rural economy. Fox argues that the small peasants sent their younger sons to the army to supplement their families' income.[13] But actually, the salaries of the privates were adequate only for the basic necessities of life. Till 1911, the privates were paid Rs. 7 per month. In 1861, the government had to spend to Rs. 9 per month for each soldier's ration. The commissariat supplied rations to the soldiers only during emergencies. In ordinary circumstances, the soldiers had to buy their own food. Even if we assume that the privates took a less varied diet than that provided by the commissariat, their salaries, after various deductions for clothing, etc., were just enough for subsistence.[14] This is clear if we compute the cost of a soldier's basic necessities from Table 4.1. However the Indian officers' salaries, as evident from Tables 4.2 and 4.3, were large enough to allow savings.

TABLE 4.1: PRICES OF NECESSARY COMMODITIES

Date	Region	Cost of Essential Goods	Remarks
1860	West India	1 *Maund* of Salt = Re. 1 1 *Seer* 12 *Chattak* of Ghee = Re. 1 7 *Seer* of Pulse = Re. 1 15 *Seer* of Rice = Re. 1 17 *Seer* of Wheat = Re. 1	1 *Maund* = 40 *Seer* 1 Seer = 2 lb = 16 *chattaks*
1875	India	11 *Seer* 15 *Chattak* of Wheat = Re. 1 11 *Seer* 10.5 *Chattak* of Pulse = Re. 1 1 *Seer* 15 *Chattak* of Ghee = Re. 1 3 *Seer* 4.5 *Chattak* of Sugar = Re. 1 7 *Seer* 12 *Chattak* of Salt = Re. 1 5 *Seer* of Tobacco = Re. 1	
1890s	India	15 *Seer* of Rice = Re. 1 17 *Seer* of Wheat = Re. 1	A soldier consumed 30 *seer* of wheat or Rice, 3 *seer* of pulse, 30 *chattaks* of ghee, 7.5 *Seer* of sugar, 10 *chattaks* of salt and 1 *seer* 14 *chattak* of tobacco every month. Further each soldier required 1.5 *Maunds* of firewood every month for cooking his food.
1900s	India	10 *Seer* of Rice = Re. 1 13 *Seer* of Wheat = Re. 1	

Sources: Michelle McAlpin, 'Price Movements and Fluctuations in Economic Activity (1860–1947)', in D. Kumar, ed., *The Cambridge Economic History of India, 1757c.1970*, vol. 2, 1982, reprint, Delhi: Orient Longman in association with Cambridge University Press, 1991, pp. 881–2; Barat, *Bengal Native Infantry*, p. 309; W.J. Wilson, *History of the Madras Army*, vol. 1, Madras: Government Press, 1882, pp. 113–14, vol. 3, Madras: Government Press, 1884, p. 93; Prices in Ajmer, December 1860, Signed Captain A.G. Davidson, Asst. Commissioner, Ajmer, Progs. no. 315, 1 December 1861, MDP, March 1861, NAI; *Copy of Recent Correspondence on the Subject of the Organization of the Indian Army*, London: George Edward Eyre and William Spottiswode, 1877, Appendix B, Return showing the Comparative Cost of Living and the Price paid for Articles of necessaries by a Sepoy between 1848 and 1875, Colonel William Merewether Collection, MSS.EUR.D.625/4, OIOC.

TABLE 4.2: PAY OF REGULAR INFANTRY

Rank	Amount Per Month			Remarks
	1860s	1870s	1912	
Subedar-Major		Rs. 125		
Subedar			Rs. 119	
- 1st Class	Rs. 70	Rs. 100		
- 2nd Class	Rs. 52			
- 3rd Class	Rs. 42			
Jemadar	Rs. 28 *anna* 8	Rs. 30	Rs. 40	
Regimental-Havildar	Rs. 24			
Havildar-Major		Rs. 21		
Havildar	Rs. 14			
Naik	Rs. 12	Rs. 16		
Private	Rs. 7		Rs. 13	In 1860, at Pegu a labourer earned Rs. 9 per month (but his job was irregular).

Sources: Shakespear, *Sirmoor Rifles*, p. 29; *Army Committee*, vol. 3, p. 651; Colonel G. Balfour, Chief of Military Finance Department, to the Secy. to the GoI, MD, Calcutta, Progs. no. 330, 17 August 1861, MDP, October 1861; Minute on the organization of the army of India, Ch. 2, Pay, para 18, 11 October 1875, Norman Minutes, NAI; Organization, Indian Army, Correspondence and memoranda on the organization of the Indian Army, 22 September 1873, Statement showing pay and allowance, H.W. Norman, Records of Chief Commands, 1865–76, Notes and Minutes by Napier of Magdala, MSS.EUR.F.114, 5 (3) (4), OIOC; From Col. H.K. Burne, Secy. to the GoI, MD, to the Resident at Hyderabad, no. 6C, 1 January 1877, L/MIL/7/14966, OIOC.

The British officers after the 1857 Mutiny till the onset of the First World War were apprehensive that the soldiers' wages were inadequate. They argued that the pay should be increased, because prices of necessary articles and civilian wages were rising. Moreover, they were worried that if the pay was not raised, then the 'martial' groups would prefer the police instead of the army.[15] In 1875, the army calculated that the average monthly cost of necessaries for the sepoys between 1860 and 1875 had increased by Re. 1, *anna* 8, *paise* 7. The total cost of living for a sepoy in 1875 came to about Rs. 7, *anna* 2, *paise* 5.[16] Both the field commanders and successive Commanders-in-Chief

TABLE 4.3: PAY OF THE IRREGULAR CAVALRY

Rank	Amount Per Month		Remarks
	1860s	1890s	
Resaldar	Rs. 150		In real terms the sowars were not paid more than the sepoys because the former had to contribute for buying their horses. Further, the sowar had to spend Rs. 3 *anna* 8 per month to maintain a grass cutter who cut grass for the horses. Each horse needed 14 seer of grass daily. Grass was also available in the market at the 5 seer for *anna* 1.
Resaidar	Rs. 80		
Naib-Resaidar	Rs. 50		
Jemadar	Rs. 50		
Dufadar	Rs. 30-5	Rs. 41	
Naib-Dufadar	Rs. 28		
Nishanburdar	Rs. 24		
Trumpeter	Rs. 24-30		
Sowar	Rs. 25	Rs. 31	

Sources: Goodenough and Dalton, *The Army Book*, p. 468; *Supplementary Report*, Appendix A, p. 18; Colonel J. Brind, commanding Artillery Division, to the Asst. ADG, Bengal Artillery, Meerut, Lieutenant Colonel C.H. Blunt, commanding 4th Troop, 3rd Brigade Horse Artillery, to Major Bishop, ADG, 3rd Brigade, Ambala, Progs. no. 227, 10 April 1861, 23 April 1861, MDP, October 1861; Lieutenant Colonel C.G. Becher, commanding 1st Regiment Beatson's Horse to Captain J.H. Champion, Asst. ADG, MD, Camp Kotah, Progs. no. 143, 2 February 1860, MDP, March 1860, NAI; From H.K. Burne, Secy. to the GoI, MD, to the Resident at Hyderabad, No. 6C, 1 January 1877, L/MIL/7/14966, OIOC.

repeatedly stressed the necessity of increasing wages. In 1864, the Commander-in-Chief Hugh Rose privately warned John Lawrence the Viceroy: 'The pay of the native infantry ought to be raised due to increasing price of food and clothing'.[17] One field commander Major-General Blake wrote to the Commander-in-Chief Frederick Haines around 1872 that the good Hindu and the Muslim families were too proud to serve in the ranks for a private's pay.[18] General Robert Napier also realized the necessity for periodic increase in pay but found finance the principal obstruction. In 1873, he informed the Adjutant General's office that due to rise of food prices and better prospects in trade and agriculture, military service is losing its popularity. At the same time, he noted down his frustration in the following words: 'As the *bazar* prices are increasing, the sepoys pay should be raised, otherwise they would starve and their physique would decline. . . . In treating this subject of increase of pay, our chief stumbling block is expenditure, and we are told that where we propose an increase there must be a corresponding decrease. There lies the great difficulty'.[19] The officers commanding Bengal cavalry regiments supported Napier's statement. In 1875, they informed the army headquarter that the recruits with good physique were not coming forward in such numbers, as was the case formerly. This was because due to rise in the price of land and its produce, the small farmers were investing their cash in land. The officers claimed that only those who were unable to do hard work that cultivation required were joining the army.[20]

To tide over the price fluctuations of foodgrains, the army paid extra money, known as *batta*, to the soldiers. In the first half of the nineteenth century, *batta* was paid to the soldiers for service in 'foreign' areas like Punjab and Sind. But, when the Company annexed these two regions, *batta* for the units deployed there was abolished, despite the high price of foodgrains there. This angered the soldiers and was one of the factors of upheaval in 1857.[21] In the immediate aftermath of the 1857 Mutiny the imperialists were split regarding whether *batta* should be retained or abolished. Bartle Frere, the Commissioner of Sind, argued that abolition of *batta* was a mistake as a private could serve in the Ganga Valley for Rs. 7 per month, but it was impossible for him to serve in Sind even for Rs. 10 per month. George Clerk argued against this, saying that *batta* should not be paid for service in north-west India as the cost of foodgrains in that region had declined.[22] However, Frere carried the day, probably because the British were nervous after the Great Mutiny. And after 1857 *batta* was paid for service inside as well as outside India.[23] After 1859, if the prices of food at certain regions registered a rise, then the army paid its personnel extra money. Each soldier, according to the army's calculations, spent Rs. 3, *anna* 8 per month on his diet. But in 1860, when the prices of foodgrains increased, the authorities calculated that each soldier had to spend more and the army provided the extra money for this.[24] In 1887, the government sanctioned Rs. 2 *anna* 8 per man to all soldiers of the Sepoy Army proceeding on foreign service.[25] In 1890, field *batta* was introduced for active service both inside and outside the subcontinent.[26] At times, *batta* was also paid in kind instead of in cash. In 1893, when the 23rd Pioneer Regiment was employed in policing Gilgit and Chitral, which were infamous for their climate and terrain, the Commander-in-Chief General Geo S. White ordered that 'The 23rd Pioneers should be granted warm clothing and free rations while employed in Gilgit and Chitral'.[27]

To prevent the possibility of any mutiny from retrenched soldiers, the army sweetened the pill by offering them gratuities. The quantum of reward was directly proportional to the length of service to the Raj. When the 13th Punjab Infantry's personnel were invalided at Meerut in 1861, those with twenty years of service got pensions as well as gratuity which amounted to nine months' pay, and those with less then twenty years of service were awarded pensions plus gratuity equivalent to six months pay.[28]

There was no retirement age for the soldiers in the pre-British Indian armies, nor was there any provision for old age or disability pensions. In the 1760s, the French Army introduced pensions. Following the French the British introduced such European techniques in the subcontinent, but they did not introduce pension in all the colonial armies. The *askaris* of the King's African Rifles were denied pension even in the twentieth century.[29] From 1796 onwards in the Sepoy armies of British-India, there were two types of pension—life and family pensions. For those personnel who were discharged because of physical infirmities, or who had taken voluntary retirement or whose terms of service were over, the army paid money every month till their death, keeping in view their past service. In the 1860s, privates with twenty years of service got pensions of Rs. 3.5 per month, while those with forty years of service got Rs. 7 per month.[30] A scheme was designed to provide extra money to activate loyalty among the troops for combat against possible rebels. For signal service against the mutineers of 1857, Mowla Buksh of the irregular cavalry, after serving for thirty-six years and two months, got the pension to which he would have been entitled only after 40 years of service.[31] Soldiers who showed extraordinary bravery in campaigns also acquired higher pensions. Naib-Resaldar H.M. Khan of the Poona Horse retired in 1861 after serving for forty-three years. He was eligible for a pension of Rs. 20 per month, but because of his excellent performance in the assault on Asirgarh fortress of the Marathas during 1818, he was granted an extraordinary pension of Rs. 50 per month.[32]

In the pre-colonial Indian armies, family pension was available only to the officers. When they died, their relatives were given villages by the king. The British converted this welfare measure into cash and extended it to the privates. The imperial scheme of family pensions aimed not only to integrate the soldiers, but also their families to the service of colonialism. The pensions were paid to the heirs till their death. If dead soldiers had no surviving parents, then the pensions were paid to their wives till their death. If the soldiers left no wives then the pension was paid to the dead soldiers' sons till they became adults, or to their daughters till their marriages.[33] If soldiers died fighting gallantly, then an extraordinary sum, instead of a mere family pension, was granted. In 1860 the mother of one brave Resaldar Wachan Singh, received Rs. 1,000 after his death.[34] Such payments were designed to generate aggressiveness among the soldiers during combat, as the troops were sure, that even if they died fighting, their loved ones would be cared for by the government.

The army hoped to activate the soldiers' combat ardour through the 'wound' pension, which was introduced in 1852. This pension was given to personnel who lost their limbs while fighting, or became so seriously wounded that they had to be discharged from the army. The magnitude of this pension depended on the nature of the wounds. Privates with minor injuries received Rs. 4 per month while those with serious wounds received Rs. 5 per month.[35] The period between 1873 and 1874 acted as a microcosm for the later half of the nineteenth century. In that year, the total number pensioned off due to injury and sickness were 3,187 men from the Bengal Army, 2,000 from the Madras Army and 1,804 from the Bombay Army.[36]

Before combat, the Rajput soldiers used to take opium to reduce their nervousness. The British replaced opium with alcohol, because contemporary British medical opinion believed that alcohol cured many diseases, and during epidemics, liquor flowed freely. John Keegan writes that drink was an important palliative of nervous tension while waiting for action. Just before battle, it was a psychological necessity. Drinking alcohol before battles was common in the European armies, and the British introduced this custom in India. When the Indian soldiers faced extra strain, as during campaigns or overseas deployments, they were provided with extra rations of rum and malt liquor to keep their morale intact. Each soldier in peacetime was supplied with one dram of rum per day; but during war and epidemics this was increased to two drams per day. Sick soldiers were allowed to buy rum at a subsidized price from the army canteens. Alcohol was also considered the best antidote to boredom inherent during the long garrison duties.[37]

Some aspects of the Sepoy Army's reward structure were unique by European standards because the British absorbed several indigenous elements. Land grants to the soldiers, which the British retained for the Sepoy Army, had no place in the professional European armies. This incentive was a modified continuation of the pre-colonial military tradition of issuing hereditary land grants (*jagirs*) to the soldiers. Most of the soldiers came from small peasant families, and had a stake in the land.[38] The army encouraged them by dangling the prospect of *jagirs* in front of them. For exceptional performances, like raising soldiers for the Raj, saving the lives of British officers, suffering wounds in battles, etc., the army awarded land to such personnel. Aitah Mohammed Khan was a Resaldar in the Bunoo Police Cavalry. During 1857, he volunteered for service in Hindustan along with 112 of his tribesmen. They joined the Multan Horse and fought against the rebels in Delhi. After the rebellion, he and his followers were granted *jagirs* (each worth Rs. 1000), in perpetuity.[39] Subedar-Major Sangbir Thapa of the 2nd Gurkha Rifles got a piece of land in 1868 for his loyal service throughout his long tenure.[40]

Bazars were another indigenous tradition which the British retained. When it was not possible to provide cooked food to the soldiers during emergencies, the army provided raw food grains (which the soldiers had to cook) at controlled prices in the *bazars* set up under military supervision. Such markets with at least three days' supplies were also set up when local supplies were not forthcoming. The commanding officers maintained

registers which contained the names of all the *banias* who were
allowed to join the market. The *banias* had to pay a certain sum
to the regiments for being allowed to do business. One *bania*
supplied either a company or half a squadron of cavalry. The
banias occasionally supplied on credit. No *mahajans* were
allowed in the *bazars*, because the army feared that the soldiers
might contract debt. Indian officers were appointed as *kotwals*,
who inspected the quantity and quality of the cereals supplied
by the *banias*.[41]

The history of warfare shows, that soldiers were not willing to
die just for tangible incentives. The missing link was symbolic
rewards. Such tokens conferred honour and glory; the intangible
factors that motivated men to encounter the ugly and deadly
'face of battle'. The pre-colonial armies had at their disposal robes
of honour, daggers, etc., which were awarded to exceptional
warriors. These were replaced by the British with rewards
imported from the West, like medals. Charles I in 1643 first
introduced the silver medal for those men who had performed
well under difficult circumstances. Individual loyalty and
gallantry were honoured by supplying Distinguished Service
Medals to the Indian soldiers for extraordinary performances.[42]
For honouring regimental pride, the 2nd Gurkha Rifles, which
participated in the successful Kabul-Kandahar march, was
awarded bronze stars in February 1882.[43] Though such medals
were of little intrinsic worth, they were highly regarded within
the armed forces. John Keegan rightly says that the cultural ethos
of the military organizations was different from the civilian
world.[44] In 1837, Bentinck introduced the Order of Merit. The
Indian Order of Merit (IOM) was given for showing extraordinary
bravery in combat. Those who bagged this award had their
salaries and pensions increased, and were allowed to put the
letters IOM beside their names.[45]

II

WELFARE MEASURES AS A DISCIPLINARY MECHANISM

By making our men comfortable and happy we must undoubtedly make
them more loyal.

Major-General Charles Reid[46]

Incentives were supplied to the soldiers with the aim of extracting proper behaviour. When the soldiers misbehaved, welfare measures were denied to them. The commanding officers had the discretionary power to give non-military jobs to soldiers, either during their service tenure, or after their retirement. Such jobs involved less strenuous duties and the soldiers continued to draw military salaries or pensions along with the wages of the extra-military jobs. For such jobs, soldiers required recommendations and good character certificates from their officers. This became a technique for encouraging obedience from soldiers. One Havildar of the 48th Madras Infantry, Munniapah, being in the good books of his commanding officer, became a Sub Overseer in the Public Works Department in Moulmein in 1861. If the soldiers on deputation misbehaved, they were removed from the civil departments.[47]

Good Conduct Pay was another scheme introduced in 1837 for disciplining the soldiers. Under this scheme, those who served obediently received extra pay and Good Conduct badges. The army's plan was to encourage long-term loyalty. The longer the soldiers remained loyal, the greater was their Good Conduct Pay. After six years of service it became Re. 1 per month and after ten years of service, it increased to Rs. 2 per month. However, the commanding officers could deny this extra pay on grounds of misconduct. There was disagreement over this scheme as some officers wanted to link discipline with combat effectiveness. They argued that the higher pay should depend, not merely on the proper conduct and length of service, but also on the tactical efficiency of the troops.[48] In 1888, the Government of India appealed to the Secretary of State Viscount Cross to raise the rate of the Good Conduct Pay in the Hyderabad Contingent to Rs. 2 and 3 per month after six and ten years services respectively. The problem was that the monthly expenditure on Good Conduct Pay amounted to around Rs. 40, 476 per month.[49]

The breakdown of discipline in 1857 forced the army to strengthen the link between obedience and wages. The Punjab School argued that ambition and satisfaction could be induced among the soldiers by a graduated scale of pay for each rank. The authorities hoped that this would satisfy the loyal veterans, and would discourage rebelliousness among the junior troops, as they were bound to gain economically by remaining loyal in the long run. This scheme was geared to encourage loyalty among the younger soldiers, as the life pension scheme had attractions only for the old soldiers who had twenty years service behind them and were going to retire. Most of the rebels of 1857 had been newly enlisted recruits. Under the new scheme the privates got Rs. 6 per month for the first year of service, Rs. 7 per month from the second year, and Rs. 8 per month after fifteen years of service. Finally, after twenty years of service, they received Rs. 8.8 per month. Graduated scales of pay existed for the Indian officers also, but they were based not only on seniority, but also on merit as assessed by the British officers. This tangible incentive was an instrument of control in the hands of the British officers.[50]

A group within the army wanted to increase the life pension of the Indian officers and the privates just before the First World War. This group argued that the Indian officers, with their high social position and influence in their local communities, should not be alienated. Colonel L.C. Dunsterville, Commandant of the 20th Punjab Regiment in 1912, warned that the low pension of the privates was a source of discontent among the Sikhs. Major-General F.J. Aylmer argued that the army introduced life pension with the aim of extracting long-term good behaviour from the soldiers. The underlying assumption was that the troops, in the hope of getting a pension after retirement, remained obedient as 'misbehaviour' would result in discharges. Hence, the pension that had remained the same for the last hundred years should be raised. W. Meyer, a civilian official, challenged this line of thinking. Meyer argued that it was improper to pamper the soldiers, who were mercenaries. Moreover, he continued, in the civil departments, one received a pension after thirty years of service while conditions in the army were improving. Before 1857, soldiers received a pension after forty years of service. In 1878, they received pension after thirty-two years of service. And now they were receiving it after twenty-five years of service. Aylmer counter-argued that since the soldiers' job was more arduous than that of the civilians and there was no other option other than to keep the mercenaries contented.[51] In the end, however, the army's penny-pinching policy won, and pensions were not raised despite the threat to discipline.

Frequently in history, the breakdown of supplies resulted in the disintegration of military forces. Lack of food resulted in decline of morale, leading to desertions and the weakening of discipline, culminating in pillage and plunder by the troops, and resulting in peasant violence against the former. The best example of this was the dissolution of the French Army in Spain while combating insurgencies during 1808. In India, the Maratha Army did not accept the burden of feeding the soldiers directly during wartime. Contractors were assigned pieces of land temporarily. From its revenues they were supposed to supply the army. The Marathas also depended on the *banjaras* (itinerant merchants) who not only charged exorbitant prices, but also vanished during campaigns and occasionally sold grain to the enemy forces. This clumsy system resulted in the Maratha field armies disintegrating during protracted campaigns. In India the princely armies commandeered supplies, which in turn alienated the peasants. By contrast, Arthur Wellington paid for all his supplies during his campaign against Mysore and the Marathas. This made the peasants pro-British and they not only brought all the provisions to the Company's force they also supplied the British with information about the enemy's movements. A contented peasantry made the British rear secure, and an effective supply system possible. The Company's sepoys fought badly against the Sikhs at Ferozeshah on December 1845 because they were without provisions. But when well fed, before the fight at Aliwal on January 1846, they performed admirably.[52]

To prevent losses of men and animals through malnutrition, and to raise the fighting spirit of the troops, the military establishment was concerned about ensuring supply of food for the soldiers and forage for their horses. During famines, or when the army functioned as an Imperial Fire Brigade, local supplies either became too costly or were just not available. The commissariat then came to the soldiers' assistance. Rations were supplied when the troops were deployed in China, as the provisions could not be procured there.[53] This kept the Indian soldiers well disciplined and tactically effective. During emergencies, when local food supplies collapsed, the more disciplined Indian regiments got preferential treatment from the commissariat, in order to encourage obedience among other units. In 1861, when due to famine in Rajasthan, the units stationed there failed to acquire local supplies at normal rates, the commissariat issued a special allowance first to the Mharwara Battalion as it had remained loyal during 1857.[54]

In general, the soldiers were provided with some money known as hutting allowance, for constructing their lines when they were shifted from one place to another. To set an example, loyal and disciplined units were always allowed the first claim on hutting money. The soldiers cut wood from the nearby forest and carried it to the site of building on commissariat carts. In 1864, the 10th Infantry Regiment built their lines at Poona with their hutting allowance plus Rs. 300 advanced by the army headquarter. But, gradually the army took over the task of constructing barracks (lines) for the soldiers.[55]

The army in Britain started building barracks from the seventeenth century, and this probably influenced the British in India. The argument was that billeting the soldiers in the civilian houses harmed group cohesion as the regiments had to be broken into small groups. This also made it difficult for the authorities to monitor the soldiers. The European armies believed that an essential factor of military conditioning was the barrack, which separated the soldiers from the civilian world. Similarly the colonial authorities felt that if the troops were exposed to the 'seditious' influence of the civilians then their loyalty would undergo a severe strain. Moreover British military and medical thinking in the nineteenth century saw Indian society as the agency of moral and physical degradation. This in turn required segregation of the soldiers for checking moral and physical infection. So, the soldiers' lines were constructed and repaired at the state's expense.[56]

From its retired personnel, the army created a landed gentry to police the countryside. In the British conceptual framework, the landed gentry was respected in India. It was the imperial belief that land grants increased the prestige of the ex-soldiers, and indirectly that of the army, in rural society. The army created military colonies. Such measures also benefited the soldiers' families and encouraged them either to remain loyal or serve in the army. The military colonies were the continuation of the Invalid *thanahs*, which the Bengal Army established in the early-nineteenth century. It was easier for the army to keep watch over the retired soldiers concentrated in the colonies, rather than scattered throughout the countryside. Their sons grew up in such colonies and were potential reservoirs of recruits. For the imperialists, soldiers were more vital than the Raj's local collaborators—the zamindars. While constructing the colonies, the government deliberately encouraged zamindar-soldier rivalry to prevent any bonhomie between the 'natural leaders' of Indian society and the Raj's sword arm. In 1861, the government forcibly took 3,000 acres of land from the zamindars in Dehradun for a military colony to settle the Gurkhas who had aided the British in reconquering Delhi from the rebels in 1857. The retired Gurkhas cultivated the land and paid a very low tax fixed specially for them by the government.[57]

For retaining the orders and the medals, the soldiers had to behave well, as they were liable to lose these privileges for misconduct, or if they had to appear before the courts martial.[58] Ranks were a sort of 'carrot' which, the British believed, encouraged the soldiers to risk their lives repeatedly. This was because higher ranks meant greater prestige, along with financial perquisites. Troops were promoted for gallantry in combat, but good behaviour on part of the soldiers was also necessary for promotions. One Mohammed Afzul, a trooper of the 1st Punjab Cavalry, on 23 October 1857 attacked the rebels in Kanauj. But, due to his previous record of bad conduct, he was not promoted to a non-commissioned officer. However, Ranjit Singh, a private who was wounded in action was promoted to a Naik, as his previous service record was satisfactory.[59]

The British strategy was to co-opt Indian officers[60] by offering them greater quantities of tangible and non-tangible rewards, and so divide them from the privates. The imperial belief was that privilege and self-interest would dominate over the collective interest, and the struggle for power, prestige and privilege would prevent the Indian soldiers from acting as a monolithic group against the British officer corps. In return for more facilities than the privates the Indian officers were responsible for the conduct of their troops. The excuse that they had no knowledge about the privates was no more accepted after 1859. Resaldar-Majors and Subedar-Majors became the confidential advisors of the British commandants about the disciplinary state of the Indian privates, and aided the British officers in controlling the troops.[61]

When the Bengal Army rebelled in 1857 it was the Punjab Irregular Cavalry[62] that aided in its suppression. So, the latters' pay was increased after 1859. The British assumption was that the influence of the Indian officers over the privates was directly proportional to the formers' seniority—higher the rank, greater was the pay packet. While Resaldars' salaries were doubled, the lower officers like Dufadar and Kote-Dufadars' salaries increased by Rs. 10 and Rs. 7 respectively, and the sowars' pay was raised only by Rs. 5.[63] In the barracks there were special quarters for the Indian officers, for extra comfort and privacy.[64] Higher the rank, greater was the hutting allowance. And in the 1860s, a Subedar got Rs. 30, a Jemadar Rs. 15, a Havildar Rs. 10 and a private only Rs. 3 as hutting allowance.[65] The Orders of British India were granted only to the Indian officers for long, honourable and faithful service. Those who got these awards received the honorary titles of 'Sirdar Bahadur' and 'Bahadur' and after retirement got the honorary rank of Lieutenant or Captain. In addition to their salaries or pensions, they got Rs. 30–60 per month. Every year, about 100 officers were given such awards.[66] Though the Indian Order of Merit was open to both the Indian officers and the privates, the lion's share went to the commissioned ranks. In fifty years twenty-three persons of 1st Punjab Cavalry got this order—of whom 16 were officers.[67]

For enhancing group morale among the soldiers and to make them more amenable to discipline, the armies were provided with uniforms, a novelty for soldiers in India. The Sepoy Army supplied uniforms annually, free of cost, to those soldiers who went abroad.[68] An allowance was provided to all the soldiers, for mending and cleaning their uniforms.[69]

III

WELFARE MEASURES, ÇOMBAT EFFECTIVENESS
AND FINANCIAL INTERESTS OF THE RAJ

Some welfare measures while ensuring loyalty and discipline of the troops aided the financial interests of the army, other incentives' however, harmed the military capability and monetary dimensions of the colonial state. Non-military jobs awarded to soldiers were financially helpful to the state, because this technique enabled the army headquarter, to honour loyal and brave officers for whom vacancies did not exist in the army. It was also cheaper for the government to man the PWD with Indian officers. In addition, the army headquarter considered the Indian officers were more efficient because unlike the European Sergeants, they were not habitual drinkers.[70]

Though the gratuity scheme raised the army's budget it also raised the army's combat potential. Gratuities enabled the army to get rid of aged personnel no longer capable of arduous campaigning. There were many units which possessed soldiers with more than two decades of service. One such unit was the Nagpur Irregular Force. To get rid of 143 aged men, the army had to spend Rs. 22,195. Those privates with twenty-six years of service were given Rs. 160 each.[71] Those soldiers who were unfit for soldiering but had not yet earned their pension (20 years of service) were encouraged to take discharge in exchange for gratuities. In 1870, the army introduced a policy under which soldiers with five or ten years of service, willing to take discharge got gratuities amounting to three months' and six months salary respectively.[72] This scheme was geared to create an army of young men, probably in response to the growing Russian threat on the North-West Frontier. Similarly, the scheme of Good Conduct Pay certainly strengthened discipline of the soldiers but the annual cost came to about Rs. 74,400.[73]

Wound pensions for the irregular cavalry sowars involved an obligation on part of the army to replace the dead horses. This expenditure was aimed to raise the combat power and loyalty of the irregular troopers. Such troopers were responsible for buying their own horses. When they lost their horses in action, the troopers received financial aid from the *chunda* funds (each regiment had a fund created out of collective contribution of the sowars) for buying new horses. But, when the irregular regiments were engaged in heavy fighting and lost many horses, then the *chunda* funds were unable to replace all the horses. The *chunda* fund provided only Rs. 150 to the sowars on the death of their horse. But, a horse cost Rs. 450. In the long run this encouraged a tendency among the troopers to shy away from combat, so as to avoid casualties to their horses. Hence, the army intervened and paid monetary compensations known as wound pension to encourage the troopers to fight. When the 4th Sikh Cavalry lost many horses in action against the mutineers of 1857, the army paid each trooper Rs. 150 in addition to the Rs. 150 each trooper got from the *chunda* fund.[74] This measure was a marked improvement on the custom prevalent in the princely armies, in which the troopers were responsible for their horses. If their mounts died, then the troopers were discharged. This explains the frequent desertions and reluctance of the cavalry of the indigenous powers to clash with the Raj's mounted force.[75]

Mark Harrison writes that health care for soldiers raised the army's cohesion, which in turn increased its military efficiency.[76] Again, epidemic diseases more than the indigenous opponents of Afro-Asia as well as in the New World frequently brought death and disaster on the military forces of the colonial powers.[77] Diseases and death rates also led to desertions.[78] The British in India understood that keeping the soldiers healthy raised their combat potential and loyalty against internal and external threats. Thus the army made arrangements for supplying food to the units deployed overseas as units stationed abroad could not cook their own food and suffered an extraordinary rate of sickness. A case in point is 1867 when the Indian soldiers stationed in Aden suffered from scurvy.[79] The army then evolved a long administrative tail for providing food and water to the soldiers who were deployed outside India. Each infantry regiment stationed abroad had ten coolies, twenty water carriers, ten sweepers and one cook. The army's initial expenditure in making arrangements to feed the soldiers reduced the long-term financial loss from gratuities it had to pay to the soldiers demobilized due to sickness.[80]

The army was convinced that the ordinary populace was disease prone. If any epidemic broke out among the civilians (who were considered more vulnerable to such diseases), the soldiers would catch such ailments if lodged with them. Lieutenant-General Lord Napier of Magdala asserted in 1869 that the Indian soldiers were infected by the civilians in the dirty towns. Periodical fairs in the town further spread the cholera among the civilians of various regions. However, the colonial state was unwilling to take over the duty of general supervision of health of the Indian population. So, the soldiers were segregated from the civilians by accommodating the former in lines. In the 1860s vaccination against small pox was made mandatory for the recruits.[81] In the second half of the nineteenth century, the hutting allowance for each regiment cost the army Rs. 3,116 annually.[82] The British believed that accumulated dirt gave rise to health problems. The only way to check it was by building new lines. Again, when diseases like small pox spread, the British medical opinion advised the army to demolish the old lines and construct new ones in their place. Those lines which were more than forty years old were demolished and new lines were constructed for better hygiene.[83] In 1860, when the line of 36th Infantry Regiment became unhealthy after rainfall, the army immediately reconstructed them. The army did re-roofing and re-thatching of the lines. Beams, doors and windows were also supplied to the soldiers for constructing the lines. Strict instructions were given for making the barracks spacious.[84] In order to check the spread of cholera, the army ordered that there should not be any stagnant pool of water in front of the soldiers' lines. The Bombay authorities in 1864 thought of constructing underground drains though this was costly, to prevent any accumulation of stagnant water during rainfall in front of the lines.[85] In 1864, the Commander-in-Chief William Mansfield sanctioned the building of lines for the sepoys on an improved plan. The sanitary conditions were taken care of and more spacious huts that allowed free circulation of air were constructed. When the army took over the duty of building lines with bricks, lime, sand and clay, the cost went up drastically. The cost of building lines for the fourteen regiments of the Bombay Army in 1864 amounted to Rs. 262,142.[86] Between 1866 till 1868, the government spent Rs. 4,085 in repairing the lines of the Madras regiments. For 1869 to 1870, the expenditure was higher—the bill came to Rs. 3,515.[87]

The army provided recreational facilities for the soldiers in barracks. Each unit was encouraged to build gardens, which provided an atmosphere necessary for the development of healthy mind. Fresh air, fruit and vegetables, necessary for good health, were available from the gardens. The authorities provided seeds, tools, land and gardeners freely. In the first decade of the twentieth century, the 6th Poona division got Rs. 400 per year for maintaining such gardens.[88]

There was a direct linkage between sickness and the frontline strength. The Marathas considered hospital arrangements unnecessary. Hence, epidemics frequently decimated their forces. In 1876, the British found out that generally a regiment with a ration strength of 700 personnel when ordered to take field, leaves 10 per cent sick in hospitals and another 10 per cent became *hors de combat* (sick plus footsore) before the regiment had been five days in the operational zone.[89] During the Second Afghan War (1878–80), the 1st Gurkha Rifles suffered more casualties from disease than from the Afghan enemy. In 1884, about 2 per cent of the Madras Army personnel were in the hospitals.[90] The British in India were influenced by the European military establishments' assumption that providing medical care for the sick soldiers raised morale and encouraged them to fight. The Sepoy Army provided extra health care for treating battlefield wounds during campaigns. Each infantry regiment had one doctor during peacetime, but when it was on active service, it was awarded one surgeon, one assistant surgeon, one assistant apothecary and one dresser.[91]

An attempt was made to utilize research done in the field of medical science for the benefit of the soldiers. Cholera ravaged the health of both the British as well as Indian soldiers. Cholera was regarded as a water borne disease and attempt was made to provide fresh drinking water to the soldiers. Still soldiers fell victim to cholera. Major-General Robert Napier Commander-in-Chief of the Bombay Army in 1869 issued an order that in case any soldier fell victim to cholera then some sample of water drunk by them should be collected in bottles which then should be corked and sealed and sent to the Inspector General of the Medical Department at Bombay.[92] The Sepoy Army's high command always made detailed enquiry about how many soldiers were ill at a time, and the type of disease(s) they had contracted. The army utilized technology to check the spread of epidemics. The senior military officers used the telegraph for quick exchange of information, to know where epidemics like cholera had broken out, and to implement counter-measures to suppress the disease.[93] Annual inspection of the presidency armies was conducted by the officers sent by the high command in order to inform the latter regarding the state of health of the soldiers in the lines. The annual inspection report of the Madras Army for 1874–5 pointed out that the average death rate was 6.8 per 1000. In addition, the Inspecting Officer Major-General Blake pointed out that the 3rd Infantry Regiment's personnel stationed at Secunderabad were unhealthy because the lines were bad.[94]

The effectiveness of the army depended not only how quickly it could suppress the spread of diseases, but also on the speed of processing the sick and wounded soldiers and transferring them back to the battle zones. In 1870, hospital facilities were available for 5 per cent of the colonial soldiers.[95] Attempts were made to improve and expand the hospital facilities. The *kuccha* hospitals were thatched, and hence vulnerable to fire and moisture destroyed the walls. So these hospitals were reconstructed with concrete. The hospital at Aurangabad was situated near the market where the patients were disturbed by continuous noise. Again, due to faulty construction, neither air nor light entered the hospital. The accommodation facilities were also inadequate. Thus a new spacious building, 6000 sq ft in area, was constructed at a new site where there were trees to provide shade to the sick and for cooking meals.[96] Hospitals with low roofs were reconstructed. Under the new plans, some cavalry hospitals had tiled rooms.[97] In addition, the army supplied bedding and blankets to the hospitals. In the cold, damp regions, socks and flannels were also issued to the soldiers. Bad sanitation claimed many soldiers' lives and so the authorities regularly enquired about the sanitary state and conditions of the latrines, and took steps to improve them.[98]

When the army was unable to provide health care, it financially compensated those who had suffered. The army hoped that this would strengthen the conviction among the soldiers that the military bureaucracy cared for them, which in turn would strengthen their bonds of loyalty with the army. The army supplied a doctor whenever a detachment of a regiment marched from one place to another place. A soldier, Bani Ram, became blind from ophthalmia. He contracted it in 1860, when a party of his regiment was marching from Gonah towards Jhansi, and there was no doctor in his unit. The commandant was ordered to explain why no doctor was accompanying the unit as per the regulations. Ram had to be demobilized, but since he had served for only two years, he was ineligible for pension. As a special case, on humanitarian ground, he was paid Rs. 66.[99]

In the nineteenth century, the evolution of the Sepoy Army's uniforms reflected a trend towards greater comfort. Occasionally, comfortable uniforms cost the army more, but at the same time they raised the soldier's combat effectiveness. The dress of the

Peshawar and the Hazara Mountain Levies was troublesome as their tight trousers were unsuitable for climbing the hills, and the sleeves of the jackets had to be cut near the armpits while loading and unloading the pack animals. This uniform was subsequently replaced by a khaki blouse and loose trousers which were better adapted for combat in the hills. As these uniforms required more cloth, the army had to spend *anna* 8 more for each uniform.[100] The annual cost for uniform for 800 privates of a regular infantry regiment came to about Rs. 3,840.[101] In 1893, the Commander-in-Chief warned the commandant of the 2nd Battalion of the 2nd Gurkha Rifles in the following words: 'More attention is necessary in fitting clothing and khaki coats should always be made loose enough to admit of jerseys and other warm under-clothing being worn on winter campaigns without uncomfortable restraints'.[102]

Some welfare measures strengthened loyalty but simultaneously harmed the combat potential and were financially expensive for the state. In order to portray a benevolent image among its service personnel, the army gave pensions to the combat ineffective troops even though they were technically not eligible for such rewards. Those soldiers who became physically unfit for military duties after fourteen years of service were deliberately retained for another year, so that they became eligible for life pensions.[103] In December 1874, about 33,690 personnel of the Bengal Army were in receipt of pension.[104] In 1888, pensions for the retired personnel of the Hyderabad Contingent came to about Rs. 16,179 every month.[105] Not only were these persons were militarily useless, their pensions involved a huge financial outlay for the government. But, pensions had to be given to them for the sake of strengthening loyalty.

The pre-British Indian militaries followed the notorious practice of going into campaigns with the soldiers' families. This not only reduced such forces' mobility but also created enormous logistical problems. One of the primary reasons for the destruction of the Maratha Army in the Third Battle of Panipat in 1765 was due to the presence of an enormous host of non-combatant followers. Though the British abolished this practice they kept the soldiers' spirits high by allowing them furlough to visit their villages. Furlough was introduced in 1796, a measure that was necessary as most of the soldiers were married. Except in the Madras Army (where the wives stayed with the regiments within the regimental lines but were not allowed to follow the units during campaigns), only 15 per cent of the troops were allowed to bring their wives to the cantonments. The rest of the soldiers' wives remained in the villages. To further motivate the soldiers, those regiments which participated in operations and suffered combat losses were awarded extra furlough. Again, for encouraging overseas service, those units which volunteered for duties abroad, were allowed a furlough of 3.5 months after the deployments. As a rule the soldiers were generally allowed 3.5 months furlough each year. If, they contracted illness in the meantime, then the army, extended the furlough period by another two to four months.[106]

This welfare measure though good for the morale and loyalty building, compromised the army's fighting potential. Because of furlough, the corps were 15 per cent weaker between April to November. Units stationed in strategically vulnerable areas like the North-West Frontier, where the living conditions were exceptionally harsh, got extra furlough. Such units were always 34 per cent below strength.[107] This proved to be a problem especially during the Second Afghan War and some officers of the Raj were against the continuation of the furlough. However, on 30 June 1880, Hartington from India Office warned the Governor-General in the following words:

I have learned with great regret from these despatches that there has been extreme difficulty of late in obtaining recruits for the Indian Army. . . . The dislike to enlist in Indian Army which is now apparent is due to the unwillingness of Indians to encounter the prospect of prolonged service in Afghanistan; nor is this a matter for surprise, when it is considered that service in that country occasions much discomfort to the sepoys, that a number of regiments have been greatly weakened by invaliding and deaths, and that it is impossible for the soldiers while serving there to obtain the usual and much prized privilege of leave of absence to their homes.[108]

As the war clouds gathered at the beginning of the second decade of the twentieth century, one lobby in the army was against allowing so much leave, since furlough reduced the frontline strength. But, in 1912, Major-General Birdwood cautioned that furlough was necessary for smooth recruitment. Furlough was vital to the soldiers for both economic and mental reasons. Most of the soldiers were from the agricultural families and during harvests, when extra hands were necessary on their farms, they demanded leave. If they were not allowed leave, Birdwood warned, then not only would they be alienated, but in future no younger sons of small farmers would join. Again, enough accommodation for all the soldiers' wives did not exist in the lines so for domestic reasons, soldiers were allowed to visit their families. Birdwood's view was similar to the report submitted by the Punjab School in 1857. To prevent another mutiny, the British attempted to learn about the Indians in greater detail and the Punjab School was ordered to gather information about the soldiers' thought processes. The Punjab School claimed that the soldiers' mentality could be reconstructed from their ballads and proverbs. The Punjab School argued that the ballads and proverbs portray from which it was clear that the soldiers hated being away from their land and families for a long time.[109]

IV

ARMY BUREAUCRACY AS SUPPLIER OF WELFARE INCENTIVES

The army crafted an enormous bureaucratic apparatus for the quick and efficient delivery of rewards. This focus on the colonial army's internal administration is relevant to the evolution of the colonial state. Anand Yang claims that the presence of the Raj's bureaucracy was very limited in indigenous society as most of the apparatus of power remained with the local notables and in his view, the British Indian state's reach was limited.[110] This minimalist position is challenged by D.M. Peers who points out that the colonial state was authoritarian, as it was backed by powerful armed forces.[111] Actually, the British attempt to introduce European-style army administration was one of the principal imperatives behind the colonial state's expansion. One of the key duties of the military establishment was the methodical distribution of largesse to the soldiers. This administrative task forced the colonial authorities to collect information about the Indians and to introduce bureaucratic mechanisms which penetrated to the lowest level of indigenous society.

The army crafted a surveillance scheme for keeping the retired soldiers on its side which forced it to create new administrative posts which extended the reach of the state to all the towns and villages. Pension was distributed through the Pension Pay Masters and as the country was divided into many administrative circles, for each circle there was such an official. They (Pay Masters), along with the District Officers, monitored the conduct of the retired troops and pensions were stopped if ex-soldiers were caught indulging in disloyal activities.[112]

For distributing family pension, the state had to collect information about the private lives of the soldiers—when and whom they married, where their families were stationed, who else constituted the families, the ages of the family members, etc. All this resulted in the fusion of public and private domains of the soldiers. The Adjutant General's department was responsible for providing salaries, pensions and gratuities to the soldiers. For investigating the claims of family pensions, and to settle the estates of the dead soldiers, Recruiting Staff Officers were appointed and resulted in an expansion of paperwork. Nominal rolls of the soldiers, maintained both in English and in the vernacular, contained information about the soldiers' careers, the names of their family members and the villages in which they resided. When military personnel died, then notices in vernacular languages were sent to their heirs containing information about when and where they should present themselves. Occasionally civil administration got fused with the military set-up for aiding in such tasks. For instance, the soldiers' relatives from Purniah and Darjeeling applying for family pension had to correspond with the Collectors of the respective districts.[113]

The army's demand for plots forced the expansion of Raj's rural administrative set-up and this process started in the last half of the eighteenth century. The Residents in the courts of the Indian princes and the Collectors (Revenue Department) were in charge of acquiring land. These officials had to maintain registers containing the names, ranks and ages of the soldiers, and details of land grants. These documents were then sent to the Governor-General who passed them on to the Board of Revenue. The grantees were given money by the government for buying agricultural implements. This money was distributed through the Collectors, who had also to inform the Army Pay Masters every month about the activities of the grantees. After retirement, many soldiers got plots from the army, where they constructed their own houses. On the death of the soldiers, the land passed to their heirs who paid one-tenth of the produce to the zamindars and a low rent to the government. If they failed to pay the zamindars and the *Sarkar*, the plots were taken away and sold to the highest bidder.[114]

Napoleon's statement that an army marched on its stomach is well known. But, the colonial army's top brass was so concerned with supplying liquor to the soldiers that it seemed that the troops marched on liquor as well. Due to lack of organized recreation, the soldiers of the British Army found solace in drinks. However, from the late-nineteenth century onwards, regimental libraries and clubs were opened for the personnel.[115] Such schemes were absent for the brown soldiers of the Sepoy Army. The Commissary General in India was in charge of storing and distributing the liquor to the soldiers. This in turn resulted in the expansion of the commissariat infrastructure. The two big depots of liquor were at Calcutta and Kanpur and the latter was the centre from which liquor was sent to various places in north and north-west India for distribution among the detachments.[116] But the godowns pured inadequate and so in the 1860s the army went on a godown-building spree for storing liquor. In 1860, Rs. 2,863 was spent on converting cattle sheds in Kanpur into liquor godowns to prevent loss due to evaporation from the casks. In 1861, for converting an unfinished barrack at Peshawar into a liquor godown, the army spent Rs. 10,000. Occasionally, the army was more interested in storing liquor than accommodating sick Indians. At certain places, like in Dinapur, the army encroached on the civilian hospitals and used them for storing liquor.[117] The Commander-in-Chief was alarmed at the rising rate of liquor consumption among the soldiers who apart from army ratios also bought large amounts of alcohol from the *bazars*, and got into debt. This led to canteens being opened in 1862 which provided the soldiers with limited amounts of alcohol.[118]

The Quartermaster General's task was housing the soldiers and the maintenance of their barracks. The soldiers demolished old lines themselves. But, when they constructed new lines, the PWD co-operated with the commanding officers, if the task exceeded the capacity of army's military engineers. To stop cholera from spreading, the Indian soldiers were prevented from drinking impure river water. Each barrack was therefore provided with deep wells which did not run dry even during summer. Boring apparatuses for the wells were provided by the PWD.[119]

Construction and repair of latrines, and construction of watering troughs (for watering the horses) were done by the Military Works Service. Some soldiers in each company were trained to built special trenches for disposing of excreta and refuse. In 1911, some of the regiments deployed in Burma were provided with incinerators. In each station, the medical officers guided the commanding officers in regard to sanitation. The sanitary officers were also responsible for testing the liquor supplied to the soldiers. For all the above mentioned tasks, meant that the army needed many doctors even in peacetime. From less than a hundred doctors and surgeons in the 1780s, the Indian Medical service of the army by the early 1900s had grown to a corps of six hundred men. The army wanted Indian doctors, as they were cheap and easily available. The army's demand for medical personnel probably forced the government to establish medical colleges, and this encouraged the growth of the medical profession in India. The army recruited Indian doctors from the medical colleges of Calcutta and Agra.[120] When the hospitals constructed by the Military Works Service failed to satisfy the demands of the army headquarter, the former faced flak from the latter. In 1893, Major W.B. Wilson, the Assistant Secretary of the Military Department complained to the Director General of the Military Works that the hospital building of the 15th Bengal Lancers was constructed badly as the heat was unendurable during the hot weather and further, that it was deficient in accommodation by about eighteen beds.[121]

V

SOLDIERS' GRIEVANCES AND THE ARMY'S RESPONSES

It is well known that there is no subject on which the sepoy is more tenacious than on questions of pay and allowances.

Lord Hartington.[122]

The limits of British policy to construct loyalty through the welfare bureaucracy become clear from the soldiers' perceptions, which are evident from their petitions. An action-reaction dialectic shaped the interaction between the army personnel and the military bureaucracy. The troops demanded redress if they perceived a qualitative or quantitative decline in the distribution of incentives. The bureaucracy responded favourably. The texture of demands and the army's response were shaped by the theoretical paradigm through which the soldiers viewed the army and vice versa. At times the soldiers bargained because they felt that the army had not fulfilled all the obligations of the contract. The troops viewed their relations with the army as partly contractual and partly patriarchal.

As the Raj monopolized the military labour market of India, the potential soldiers had no other employers to fall back upon. Being aware of their weak position in the power game, they never challenged the *Sarkar* directly. So, the demands of the soldiers were always clothed as 'humble petitions'.[123] Being dependent on the army for sustenance, the soldiers conceived the war machine as their 'mother' who breast-fed and cherished her sons.[124] By destroying the army they would get nothing, so to get their dues, they pressured the army bureaucracy, but never aimed to break it. The realities of the power structure and the soldiers' intellectual paradigm made them somewhat fatalistic. The soldiers' view as regards service in the army was *Kabhi sukh aur kabhi dukh, Angrez ka naukar.*[125]

After 1857, the British were neither bent on revenge on all the Indians, nor did they want to stop their recruitment in the army. With the limited number of white troops available to them, they had to depend on the Indians whether they liked it or not. For the 1857 catastrophe, the British partly held responsible their faulty policies and not the soldiers' mentality. The annexation of Awadh and mismanagement by the British officers were regarded as the principal causes of the uprising.[126] The Indians were portrayed neither as untrustworthy by nature, nor as incarnations of evil; neither as machines nor as animals. The soldiers in imperial view, were not automatons, but ordinary men of flesh and blood with feelings, passions and prejudices, who must be treated and sympathetically. The British officers were warned that their arrogance and intolerance had caused 1857. The declared policy was that the religious customs and prejudices of the Indians should be respected.[127]

Occasionally the soldiers' demands were shaped by their

religious scruples, and the authorities gave in to the soldiers' pressure. In 1860, a Sikh regiment demanded borax and *ghee* for washing their hair. On religious grounds, they refused to use the soap provided by the army. In the end, the army, instead of supplying two maunds of soap, offered to each regiment eight maunds of borax and ten maunds of *ghee*.[128] When the ordinary Indians were not getting enough rice to eat, the soldiers, aware of their special bargaining power, got costly *ghee* from the army.

The army could not afford to be tough while discharging soldiers, because its aim was to craft a special collaborative relationship with the Indian populace who manned the Raj's ultimate line of defence. During the demobilization of the 13th Punjab Infantry's personnel at Meerut in 1861, the army decided to provide all the men with over eight years service, with gratuities amounting to twelve months' pay. This scheme failed to satisfy them, so, to stifle protests many were promoted before being discharged. The rest were absorbed in the Meerut Police. The latter scheme enabled them to enjoy social status, pay and other privileges.[129]

Frequently, the Indian officers protested and as they were politically and militarily more important than the privates, the army could not afford to alienate them. In 1861, the Central Indian Horse was amalgamated with the Meade's Horse as part of the overall military policy to reduce the Indian Army's size in the aftermath of the 1857 Mutiny. The amalgamation of these two units demanded the discharge of twenty-two Jemadars and forty-nine Dufadars. To get rid of them, the army offered gratuity amounting to six months' pay. They rejected this offer and demanded bigger gratuities along with employment in the mounted police of Punjab. The salary of the mounted police was higher than that of the irregular cavalry. In addition, the Indian officers demanded promotion. Colonel J. Travers, the officer on the spot, lost his nerve, and urged the government to accept the demands. He warned that otherwise there would be gross indiscipline. The storm of 1857 had just subsided and the government decided not to take any risk. The gratuity was increased to twelve month's pay and all the discharges in the Bengal Cavalry were made voluntary.[130]

These incidents also unnerved the Secretary of State in London. To prevent any probable outbreaks, Charles Wood decided to play safe by ordering that those *Purbiya* regiments, which had remained loyal during 1857–9, should be retained. He reminded the army that when the units were raised, the men had had natural expectations of permanent employment. So, argued Wood, even if total disbandment of some of the units was necessary, in order to avoid large-scale disturbances, as many personnel as possible should be transferred to the other units and the rest should be discharged with bigger gratuities.[131]

Mir Jafir, the late commandant of the 2nd Jezailchee Corps complained in 1860 to General Robert Napier that about a year and a half back, the government had promised him a pension of Rs. 200 per month. However, he was yet to receive any money. Napier immediately sent the petition to Fred Roberts who was looking after the pensioners' claims.[132]

Occasionally the army acted without any direct pressure from below. It assumed that if it did not reward the soldiers then there might be mutinies. This over-reaction on part of the sahibs was probably due to an acute sense of powerlessness. The Indian population ran into millions, while white power was represented by a small force of British soldiers.[133] The British were conscious of the necessity of not alienating the collaborators needed for manning a coercive machinery. To meet the emergency during 1857, the army raised many temporary local levies and also expanded the size of the existing irregular units. After the crisis was over, the army did not have much use for units like the Awadh Police Cavalry and Hodson's Horse. Even though these men, facing discharge, did not pose any direct threat, the army was reluctant to throw them out without any monetary compensation. However, the volume of rewards awarded was linked with the level of loyalty displayed. The army favoured the Punjabis who actively aided in crushing the revolt and discriminated against the men from the Ganga-Jamuna doab who actually engineered the rebellion. Those Indians who joined the British side before November 1857, when imperial victory was uncertain, were given gratuities amounting to six months' pay (to those from Punjab) and three months pay (to the personnel from the Ganga-Jamuna doab) on being discharged. Again, those who joined the British after November 1857 when the rebel cause was hopeless were given gratuities amounting to three month' pay (to the Punjabis) and two months pay (to the Hindustanis), on being discharged.[134]

At times rather than the higher echelons of the military bureaucracy, the men on the spot being in immediate contact with the soldiers were more sensitive to the gravity of the threat posed by the soldiers' demands. In June 1869, the commanding officer of the 3rd Light Cavalry from Saugor wrote to the Quartermaster General of the Madras Army about the necessity of expanding the troopers' lines. The commanding officer insisted:

The authorities here have refused to allow me horse lines, and the horses are picketed between the lines of the men's huts. This I need scarcely remark, is repugnant to the feelings of the Muslim sowars, whose privacy is to a certain extent invaded, for men riding on horseback in the lines can, by going near the enclosures and looking over the bamboo matting which surrounds them, see females, [wives, daughters and sisters of the Muslim Sowars] who according to Muslim customs should be kept in the strictest seclusion.[135]

Whenever the higher authorities attempted to reduce the perquisites of the soldiers, the regional commands obstructed such moves fearing that any reduction in the tangible incentives offered to the sepoy and the sowars might spark off a mutiny. In 1882, when the Commander-in-Chief of India Donald Stewart tried to abolish marching *batta* (allowance for marching within India), the Madras and the Bombay officers obstructed this move.[136]

CONCLUSION

The army supplied a host of incentives to the soldiers to project a benevolent image in order to legitimize its authority over its personnel and to extract sacrifices from them. A disciplinary infrastructure to control the troops was enmeshed with the army's policy of 'caring' for its men. However, the army's control over the soldiers was mainly hegemonic rather than coercive. The imperialists aimed to drive a cleavage among the Indian privates and the officers by supplying the latter with a greater amount of rewards. The welfare scheme gave adequate space to the soldiers for protest by petitions. And the soldiers were conscious of the special position they enjoyed *vis-à-vis* the Indian civilians in the colonial framework. Due to the presence of an extensive bureaucratic machinery, the army, by its quick response to the soldiers' demands, was able to contain the latters' grievances. Thus the army was able to keep its loyalty mechanism intact.

1857 represented not only break but also continuity as far as evolution of the welfare bureaucracy was concerned. The Mutiny was no break for incentives like military *jagirs,* etc. Nevertheless in the pre-1857 period, due to Bentinck's policy of reducing expenditure, the state abolished many privileges like *batta,* etc. But, after 1857, as a reaction to the rebellion, the state became more generous. Privileges were not only reintroduced but also elaborated and systematized. Further, the imperialists learnt from the 1857 experience and became more sensitive to the religious sensibilities of the Indians. Another reason for the implementation of the elaborate welfare network in the second half of nineteenth century was that the army was anxious that the quantum of welfare measures provided were probably inadequate for generating loyalty. As the British were not confident of their position, there was much debate within the army about how best to implement the welfare mechanism. The starting point of this programme was 1859: the immediate aftermath of the Mutiny; and it reached its peak just before 1914 because of the imperial attempt to gear the army up in response to the worsening international scenario.

The colonial army provides us a window to see the colonial state's structure. Since, the army lacked the requisite administrative machinery for distributing supplies, it cooperated with the Raj's civilian bureaucracy, like the Collectors, PWD, etc. The multifarious demands of supplying the soldiers and the necessity of watching their activities transformed the 'Night Watchman State' into an ever expanding bureaucratic state. The colonial state consolidated itself by a balanced synthesis of indigenous elements (like *bazaars,* land grants, etc.) and imported Western techniques (like gratuity, pension etc.). To sum up, colonialism depended on collaboration, and military collaboration was most vital. The welfare mechanism was vital in preventing rebellions among the indigenous military collaborators. Further, welfare measures directed towards the units stationed outside the subcontinent made it possible for the British to use the Sepoy Army as an instrument of power projection throughout Asia.

NOTES

1. Notes on the Indian Army of Bengal; Its Present Material and Organization as compared with the Past, September 1875, p. 6, L/MIL/ 17/2/468, OIOC.

2. William Irvine, *The Army of the Indian Moghuls: Its Organization and Administration*, 1903, reprint, New Delhi: Low Price Publications, 1994, pp. 3–27, 36–44, 296–300.

3. R.K. Saxena, *The Army of the Rajputs: A Study of Eighteenth Century Rajputana*, Udaipur: Saroj Prakashan, 1989, pp. 2, 15, 23.

4. Smith, *A Sketch of the Rise, Progress and Termination*; Herbert Compton, *A Particular Account of the European Military Adventurers of Hindustan from 1784 to1803*, 1892, reprint, Karachi: Oxford University Press, 1976; B.K. Sinha, *The Pindaris: 1798–1818*, Calcutta: Bookland, 1971, pp. 4– 5, 15–16, 184–5; Henry Steinbach, *The Country of the Sikhs*, 1845, reprint, New Delhi: KLM Book House, 1977, pp. 28–9, 72–86; Fauja Singh Bajwa, *Military System of the Sikhs during the Period: 1799–1849*, Delhi: Motilal Banarsidass, 1964.

5. Frank Tallett, *War and Society in Early Modern Europe, 1495–1715*, 1992, reprint, London: Routledge, 1997, p. 80; Martin Blumenson, 'The Development of the Modern Military', *Armed Forces and Society*, vol. 6, no. 4 (1980), pp. 670–82.

6. H.L. Wesseling, 'Colonial Wars: An Introduction', in idem. and J.A. de Moor, ed., *Imperialism and War: Essays on Colonial Wars in Asia and Africa*, Leiden: E.J. Brill, 1989, p. 11.

7. Colin Jones, 'The Welfare of the French Foot Soldiers', *History*, vol. LXV (1980), pp. 193–213; J.A. Lynn, 'The History of Logistics and Supplying War', in idem, ed., *Feeding Mars: Logistics in Western Warfare from the Middle Ages to the Present*, Colorado/Boulder: Westview Press, 1993, pp. 23–4; Lorenzo M. Crowell, 'Logistics in the Madras Army circa 1830', *War & Society*, vol. 10, no. 2 (1992), pp. 1–33; Tan Tai Yong, 'Maintaining the Military Districts: Civil–Military Integration and the District Soldiers' Boards in the Punjab, 1919–30', *MAS*, vol. 28, no. 4 (1994), pp. 833–74. In his monograph, Young devotes one chapter (i.e. chapter 2) explaining the British grant of landed resources to the Sikhs. Tan Tai Yong, *The Garrison State: The Military, Government and Society in Colonial Punjab, 1949–1947*, New Delhi: Sage, 2005, pp. 70–97.

8. For an account of the Sepoy Army's attempt to ensure discipline and combat effectiveness among the personnel by providing food see Kaushik Roy, 'Feeding the Leviathan: Supplying the British–Indian Army, 1859–1913', *JSAHR*, vol. 80, no. 322 (2002), pp. 144–61.

9. A.S. Kanya–Forstner, 'The French Marines and the Conquest of the Western Sudan, 1880–99', and David Killingray, 'Colonial Warfare in West Africa: 1870–1914', in Moor and Wesseling, ed., *Imperialism and*

War: Essays on Colonial Wars in Asia and Africa, Leiden: E.J. Brill, 1989, pp. 138, 140, 146, 154–5.

10. An abridged version of Sections I, II and III have been published in Kaushik Roy, 'Logistics and the Construction of Loyalty: The Welfare Mechanism in the Indian Army, 1859–1913', in P.S. Gupta and Anirudh Deshpande, ed., *The British Raj and Its Indian Armed Forces: 1857–1939*, New Delhi: Oxford University Press, 2002, pp. 98–124.

11. Hartington to the Governor General, no. 25, 30 June 1880, Colonel William Merewether Collection, MSS.EUR.D.625/5, OIOC.

12. Barat, *The Bengal Native Infantry*, pp. 139–40; H.L.O. Garrett, ed., C. Grey, *European Adventurers of Northern India, 1785–1849*, 1929, reprint, Madras: Asian Educational Services, 1993, p. 29; Lieutenant-Colonel Eden Vansittart, *Handbook for the Indian Army: The Gurkhas* (Calcutta: office of Supdt. of Govt. Printing, 1906), p. 44; Major D.M. Probyn, commandant of 1st Sikh Cavalry, to Colonel W. Mayhew, ADG, Calcutta, Progs. no. 594, 14 March 1861, MDP, March 1861; Major General J. Michael, Commanding at Aden, to the ADG of the Bombay Army, Mhow, Progs. no. 143, 6 September 1859, MDP, March 1860, NAI.

13. Clive Dewey, 'Some Consequences of Military Expenditure in British India: The Case of Upper Sind Sagar Doab, 1849–1947', in idem, ed., *Arrested Development in India: The Historical Dimension*, New Delhi: Manohar, 1988, pp. 93–169; Omissi, *Sepoy and the Raj*, pp. 59–61, 67; Fox, *Lions of the Punjab*, pp. 43–4; Rajit K. Mazumder, *The Indian Army and the Making of Punjab*, Delhi: Permanent Black, 2003, pp. 5, 143, 163–4.

14. Colonel E. Green, ADG, to the Secy. to the Govt. of Bombay, MD, Poona, Progs. no. 114, 30 November 1859, MDP, March 1860; Mayhew, ADG, to the Secy. of GoI, Calcutta, Memorandum from Major-General A. Becher, QMG, to the ADG, Calcutta, Progs. nos. 111, 338, 6 August 1861, 31 August 1861, MDP, October 1861.

15. *Supplementary Report*, pp. 4, 16, 19; *Army Committee*, vol. 1–A, *Minority Report*, p. 158.

16. *Copy of Recent Correspondence on the Subject of the Organization of the Indian Army*, London: George Edward Eyre and William Spottiswode, 1877, p. 16, Appendix B, 1698, Merewether Collection, MSS.EUR.D.625/4.

17. Hugh Rose to John Lawrence, Private, 28 April 1864, The Commander-in-Chief to the Viceroy, 1864–67, John Lawrence Collection, MSS.EUR.F.90/59, OIOC.

18. Extract from a letter by Major-General Blake, commanding at Burma, to F. Haines, Rangoon, 20 July 1872, Records of Chief Commands, Notes and Minutes by Napier of Magdala, MSS.EUR.F.114, 5 (2), OIOC.

19. Organization, Indian Army, ADG's office, Simla, 22 September 1873,

Correspondence and Memoranda on the Organization of the Indian Army, Records of Chief Commands, 1865–76, Notes and Minutes by Napier, MSS.EUR.F.114, 5 (3).

20. Appendix E, Abstract of replies from officers commanding regiments of Indian cavalry as to the difficulty of obtaining recruits, Records of Chief Commands, Notes and Minutes by Napier, MSS.EUR.F.114, 5 (3).

21. Barat, *Bengal Native Infantry*, pp. 299, 301.

22. *Supplementary Report*, p. 57; *Peel Committee*, p. 45.

23. Charles Wood to the Governor-General, no. 58, 14 January 1860, Military despatches of the Secretary of State, NAI.

24. Colonel H.W. Norman, to Secy. to the GoI, MD, Calcutta, Progs. no. 36, 6 July 1861, MDP, October 1861.

25. General Frederick Roberts, *Short Report on Important Questions dealt with during the tenure of command of the Army in India: 1885–93*, p. 134, L/NIL/17/5/1613/OIOC.

26. Roberts, *Short Report on Important Questions*, p. 133.

27. Confidential note by the Commander-in-Chief, Simla, 10 June 1893, 1Q/6, George White Collection, MSS.EUR.F.108/24, OIOC.

28. Roll of the men of 13th Punjab Infantry who appeared before the invaliding committee at Meerut, 20 May 1861, Lieutenant T.H. Scott Commanding late 13th Punjab Infantry to the Asst. ADG, Calcutta, Progs. nos. 104, 187, 10 July 1861, 15 July 1861, MDP, October 1861.

29. Timothy Parsons, 'All *askaris* are family men: Sex, Domesticity and Discipline in the King's African Rifles, 1902–64', in David Killingray and David Omissi, eds., *Guardians of Empire: The Armed Forces of the Colonial Powers c. 1700–1964*, Manchester/New York: Manchester University Press, 1999, p. 170.

30. Mason, *A Matter of Honour*, pp. 201–2; Colin Jones, 'The Military Revolution and the Professionalization of the French Army under the *Ancien Regime*', in Clifford J. Rogers, ed., *The Military Revolution Debate: Readings on the Military Transformation of Early Modern Europe*, Colorado/Boulder: Westview Press, 1995, p. 164; K.S. Lal, 'The Striking Power of the Army of the Sultanate', *JIH*, vol. LV, (1977), p. 106; *Supplementary Report*, p. 37; Roll of men of Nagpur Force transferred to the pension establishment, Progs. no. 388, 28 August 1861, MDP, October 1861.

31. Lieutenant H. Collier commanding Ramgarh Cavalry to the ADG, Calcutta, Colonel H.W. Norman, Deputy ADG, to the Secy. to the GoI, MD, Calcutta, Balfour, to the Secy. to the GoI, MD, Calcutta, Captain B.E. Bacon, Asst. Secy. to the GoI, MD, to the ADG, Fort William, Progs. nos. 24–6, 37, 28 June 1861, 30 July 1861, 17 September 1861, 1 October 1861, MDP, October 1861.

32. Capt. R.H. Westropp, commandant Poona Horse to the Asst. ADG, Poona, Colonel W.F. Marriot, Secy. to Bombay Govt. MD, to the Secy.

to the GoI, MD, Report by Lieutenant-Colonel J. Hannyngton, offg. Controller of Military Finance, Fort William, Progs. no. 421, 13 September 1860, 22 October 1860, 28 December 1860, MDP, March 1861.

33. Ravindra Kumar Sharma, 'The Military System of the Mewar (Udaipur) State (*Ca*. 800 to 1947)', *Central Asiatic Journal*, vol. 30 (1986), p. 120; *Supplementary Report*, p. 136; Extract from the proceedings of the GoI in the FD, Progs. no. 313, 20 January 1860, MDP, March 1860.

34. To the Governor-General from C. Wood, London, no. 139, 3 April 1860, Military despatches of the Secretary of State.

35. Barat, *Bengal Native Infantry*, pp. 145–6; Major H.K. Burne, offg. Deputy Secy. to the GoI, MD, to the Deputy ADG, Fort William, Progs. no. 262, 8 March 1860, MDP, March 1860.

36. From Colonel P.S. Lumsden, offg. ADG in India, to Colonel H.K. Burne, Secy. to the GoI, MD, Simla, no. 2837/B, 16 November 1874 in *Copy of Recent Correspondence on the Subject of the Organization of the Indian Army*, C 1698, Merewether Collection.

37. Tony Hayter, 'The Army and the First British Empire, 1714–83', in David Chandler and Ian Beckett, eds., *The Oxford Illustrated History of the British Army*, Oxford: Oxford University Press, 1994, p. 111; John Keegan, *A History of Warfare*, 1993, reprint, New York: Vintage Books, 1994, p. 249; Idem., *The Price of Admiralty: The Evolution of Naval Warfare*, 1988, reprint, New York: Penguin, 1989, p. 70; R.K. Saxena, *Army of the Rajputs: A Study of Eighteenth-century Rajputana*, Udaipur: Saroj Prakashan, 1989, p. 355; *Army Regulations, India: Regulations and Orders for the Army*, vol. 2, Calcutta: Superintendent of Govt. Printing, 1913, p. 115; Circular by Lieutenant-Colonel E.B. Johnson, offg. ADG, ADG's office, Simla, no. 3061, 25 June 1862, ADG's circulars, vol. 2, NAI.

38. Sarkar, *Art of War*, pp. 75–86; Omissi, *Sepoy and the Raj*, p. 50; Minute on the Organization of the Army, Ch. 2, Bengal Army, para 66, 11 October 1875, Norman Minutes, NAI.

39. Captain J.B. Lind commanding Pathan Cavalry, to Major R.C. Lawrence, Military Secy. to the Punjab Govt., Lahore, Progs. no. 180, 13 July 1861, MDP, October 1861.

40. Shakespear, *The Sirmoor Rifles*, p. 99.

41. Sarkar, *Art of War*, p. 191; *Army Regulations*, p. 82; *Peel Committee*, p. 4.

42. Ian Roy, 'Towards the Standing Army, 1660–1702', in Chandler et. al., *History of the British Army*, p. 44; Keegan, *History of Warfare*, p. 270; *Army Regulations*, pp. 67, 70 ; Z.A. Desai and W.E. Begley, ed., *The Shah Jahan Nama of Inayat Khan*, tr. by A.R. Fuller, Delhi: Oxford University Press, 1990, pp. 91–2; To the Governor-General from Wood, London, no. 3, 8 January 1861, Military despatches of the Secretary of State.

43. Shakespear, *Sirmoor Rifles*, p. 104.

44. Keegan, *History of Warfare*, p. XVI.

45. Barat, *Bengal Native Infantry*, p. 146; Wilson, *Historical Records*, p. 66; *Army Regulations*, pp. 69–70; To the Governor-General from Wood, London, no. 50, 24 January 1860, Military despatches of the Secretary of State.

46. Inefficient state of the Indian Army and difficulty in recruiting, Memorandum no. 2, Barrackpur, 25 December 1867, Merewether Collection, MSS.EUR.D.625/3 (b).

47. *Army Regulations*, pp. 89, 267; Extract from the proceedings of the Governor-General of India in the MD, Progs. nos. 412, 614, 18 March 1861, MDP, March 1861; Memo by Colonel E. Haythorne, ADG, ADG's office, Ambala, no. 63/N, 27 March 1865, ADG's circulars, vol. 5.

48. Omissi, *Sepoy and the Raj*, p. 67; *Army Committee*, vol. 1–A, *Minority Report*, p. 159; Circular to officers commanding divisions, districts and infantry regiments, by Haythorne, ADG's office, Simla, no. 97/N, 17 August 1864, ADG's circulars, vol. 4, Minute on the Organization of the Army, Ch. 2, Bengal Army, para 26, 30, 11 October 1875, Norman Minutes; Roberts, *Short Report on Important Questions*, p. 134.

49. To Viscount Cross, Secy. of State for India, Fort William, MD, para 3, no. 59, 27 March 1888, L/MIL/7/14966, OIOC.

50. *Supplementary Report*, pp. 18, 36, 55; Minute on the organization of the army, Ch. 5, Pension system, para 2, 11 October 1875, Norman Minutes.

51. *Army Committee*, vol. 1–A, *Minority Report*, p. 158, vol. 3, pp. 651–2, 904.

52. Richard Holmes, 'Battle: The Experience of Modern Combat', in Charles Townshend, ed., *The Oxford Illustrated History of Modern War*, Oxford/ New York: Oxford University Press, 1997, p. 205; A.G. Macdonell, *Napoleon and His Marshalls*, 1934, reprint, London: Prion, 1996, pp. 131, 149; Jac Weller, *Wellington in India*, London: Longman, 1972, pp. 33–248; M.R. Kantak, *The First Anglo–Maratha War, 1774–83: A Military Study of Major Battles*, Bombay: Popular Prakashan, 1993, pp. 228–31; Hugh Cook, *The Sikh Wars: The British Army in Punjab, 1845– 49*, Delhi: Thomson Press, 1975, pp. 69, 82.

53. Colonel W.B. Thomson, Commissary General, to the Secy. of the GoI, MD, Fort William, Progs. no. 208; 25 February 1861, MDP, March 1861; To the Governor-General from Wood, London, no. 50, 10 February 1860, Military despatches of the Secretary of State.

54. Colonel G.S.T. Lawrence, Agent for the Rajputana States, to the Undersecretary, to the GoI, FD, Progs. no. 315, 29 January 1861, MDP, March 1861.

55. Hannyngton, to the offg. Secy. to the GoI, MD, Becher, to the Secy. of the GoI, MD, Calcutta, Major F.D. Atkinson, to the offg. Controller of Military Finance, Fort William, Progs. nos. 390, 392, 720, 722, 25 January 1861, 21 March 1861, 28 March 1861, MDP, March 1861; Memo by

Napier of Magdala on Sepoys building their own lines, Notes and Minutes by Napier, Commander-in-Chief Bombay, 1866–9, MSS.EUR.F.114 1(C).

56. Tallett, *War and Society*, pp. 141–2; John Childs, 'The Restoration Army, 1660–1702', in Chandler et al., ed., *History of the British Army*, p. 62; Douglas M. Peers, 'Imperial Vice: Sex, Drink and the Health of British Troops in North Indian Cantonments, 1800–58', in Killingray and Omissi, eds., *Guardians of Empire*, p. 31; *Army Regulations*, p. 81; Memorandum by Norman on the distribution of the armies of India, para 10, 26 September 1872, Minute on the Organization of the Army, Ch. 2, Bengal Army, Localization of regiments, para 11, 11 October 1875, Norman Minutes.

57. Alavi, *The Sepoys and the Company*, pp. 95–139; Extract from the proceedings of the Governor-General in the HD, camp Kylwara, Atkinson, to the ADG, Fort William, Progs. nos. 618–19, 4 January 1861, 15 March 1861, MDP, March 1861.

58. *Army Regulations*, pp. 68–70.

59. *History of the 1st Punjab Cavalry*, Lahore: Civil Military Gazette Press, 1887, p. 40; Circular to the officers commanding divisions, districts and brigades, circular by Johnson, ADG's office, Lucknow, no. 568, 27 January 1863, ADG's circulars, vol. 3; To the Governor-General from Wood, London, no. 77, 24 February 1860, Military despatches of the Secretary of State.

60. For the rank structure of the Indian commissioned and non-commissioned officers see Appendix 3.

61. *Army Regulations*, p. 104; *Supplementary Report*, p. 37.

62. Irregular cavalry regiments of the Punjab Frontier Force were called Punjab Irregular Cavalry.

63. *Supplementary Report*, pp. 16–18.

64. Note on the garrison and fortress of Agra, Indian troops, Calcutta, 31 December 1873, Norman Minutes.

65. Hannyngton, to the offg. Secy. to the GoI, MD, Progs. no. 392, 25 January 1861, MDP, March 1861.

66. Wilson, *Historical Records*, p. 66.

67. *1st Punjab Cavalry*, Appendix II–III, pp. IV–V.

68. Tallett, *War and Society*, p. 120; S.N. Sen, *The Military System of the Marathas*, 1928, reprint, Calcutta: K.P. Bagchi, 1979, p. 72; To the Governor-General from Wood, London, no. 58, 14 February 1860, Military despatches of the Secretary of State; From the Secretary of State for India to the MD, Fort William, Progs. no. 215, 11 March 1861, MDP, March 1861.

69. *Army Regulations*, p. 112.

70. Extract from the proceedings of the President of the Council of India, Fort William, 26 November 1860, From the ADG, to the Secy. to the

GoI, MD, Progs. no. 614, 3 January 1861, MDP, March 1861, Circular to officers commanding divisions and districts, service soldiers, memos, by Haythorne, ADG's office, Ambala, nos. 62/N, 63/N, 27 March 1865, ADG's circulars, vol. 5.

71. Roll of men of the Nagpur Force transferred to the pension establishment, Progs. no. 388, 28 August 1861, MDP, October 1861.

72. Minute on the Organization of the Army, Ch. 4, Pension system, para 8, 28, 11 October 1875, Norman minutes.

73. *Copy of Recent Correspondence on the Subject of the Organization of the Indian Army*, Appendix D, 1698, Merewether Collection.

74. *Supplementary Report*, p. 19; To the Governor-General from Wood, London, no. 77, 24 February 1860, Military despatches of the Secretary of State; Scinde Horse, Brigadier Park's Report, Bairseah, Progs. no. 143, 11 October 1859, MDP, March 1860; Memorandum by Brigadier General T. Wright commanding Hyderabad Contingent, Aurangabad, Progs. no. 107, 25 May 1875, L/MIL/7/14966, OIOC.

75. Irvine, *Army of the Indian Moghuls*, pp. 298–9.

76. M. Harrison, 'Medicine and the Management of Modern Warfare', *History of Science*, vol. 30, no. 106 (1996), pp. 379–410.

77. J.A. de Moor, 'Warmakers in the Archipelago: Dutch Expeditions in Nineteenth Century Indonesia', and J.L. Miege, 'The French Conquest of Morocco: The Early Period, 1901–11', in Moor, and Wesseling, ed., *Imperialism and War: Essays in Colonial Wars in Asia and Africa*, 1989, pp. 66, 202.

78. Christon I. Archer, 'Combating the Invisible Enemy: Health and Hospital Care in the Army of New Spain, 1760–1810', in Douglas M. Peers, ed., *Warfare and Empires: Contact and Conflict between European and Non–European Military and Maritime Forces and Cultures*, Aldershot, Hampshire: Variorum, 1997, p. 50.

79. Annual relief of troops at Aden, Minute by Robert Napier, 20 April 1867, Notes and Minutes by Napier, Commander-in-Chief Bombay, 1866–9, MSS.EUR.F.114, 1©.

80. Major G. Casserly, *Life in an Indian Outpost*, London, n.d., p. 23; Abstract return of the 19th Punjab Infantry Regiment, signed Capt. J. Doran, Commandant, Barackpur, Progs. no. 136, 1 December 1859, MDP, March 1860, Commissariat department, office of the Controller of Military Finance, signed Lieutenant-Colonel T. McGown, Controller of Military Finance, Fort Saint George, Progs. no. 329, 7 May 1861, MDP, October 1861.

81. Mark Harrison, 'Disease, Discipline and Dissent: The Indian Army in France and England, 1914–15', in idem., Roger Cooter and Steve Sturdy, ed., *Medicine and Modern Warfare*, Amsterdam–Atlanta, GA: Rodopi, 1999, p. 187; Proceedings of a committee assembled at Allahabad by the order of Brigadier Fordyce to report upon the cantonment of

Allahabad, Progs. no. 14, 10 July 1860, MDP, October 1860; Circular by Johnson, ADG's office, Simla, no. 1125, 15 April 1862, ADG's circulars, vol. 2; Memo by Napier, 18 June 1868, Notes and Minutes by Napier of Magdala, 1866–9.

82. Hannyngton, to the offg. Secy. to the GoI, MD, Memorandum from Capt. H. Hyde, Undersecretary to the GoI, to the offg. Secy. to the GoI, MD, Progs. nos. 392–3, 25 January, MDP, March 1861.

83. *Army Regulations*, p. 81; Lieutenant-Colonel C. Davidson, Resident at Hyderabad, to Major-General R.J.H. Birch, Secy. to the GoI, MD, Governor-General's camp, Mirzapore, Progs. nos. 158, 368, 1 and 14 February 1861, MDP, March 1861; Circular to officers commanding divisions, districts, brigades, stations and cantonments, no. 32/E, 22 February 1865, ADG's circulars, vol. 5.

84. Note on the garrison and fortress of Agra, Calcutta, 31 December 1873, Norman Minutes; Proceedings of a committee assembled by the order of Lieutenant-Colonel Pelly commanding at Aurangabad to report upon the lines of the Hyderabad Cavalry, Proceedings of a committee assembled by order of the officer commanding at Aurangabad to examine and report on the infantry lines of the Hyderabad Contingent, Major B.R. Powell, President of committee on lines at Aurangabad to the staff officer at Aurangabad, Progs. no. 371, 5 December and 6 December 1860, MDP, March 1861.

85. *Report of the Sanitary Commission for Bombay 1864,* Bombay: Education Society's Press, Byculla, 1865, p. 214.

86. Memo by Napier on Sepoys building their own lines, Notes and Minutes by Napier of Magdala, 1866–9.

87. Appendix B, Expenditure, signed by H.W. Norman, 1872, Records of Chief Commands, Notes and Minutes by Napier of Magdala.

88. *Army Regulations*, pp. 83–4.

89. Sen, *The Military system of the Marathas*, p. 134; Inefficient state of the Indian Army, laid before the Duke of Cambridge, Memorandum on the Indian Army by Lieutenant-General Charles Reid, 1 July 1876, Merewether Collection, MSS.EUR.F.D.625/3 (c).

90. Gaylor, *Sons of John Company*, pp. 59, 326; Roberts to the Duke of Cambridge, Ootacamund, 1 August 1884 in General Roberts, *Correspondence with England while Commander–in–Chief in Madras*, p. 202, Part 2, Indian Series, L/MIL/17/5/1615, OIOC.

91. Tallett, *War and Society*, p. 111; Wilson, *Historical Records*, p. 45; Shakespear, *Sirmoor Rifles*, p. 3; Colonel H. Marshall, Acting Secy. to the GoI, MD, to the offg. Secy. to the GoI, MD, Fort Saint George, Progs. no. 41, 3 February 1860, MDP, March 1860.

92. Memo by Napier, Poona, 16 May 1869, Notes and Minutes by Napier of Magdala, 1866–9.

93. Circular by Johnson, ADG's office, Simla, no. 1125, 15 April 1862, ADG's circulars, vol. 2.

94. Inspection report of the Madras Army, 1874–5, Records of Chief Commands, 1865–76, Notes and Minutes by Napier, MSS.EUR.F.114, 5(4).

95. Minute on the Organization of the Indian Army, Ch. 2, Bengal Army, para 36, 43, 11 October 1875, Norman Minutes.

96. Proceedings of a committee assembled at Aurangabad under instruction received from the QMG for the purpose of fixing the site of the lines of Aurangabad station, Progs. no. 370, 24 December 1860, MDP, March 1861.

97. Note on the station of Morar and fortress of Gwalior, Accommodation for the troops, Calcutta, 19 January 1874, Norman Minutes.

98. Barat, *Bengal Native Infantry*, p. 172; *Army Regulations*, p. 83; Memorandum on possible military operations beyond our trans Indus frontier, para 8, Minute on the Organization of the Army, Ch. 2, Bengal Army, para 36, 43, 45, 11 October 1875, Norman Minutes.

99. Major S. Becher, Deputy ADG, to the Secy. to the GoI, MD, Bacon, to the offg. Deputy ADG, Fort William, Progs. nos. 200, 202, 17 October 1860, 9 March 1861, MDP, March 1861.

100. R.H. Davies, Secy. of Punjab Govt. MD, to the Secy. of GoI, Progs. no. 285, 17 December 1860, MDP, March 1861.

101. Memorandum of proposals relative to the Hyderabad Contingent submitted by Brigadier-General T. Wright, para 5–6, Progs. no. 107, May 1876, L/MIL/7/14966.

102. Report on 2nd Battalion 2nd Gurkha Rifles, 13 April 1893, Annual confidential reports on the regiments, L/MIL/7/17008, OIOC.

103. Minute on the Organization of the Army, Ch. 4, Pension system, para 9, 11 October 1875, Norman Minutes.

104. Bengal Army, ADG's office Head quarter, Simla, Major-General P.S. Lumsden, ADG in India, 16 June 1875, Records of Chief Commands, 1865–76, Notes and Minutes by Napier.

105. To Viscount Cross, Secy. of State for India, Fort William, MD, para 3, no. 59, 27 March 1888, L/MIL/7/14966.

106. P.L. Mehra, 'The Panipat Campaign', in Hari Ram Gupta, ed., *Marathas and Panipat*, Chandigarh: Punjab University Press, 1961, pp. 173–243; *Army Regulations*, pp. 43–4; Shakespear, *Sirmoor Rifles*, pp. 102–3; Barat, *Bengal Native Infantry*, p. 141; Atkinson, to the ADG, Fort William, Progs. no. 350, 15 March 1861, MDP March 1861; Minute on the Organization of the Army, Ch. 2, Bengal Army, para 66, 11 October 1875, Norman Minutes.

107. *Army Regulations*, p. 43; Memorandum on the distribution of the army in Bengal, para 13, Muzaffarnagar, 14 March 1863, Norman Minutes.

108. Hartington to the Governor General, no. 25, 30 June 1880, Merewether Collection, MSS.EUR.D.625/5.

109. *Supplementary Report*, p. 30; *Army Committee*, vol. 3, p. 548.

110. Anand A. Yang, *The Limited Raj: Agrarian Relations in Colonial India, Saran District: 1793–1920*, Delhi: Oxford University Press, 1989.

111. Peers, *Mars and Mammon*.

112. Circular by Norman, ADG, ADG's office, Calcutta, no. 2493/A, 25 June 1861, ADG's circulars, vol. 1; A.P. Macdonnell, Secy. to the GoI, HD, to the Chief Secy. to the Bengal Govt., Simla, Progs. no. 7056, 8 July 1887, Proceedings of the Lieutenant-Governor of Bengal, August 1887, Judicial Department, WBSA.

113. Vansittart, *Gurkhas*, pp. 149, 161, 166; Circular by Norman, ADG's office, Calcutta, no. 2493/A, 25 June 1861, ADG's circulars, vol. 1.

114. James Colebrook, *Supplement to the Collection of Regulations* (Calcutta, 1807), Regulations for invalided sepoys, 18 February 1789. (This document is unpaginated).

115. E.M. Spiers, *The Army and Society: 1815–1914,* Harlow/London: Longman, 1980, pp. 60, 62, 66.

116. Thompson, to the offg. Secy. to the GoI, MD, Lieutenant G. Newmarch, Asst. to Chief Engineer, Punjab, to the Military Secy. to the Govt. of Punjab, Lahore Progs. nos. 441, 444, 3 January 1861, 15 February 1861, MDP, March 1861.

117. H. Andrew, Executive Engineer, Dinapur division, to the Superintending Engineer, Bihar Circle, Newmarch, to Major G. Hutchinson, Military Secy. to Govt. of Punjab, Lahore, Thompson, to the offg. Secy. to the GOI, MD, Fort William, 12 January 1861, 25 January 1861, 5 February 1861, Progs. nos. 442–3, MDP, March 1861.

118. Circular by Johnson, ADG's office, Simla, no. 3061, 25 June 1862, ADG's circulars, vol. 2.

119. *Army Regulations*, p. 81; Circular to officers commanding divisions, districts, brigades, stations and cantonments, no. 32/E, 22 February 1865, ADG's circulars, vol. 5; Lieutenant-Colonel R. Phayre, QMG, to the Secy. to the Bombay Govt., MD, From the offg. Deputy QMG, to the QMG, Davidson to Birch, Balfour and Lieutenant-Colonel R.S. Simpson, Military Finance Commissioners, to the Secy. to the GoI, MD, Progs. nos. 362, 368–9, 411, 9 January 1861, 31 January 1861, 1 February 1861, 6 March 1861, MDP, March 1861; Memo by Lieutenant General Napier of Magdala on cholera, 16 May 1869, Notes and Minutes by Napier, MSS.EUR.F.114, 1 ©.

120. David Arnold, *Colonizing the Body: State Medicine and Epidemic Disease in Nineteenth Century India*, Delhi: Oxford University Press, 1993, p. 62; *Army Regulations*, pp. 83, 115; Dr. J. Forsyth, Inspector General, Medical Department, to Birch, MD, Fort William, Progs. no. 147, MDP March 1861; Sanitary Report Maneuvers, Mandalay Brigade, 1911, p. 3, GP62375(591)B927, National Library, Kolkata.

121. From Major W.B. Wilson, offg. Asst. Secy. to the GoI, MD, to the Director General of Military Works, Enclosure no. 21, Annual

confidential inspection reports of the Bengal Army and the Punjab Frontier Force, 1893, L/MIL/7/17008.

122. To the Governor-General, para 12, no. 25, 30 June 1880, Merewether Collection, MSS.EUR.D.625/5.

123. For example: The humble petition of Mir Jafir, late commandant of 2nd Jezailchees and Subedar in Coke's Rifles, to General Robert Napier, MD, Fort William, Progs. nos. 449–50, 14 October 1861, MDP, October 1861.

124. Wilson, *Historical Records*, p. 71.

125. MacMunn, *The Armies of India*, p. 212. A meaningful translation would be 'Sometimes pleasure, Sometimes pain, I am the servant of the English'.

126. Roberts, *Forty-one Years*, pp. 231–44; MacMunn, *The Armies of India*, pp. 82–105; *Supplementary Report*, pp. 97.

127. *Supplementary Report*, pp. 30, 65–6; *Army Regulations*, p. 94; To officers commanding districts, divisions and brigades, by Haythorne, ADG's office, Simla, circular no. 77/N, 23 July 1864, ADG's circulars, vol. 4.

128. Thompson, to the offg. Secy. to the GoI, MD, Fort William, Progs. no. 43, 22 February 1860, MDP, March 1860.

129. Scott, to the Asst. ADG, Calcutta, 10 July 1861, Roll of the 13th Punjab Infantry who appeared before the invaliding committee, Meerut, Progs. no. 103, 20 May 1861, MDP, October 1861.

130. Extract from the proceedings of the GoI, in the FD, Progs. no. 538, 15 March 1861, MDP, March 1861; Circular to officers commanding divisions, districts and regiments of cavalry, by Haythorne, no. 82/N, 19 August 1863, ADG's circulars, vol. 3.

131. To the Governor-General from Wood, London, nos. 59, 98. 14 February 1860, 8 March 1860, Military despatches of the Secretary of State.

132. Mir Jafir, to Napier, Progs. nos. 449–50, MDP, October 1861.

133. Chesney, *Indian Polity*, pp. 206, 208, 211, 216, 223.

134. From the Secy. to the GoI, MD, to the ADG, Fort William, Progs. no. 726, 11 March 1861, MDP, March 1861.

135. Copy of a letter from the officer commanding 3rd Light Cavalry to the QMG, Saugor, no. 157, 1 June 1869, Records of Chief Commands, 1865–76, Notes and Minutes by Napier, MSS.EUR.F.114, 5 (2).

136. Roberts, *Short Report on Important Questions*, p. 133.

FIVE

Construction of Regimental Loyalty

Can we expect men to fight just for tangible and non-tangible rewards? Military philosophers from the dawn of civilization have tried to answer this question. Sun Tzu, the Chinese military theoretician, writing about 2,400 years ago and viewing history 'from above', gives credit to the initiative of the leaders who drove the soldiers towards victory.[1] Xenophon (430–350 BC), the Greek military intellectual, spoke on the mercenary aspects of the soldiers' service. But he acknowledged that tangible incentives by themselves were inadequate for propelling men forward. He hinted at an *esprit de corps*, an abstract identity, which bound men from different communities, who had fought together over a long period.[2] The great Clausewitz focused on raising the combatants' passions and emotions in order to kill the enemy.[3] But, pugnacity had to be properly directed. For this, an organizational machinery was necessary. Early modern Europe had such an organizational structure in the shape of regiments, which were lineal descendants of the Roman legions. The legions, as a framework for structuring armies, survived in the Byzantine Empire and re-emerged in Europe with the reforms of the Nassau brothers. The Spanish *tercio* was the last step in the conversion of the legions into regiments.[4]

Back in India, why did the sepoys and the sowars fight for the British? The officer-soldier relationship, along with the incentive structure constructed by the British, definitely constituted important components of the command structure. Another factor behind the British success in constructing a combat effective loyal army was their ability to incorporate the sepoys into a professional combat organization, through the regimental structure. The regiment was one of the chief determinants of the standing armies which were the products of the 'Military Revolution' in the West.[5] The regimental culture was imported from Europe and replaced the *mansabdari* structure, the basis of pre-colonial forces. Under the *mansabdari* system, the chieftains were granted land for maintaining troops. They, and not the princes, were responsible for recruiting, disciplining and leading the soldiers. This resulted in divided loyalty and frequent desertions. Cohesion was dependent on the heroic leadership of the *mansabdars*. The war bands formed around individual *mansabdars* were replaced by the regimental institution under the Raj.[6] The British were able to construct impersonal bonds of cohesive loyalty with the help of the European regimental structure. However, the colonial scenario modified the process of regimental construction in ways, which can be traced back to the pre-1857 era.

Along with unit pride, Omer Bartov emphasizes the role of ideology in motivating men during war.[7] The post-Mughal polities exploited the religious fervour of the mercenary bands like the Naga *sanyasis* who were deployed as shock troops.[8] However, the East India Company did not utilize the military honour of such *sanyasi* warriors. Since the British could not utilize nationalism in the construction of regimental pride for their Indian armed personnel, they tried to motivate the sepoys of the Bengal Army before 1857 by pampering caste feelings. The British officers paid deference to the rituals for fostering caste pride among the two high castes—the Brahmins and the Rajputs of north India. To please these upper castes, the low castes were not enlisted. By 1852, about 70 per cent of the Bengal Army's personnel were *Purbiyas*. As each regiment was composed of mostly these two castes drawn from more or less the same district, thus constituting a brotherhood, it became impossible to instill discipline. The caste experiment collapsed with the *Purbiya* rebellion in 1857. The British then aimed to generate regimental ethos by constructing racial identities for the various groups who were dubbed 'martial' in late-nineteenth century.[9] *Esprit de race* became the secret of creating battlefield morale.

This chapter attempts to chart the trajectory of the evolution of the regiments in the aftermath of the 1857 Mutiny.[10] The process of regimental construction involved two aspects. Different 'martial' communities were constructed from the diverse groups which entered the Sepoy Army, and their community ethos was then amalgamated with the ethos of the units. In the nineteenth century, the British Empire invented several 'martial' communities like the Scottish Highlanders and the Nigerian warriors by redefining cultural and tribal relations.[11] The Highlanders in scarlet and tartan with bonnet and plaid were, to quote John Prebble 'the first of Britain's colonial levies, called to arms to police their own hills and then to fight in the crown's imperial wars'.[12] Construction of the warrior communities in India was part of the same process. But the different contexts involved region specific modulations. In India the western regimental structure, by soaking up certain indigenous traits, mutated into a hybrid organization.

I

CONSTRUCTION OF MARTIAL IDENTITIES

The British constructed several 'martial' communities from the subcontinent's manpower and their group consciousness probably sustained them. The imperial belief was that the men could be typecast under different racial communities on the basis of their biological origin, as well as their varying social and cultural mores. For Major A.H. Bingley, the Jats and the Sikhs, despite their similar biological origin, constituted separate races because of their religious difference.[13]

This section focuses on the British policy of shaping the identities of the Gurkhas, the Rajputs and the Sikhs, as the share of these groups in the post-1859 army was considerable. Between 1885 and 1912, the percentage of these communities increased significantly. For the Gurkhas, the increase was from 5 per cent to 11.5 per cent; for the Rajputs, from 6.7 per cent to 7.7 per cent; and for the Sikhs, from 13.5 per cent to 22.5 per cent. In absolute numbers, the increase was greatest for the Sikhs. From 17,774 their number rose to 32,702 men, while the Rajputs rose from 8,291 to 12,051, and the Gurkhas from 6,684 to 18,100. The size of the Sepoy Army at that period fluctuated between 130,000 and 158,000 men.[14]

Certain historical factors were conducive for manufacturing a separate identity for the various tribes of Nepal. There was much tension between the Nepalis and the Hindus of north India. The Nepalis looked down upon the Hindus of the Gangetic plains because the Muslims had conquered the latter in the medieval era. There were also linguistic differences between these two groups. All these distinctions were further exacerbated by the difference in the religious practice of those Nepalis who had accepted Hinduism. The *Thakurs* (high castes) among the Nepalis did not accept the *janeo*, which was the primary symbol of Hinduism in the plains. Nor did the *Thakurs* accept the strict food habits of the high caste Hindustanis. Since, the Nepali Hindus rejected many of the caste principles of the orthodox Hindus, the north-Indian Hindus conceived the former as 'unconverted barbarians' and called them *Pahariyas*. This was an abusive term meaning outcaste highlanders. In return, the Nepalis termed the Hindustanis as inferior *Madhesias* (inferior men from the plains).[15] All these distinctions not only created a distinct sense of identity among the recruits from Nepal, but also fitted into the imperial game of 'divide and rule'. The imperial belief was that the physiognomy of the Nepali tribes was distinct from that of the Hindustanis. For the British, this was one of the principal reasons for ascribing a separate identity to the Nepalis. The imperial ethnographers claimed that the aboriginal tribes of Nepal were of Tibeto-Mongolian stock.[16]

The British took the term Gurkha from a district north-east of the Gandak basin in Nepal. The Magars, Gurungs, Khas and the Thakur tribes inhabited this locality. A dynasty called Gorkha ruled over the region from the eighteenth century. For several reasons, the British mainly used the inhabitants of the Gorkha district to forge the Gurkha community. Under the Gorkha dynasty, the people of this region conquered Nepal. The Raj's officials believed that martial prowess was hereditary.[17] The Khas, the Magars and the Gurungs constituted the Gorkha or Nepali Army. By enlisting these tribes, the Raj wanted to utilize an existing military tradition to build a warrior community. In the local society of the Khas, military service was regarded as honourable. Those Khas who ran away from battle became outcastes in their own society and their wives refused to accept them. However, the British favoured the Magars and the Gurungs (who constituted the rank and file of the Nepali Army), more than the Khas. This was because the latter dominated the officer corps of the Nepali Army and the Raj could not offer high officer ranks to the South Asians. Probably, the British also conceived the Khas as too skilled, and hence dangerous, to be inducted into the Sepoy Army in large numbers. The Magars, Gurungs and the Limbus were also eager to join the Sepoy Army because they had lost their ancestral lands to the high castes in Nepal. The pay and pension derived from the imperial military service enabled them to buy back their family land and acquire social prestige.[18] Though clans like the Limbus and the Rais were not inhabitants of the Gorkha district, they were also given the Gurkha identity. Limbus were recruited by the British because, being hunters, they were skilled marksmen. Their familiarity with the hilly jungles made them excellent light infantry skirmishers who could be used for high-altitude warfare both in north-east and north-west India.[19]

The British never included any tribes from west Nepal, as enlisting them would run counter to the programme of establishing a Gurkha identity distinct from the Hindustanis. This was because the customs and traditions of the Ganga Valley Hindus were very similar to the tribes of west Nepal, on account of the continuous immigration of the Brahmins and the Rajputs into that region from the twelfth century onwards.[20]

The British used certain techniques to transform the various Nepali tribes into a homogeneous Gurkha community. But they had to be cautious, because the Kathmandu government was also at the same time constructing the Nepali Army from the same tribes. The Nepali *sardars* with the aid of the *Purbiya* deserters from the Bengal Army eagerly followed the British practice of drilling the recruits in order to transform them into infantry on the Western model. In 1814, the Nepali Army had 12,000 men organized in regiments. When Nepal fought Tibet in 1864, each of the Nepali regiments deployed 650 men.[21]

The British policy of structuring the Gurkha community was geared to prevent an amalgamation of identities between the Nepali Army's soldiers and the Gurkhas of the Sepoy Army. The Sepoy Army, unlike the Nepali Army, never went for mono-tribal units but mixed the various tribes to create a supra-tribal identity: the Gurkha community. Kathmandu's military establishment used tribal identities while organizing their regiments. The Bhairanath Regiment of the Nepal Army was composed of the

Limbu tribe of eastern Nepal, whereas the Sepoy Army never had any Limbu regiment. The Limbus and the Rais were mixed together in 1890 within the 1st Battalion of the 10th Gurkha Rifles in an attempt to integrate these two groups within the Gurkha identity. Till 1877, the 6th, 7th and 8th Gurkha Rifles accepted the Limbus and the Rais. But, the dominant majority in these units were the Magars and the Gurungs. The Nepali Army also had Gurung regiments. The Gurung tribe was divided into Charjat and Solahjat clans. For using clan identities to build up primary group loyalties, the Kali Bahadur Regiment of the Nepali Army enlisted only the Charjat Gurungs. None of the Indian regiments was composed only of the Charjat clan of the Gurung tribe.[22]

Much has been written about the *kukri* being the traditional weapon of the Gurkhas. The Nepali soldiers also used *kukris*. It was the distinct uniform evolved by the Raj, rather than the *kukri*, which played an important role in establishing the distinct Gurkha ethos. In the 1790s, the Nepali military introduced Western dress for their personnel. They wore red jackets with white facings and white cross belts. The elite units wore blue cotton tunics and *pyjamas* of the same colour. Their headdress was a skullcap, with thick, tightly rolled coils adorned with brass wires. The Gurkhas of the Sepoy Army wore rifle green shirts, and trousers with Kilmarnock caps. The British introduced Western dress among the Gurkhas slowly and steadily, as rapid and forcible introduction could have prompted a reaction. When the 2nd Gurkha Rifles was raised between 1815 and 1818 from the prisoners of war from the Anglo-Nepal conflict (1814–15) and the disbanded Nepali soldiers, they preferred their mountaineers' dress, their own shoes and traditional headgear, rather than *pugris* or European dress.[23]

The British deliberately gave their Gurkha regiments titles and numerical designations which were different from the Nepali Army units. The latter had names of Hindu gods like 'Ram Dull', 'Gorucknuth', etc. The British numbered their Gurkha regiments from one to ten depending on their year of raising. All these units had subsidiary titles, which bore a connection with the places where the units were originally raised. The 1st Gurkha Rifles was raised at Malaun fortress in 1815. So its subsidiary name was the Malaun Regiment. The 2nd Gurkha Rifles was raised later in the same year at Nahan in Sirmoor. So, its subsidiary title was the Sirmoor Rifles.[24]

The British modified religion while constructing both the Gurkha and the Rajput 'martial' races. The 'Gurkha' community, an amalgam of six tribes, had no uniform religion. The Swedish Army of the seventeenth century encouraged Lutheranism among the personnel of the regiments to make the units coherent entities.[25] Religion, the British perceived, was an essential aspect of community feeling that enhanced collective ethos. The Khas were strict Hindus, while the Magars and the Gurungs were lax in their practice of Hinduism, and the Limbus were Buddhists. The British, in their attempt to encourage homogeneity over this heterogeneous group, encouraged them to practise a single religion—Hinduism. Indigenous social dynamics also influenced British policy regarding identity formation. The British decided to Hinduize the Gurkhas instead of encouraging Buddhism, because Nepali society itself was moving towards Hinduism. The Kathmandu government regime imposed the caste hierarchy on society to strengthen the position of the high-caste ruling elite (the Brahmans and the Chetris) over the tribes. The distinction between the high castes and the low castes became very rigid, and the Brahmins enjoyed several privileges in Nepali society. The penal code was based on Hindu scriptures. For instance, in Nepal killing a cow was punishable by death.[26] Seema Alavi writes that Prithvi Narayan, the king of the Gorkhas who conquered Nepal, used the Hinduism of north India to provide *Kshatriya* identity to his tribal soldiers.[27] Hence, the British created 'Hill Hinduism' for the Gurkhas to give them a separate ethos from the Hindus of north India and the soldiers of Nepali Army.

The Raj invented Gurkha Hinduism for the Gurkhas by negating certain caste rules, which hampered the army's operational capacity, and by appropriating and modifying certain tribal customs. Occasionally, the British modified the religious customs of the Nepali tribes to suit their project of popularizing Hinduism among them. When the Gurungs of the regiments got married under British patronage, instead of the *Lamas*, the Brahmins were called to preside over the marriage ceremonies.[28] This was a case of the imperialists interfering in the personal lives of their armed personnel.

If the religious superstition of the Gurkhas fell within the ambit of Hinduism, then the Sepoy Army went out of its way, by bending its service rules, to promote such customs. The Nepali Hindus worshipped Hindu deities like Deorali, etc., and this trend was encouraged. Epidemics were believed to be angry visitations by the goddesses. When in March 1899, a Gurkha woman died of cholera in the Gurkha recruiting depot at Gorakhpur, all the Gurkha soldiers contributed to a fund from which goats and fowl were purchased and then sacrificed to pacify the deities. To please the soldiers, even the British officers contributed financially, and then participated in the rituals of the sacrifice.[29] Imperial participation in indigenous customs was part of the British programme of constructing a special identity for their favoured 'martial' group.

The regimental officers were ordered that Hindu festivals like *Dussehra* should be organized in the camp, or in the field if the unit was on the march. All the personnel contributed towards purchasing animals that were to be sacrificed. The festival was transformed by the army into a symbolic spectacular event, which was incorporated into the collective memory. Spectators were invited to see how quickly the Gurkhas could sever the heads of the sacrificial buffaloes. In addition to the aim of encouraging Hinduism, the British emphasized such ceremonies probably because they believed that such 'martial' rituals would activate the warrior instinct among the soldiers. Before the introduction of Shamanistic Buddhism from Tibet and Hinduism from north India, the tribes of Nepal were animal worshippers. Sacrificing buffaloes was an essential feature of their animistic religion. The British, in evolving Gurkha Hinduism, absorbed this strand.[30]

The army not only absorbed elements of traditional religion but also added new elements to suit imperial demands. To ensure the split between Nepali Hindus of the Gurkha regiments and the north Indian Hindus, the army invented a distinct tradition of Durga *puja*. In the Gurkha units' Durga *pujas*, the Brahmins sowed barley at the place of worship, rather than having clay images of Goddess Durga made, as in Bengal. To build a religious tradition separate from north-Indian Hinduism, every Gurkha regiment had a shrine of the goddess Deorali, which the whole battalion if not deployed for war away from the depot, visited during the *Dussehra* festival. The Sepoy Army used Hinduism to raise the morale of the troops. During Durga *puja*, the Gurkhas asked for protection for themselves, and blessings, for their weapons and regimental colours, from the warrior goddess Durga.[31]

Unlike the Gurkhas, for the north-Indian Hindus, caste rituals were vital and these had adverse effect on matters military. The high castes took many baths and their elaborate rituals meant that four hours a day were required for cooking, bathing and eating. H.G.W. Smith declared in 1859 that, if the *Purbiyas* were cooking, and an order for duty came or if somebody's shadow fell over their earthen oven, they threw away their victuals and would not cook again that day. He asserted that such caste taboos reduced the army's fighting power. During the First Sikh War (1845–6) his three *Purbiya* regiments lost their baggage, which contained their cooking pots and their vessels for drinking water. Though provisions were readily available and they were hungry, they refused to cook using the utensils belonging to others. Hungry soldiers fought badly and this probably explains the *Purbiyas'* inefficient performance against the *Khalsa* Army. Viscount Melville claimed that, when ordered to dig trenches, the *Purbiyas* protested saying that they were not coolies. Such menial tasks would have undermined their caste pride.[32]

The British-tailored Gurkha Hinduism encouraged its followers to throw to the winds the upper-caste north Indian concept of Hindu ritual purity. This, besides giving the Raj's Nepali mercenaries a distinct tradition, also aided British military deployments. The Gurkhas joked at the *Purbiyas'* custom of taking a bath before eating. Unlike the *Purbiyas*, on active service the Gurkhas finished their meals in half an hour. Also the Gurkhas, unlike the high castes, did not find carrying provisions on their back degrading. Further, the Gurkhas did not consider foreign service polluting. In crossing the *Kalapani*, they saw only the prospects of glory and spoils.[33]

The high-caste taboo against taking food together created a logistical burden, as every caste had to carry their own cooking utensils for preparing their food separately. The Brahmin soldiers ate alone. But, eating and drinking in a common mess was necessary to generate a sense of oneness. Socializing together produced intense personal bonding among the soldiers, which in turn strengthened group spirit. And this was necessary for creating the 'will to fight'. The army, in order to create strong primary bonds among the men, tried to encourage common messing among all the soldiers.[34] About the success of the messing system, Frederick Roberts in 1884 wrote to Robert Napier: 'Messes for recruits have been established in every regiment, and are gradually becoming popular. Bachelor sepoys have asked to be allowed to join them.'[35] The mess system was not accepted without any demur. In 1893, the Rajputs of the 8th Madras Infantry Regiment refused to attend the regimental mess because men of low and middle castes also ate their food there. The Commander-in-Chief of the Madras Army ordered the commanding officer that no personnel should be excused from attending the mess. The regimental commandant took care of the caste sensibilities of the Rajput sepoys and established a separate mess for them.[36] Initially the Gurkhas, like the high castes, ate in small groups varying from three to twelve men. The soldiers were encouraged to eat game acquired by hunting together. The various Gurkha clans were unwilling to eat rice in a mess. Hence, a custom was introduced that allowed rice cooked in *ghee* to be eaten together by all the clans.[37]

Just as in the case of the Gurkhas, the British also encouraged Hinduism among the Rajputs. The practice of Hinduism among many Rajput clans was ambiguous before the British intervened. In order to establish religious homogeneity within the Rajputs, the British suppressed other forms of worship, like serpent worship, which was originally a Scythian practice. The tribal totem of the Bais Rajput clan of Farrukhabad was the cobra. But when they joined the army, serpent worship was disallowed.[38]

The territorial identification of the Rajput clans settled along the Ganga-Jamuna rivers with Hindustan, and those Rajput clans west of the river Chambal with Rajputana, enabled the British to divide the Rajput community, despite all of them being Hindus, into eastern Rajputs (north-Indian Rajputs) and western Rajputs (Rajasthani Rajputs). This was somewhat similar to the nineteenth century Chinese government's plan of dividing the Muslims into various groups according to their territorial locations. Social and cultural factors further helped the British to create divisions within the Rajputs. The western Rajputs had fewer caste prejudices as regards eating and drinking. In the second-half of the nineteenth century, the British favoured the western Rajputs against the eastern Rajputs for several reasons. The former enjoyed a higher status in India, so the British, like the Mughals, tried to harness the greater Rajput tradition by attempting to enlist the Rajputana Rajputs. Further, the disloyalty of a big chunk of the north-Indian Rajputs during 1857 pushed the British towards the western Rajputs. But, this shift was not total, as clans of Hindustani Rajputs, like the Pundirs of Saharanpur who remained loyal during 1857, were enlisted. [39]

The army took pains to provide martial reputations for the various sub-units (clans) which constituted the 'martial' groups, probably in the hope that this would enhance the troops' combat morale. The British constructed the military tradition of the Bhaduriya Rajput clan of Kanpur who provided soldiers by claiming that they fought well under the Mughals. The army also tried to ascribe a martial tradition to the community as a whole. The Rajputs were assumed to be pre-colonial India's sword arm. The Rajputs were encouraged to believe that they were the true *Kshatriyas*. The Raj encouraged the traditional Indian ethos of *Kshatra-dharma* which emphasized personal loyalty, chivalry and aggressiveness in the battlefield. Occasionally a communal tinge was added as part of the 'divide and rule' policy, to prevent an amalgam of the martial tradition of all the 'martial' groups. The Rajputs were made to believe that, even in the hour of desperation, they fought bravely against the Muslim invaders of north India. [40] Between 1885 and 1912, the size of the Muslim contingent in the Sepoy Army rose from 50,000 to 55,000. [41] The Raj was apprehensive about the large number of Muslims in the force, and about their loyalty. [42] So, any Rajput-Muslim tension was favoured by the British.

The British also encouraged distinct war cries for different groups. Besides creating separate traditions, the battle cries gave the soldiers martial ardour in the high-risk encounter zones. The Sikhs shouted *Fateh* or *Wa Guru* and the Punjabi Muslims cried *Allah, Allah*. Unlike these religious war cries, the Gurkha and the Pathan battle cries were secular. Instead of drawing inspiration from the religious faith, the Gurkha war cry emphasized on 'Gurkha' greatness. The Gurkhas shouted *Maro Sangin, Gorkhali Ki Jai*. The Pathan battle cry was *Bal, Bal, Bal*. [43]

However, imperial inputs did not completely shape the identity of the 'martial' communities. [44] Local tradition also modulated the imperial-sponsored identity formation process. Occasionally the imperial attempt to include newer groups in a community suffered checks due to the customs of traditional society. The British attempt to include the Damais and the Sarkis in the Gurkha brotherhood faltered due to opposition from the Magars and the Gurungs. They considered the first two groups as 'menial'. So, the Damais were enlisted as buglers and the Sarkis as armourers, and not as soldiers in the Gurkha regiments.[45]

In order to construct a martial culture, the British could not enlist clans with low status. Civilian socialization of the personnel was vital in generating positive group dynamics. Stanford W. Gregory argues that a soldier's fighting qualities depend on how civil society perceives him.[46] The Magar tribes had many clans. The Paria clan was never enlisted as they were regarded as outcastes within the Magars. The Rana clan was favoured because a family, which had lost three generations of ancestors in warfare, got the title of 'Rana'.[47]

The imperial identity-formation scheme had a massive impact on indigenous society. The army strengthened Sikhism among the Sikh recruits, not only to give them a separate religious identity, but also because the imperial belief was that Sikhism, being a 'martial' religion, imparted a martial ethos to those Jats who embraced Sikhism. W.L. McGregor, a British officer, representing the pre-1857 army's views claimed that Sikhism demanded that its followers should never renounce their weapons before death.[48]

Major G.F. MacMunn voiced the post-Mutiny army's view when in 1911 he wrote:

Sikhism is an austere faith, demanding some simplicity and rigour of life from its adherents. So much is this so, that for many years there has been a tendency for young men to avoid the *pahul* and grow up as ordinary Hindus, for whom life has few irksome restrictions. But as the value of the Sikh as the simple, faithful soldier, has lain in his adherence to the simple tenets and hardy life of his forebears, no non-baptized Sikh is admitted into a regiment of the Indian Army. So careful are regiments in this matter, and so much are regiments the home of the old martial and simple Sikh principles, that it has been said, not without some shadow of truth, that it is the British officer who has kept Sikhism up to its old standard.[49]

The British preference for the Jat Sikhs encouraged many Hindu Jats to accept Sikhism. In 1891, there were 250,000 male Sikhs in Patiala. Despite heavy enlistment in the army, their numbers rose to 323,000 in 1900.[50] Many Hindu Jats of Hoshiarpur district accepted Sikhism for enlistment.[51] Uniforms were another technique to create distinctive religious identities for different groups. The *pugri* was designed for the Punjabis by British officers. This headgear became so common that even now the Sikhs identify the *pugri* as a crucial element of their religious identity. Thus, the modern Sikh identity was partly the creation of the alien colonial state.[52]

The imperial attempt to differentiate various communities had certain aspects which the Indians exploited for their own gains. After 1859, the British perceived the Brahmins of north India as disloyal. So the army did not enlist them in significant numbers, but recruited the Rajputs. The officers differentiated the Rajputs from the Brahmins by means of the sacred threads which they wore around their shoulders. The Rajputs' threads were shorter and had knots. Those Brahmins eager to enter the military service for economic or social reasons bluffed their way into the army by imitating the Rajput sacred thread.[53] The Jats were considered by the British as hardy yeomen farmers and perceived as possessing endurance, an essential component of soldiering. However, the low castes like Chakers and Daroghas in Rajasthan joined the army by assuring the British recruiting officers that they were Jats.[54]

II

CONSTRUCTION OF REGIMENTAL TRADITIONS

I see. You really have no Indian Army with *esprit de corps* as such. You have a large number of small armies—some very small—all jealous of one another, and each probably thinking itself superior to the rest.

Field Marshal Kitchener[55]

Once community consciousness was created, it was fused with the regimental fabric. The Sepoy Army was a collection of regiments. And each community provided a group of regiments.

By 1911, the Gurkhas supplied ten regiments. Each Gurkha regiment had two battalions of 912 men each.[56] Primary group solidarity among the soldiers encouraged them to fight. This group cohesion increased among the personnel of a unit if they were made to believe that they were distinct from society, and from other units of the army.[57] From the 1850s, writes John Keegan, the British regiments generated distinct identities by buying silver and furniture, commissioning portraits and histories, etc. Douglas Porch while analysing the French Foreign Legion writes that regimental tradition was an important element in fostering unit cohesion and especially in projecting a positive image of the Legion as an elite fighting force.[58] All the Gurkha units were encouraged to possess a distinct Gurkha identity vis-à-vis the other groups. The Raj tried to generate this feeling among the troops by providing the units of particular communities with separate identities. The imperialists also attempted to create through several organizational techniques, a distinct identity for each unit. The institutional mechanism was also geared to establish traditions for both the class company regiments and the general mixed regiments.

Every regiment was given its own home (depot) to foster distinct custom. Each Gurkha battalion had a separate depot. The 1st and 2nd battalions of the 2nd Gurkha Rifles had depots at Dharamsala in the Kangra Valley of Punjab, and Dehradun.[59] The regimental depots were situated at the centre of each regiment's recruiting base. The depot of the 14th Madras Infantry Regiment was Bangalore, because this unit enlisted the Tamils and Deccani Muslims from Karnataka, Tanjore, Madras and Mysore.[60] The recruiting parties went out from the regimental depots and returned there with the newly enlisted men. The recruits were stationed and trained there, before joining the units which were on active service. The reservists of the regiments were trained at each unit's depot. The regimental centre of the 20th Punjabi Infantry Regiment was Lahore. Even though this unit's Pathans were enlisted from the Indus frontier, for fostering unit spirit, they were brought all the way to the depot at Lahore for training. The reservists were then distributed in the various companies according to their communities. Senior military commanders inspected the units on parades at the depot parade grounds, and occasionally distributed medals for gallantry.

Further, the annual examination of the Indian officers of the regiments, and the musketry instruction classes, were held at each regiment's depot.[61]

For building up unit spirit, even non-Western forces like the Burmese, used flags and standards. In November 1885 during the Third Burma War, after being driven from the Thitkokkuin village by the British column under Captain F.D. Raikes, the Burmese militia left three standards behind. Each standard had the picture of a dragon.[62] For the British, the standard (in the case of the cavalry) or the colours (in the case of infantry) were an essential part of the regiment. In the West, the tradition of using standards to provide regiments with a continuous and coherent identity dated back to Rome. Marius provided each regiment with a standard, and Emperor Julius gave a particular number to each legion, which was inscribed on its standards, to distinguish the legions from each other. In the mid-eighteenth century, Marshal Saxe re-introduced these techniques for creating distinct identities among the different French regiments.[63]

Following this tradition, the British gave each regiment a standard or colours. In 1788, the Madras Light Cavalry Regiment was first issued with a standard. The British tried to design the regimental flags of the Sepoy Army units in conformity with the military customs of the metropole. In 1801, Fort Saint George was ordered to transmit to the Adjutant General's office an indent for a set of colours for the respective units, which would be made in imitation to the flag of the United Kingdom. The colours were generally kept in the regimental headquarters, but during battle the colours were carried into actions by special officers—the Colour-Havildars—to provide moral encouragement to the men. The colours were presented to the units in formal public ceremonies so that the 'great' events were engrained in everybody's mind. Each regiment received its colours under a general salute and guns were fired in celebration of the event.[64] This public spectacle aided in the production of a unit tradition. Occasionally, senior political elite participated in such 'dramas', to provide added grandeur. On 28 October 1899, the commandant of the 44th Merwara Regiment announced to the men that the Viceroy would present the new colours to the unit. The soldiers were made to understand that this was indeed a rare honour for them, as the Viceroy rarely performed such a duty.

On 1 November 1899, the regiment staged a parade held for the presentation of new colours by the Viceroy. The colours, which functioned as the regimental flag after the presentation on 1 November were, in the Viceroy's words, to be the guarantee of orderly conduct and good discipline of the unit, and the symbol of loyalty and allegiance. He told the men to regard the colours as a gift from the Queen, which must be guarded properly. The regiment as a whole swore loyalty to the colours and assured the Viceroy that the loyalty, which they had displayed for the last seventy years, would continue and that no stain would be allowed on the regiment's reputation.[65]

The belief was inculcated among the soldiers that to lose their colours was worse than death. When the colours wore out, they were replaced at the government's expense. The imperial technique for constructing regimental ethos by awarding colours had both pros and cons. In the late nineteenth century colours proved to be an Achilles heel for the regiments in the battlefield. Due to rise in firepower, the troops needed to be scattered in the battlefields, instead of being concentrated around the colours which were meant to provide the rallying points. Colours, in this case, became an obstacle as they attracted enemy firepower.[66]

Different regiments were allowed and encouraged to possess different types of uniforms (facings, laces, *pugris*, badges, mottos and cuffs) for making each unit a distinct entity. The army assumed that these external markers functioned as symbols of distinction, and so created a separate unit ethos and heightened each unit's prestige. Uniforms which were worn by famous units, asserts John Keegan, instantly turned the recruits of those regiments into battle-hardened warriors.[67] In the post-1859 era, the 1st Bengal Cavalry had yellow uniforms, black facings, gold lace and badges inscribed with the words 'Bharatpore' and 'Kandahar 1842', commemorating the successful battles in which this unit had participated. The 1st Punjab Cavalry's dress was different. It was dark blue with blue and scarlet *pugris*. Delhi and Lucknow were inscribed on their badges, to remind the unit's personnel of their loyal behaviour during the stormy days of 1857-8.[68]

Details of uniforms were a technique, not only to differentiate various regiments, but also to introduce distinctions between the units of different communities. The British drove a wedge between the Gurkhas and the Punjabis, by giving the former the circular pill-box type caps known as Kilmarnock forage caps, instead of the *pugris* worn by the latter group.[69]

The symbolic markers of status were awarded to a loyal and brave unit for establishing its special position within the military hierarchy. Providing elite status to a unit, claims an American sociologist Anne Hoiberg, raised its members' sense of importance and self-esteem, which in turn enhanced the military staying power of the regiment. The 2nd Gurkha Regiment was given a special identity, by putting it at par with an elite white unit, because the Gurkha Regiment had remained loyal during 1857 and fought well with the 60th Rifles against the rebels in Delhi. For its extraordinary comradeship with the 60th Rifles at the Delhi Ridge, the dress of the 2nd Gurkhas was made similar to that of the crack white unit. So all the Gurkha soldiers of that regiment wore the distinctive scarlet facings of the 60th Rifles. In 1858, the 2nd Gurkhas was given the prestigious title of the 'Rifles'. Hitherto only famous British Infantry regiments, and no Indian units, had been designated Rifles. Each member of the 2nd Gurkhas was designated a rifleman instead of a sepoy.[70]

In 1891, all the Gurkha regiments in the Sepoy Army were given the prestigious title of Rifles to distinguish them from regiments formed of other communities. Each Gurkha regiment maintained its own distinct identity, which also kept alive competition among them. The 2nd Gurkha Rifles' 2nd Battalion, unlike other Gurkha battalions, wore white helmets. Every soldier was ordered to wear the regimental badge, to inculcate the feeling that he was a member of a particular family. The badges of the Gurkha units had *Kukris* painted on them, which strengthened the Gurkha community's identity. But, the numerals painted between the *Kukris* varied, as they represented the regimental number of the particular units. For example the 7th Gurkha Regiment's badges had the numeral 7 between the *Kukris*.[71]

Though the regimental badge was a European concept, the imperialists accommodated indigenous elements like the *Kukris* within it. A similar mixture of the Oriental and the Occidental traditions was evident in the case of the evolution of the soldiers' dress. Initially the British tried complete Europeanize the uniform of the Indian troops, but the Vellore Mutiny forced them to go slow. In May 1806, the 2nd Battalion of the 4th Madras Infantry Regiment declined to use cockades and stocks of leather. The Indian personnel complained that the leather was made from hogs and cows. Both the Hindu and the Muslim soldiers considered it as an affront to their religion. After the suppression of the Vellore Mutiny, the Westernization of uniforms slowed down, but did not stop. Till 1812, the personnel of the 14th Madras Infantry Regiment were allowed to use slippers, then had to change to boots. Similarly, in 1787 the 9th Bombay Infantry Regiment's men were asked to wear pantaloons instead of drawers.[72]

As a reaction to 1857, the British became more sensitive to the feelings of their brown soldiers. By 1864, the metal helmets with leather chin straps which the Hindus considered unclean were replaced by the *pugris*. The aim was to create consciousness among the soldiers that the regimental dress was not a totally alien construction. The amalgamation of the Eastern and the Western elements in uniforms was evident in the case of 28th Bombay Infantry Regiment. By 1880, the men wore socks, boots and Khaki coats, along with *pugris* and pyjamas. The uniforms, while representing regimental uniqueness, also took into account the men's cultural sensibilities and climate. In the hot climate of India, loose pyjamas were more comfortable than tight trousers. Occasionally a contradiction developed between cultural and professional requirements. When, in November 1880, the 28th Bombay Infantry Regiment was ordered to serve in Afghanistan, the men were asked to wear tunics, great coats and trousers, though they preferred pyjamas and *dhotis*. In the case of the 4th Battalion of 9th Jat Regiment, Eastern traditions dominated over Western elements in the uniforms. The men used dark blue turbans, cummerbands, serge pyjamas and red serge blouses, but black leather ankle boots. On one hand, uniforms re-presented regimental collectiveness because all the personnel of the unit wore more or less similar dress. But, symbolic distinctions in the details of the uniform of the same unit reflected hierarchy. The Indian officers of this unit, unlike the privates, used brown leather gloves and their cummerbands had golden lines within dark blue.[73]

Regimental identities were also strengthened with the help of inter-unit games like the three-mile cross country races, football tournaments, firing competitions, etc. The officers organized such games even in the British Army. The soldiers participated in them as representatives of particular units and tried their best to keep up their regimental status. All these sports, besides keeping the troops occupied, also kept them physically fit. Sporting competitions to encourage competitive spirit, and hence better performance, were held even in the post-1945 Western armies like the Soviet Army. Rifle shooting competitions in the Sepoy Army, apart from forging a regimental ethos, also raised the units' combat potential by upgrading individual marksmanship of the participants, a necessary skill required for fighting in the mountains of the North-West Frontier. In the Quetta District Rifle Competition, the participants had to shoot over ranges of 800 yards and 500 yards. The first prize was Rs. 15, descending from there to Rs. 8, 5, 4, 3, 2, and Re. 1 which was given as the last prize. In 1890, at the rifle shooting test organized by the Bengal Punjab Rifle Association at Meerut, the 5th prize was won by the soldier from the 2nd Gurkha Regiment.[74] In 1900, twenty-six regiments (Gurkhas, Madrassi, Garhwali, Sikh and Pathan, etc.) participated in the annual musketry competition. Representatives from each regiment were to shoot at targets set at a distance of 200, 600 and 800 yards. The 2nd Battalion of the 2nd Gurkha Rifles won the Silver Cup. The Magdala Gold Medal went to the best shot, Lance Havildar Man Singh Bohra of the 2nd Battalion of the 2nd Gurkha Rifles. To ensure seriousness of such competitions, the Commander-in-Chief himself distributed the prizes.[75]

The company was both an administrative and a tactical unit. In the 'small' colonial campaigns, not the regiments as a whole, but the various companies had to fight separate scattered actions. One example was at Burma on 17 November 1885, where Colonel Simpson and Major Hill, operating under Major-General Harry Prendergast, captured the Minhala masonry redoubt with a company of the 12th Madras Infantry Regiment and a company of the 11th Bengal Infantry Regiment, under Lieutenant Downes, supporting this attack. Another was on the night of 26 July 1897, when Lieutenant E.W. Costello, with a company of the 24th Punjab Infantry, repulsed a tribal attack on a field hospital in Malakand.[76]

How was cohesion maintained among such small groups in

dispersed actions? The personal heroics of the British officers, which traditional historiography emphasizes,[77] is an inadequate explanation. The construction of a distinct ethos for each company enabled it to face such scattered fights. The creation of a distinct tradition for each company was especially vital in the case of mixed regiments. The 8th Bombay Infantry Regiment was a polyethnic unit. In 1884 it comprised of seventeen Indo-Portuguese, eighteen Jews, fifty-one Sikhs, 186 Muslims and 502 Hindus. The personnel were further divided on caste and territorial lines. Among the Hindus, forty-seven were Brahmins and twenty-seven were from the low castes. Of the middle castes, the Marathas dominated, as there were 355 of them. The Muslim community was differentiated both on regional and on cultural lines. There were ninety-three Deccani Muslims who were Shias from the Bombay region, eight Hindustani Muslims from north India, fifty-nine Muslims from Punjab. Of them fifty-one were Rajputs who had converted to Islam. To cap it all, there were twenty-five Pathans who were Sunnis from the North-West Frontier. This polyglot mixture with its religious, linguistic and cultural heterogeneity was organized into eight companies. The British tried to generate a company ethos by holding annual musketry competitions within the various companies of the units in the hope that it would create a competitive spirit among the various sub-units. The annual musketry competition for 1884 was held on 31 March. In that competition, B Company came first with ninety-five points and E Company came last with eighty-one points.[78]

The British tried to make the regiments a sort of community enterprise for the soldiers. The dominant imperial view, in the post-1857 era, as propounded by Major-General H. Hancock, was that long service allowed the Indian recruits to make army service a lifetime career. The regiments in general, and the companies in particular, became their homes, thus enabling them to identify their interest with the unit. But, short-service commissions would make their loyalty precarious, as their ties with the units would be temporary.[79] There was another reason for introducing long-term volunteer service for the Indians. The Eden Commission in 1879 voiced the Raj's fear:

It must be remembered that our native army is a mercenary force, serving an alien government. . . . And it would be politically inadvisable to adopt for India short-service system of Europe, whereby the largest possible number of men are passed through the army, returned into the general population, and are kept by periodical training in a state of military efficiency. There can be no advantage and there might be much risk in scattering hundreds of thousands of trained reservists over the several provinces of India.[80]

Military theorists as well as military commanders agree that the stability of the personnel in the unit gives rise to cohesion. Close personal ties among the troops were an essential ingredient for their willingness to enter the battle zones. Sun Tzu II, who lived 100 years after Sun Tzu, had written that victory depended on trust and loyalty among the soldiers.[81] Ardant Du Picq, a French military scholar of the late-nineteenth century, wrote that four brave men who did not know each other would not dare attack a lion. But, four less brave men knowing each other well, sure of their reliability and mutual aid, would attack resolutely.[82] Field Marshal Von Manstein asserted that the mutual acquaintanceship and trust which comes after fighting battles together are important.[83] Historical case studies support these assumptions. For sustaining *esprit de corps* in the 51st Highland Division during the Second World War, the commanding officers demanded that the unit recruit as many Scots as possible and that there should not be any transfer within the Highland regiments which constituted the division.[84] The frequent transfer of personnel within the American regiments stationed in Europe during the Second World War resulted in men serving with strangers. The American Army in Vietnam also suffered from instability as the men remained in their units for only one year. The net result was low morale and high desertion rates.[85]

The British aimed to create a sort of joint enterprise in the regiments by not transferring the long-service Indian personnel from one unit to another. The absence of inter-unit transfer was geared to encourage 'buddy feeling' among the members of the regiment.[86] When the privates of the 13th Punjab Infantry were invalided in May 1861, most of them had more than twelve years service behind them. When Subedar-Major Rana of the 28th Bombay Infantry Regiment retired in 1895, he had completed thirty-three years service in the same unit. Subedar Mussunjie of the 8th Bombay Infantry Regiment was pensioned off in August 1878 after thirty-five years of service in that unit.[87] Because of the long service by the Indian volunteers, the turnover in the Indian regiments was very low. And this was in turn reflected in the small number of recruits required annually. The 2nd and 3rd Lancers of the Hyderabad Contingent between 1890–1 enlisted only thirty-seven and thirty-eight personnel respectively,[88] and such examples were numerous.

The British Army used short-service recruits from 1871 onwards under the Cardwell system,[89] because, unlike the Sepoy Army, it could afford to utilize nationalism. However, Cardwell's scheme was not truly a short-service scheme in the European sense. After 1868, a conscript in the Prussian Army served for three years with the colours and another four years with the reserve. But a British soldier served six years with the colours and another six years with the reserve.[90] Under the Cardwell scheme, each battalion recruited from a particular district to encourage local connections. G.J. Wolseley, a British commander, believed that territorial connections strengthened *esprit de corps.*[91]

In the Sepoy Army, to take advantage of clan and family feelings and territorial links, each company recruited men of a particular clan from a particular district. Men from a community liked to join the companies which had their clans, for reasons of familiarity. The troops felt comfortable among their relatives and friends, and such personal ties heightened unit cohesion. In the high risk action zones, the men wanted to be surrounded by others whom they could trust, whom they knew and who came from the same neighbourhood and had same culture and dialect. If someone was unable to get furlough, then others from his company, who belonged to the same clans and villages, conveyed the news back to his family and brought to him information about his domestic affairs. All this created strong inter-personal bonds among the men, and helped the growth of unit spirit.[92]

An example of the companies utilizing territorial links was the 4th Battalion of the 9th Jat Regiment. In 1903, this unit was allotted Ludhiana and Ferozepur divisions for recruitment. By 1908, this class company regiment had four Rajput companies (A, B, E, and F), two Gujar companies (C and D), and two Muslim Jat companies (G and H). A, D and G companies were recruited from Ferozepur, Faridkot and Bhawalpur districts. B, C and H companies enlisted men from Ludhiana, Maler Kotla and Nabha districts. E Company acquired its personnel from Ambala, Patiala and Karnal districts. And F Company derived its manpower from Rohtak and Hissar districts.[93]

In the Sepoy Army, the soldiers' offsprings who were born and brought up in the regimental lines received free education in the garrison school, and they were designated as recruit boys. Many of them enlisted in their fathers' regiments. The army hoped that this policy would make the serving soldiers more loyal and also that those recruits who were growing up in the regimental lines would imbibe the traditions of service and loyalty.[94] Such beliefs also shape the policies of modern military establishments. It is interesting to note that the Soviet Army believed that what a child was taught during his formative years had a lasting impact on the beliefs carried into adulthood. So, in the Soviet Union the militarization of youth started at an early stage.[95] About twenty-four boys were attached in each regiment of the Bombay Army. They were sons of soldiers and orphans were given preference. They were enlisted at a very early age and received half pay. They wore the uniform of the regiment which was paid for by the regiment and went to the regimental schools. Many soldiers told Robert Napier Commander-in-Chief of the Bombay Army (1866–9): 'I was born in the Regiment, as was my father before me. I have no other home.'[96] The Madras Army units being mostly general mixed regiments (comprised of Tamils, Telugus, and the Deccani Muslims) had weak ethnic loyalties to back up their regimental ethos. Hence in the Madras regiments, the sons and relatives of the soldiers brought up in the regiment (known as line or recruit or pension boys)[97] were given special preference when vacancies occurred. From the regimental records of the 14th Madras Infantry Regiment it is clear that the recruit boys constituted 30 per cent of the unit's manpower.[98] Between 1890–1, in the 3rd Lancers of the Hyderabad Contingent about 18 per cent of the recruits enlisted were recruit boys.[99] Overall, in the Hyderabad Contingent about 27 per cent of the recruits enlisted were recruit boys.[100] In 1892, T.J.C. Plowden, the officiating Resident at Hyderabad wrote in a despatch to the Military Department of the Government of India: 'The enlistment of the line and pension boys be restricted to 25 per cent of the strength in cavalry and to 10 per cent in artillery and infantry.'[101] Why did a regiment not depend totally on recruit boys? We could hazard a guess that the British were probably afraid that to convert a regiment into a set of family monopolies would result in a very narrow base which might prove to be dangerous in the long run.

Not only did the regiments have soldiers' sons, but other relatives from the same locality also served in the same unit. In 1857, the 1st Punjab Cavalry Regiment had three Dufadars and twenty troopers who were Ranghars from Hansi and Rohtak districts of Haryana. They were all related to each other. Then there were two brothers Naib-Resaldar Firoz Khan and Lance-Dufadar Akbar Khan.[102] The 1st Regiment of Beatson's Horse raised in March 1858 had about 579 troopers and several of them had their relatives serving in it. Sowar Imam Ali was the son of Resaldar Rustum Ali Khan. Mahmud Khan, a trooper, was the uncle of Naib-Resaldar Abdullah Khan. Another Afzal Khan was the father of Naib-Resaldar Hakim Khan.[103] In 1861, the 24th Madras Infantry Regiment had two privates named Mahmud Hussain and Moonerpah, who were cousins.[104]

The Indian officers in charge of enlistment generally acquired men from their own villages, and frequently enlisted their relatives. A typical example was sepoy Sitaram who was enlisted in 1812 by his uncle, who was a Jemadar. Both were Brahmins, who came from Tilowee village in Awadh, and both served in the same regiment throughout their lives.[105] It was the army's policy to encourage soldiers on furlough to bring recruits. The aim was to utilize the already existing inter-personal bonds for the construction of group cohesion. So each company became a caucus for a particular clan from a particular locality, and these clans resisted the entry of other clans in their companies. This policy was geared to create a sense of emulation among the various companies of a regiment.[106] The British felt that the military clans looked down upon other clans, and if these clans were mixed within the companies, then the *esprit de corps* would disintegrate. Many non-Rana Gurung recruits tried to enlist along with the Rana clan of the Gurung tribe. This was because Rana clans enjoyed more prestige both in Nepali society as well as in the eyes of the British. The army, to ensure clan homogeneity in the companies took care to ask the recruits what clan they belonged to, from which districts they hailed, and what their family backgrounds were.[107] Thus the regiments became a network of families of particular clans. The 5th Gurkha Rifles recruited mostly members of the Thapa clan of the Magar tribe and people from the Srisht clan of the Newar tribe. The catchment area of this regiment was Nepal Valley in central Nepal. Most of the officers were from the Kala family of the Thapa clan. Many officers of the 8th Gurkha Rifles were from Nagarkoti family of the Srisht clan of the Newars.[108]

The companies of the polyethnic regiments also harnessed clan and family loyalties. The 20th Punjabis was a class company regiment. In 1912 it had eight companies with a total of 912 men. This unit had two companies of Jat Sikhs and two Dogra companies (the Rajputs and not the Brahmins of this community were enlisted). And the other four companies (B, C, F, and G) were composed of trans-Indus tribes. Though only four companies (the Jat Sikhs and the Dogras) were enlisted from Punjab, the unit as a whole was still given the title of 'Punjabis' to create an artificial territorial identity. As the companies were of distinct groups, they were never mixed, but functioned as separate entities. For small unit actions, the companies were divided into sections. Each section had a minimum of sixteen men. And, for making use of the familial and territorial ties, each section was composed of a single clan. In 1912, Colonel L.C. Dunsterville, the commandant of 20th Punjabis commented that new clans should not be inducted in the sections as it would create obstacles in the evolution of a clan spirit. Hence the personnel of different sections were never mixed. Training was based on sections. B and G companies were filled with Afridi tribe. B Company had four sections. They were filled with Adam Khel, Malikdin Khel, Kuki Khel and Zakka Khel Afridis. G Company was filled with Kambhan Khel Afridis. The Pathans were in F Company. Two sections of this company were filled with the Sagri Khattak clan and the other two sections had Bangi Khel and Barak Khel Pathans.[109]

CONCLUSION

The creation of an identity was not an event, but a process extending over a century. In one sense, 1857 caused changes in the perspective of regiment construction. British rule now was tinged with 'racial' pride. But there were also elements of continuity—the use of colours and standards for establishing regimental pride and family ties for generating regimental ethos.

The regiment building process included both indigenous and foreign strands. The British imported modern institutions like the regiment to India. But, in the subcontinent it appropriated traditional elements like tribal and clan consciousness. The uniforms of the regiments' bore evidence of ethnic content, and the end product, the Indian regiments, were an amalgam of tradition and modernity. In fact, the construction of regiments moulded many supposedly 'pre-colonial' trends, like religious consciousness, in Indian society. In the long run, the regiments by emphasizing distinct ethnic ethos strengthened communalization of the Indian society.[110] Lionel Caplan has asserted that for the various communities the British manufactured images, which reflected those very traits which the imperialists admired in themselves,[111] but the imperial construct was more complex than that.

Since national ideology could not be utilized to propel colonial soldiers into the field of fire, the only option for the imperialists was to generate regimental cameraderie. The organizational gamut of the regiment was designed to reduce individuality at the cost of bureaucratization, in an attempt to transform the soldiers into a set of automatons. Distinct regimental traditions, by appropriating certain loyalty traits, gave rise to a group ethos, which enabled the sepoys and the sowars to tolerate the inhuman 'face of battle'. Simultaneously, regimental loyalties also prevented mutinies among the colonial soldiers. Professional soldiers did not fight merely for monetary rewards, but also for corporate ethos.[112] Most nineteenth century officers dubbed the Sepoy Army as a mercenary force. When Major Von Wachs commanding 4th Pomeranian Infantry at Thorn in Prussia, visited India in 1884, he described the sepoy as a hireling.[113] Regimental loyalty is indeed instrumental for recruiting and welfare measures. The titles, prizes and details of uniform all built on that. The sepoys were motivated not only by tangible incentives but also by the regimental consciousness which the British manufactured. Therefore, the Sepoy Army cannot be typologized as a purely mercenary army. It was also partly a professional force.

How successful was the British policy? All went well till the mass casualties of the First World War destroyed the intricate clan and family networks within the Indian regiments. But, then, the Sepoy Army was designed for 'small wars' and not for modern industrial warfare, which also destroyed the most effective combat force of contemporary time, the *Kaiserheer.*

NOTES

1. Sun Tzu, *The Art of War,* tr. by Yuan Shibing, 1990, reprint, Hertfordshire: Wordsworth, 1993, pp. 91–3, 104, 110.
2. J.K. Anderson, *Xenophon,* London: Duckworth, 1974, pp. 75, 121–2.
3. Anatol Rapoport, ed., Carl Von Clausewitz, *On War,* tr. by J.J. Graham, 1908, reprint, London: Penguin, 1982, pp. 251–6.
4. Warren Treadgold, *Byzantium and Its Army: 284–1081,* Stanford/ California: Stanford University Press, 1995; Michael Roberts, 'The Military Revolution, 1560–1660', and Parker, 'The "Military Revolution, 1560–1660"—A Myth', in Clifford J. Rogers, ed., *The Military Revolution Debate: Readings on the Military Transformation of Early Modern Europe,* Colorado/Boulder: Westview Press, 1995, pp. 13–35, 37–54.
5. For the view that there was Military Evolution and no Revolution see Jeremy Black, 'A Military Revolution? A 1660–1792 Perspective', in Rogers, ed., *Military Revolution Debate,* pp. 95–114.
6. Irvine, *The Army of the Indian Moguls,* pp. 3–61; Channa Wickremesekera, *'Best Black Troops in the World': British Perceptions and the Making of the Sepoy, 1746–1805,* New Delhi: Manohar, 2002, p. 50.
7. Omer Bartov, 'Indoctrination and Motivation in the *Wehrmacht*: The Importance of the Unquantifiable', *JSS,* vol. 9, no. 1 (1986), 16–34; idem., 'Daily Life and Motivation in War: The *Wehrmacht* in the Soviet Union', *JSS,* vol. 12, no. 2 (1989), 200–14.
8. Jadunath Sarkar, *Fall of the Mughal Empire: 1771–88,* vol. 3, 1938, reprint, New Delhi: Orient Longman, 1991, pp. 15, 189.
9. Bingley, *Rajputs,* pp. 20–24; *Hancock Report,* pp. 27, 32.
10. An abridged version of this chapter has been published as 'The Construction of Regiments in the Indian Army: 1859–1913', *War in History,* vol. 8, no. 2 (2001), pp. 127–48.
11. Hugh Trevor-Roper, 'The Invention of Tradition: The Highland Tradition of Scotland', and Terence Ranger, 'The Invention of Tradition in Colonial Africa', in Eric Hobsbawm and Ranger, ed., *The Invention of Tradition,* 1983, reprint, Cambridge: Canto, 1985, pp. 16, 19–23, 211, 224.
12. John Prebble, *Mutiny: Highland Regiments in Revolt, 1743–1804,* 1975,

reprint, Harmondsworth, Middlesex: Penguin, 1977, pp. 13, 15. The quotation is from p. 20.

13. The imperial concept of a racial community is similar to Cynthia H. Enloe's concept of an ethnic group. Enloe, *Ethnic Soldiers: State Security in Divided Societies*, Harmondsworth, Middlesex: penguin, 1980, pp. x, 1–2; Bingley, *Sikhs*, pp. 2, 18, 50, 54.

14. *Army Committee*, vol. 1-A, *Minority Report*, p. 156.

15. Vansittart, *Handbooks*, pp. 8, 10–11, 65, 71.

16. Vansittart, *Notes*, pp. 56–7, 84.

17. Lionel Caplan, 'Martial Gurkhas: The Persistence of a British Military Discourse on "Race"', in Peter Robb, ed., *The Concept of Race in South Asia*, Delhi: Oxford University Press, 1995, p. 261.

18. Caplan, *Warrior Gentlemen*, pp. 28–55.

19. Vansittart, *Gurkhas*, pp. 24–35, 48, 60, 71, 118; Hamilton, 'Ochterlony's Campaign', 137–56.

20. Vansittart, *Gurkhas*, p. 10.

21. Ibid., pp. 33, 51; To Lieutenant Ball Noughton in charge of the Gurkha force, from G. Ramsay, Resident of Nepal, no. 15, 29 January 1858, Return showing the number of each rank and subsistence allowance drawn by each individual per mensem in the Nepal regiments forming a part of the Saran Field Force, List showing the number of each grade and the subsistence allowance drawn by each individual per mensem in the force under the command of Maharaja Jung Bahadur, signed H. Byers, 17 July 1858, Military letters from Nepal, NAI; Ethnic elements of the Indian Army, Records of Chief Commands, 1865–71, Notes and Minutes by Napier of Magdala, MSS.EUR.F.114, 5(4), OIOC.

22. Vansittart, *Gurkhas*, pp. 34, 81, 89, 97, 99, 101–2; Gaylor, *Sons of John Company*, pp. 235–40, 244–5.

23. Pemble, *The Invasion of Nepal*, pp. 26–7; Vansittart, *Gurkhas*, p. 44; MacMunn, *The Armies of India*, p. 164, plates 58, 60–1; Shakespear, *Sirmoor Rifles*, pp. 1–2, 4.

24. Gaylor, *Sons of John Company*, pp. 219, 221, 223; To Colonel H. Rowcroft, commanding Saran Field Force from Ramsay, no. 11, 21 January 1858, Return showing each rank and the subsistence allowance drawn by each individual per mensem in the Gorucknath and Burruck regiments, Abstract of sum paid in advance to the Gurkha force under the command of Bukht Jung and Khurg Bahadur from 12 January 1858 to 11 Feb. 1858, Byers, Nepal Residency, 27 July 1858, Military letters from Nepal.

25. Alf Aberg, 'The Swedish Army from Lutzen to Narva', in Michael Roberts, ed., *Sweden's Age of Greatness: 1632–1718*, London: Macmillan, 1973, p. 272.

26. Vansittart, *Gurkhas*, pp. 52, 65, 77; Kumar Pradhan, *The Gorkha Conquests: The Process and Consequences of the Unification of Nepal*

with Particular References to Eastern Nepal, Calcutta: Oxford University Press, 1991, pp. 155, 160–3.

27. Alavi, *The Sepoys and the Company,* pp. 6–7, 264–90.
28. Vansittart, *Gurkhas,* pp. 49, 51.
29. Ibid., pp. 54–5.
30. Ibid., pp. 55, 129–30.
31. Ibid., pp. 55–6, 119.
32. Cook, *The Sikh Wars,* pp. 9, 48; *Peel Committee,* pp. 8–9, 48.
33. Vansittart, *Gurkhas,* p. 57.
34. William L. Hauser, 'The Will to Fight', in Sam C. Sarkesian, ed., *Combat Effectiveness: Cohesion, Stress and the Volunteer Military,* Beverly Hills/London: Sage, 1980, p. 190; Bingley and Nicholls, *Brahmins,* p. 43.
35. Roberts to Napier, 10 October 1884 in Roberts, *Correspondence with England while Commander-in-Chief in Madras,* p. 216, Indian Series, Part 2, L/MIL/17/5/1615, OIOC.
36. Inspection report of 8th Madras Infantry Regiment, From Brigadier General H.R. Hope, Secy. to the Madras Govt. MD, to the Secy. of GoI, MD, 26 October 1893, Ootacamund, Enclosures to general letter no. 6, Annual confidential reports on the regiments, L/MIL/7/17008, OIOC.
37. Vansittart, *Gurkhas,* pp. 56–7; Bingley and Nicholls, *Brahmins,* p. 43.
38. Bingley, *Rajputs,* pp. 39, 145, 149.
39. Ibid., p. 44, Appendix B; Dirk Kolff, *Naukar, Rajput and Sepoy,* pp. 71–4; Lanny Bruce Fields, 'Ethnicity in Tso Tsung-Tang's Armies: The Campaign in Northwest China, 1867–80', in Cynthia H. Enloe and DeWitt C. Ellinwood, ed., *Ethnicity and the Military in Asia,* New Brunswick/London: Transcation Books, 1981, pp. 54–5.
40. Bingley, *Rajputs,* pp. 7, 9, 50–1; B.N.S. Yadava, 'Chivalry and Warfare', in Jos J.L. Gommans and Dirk Kolff, ed., *Warfare and Weaponry in South Asia: 1000–1800,* New Delhi: Oxford University Press, 2001, pp. 66–98.
41. *Army Committee,* vol. 1-A, *Minority Report,* p. 156.
42. The Muslims were considered as 'fanatic' and 'treacherous' by the Martial Race lobby, which ruled Indian Army from the 1880s. Kaushik Roy, 'Recruitment Doctrines of the Colonial Indian Army: 1859–1913', *IESHR,* vol. 34, no. 3 (1997), p. 351.
43. Chaudhuri, 'The Martial Races of India', *Modern Review,* vol. XLIX, no. 1 (1931), p. 79; Shakespear, *Sirmoor Rifles,* p. 23.
44. Fox in *Lions of the Punjab* argues that the Sikh identity was totally an imperial construct.
45. Vansittart, *Gurkhas,* p. 145.
46. Stanford W. Gregory Jr., 'Towards a Situated Description of Cohesion and Disintegration in the American Army', *Armed Forces and Society,* vol. 3, no. 3 (1977), 476–81.
47. Vansittart, *Gurkhas,* p. 88.

48. McGregor, *The History of the Sikhs,* vol. 2, pp. 51, 88–9.
49. MacMunn, *The Armies of India,* p. 135.
50. Bingley, *Sikhs,* pp. I, II, VI, 41, 49, 53, Appendix A.
51. Bingley, *Jats and Gujars,* p. 31.
52. Bernard S. Cohn, 'Cloth, Clothes, and Colonialism: India in the Nineteenth Century', in idem., *Colonialism and Its Forms of Knowledge: The British in India,* Delhi: Oxford University Press, 1997, pp. 106–11.
53. Bingley, *Rajputs,* pp. 149, 170-1.
54. Radhika Singha, 'Settle, Mobilize, Verify: Identification Practices in Colonial India', *Studies in History,* New Series, vol. 16, no. 2 (2000), p. 162.
55. Quoted from Field-Marshal Birdwood, *Khaki and Gown: An Autobiography,* London: Ward, Lock & Co., LTD, 1941, p. 141.
56. Vansittart, *Gurkhas,* p. 145; Gaylor, *Sons of John Company,* pp. 8–9.
57. Elliot P. Chodof, 'Ideology and Primary Groups', *Armed Forces and Society,* vol. 9, no. 4 (1983), p. 570; John Keegan, 'Regimental Ideology', in Geoffrey Best and Andrew Wheatcroft, ed., *War Economy and the Military Mind,* London: Croom Helm Ltd., 1976, p. 11.
58. Douglas Porch, *The French Foreign Legion: A Complete History of the Legendary Fighting Force,* 1991, reprint, New York: Harper Perennial, 1992, p. 620.
59. Shakespear, *Sirmoor Rifles,* p. 180.
60. 14th Madras Infantry, NAI, pp. 39, 134, 198.
61. *Army Committee,* vol. 3, pp. 901, 903–4; 8th Bombay Infantry, NAI (This manuscript is unpaginated. Information is given under each date.), 28 May 1881, 13 September 1893.
62. Diary of Capt. F.D. Raikes, Deputy Commissioner Thayetmoyo with the Movable Column, eastern frontier from 16 to 30 November 1885, no. 830, Proceedings of the GoI, Burma, 1885–6, NAI.
63. General John Hackett, *The Profession of Arms,* 1983, reprint, London: Sidgwick & Jackson, 1984, p. 18.
64. Wilson, *Historical Record,* pp. 6, 33; 8th Bombay Infantry, 25 November 1886.
65. 44th Merwara Infantry, NAI (this manuscript is unpaginated and the information is given under the heading of various dates), 28 October and November 1899.
66. *Army Regulations, India,* p. 96; Circular to officers commanding infantry regiments, ADG's office, camp Mudki, no. 27/N, 15 March 1864, ADG's circulars, vol. 4; Minute on the Organization of the Army, Ch. 2, Bengal Army, Proposals for all regiments to have colours, para 31, 11 October 1875, Norman Minutes, NAI.
67. John Keegan, 'Inventing Military Traditions', in Chris Wrigley, ed., *Warfare, Diplomacy and Politics: Essays in Honour of A.J.P. Taylor,* London: Hamish Hamilton, 1986, p. 69.

68. *Manual for Bengal and Punjab Cavalry,* 1893, reprint, Delhi: Mayur Publications, 1985, p. 20.

69. Gaylor, *Sons of John Company,* pp. 222, 224–5, 328.

70. Anne Hoiberg, 'Military Staying Power', in Sarkesian, ed., *Combat Effectiveness,* pp. 238–9; Shakespear, *Sirmoor Rifles,* pp. 68–9.

71. Gaylor, *Sons of the John Company,* pp. 222, 227–8, 236, 241; Shakespear, *Sirmoor Rifles,* p. 166.

72. Menezes, *Fidelity and Honour,* pp. 100–1; Longer, *Red Coats to Olive Green,* p. 57; 14th Madras Infantry, pp. 171–2; 9th Bombay Regiment, NAI (this manuscript is unpaginated and the information is given under various dates), 1769, 1787.

73. Lieutenant (Adjutant) Carter, 28th Bombay Regiment, NAI, (this document is unpaginated and the information is given under various dates), 27 September 1860, 26 December 1870, 7 November 1880; 4th Battalion, NAI (this manuscript is not paginated and the information is given for various years), 1911.

74. Ellen Jones, *Red Army and Society: A Sociology of the Soviet Military,* Boston: Allen & Unwin, 1985, p. 129; John Keegan, *The Face of Battle: A Study of Agincourt, Waterloo and the Somme,* 1976, reprint, Harmondsworth, Middlesex: Penguin, 1978, p. 279; Pierce G. Fredericks, *The Sepoy and the Cossack,* London: W.H. Allen, 1972, pp. 102, 144, 160–3, 212, 217; Shakespear, *Sirmoor Rifles,* pp. 109, 162, 165; 28th Bombay Regiment, October 1904.

75. No. 126, 1901, pp. 85–6, GO, NAI.

76. *Army Committee,* vol. 3, p. 950; Extract from Major-General H. Prendergast's diary, para 31–2, no. 635, 17 November 1885, Burma proceedings; Evidence in the case of Lieutenant E.W. Costello, attached to 24th Punjab Infantry recommended for the reward of the Victoria Cross for bravery in presence of the enemy at Malakand on the night of 26 July 1897, no. 668, Proceedings of the GoI, Malakand 1897–8, NAI.

77. One representative is Mason's *A Matter of Honour,* pp. 384–91.

78. 8th Bombay Infantry, 1 January and 31 March 1884.

79. *Hancock Report,* p. 30.

80. *Eden Commission,* p. 87.

81. Sun Tzu II, *The Lost Art of War,* tr. with a commentary by Thomas Cleary, New York: Harper Collins, 1996, p. 44.

82. Lawrence Freedman, ed., *Oxford Readers: War,* Oxford: Oxford University Press, 1994, p. 144.

83. Field-Marshal Erich von Manstein, *Lost Victories,* tr. by Anthony G. Powell, 1958, reprint, Dehradun: Natraj, n.d., pp. 260–1.

84. Craig F. French, 'The Fashioning of *Esprit de Corps* in the 51st Highland Division from St Valery to El Alamein', *JSAHR,* vol. 77, no. 312 (1999), pp. 282–4.

85. Michael Howard, 'Leadership in the British Army in the Second World War: Some Personal Observations', in G.D. Sheffield, ed., *Leadership and Command: The Anglo-American Military Experience Since 1861,* London: Brassey's, 1997, p. 123; Martin van Creveld, *Command in War,* Cambridge/Massachusetts: Harvard University Press, 1985, p. 236.

86. Buddy relations were personal and intimate. It was generated because the men stayed within the units and shared the risks and hardships of war. For this concept see Roger W. Little, 'Buddy Relations and Combat Performance', in Morris Janowitz, ed., *The New Military: Changing Patterns of Organization,* 1964, reprint, New York: W.W. Norton & Company, 1969, p. 195.

87. Roll of men of the 13th Punjab Infantry Regiment, signed Capt. V. Tonochy, commandant, Progs. no. 103, 20 May 1861, MDP, October 1861; 8th Bombay Regiment, 28 August 1878; 28th Bombay Regiment, 2nd March 1895.

88. From Lieutenant-Colonel J.T. Cummins, Commandant 2nd Lancers, Hyderabad Contingent, to the Asst. ADG Hyderabad Contingent, Bolorum, Statement showing the caste and country of recruits enlisted in the 3rd Lancers Hyderabad Contingent between 1890–1, no. 438, 3 March 1897, L/MIL/7/14966, OIOC.

89. V.G. Kiernan, *European Empires from Conquest to Collapse, 1815-1960,* Bungay, Suffolk: Fontana, 1982, pp. 89–90.

90. Michael Howard, *The Franco-Prussian War: The German Invasion of France, 1870-71,* 1961, reprint, London/New York: Methuen, 1979, p. 21; Correlli Barnett, *Britain and Her Army: A Military, Political and Social Survey,* London: Penguin, 1970, p. 304.

91. Edward Spiers, 'The Late Victorian Army, 1868–1914', in David Chandler and Ian Beckett, eds., *The Oxford Illustrated History of the British Army,* Oxford: Oxford University Press, 1994, pp. 191, 194.

92. *Army Committee,* vol. 2, pp. 954-5.

93. 4th Battalion, 1903, 1908.

94. *Army Regulations,* pp. 118-19; Minutes on the organization of the army in India, Ch. 1, Bengal Army, British officers, para 2-3, 11 October 1875, Norman minutes.

95. William F. Scott and Harriet Scott, *The Armed Forces of the Soviet Union* (1979, reprint, Colorado/Boulder: Westview Press, 1984), p. 400.

96. Regimental Schools (Indian Regiments), Memo by Lieutenant-General R. Napier, Bombay, 1 May 1866, Notes and Minutes by Napier of Magdala, MSS.EUR.F.114, IC.

97. Line boys were very young recruit boys who generally performed chores for the British officers. Pension boys were senior recruit boys who were not recruited due to lack of vacancies but derived some allowances.

98. Wilson, *Historical Records*, p. 33; 14th Madras Infantry Regiment, pp. 28–40.
99. Statement showing the caste and country of recruits enlisted in the 3rd Lancers Hyderabad Contingent between 1890–1, Enclosure no. 1, L/MIL/7/14966.
100. From T.J.C. Plowden, offg. Resident at Hyderabad to the Secy. to the GoI, MD, no. 26, 22 February 1892, L/MIL/7/1/14966.
101. Plowden to the GoI, MD, L/MIL/7/1/14966.
102. *1st Punjab Cavalry*, pp. 27, 30.
103. Camp Bairseah, signed Captain E.G. Wood, commandant 1st Regiment of Beatson's Horse, Progs. no. 1813, 11 October 1859, MDP, March 1860, NAI.
104. Roll of men of 24th Madras Infantry Regiment, Progs. no. 74, 6 May 1861, MDP, October 1861.
105. Lunt, ed., *From Sepoy to Subedar*, pp. 3–6, 13–16.
106. Bingley, *Rajputs*, pp. 174, 176.
107. Ibid., p. 177; Vansittart, *Gurkhas*, p. 88.
108. Vansittart, *Gurkhas*, pp. 105, 109.
109. *Army Committee*, vol. 2, pp. 895–7, 900.
110. Dewitt C. Ellinwood, 'The Indian Soldier: The Indian Army and Change, 1914–18', in idem. and S.D. Pradhan, eds., *India and World War I*, New Delhi: Manohar, 1978, p. 177.
111. Caplan, ' "Bravest of the Brave" ', pp. 589–93.
112. Keegan, *A History of Warfare*, p. 270.
113. Roberts to Wachs, 9 July 1884 in Roberts, *Correspondence with England while Commander-in-Chief in Madras*, p. 195.

SIX

Sustaining Loyalty: The Sepoy Army's Disciplinary System

The greatest danger we have to apprehend is from our native army; our military force is the exclusive tenure by which we hold the government, and the fidelity of the troops ... is necessarily precarious; they are foreigners and mercenaries.

Henry Russell[1]

Besides regimental pride and incentives, coercion also played an important role in keeping the sepoys and the sowars loyal to the British. The coercive infrastructure was influenced by imperial opinions about the colonized. Initially, the British viewed the Sepoy Army as a mercenary force. In the first half of the nineteenth century, British officers like Major-General S.F. Whittingham assumed that the sepoys were attached to the British because of the prospect of economic gain. However, in the first decade of the twentieth century, Major (later Lieutenant-General) G.F. MacMunn argued that though the sepoys were mercenaries, they were also motivated by the leadership of white men.[2] Most of the contemporary officers shared the view that discipline depended on the regimental commandants and underplayed the importance of institutions in inculcating loyalty among the Indian soldiers. Among the recent historians, at least one shares such a view.[3] However, the British also evolved a disciplinary system based on force.

One of the main factors behind the Sepoy Army's military success against the indisciplined princely forces was the operation of an institutional command mechanism designed on Western mechanics of command. Since the British replaced the part-time mercenaries with full-time soldiers, the permanent military bureaucratic infrastructure aided in the emergence of a clear-cut chain of command with a hierarchy of subordinates.

This disciplinary mechanism was superior to the chaotic and the arbitrary attempts by the *jagirdars* to discipline their retainers. In the princely militaries there was no distinction between the army officers and the civilian bureaucrats. The *jagirdars* were mostly absentee landlords who raised troops during campaigns. And they remained in charge of the operational control of the army. As the Indian rulers never maintained permanent military establishments, specialized administrative machinery for inculcating military discipline never emerged in the pre-British Indian armies.[4] Even the Marathas, who introduced a Western-style infantry force, failed to evolve a stable command structure.[5] Desertions were common and the troops frequently changed sides.[6] The net result was friable indigenous militaries, which disintegrated while confronting the more cohesive Sepoy Army.

In the post-Mutiny era, the disciplinary system of the Sepoy Army underwent a transformation. From being a personalized and decentralized system based on the regimental officers, it became an impersonal centralized system centred around the army headquarter and run by the Adjutant Generals and the Commanders-in-Chief. This transition was part of the wider process of the transformation of the army's command structure. From a regiment-centric command apparatus, there emerged a centralized bureaucratic command culture. The disciplinary structure and the command system were interrelated. In the regiment-centric command system, which centred around the regimental officers, military discipline depended on their discretionary power. The proponents of the regiment-centric command culture wanted the British officers to function as paternal despots. This was not unique among the British officers of the Sepoy Army. In the European controlled African colonial armies also, the paternalist ethos that the white officers were 'fathers to the men' was dominant.[7] But, in the impersonal command, the disciplinary fabric functioned through authority based on rules and regulations fabricated by the distant military bureaucrats. This transition was achieved through a tortuous process. The vested interest of the regimental officers, the experiences of 1857, and the theoretical paradigm through which the British viewed India, acted as brakes on the army headquarter's attempt to inculcate an abstract impersonal loyalty among the soldiers in place of the troops' personal loyalty towards their commanding officers. The consideration that

Indians were 'different' encouraged some elements of the civilian and military elite to think that the local officers should have supreme power. However, the army headquarter's policy of accelerating the transition towards a top down command system won, because of the improvement in communications, and the general trend towards building professional bureaucratic armies in Europe. As standing armies emerged in Europe, the military establishments created vast bureaucratic infrastructures for administering the armed forces from the top, and bringing all the personnel under unified regulations.[8] From the late 1890s onwards, centralization in the Sepoy Army was accelerated by reforms in the military administration. By 1895, the posts of the Commander-in-Chief of the Madras and the Bombay armies were abolished. Further, Lord Kitchener grouped the regiments into nine divisions.[9]

Centralization and bureaucratization were the two components of professionalism. In the second half of the nineteenth century, the colonial army's disciplinary apparatus became more professional. However, the colonial scenario modulated the process of modernization of the army in India. The shift towards professionalism was played out within the colonial context. This chapter surveys the professionalization of the army's disciplinary structure. The first section shows the gradual reduction of the powers of the regimental commanding officers. The second section deals with the increasing role of impersonal institutions like the military court, articles of war and the oaths in controlling soldiers. The third section focuses on the evolution of bureaucratic disciplinary system controlled by impersonal institutions, in place of punishment shaped by the regimental officers. Section four highlights on the army headquarter's attempt to provide some legal immunities to the soldiers, under the framework of the military law, as part of the high command's attempt to transform the arbitrary paternal despotism of the local officers into a sort of institutional disciplinary structure.

I

REGIMENTAL OFFICERS VERSUS THE ARMY HEADQUARTER

The military authorities were divided on the issue of what constituted the bedrock of disciplinary administration: regimental officers who were the immediate superiors of the soldiers, or the distant army headquarter. One group of officers argued that the frontline commanders must have the power to discipline the soldiers, as this would help them to orient the troops' loyalty towards the regiments. But, the army headquarter wanted the concentration of power in the hands of distant military bureaucrats for constructing extra-regimental loyalty bonds. The headquarter was afraid that too much power in the hands of the regimental officers would result in the disintegration of the bonds of loyalty. The army headquarter won, but only after a fierce debate about whether commanding officers' power to punish the soldiers should be increased or decreased. The debate was also partly shaped by the British perception of Oriental character and pre-colonial polities.

A mutiny occurred on 6 May 1827 in the 3rd Cavalry Regiment of the Hyderabad Contingent. The Court of Enquiry in its report stated that the arbitrary beating of the sowars by the European officers with rattan cane for slight offences at drill resulted in the uprising.[10] As a reaction in the same year, Lord Combermere (Commander-in-Chief of the Indian Army, 1825–30) reduced the powers of commanding officers. They lost the authority to inflict corporal punishment and dismiss soldiers from service without the sanction of the superior officers. But, in 1832, Edward Barnes (Commander-in-Chief of the Indian Army, 1832–3) gave back the commanding officers, the power they previously enjoyed. They were authorized to summon courts, to carry out the proceedings and to exercise their judgement according to the nature of the cases without any interference by the superior officers. Moreover, they acquired the right to alter the intensity of punishments by taking into consideration the previous conduct of the soldier. Barnes disagreed with the view that commanding officers misuse their power.[11]

The tussle between two lobbies within the army, one for the reduction and the other for the accretion of power of the commanding officers, was going on when Governor-General William Bentinck stepped in in 1828. He believed that to strengthen the soldiers' ties with the Company, it was necessary to reduce the power of the commanding officers. Bentinck accepted that the sahib–sepoy relationship was the human lynchpin that held the Sepoy Army together. He asserted that the soldiers' loyalty was necessary to check the internal rebellions and foreign dangers. Ties like nationalism, which operated in case of soldiers in Western countries, were lacking since the population from which Indian soldiers were recruited had no natural affection towards the government. Bentinck believed that the Indian mentality being unique, they were attached only to the chiefs to whom they served, and their fidelity to their chiefs increased if the chiefs treated them with kindness. He further accepted the fact that now the British officers were in positions substituting those of Indian chiefs. So Bentinck concluded that the power of commanding officers must be reduced, to prevent the abuse of power, and to ensure that the officers could no more treat the soldiers with injustice and harshness. Bentinck pointed out a recent case where a commanding officer had misbehaved with some soldiers. And, he could do nothing due to Barnes' 'unfortunate' order which concentrated all power in the hands of the regimental officers. The faulty behaviour of the commanding officer, according to Bentinck, sent a shock wave through the entire army. He deduced that such serious matters could not be left to the caprice of the individual officers but required high-level intervention. Bentinck's response was to reduce the powers of the regimental officers in 1835, and they lost the authority to flog and dismiss the privates.[12]

In 1857, the Bengal Army rebelled and a reaction set in. Most of the British elite accepted that the loyalty mechanism disintegrated because of Bentinck's intervention, which reduced the power of the soldiers' immediate superiors (the commanding officers). So, the Mutiny strengthened the position of the advocates of the decentralized, regiment-centric disciplinary apparatus. But, the promoters of the regiment-centric command differed on the quantum of authority to be delegated to the commanding officers.

The Punjab School, Bartle Frere and Brigadier J. Christie were for a regiment-oriented command culture. They assumed that the reduction of the commanding officers' power had resulted in the disintegration of the command structure in 1857. They wanted more power in the hands of the commanding officers. This, they argued, was necessary because of the 'Oriental' character and the nature of the pre-colonial governments.[13] The Punjab School believed that the Indians respected power in their immediate superiors and not an impersonal power thousands of miles away, and were not accustomed to constitutional checks and balances. The best policy would be to make the commanding officers supreme. The soldiers should look up to them for everything. Frere corroborated the Punjab School's view by arguing that divided responsibilities, in which power was shared by the Commander-in-Chief, Adjutant General and the Brigadiers in charge of the divisions, confused the soldiers and created suspicion and discontent in their minds. Frere warned that the Indians had no faith in the laws written on paper by men whom they did not know. So, in his view, discretion and judgement on the part of the commanding officers were better than laws embodied in manuals.[14]

Such officers also assumed that a sort of 'Oriental Despotism' by their commanding officers was favoured by the Indians because of the nature of the pre-colonial regimes. Frere assumed a linkage between the despotic nature of the pre-British governments and the 'peculiar' mentality of the Indians, which was accustomed to despotic rule. His view was that the British soldiers came from races accustomed to self-government, hence conscious about their rights and obligations, but an Indian did not have respect for any other form of government except the tyrannical one, because he was familiar to absolute polity, with only one master. The Punjab School also joined the debate by saying that, for the above reasons, the Indians were not suited for constitutional liberty.[15]

Besides this ideological obsession, there was also another pragmatic dimension in the debate. Christie argued that before the 1820s, when power of the commandants was intact, the soldiers did everything to please their commandants. But, after the commandants' authority was reduced in the late 1830s, the soldiers did not care much for the orders of their superiors. As a result, discipline declined.[16] The Punjab lobby pointed out that the power of the commanding officers had decreased due to constant interference by the army headquarter in matters of the internal discipline of the regiments. This centralization of power in the hands of the Adjutant General and the Commander-in-Chief proved dangerous, as rewards and punishments were the sources of the commanding officers' power over their men, and these two were now being taken away from them. The Punjab

School argued in favour of promotions controlled by the regimental officers, as this technique forced the soldiers to do their best to remain in their officers' good books. But General Charles James Napier (Commander-in-Chief of the Indian Army, 1849–50) was afraid that promotion by merit, which was assessed by the commanding officers, put too much power in their hands and so he replaced it with promotion based on seniority. And the Punjab School criticized this order. They pointed out that whenever regimental commandants tired to supersede inefficient soldiers, the latter obstructed this move by appealing directly to the military headquarter about the 'injustice' done to them. In such cases, the soldiers got promotions and the Colonels were humiliated among their subordinates. Again, article 112 reduced the quantum of punishment which the commandants could inflict on their men. The commandants could neither give extra duties to the soldiers, nor refuse them furlough. Christie also agreed with the Punjab School that, in the ultimate analysis, the discipline of the soldiers pivoted round the commanding officer on the spot. To increase their authority was therefore the only solution.[17]

The Punjab School also came out with a formula for transforming the commandant into a type of 'Oriental Despot', by increasing his power in the following spheres: (i) the authority to dismiss privates, (ii) the power to flog the soldiers for insubordination or theft, (iii) the authority to fine the soldiers, (iv) the power to reduce the non-commissioned officers by at least one rank, and (v) the authority to imprison privates and non-commissioned officers.[18]

As a result, after 1859, the powers of the regimental officers increased. However, not everybody, and certainly not the Adjutant General (who lost authority due to the shift of power towards the regimental officers), accepted the post-Mutiny scenario without demur. Colonel E. Haythorne, the Adjutant General, kept a strict watch over the activities of the commanding officers. He attacked summary trials and the other powers of the commanding officers.

Summary trials were the trump card in the commandants' hands. In such trials, the officers could deploy their authority unchecked, away from the supervision and counselling of their superiors. This came under sustained criticism from the Adjutant

General. In 1863, an officer punished several men of his regiment because they disobeyed orders on parade and used bad language. To punish them, the officer resorted to a summary trial. The Adjutant General pointed out that there was nothing wrong in punishing the soldiers, but the method used for punishing them was faulty. Summary trials could be used only when the concerned superior officer was far away. But, in this case the officer commanding the brigade was on the spot. The Adjutant General admonished the officer commanding the regiment and felt that he should have taken recourse to a general court martial.[19] In the next year Haythorne pointed out that according to the 81st article of war, the proceedings of summary trials must be held in the presence of two commissioned officers, but in one recent case the rule had not been followed. He warned that, if the commanding officers broke the law, then they would be divested of their power of holding summary trials.[20]

The final attack came from the highest authority, the Viceroy, Lord Lawrence. With the memories of the 1857 Mutiny fresh in his mind, Lawrence concluded that misuse of power by the regimental officers resulted in the outbreak. So when Lawrence enquired about the state of regimental officer's arrogant attitude in disciplining the sepoys, the Commander-in-Chief, Hugh Rose had to write an apologetic letter to the Viceroy. On 9 March 1864 Rose wrote to the Viceroy:

I pay particular attention to the fact that Native soldiers being properly and kindly, treated by their British officers. I never fail to check or disapprove injustices or misconduct in a contrary sense. But, in justice to these officers, I am forced to say that cases of the latter type were very rare. I am a strict disciplinarian in all matters of duty; but my principle is that no discipline is good which is not based on justice. . . . If you have heard of any instances of British officers acting improperly towards their Native subordinates I should feel very much obliged if you are good enough to tell me about them.[21]

Prodded by Lawrence whose ideas were somewhat similar to Bentinck regarding the introduction of humane disciplinary structure, General William Mansfield, the Commander-in-Chief of the Indian Army from 1865 to 1870 also took steps to reduce the regimental commandants powers of. His view was that the high-handed behaviour by the commanding officers had brought the summary trials into disrepute. He cited a case where the commanding officer had acted on impulse and abused his power. In 1865, a sepoy went to his regimental officer for the redressal of some grievance but the officer instead of hearing it, called him *haramzada*. When the sepoy reacted sharply, he was flogged.[22]

Sowar Gunay Khan belonging to the 1st Light Cavalry of the Bombay Army was given extra guard duty by his commanding officer without any reason. When he demurred, the regimental commandant Colonel Ashburner summarily dismissed him. The high command took note of the arbitrary behaviour on part of the commanding officer of the regiment. Lieutenant-General Robert Napier, Commander-in-Chief of the Bombay Army (1866–9) agreed that the sowar was not guilty. But, he refused to overrule the regimental commandant's decision fearing that such a move would weaken the regimental commandant's authority to a dangerous extent and in the end might result in indiscipline. Nevertheless, Napier warned that his patience was running thin. On 24 January 1866, Napier communicated to the regimental officers the following message:

Very great powers are now placed in the hands of commanding officers, and I am most unwilling to interfere with them; but it will be impossible to continue my support to those commanding officers who do not show a due discrimination in the exercise of their authority. Colonel Ashburner's explanation of the circumstances under which sowar Gunay Khan of the 1st Light Cavalry was placed on police picket immediately after coming off standard guard is unsatisfactory. . . . Ashburner must be informed that I entirely disapprove of the severity of the sentence, under the circumstances which led to it.[23]

In 1893, the commandant of the 26th Bombay Infantry requested power to dismiss summarily any Indian officer whom he considered unsuitable. Neither the Adjutant General of India nor the Commander-in-Chief of the Bombay Army agreed to this.[24] The army higher administration again acted in 1895, to curtail the powers of commanding officers. This move was headed by the Adjutant General, G. Dec. Morton. He decreed that summary courts martial could not try offences of soldiers against their commanding officers, unless the permission of the staff officers of the divisions, districts and brigades was obtained. When their sanctions were not recorded then the commanding officers had to state the reasons for proceeding on their own authority. In

1895, it was further ordered that, though the commanding officers who held the summary courts martial alone constituted the courts, in order to check or at least to reduce the gross misuse of power, each summary court martial was to be attended by an interpreter. The army administration demanded evidence to ensure that the summary courts martial procedures were in accordance with law. An aspect of centralization from top was the army headquarter's demand for inspection of the returns regarding the summary courts martial. Hence, the commandants had to record their findings and sentences. The proceedings were to be signed by the commanding officers and all those officers in whose presence the trials were held.[25] Besides directly reducing the regimental officers' authority, the Adjutant General increased the power of the senior officers. He informed them that they were empowered by article 141 to use their discretionary power during the courts martial of which they were the confirming officers.[26]

After 1859 the Adjutant General's department by issuing directives reduced the powers of regimental officers in other spheres beside the summary courts martial. In many cases the commanding officers were awarded joint responsibility for punishing their men. Fights between the soldiers and the Indian police were common. The Adjutant General pointed out one case in 1862, when soldiers marching along the Grand Trunk Road misbehaved towards the police personnel. To prevent the recurrence of such affairs, the commanding officers of the regiments and detachments were ordered that, if such cases occurred in future, then they should report to the nearest military stations and enquiries should start under the officers in charge of the stations.[27] For serious offences committed by the soldiers in detached employments, the regimental commandants could not award them punishments without accommodating, the views of the concerned departmental officials.[28] The regimental officers were further directed to obtain the sanction of the Commander-in-Chief before giving the options of resigning from the service or of standing before the courts martial, to the soldiers who had broken discipline.[29]

Just before the onset of the Great War, though the powers of commanding officers were decreased in some areas, the army headquarter increased their authority in certain spheres. This was probably because the top echelons of the army accepted the fact that, to a large extent, the discipline of the soldiers depended on the commanding officers, who could not be dispensed with. The high command probably grasped that the Sepoy Army was always scattered in small units performing police operations against the tribals and peasant insurgents. For conducting such small-scale peacekeeping operations, devolution of power to the regimental officers was necessary. Even in the twentieth century the Western armies gave much autonomy to the junior officers to come up with innovative tactics in order to cope with rapidly changing scenario both during peacekeeping campaigns as well as in cases of inter-state war. Thus the imperative of mission or directive command (*Auftragstaktik*) probably forced the top echelon of the military bureaucracy not to eliminate the authority of regimental officers completely. The Sepoy Army had many similarities with the late-nineteenth century American Army. Both were composed of volunteers and were principally engaged in low intensity operations, and the American regimental officers played a dominant role in the American Army like their Indian counterparts.[30] Thus, the structural and functional necessities of the Sepoy Army prevented complete centralization.

However, the extent of reduction of the commanding officers' power becomes clear when we compare the power they enjoyed in 1913 with the programme of the Punjab lobby. The commanding officers lost the power to flog the soldiers. The power to award rigorous or simple imprisonment with or without solitary confinement was reduced from seventy-five days to only twenty-eight days. The officers could imprison the privates for only seven days, and lost the authority to arrest any non-commissioned officer. For misconduct, negligence and inefficiency, the non-commissioned officers and the privates could be deprived, by their commanding officers, the whole or part of the pay of the day on which the offence was committed. Previously the commanding officers had the power to also fine the commissioned officers, up to one month's pay. The senior officers got the power to remit punishments awarded by the regimental officers. A procedure came into existence to check the abuse of authority by the officers, and also to prevent them from exacting personal revenge on their men. Whatever punishments the regimental officers awarded to their men, they had to be recorded in the conduct sheets and these were sent to the army headquarter.[31]

The powers of commanding officers as regards the summary courts martial though reduced remained adequate. In such courts martial, much depended on the discretion of the commanding officers who were allowed to pass judgements legally which depended on their perceptions of the soldiers' characters. Thus, they retained the authority to deprive the soldiers of their rank.[32] The commanding officers' authority registered a quantum jump in the following spheres: the power to issue reprimands to the Indian officers and the authority to confine them to the lines. However, for increasing confinement to the lines beyond 15 days, the commanding officers had to take the Adjutant's permission. During the short-term imprisonments, the commanding officers retained control over the prisoners. For minor breaches of prison discipline by the prisoner, which were enquired into by the commanding officers, the latter could award the following punishments (i) reduction in their diet and (ii) additional hard labour and punishment drill.[33] At the discretion of the commanding officers, prisoners serving sentences of hard labour were awarded the following tasks (i) digging and carrying earth and (ii) filling up shelter trenches, etc. The details regarding the apportioning of the hours for hard labour and drill, for waking up the prisoners in the morning and locking them at night, were left to the will of the commanding officers.[34] So, enough space remained for the commanding officers to award either minor or heavy forms of punishment for the same type of crime. If the commanding officers wanted, they could make life hell for the soldiers. Hence, the latter had good reason to keep the officers in good humour.

Most of these punishments were regimental in nature, as they were carried out inside the regiments and under the supervision of the regimental officers. All these increased the leverage of the regimental officers *vis-à-vis* their soldiers, which would have been impossible in case the punishments were conducted by the extra-regimental authorities. Why did the Adjutant General's department tolerate regimental punishment? This was because, even for the high command, the colonial army remained regiment oriented. Again, regimental punishments were probably preferred because, if the accused were humiliated in front of their comrades, the fear shame deterred others from breaking the law. Thus the tussle about where the real locus of power should lie— whether with the regimental officers or with the Adjutant General's department—was shaped, not merely by the struggle between the frontline commanders and the military bureaucrats at Simla and Calcutta, but also by the civilian-military elite's conception of the Indian society and the structure of the army.

II

COURTS MARTIAL, ARTICLES OF WAR AND OATHS

The impersonal institutions at the disposal of the army head-quarter for disciplining the soldiers were the courts martial, articles of war and the oaths. Just after the 1857 catastrophe, those who favoured the decentralized regimental disciplinary structure stressed the inefficiency of such impersonal institutions and demanded more discretionary power in the hands of the commanding officers. Against their wishes, the army high command encouraged greater use of bureaucratic institutions for inculcating extra-regimental discipline.

The army possessed various types of courts martial, whose jurisdiction and composition varied. For the Sepoy Army, the British introduced, with slight modifications, the different types of courts martial which were operational in the British Army from late-eighteenth century.[35] The cases brought before the various types of courts martial depended on the gravity of the crimes and the ranks of the persons to be tried. At the top were the general courts martial. Then came the district or garrison courts martial and below them were the regimental courts martial. At the bottom were the summary courts martial which were controlled by the commanding officers under the loose supervision of the army headquarter.[36]

The courts had a wide variety of punishments to discipline the soldiers. The quantum of punishment that could be awarded decreased as one moved down the hierarchy of the courts martial. General courts martial could award death sentences, imprisonments for life, or very long-term imprisonments. District courts martial had the power to impose fines, to demote and suspend the army personnel, and could award penal servitudes for limited periods.[37] Summary courts martial could inflict purely physical punishments like lashing or purely financial punishments. The latter could be temporary (like stoppages) or permanent (like forfeitures of additional pay and pension). Such courts could also award a mixture of monetary and non-monetary punishments like imprisonments which involved loss of pay, as well as physical and mental discomforts.[38]

The higher the courts were, the greater was their power to try higher ranks and serious offences. As one goes down the hierarchy of the courts martial, the ranks and number of officers sitting in them declined. The general courts martial had power to try any rank and only such courts had the authority to judge the commissioned Indian officers. They tried serious crimes like mutinies and insubordination. Each general court martial was composed of nine officers.[39] The presidents of such courts were very high ranking officers like Brigadier-Generals or Lieutenant-Generals.[40] Each district court martial was composed of five to seven officers. The regimental courts martial tried minor offences and the officers commanding the regiments could summon these courts. Each such court had three to five officers.[41] The summary courts martial were held for such minor offences as receiving stolen goods and even European non-commissioned officers summoned such courts.[42]

The army high command was itself confused about the degree of centralization it should pursue. The quantum of power in the hands of the higher courts martial and the senior officers was directly proportional to the degree of centralization achieved. The jurisdiction of the various types of courts martial varied with time, as the army high command dilly-dallied about the quantum of power to be devolved to the various courts for maintaining the disciplinary structure.

In 1827, Combermere ordered that the regimental and not the summary courts martial apparatus could award corporal punishment and that too only when the crimes involved stealing, marauding or insubordination.[43] In 1859, the Punjab lobby demanded that those crimes which involved imprisonment of more than six months were to be tried by the district courts martial under the generals commanding divisions. They should have the power to order imprisonments upto fourteen years with transportation, but punishments beyond this should require the Commander-in-Chief's intervention.[44] For the time being, the district courts martial acquired such power. But in 1861, the army headquarter, in pursuing the policy of centralization, reduced the power of the district courts martial, and increased that of the general courts martial. It was necessary to implement prompt punishments if the disciplinary mechanism was to remain intact. But due to communication and transportation difficulties, assembling general courts martial was time-consuming—it took about three months to arrange one. So, in 1865 the power of the district courts martial was slightly increased. They acquired the power to dismiss officers and award imprisonment (not exceeding two years) with hard labour as well as solitary confinement.[45]

In some cases, senior officers enjoyed wide discretionary power *vis-à-vis* the court martial. But, how much power would be wielded by the officers, and at what level, was decided by the army headquarter's centralization scheme. Privates and non-commissioned officers who lost their arms were generally tried by the district courts martial. In 1913, the general officers commanding divisions acquired authority to order trials. However, the Commander-in-Chief could annul proceedings of such trials.[46]

The British Army like other Western armies of the nineteenth century flogged and jailed its errant personnel following a written code of punishment and laws.[47] Similarly, in the Sepoy Army the articles of war shaped punishment. The army also made use of the oaths to run the court martial mechanism and to influence the conscience of soldiers, so that they obeyed the code of conduct prescribed by the articles of war. After 1857, the army was a divided house as regards the efficacy of the oaths and the articles of war. While the regimental officers argued that the articles of war as elements of alien law should not be imposed on the Indians, the army headquarter was for modernizing the army by introducing Western laws. As regards constructing laws for the civilians, a similar debate occurred among the Raj's officials. While the anti-Macaulay group was for continuation of the existing Indian laws and practices, the pro-Macaulay-Benthamite lobby was for introducing English laws and practice.[48]

Christie was against imposing the rule of articles of war on the soldiers. He pointed out that, before 1857, the articles of war were read out and explained to the men four times a year to acquaint the troopers of the irregular cavalry regiments of the Bengal Army with the military code under which they were governed. However, the discipline of the Bengal Irregular Cavalry deteriorated when they were brought under the articles of war. In his opinion the small zamindars and their retainers, who joined the irregular cavalry, disliked rigid disciplines and the articles of war which were explained to them during the parades.[49] The members of the Punjab School agreed with Christie about the inefficiency of the Western articles of war. But, unlike Christie, they believed that the articles of war were necessary for the army's discipline. So, the Punjab School demanded separate articles of war for the brown soldiers, as they were convinced that the character of the Indians was different from that of the British. The Punjab School cautioned against the amalgamation of the rules of the British Army with those of the Sepoy Army.[50] Both Bentinck and the Punjab School accepted that the Indians were different from the Europeans, and hence it was necessary to change the articles of war. But both held different views on the changes. While Bentinck wanted 'enlightened' principles like the abolition of flogging, the Punjab School was for retention of flogging, etc.[51]

Distribution of the articles of war among the soldiers was not considered effective because of their low level of literacy. We have some figures about the literacy rate among the soldiers during 1857, and this rate more or less remained stagnant in the post-1859 period. No drivers of the artillery could read the articles of war in the vernacular, and only 10 per cent of the *golundazes* understood them. About 15 per cent of the troopers of the Punjab Irregular Cavalry were able to read and comprehend the articles of war in their own vernaculars. Only 5 per cent of the personnel in the Punjab Frontier Force were able to read the articles of war in their own vernaculars. Overall, 10 per cent of the soldiers were able to do the same. Between 1874–5, 1,086 recruits joined the Madras Army. Of them, 1,041 joined the regimental schools. Among the personnel of the Madras Army, 9,421 could read and write and 2,231 could only read. However, Madras Army was exceptional for having a significant number of literate soldiers. The communities from Nepal and north-west India were much less literate compared to the communities of South India who joined the Madras Army till the 1880s. As the entry of the 'martial races' increased under Roberts, the overall literacy rate among the personnel of the Sepoy Army went down. An idea about literacy among the late-nineteenth century soldiers could be gleaned from analysing the literacy rates among the groups who joined the army. Only 4 per cent among the Marathas, 10 per cent among the Deccani Muslims and 11 per cent among the Jat Sikhs were literate.[52]

Though the civilian-military elite just after 1857 was not enthusiastic about the efficacy of the articles of war in acting as a deterrent, the army headquarter put its faith on the public readings of the articles of war. To acquaint the personnel with the serious punishment they would suffer for breaching discipline, the Commander-in-Chief in 1865 issued orders that when the articles of war were read out, the prisoners as well as the wounded and the sick should also attend the parades. It was ordered that the articles of war were to be read in the hospitals once every three months.[53] After the Commander-in-Chief's order was issued certain officers continued to challenge the imposition of Western disicipline over the sepoys. Brigadier C.H. Brownlow commented in 1875 that the Hindustani soldiers degenerated in the first half of the nineteenth century due to the imposition of Western disciplinary structure over them.[54] In the next year, the Resident of Hyderabad, C.B. Saunders warned the higher authorities that drill and discipline merely irritated the landed magnates and their relatives who joined the Hyderabad Contingent Cavalry.[55]

The spokesmen of the regiment-centric disciplinary system displayed a casual attitude towards the oath and did not take it seriously. Christie bluntly told the men in the higher echelons that he did not remember the words of the oath which was administered to the recruits who joined the Bengal Army's Irregular Cavalry.[56] The Punjab lobby was sceptical of the policy of using the oath in strengthening the loyalty of the soldiers. No oath was administered initially in the Punjab Frontier Force, but in 1857, due to pressure from the army headquarter, it became obligatory for the men to take oaths. However, the authorities found it prudent not to humiliate old soldiers by ordering them to take an oath, as they had already served with loyalty for long. However, all the new recruits had to take the oath. After the

1857 bloodbath, the Punjab lobby argued that the oath was useless in practice, as the unconscientious soldiers would always disregard them. The Punjab lobby concluded that every solemn arrangement had its limitations and the soldiers willing to rebel could find loopholes in the oath. Still, the army headquarter took the oath seriously, and imposed it on the soldiers. The oath had been introduced in 1840 for the recruits. The oath remained unchanged even after the Mutiny.[57] The oath was simplified to the fewest possible words, as most of the soldiers were un-educated. The oath was as follows: 'I inhabitant of . . . village, . . . parganah, . . . district, . . . province; do swear before Almighty God, that I will be a faithful soldier, and servant of the British government, that I will march wherever I am directed and will obey the orders of any European officer.' The oath contained information about the soldiers' geographical origin so that they could be traced easily in case of desertion. The oath contained an obligation for general service, though it was not implemented till 1856. Its implementation caused grievance among the *Purbiyas*, which in turn accelerated the 1857 catastrophe.[58]

Unlike the recruits' oath, the court martial proceedings' oath was characterized by the appropriation of the religious identity of the different groups. This was probably because the army took courts martial more seriously. So, the oaths were designed to touch the religious belief of the soldiers in order to extract the 'truth' out of them. Each religious group's belief was invoked. For the Hindus, *Parmeshwar Bhagwan*, for the Muslims, *Khuda* and for the Sikhs the *Guru Granth Sahib* was invoked. The emphasis on conscience for each religious group differed. For the Hindus, the emphasis was on *dharma*, for the Muslims the focus was on *iman* and for the Sikhs, it was the wrath of the *Guru Granth Sahib*. The vernacular oath can roughly be translated as: 'I swear in the name of God that I will only tell the truth and I will not lie. If I lie then I will be punished.'[59]

III

TRANSITION FROM PERSONALIZED TO BUREAUCRATIC EXTRA-REGIMENTAL DISCIPLINARY SYSTEM

The disciplinary apparatus gradually became impersonal, as control passed from the regimental commanding officers into the hands of distant military bureaucrats, who functioned from Simla and Calcutta. Under their bureaucratic supervision a series of modalities which involved lot of paper work came into existence for regulating punishment. Along with bureaucratic surveillance, the nature of punishment was also transformed. From being repressive and public, it became reformative and private. This change was not due to public pressure through newspapers but due to internal bickering within the army about how best to construct the disciplinary apparatus over the soldiers.

Bentinck wanted to change the nature of punishment because of the changing material conditions and mentality of the Indians. His view was that the system of punishment had not changed since 1797, but, due to the *Pax Britannica*, education was spreading. To his mind, this had improved the character of Indians and made them more sensible of their rights. Consequently, degrading punishments could not be inflicted upon the soldiers any more. According to him, Indians were by nature attached to a government which treated them kindly, and they were very sensitive to disrespect. So, if the state wanted allegiance from them, then corporal punishment had to be abandoned. He then linked this issue with recruitment. The high castes who joined the Bengal Army were obedient and faithful by nature, so, there was no need to flog them. And if they were flogged, then it depressed them so much that they had to be discharged. Bentinck further claimed that many high castes who make 'good soldiers' avoided the army for fear of corporal punishment.[60] The argument, that flogging prevented good men from entering the army, and depressed the spirit of those who were lashed, was also put forward by a radical minority in Britain in the late-eighteenth and early-nineteenth centuries.[61] Bentinck was probably influenced by such ideas. He argued that any attempt to check crimes through terror tactics was wrong. He pointed out that even in the British Army corporal punishment was gradually reduced from 1793 onwards because it was believed that lashing was both cruel and impolitic.[62]

The Bombay Army's officers like Whittingham wanted corporal punishment to maintain discipline.[63] He argued that, corporal punishment should not be abolished in the colonial army unless flogging was done away with in the British regiments also. Otherwise the effect on the white troops would be to 'produce a dangerous feeling in the mind of the European soldier serving in the same brigade with black battalions, to find that he is still subject to a vile degradation from which his black comrade in arms has been so lately exempted'.[64]

Bentinck overruled such opinions and replaced corporal punishment with solitary confinement and dismissal from service. He wanted fines to be imposed on the prisoners during their confinement. Bentinck assumed that the termination of service was the greatest punishment for the Indian soldier. Bentinck viewed dismissal from service both as an economic loss and a social stigma for the soldier. He wrote that discharge deprived the soldiers of the chance of acquiring honour, as well as the pay which went to support their families.[65]

Lord Hardinge (Governor-General from 1844 to 1848) re-introduced corporal punishment in 1845, against the opposition of the Adjutant General. Unlike Bentinck, Hardinge was unsure, in the context of the rising crime rate within the Bengal Army, about the deterrent value of dismissal as a punishment. The premium placed on flogging as a deterrent was based on a particular British view of Indian society which was quite different from that portrayed by Bentinck. Hardinge painted a picture of the high-caste soldiers with a sense of strict honour; so flogging in public humiliated them. Fear of public humiliation, argued Hardinge, forced the sepoys to behave properly. Also, the army did not like civilian interaction with its personnel even when the latter were punished, because it was assumed that civilian company while undergoing punishment, would ruin the soldiers. Under Bentinck, flogging was replaced by hard labour, which involved the soldiers working with civilian prisoners in constructing roads. So, to avoid the contact with civilians, the army wanted restoration of flogging. Further, there was pressure from 'below' by the soldiers themselves. Many high-caste soldiers demanded flogging instead of hard labour, as repairing roads resulted in mixing with low castes and consequently loss of caste for the former, and many soldiers demanded discharge for this reason. Finally, the army wanted to stop the continuous haemorrhage of manpower, as those soldiers who were awarded hard labour on the roads never rejoined their units. The British also believed, that by implementing flogging, they were just following the age-old Indian tradition. They were convinced that flogging existed in the Indian armies long before British intervention.[66] So the oscillation between the abolition and the introduction of lashing was a complex tussle between humane liberalism and reactionary conservatism.

After the 1857 Mutiny, the Punjab School proposed the following forms of punishment: (i) imprisonment and solitary confinement, (ii) fines, (iii) reduction in rank, (iv) flogging upto thirty lashes for theft or insubordination (those who were flogged three times were to be dismissed), and (v) dismissal.[67] In contrast to the Punjab School, Frere supported Bentinck's proposal that dismissal from service was the greatest punishment for the Indian soldiers. While Bentinck emphasized both the monetary and non-monetary aspects (honour and prestige) of the service, Frere stressed only on the economic aspect. Both believed that the European soldiers were paid very little in the context of the wages prevalent in their societies. So they were unwilling to join the armies, and had to be retained by fear, generated through various forms of punishment against desertions. Frere and Bentinck believed that the sepoys and the sowars were paid quite highly in relation to other occupations in their society, so they joined voluntarily for long periods. Expulsion from service, which also involved loss of pension, was a great loss for them.[68]

By 1913, the following forms of punishment were in vogue: (i) Imprisonment, rigorous or simple, long or short-term, with or without solitary confinement. Generally imprisonment was reserved for serious and repeated offences; the guilty soldiers were confined to the lines before imprisonment, (ii) Confinement to the lines, not exceeding twenty-eight days. An award of more than fourteen days carried with it punishment drill. For minor offences, extra guard or fatigue duties were awarded, (iii) non-commissioned officers and privates were admonished. Reprimands were for the commissioned officers, (iv) deprivation of ranks.[69]

Though some aspects of punishment, like dismissal, remained unchanged for over half a century, several aspects of the disciplinary system were transformed. The shift was from flogging towards imprisonment under the extra-regimental authorities. This process started long before 1857. Sending soldiers to prison for punishment was common in the post-Napoleonic French Army.[70] Similarly in the British Home Army, the second half of the nineteenth century witnessed the replacement of flogging with imprisonment.[71] In the post-Mutiny period, for the British soldier stationed in India, imprisonment replaced corporal punishment as the most common form of punishment.[72] This trend also became widespread in the Sepoy Army. The number of lashes which could be inflicted on the soldiers, and the incidence of lashing, decreased with time. In 1806, two soldiers of the 2nd Battalion of the 4th Madras Infantry Regiment got 900 lashes each.[73] Flogging was resorted to very rarely, even after Hardinge's introduction of corporal punishment. In 1859 one officer, who had commanded a sepoy battalion for seven years, claimed to have implemented corporal punishment not even twice during his career.[74] After the Mutiny, as part of British reaction to it, flogging remained, but the maximum number of lashes which could be awarded was limited to fifty, and became increasingly rare. We have only one recorded case between 1860 and 1865, when in the latter year, a sepoy was flogged for misbehaving with his officer.[75] The real value of flogging lay in its threat and not in its actual implementation. By 1913, flogging had vanished from the army.

How did this shift occur, and what were the factors that influenced the changes in punishment? In the post-Mutiny era, in the absence of an all powerful Governor-General like Bentinck, the mantle for shaping the contours of the punishment system went by default to the Adjutant General's department. Imprisonment with hard labour, and solitary confinement, came into existence under the Adjutant General's orders.[76] Solitary confinement in military custody was carried out in the following manner. The prisoners were confined separately in the regimental cells or in the guard rooms and two prisoners were never put in a single cell. In case of rigorous punishment in military custody, the prisoners were put to hard labour, and had to undergo punishment drills.[77] The need for the combat effectiveness of the units, also shaped the type of punishment. Long periods of imprisonment, which were carried out in regimental custody, were discouraged in the army.[78] This was because such imprisonment reduced the combat efficiency of the units, as extra men had to be detached for guarding the prisoners. Moreover, finding a suitable place for imprisonment was a problem, especially when the regiments were on the move. So, the Adjutant General further ordered that short imprisonment terms should be implemented in the barrack cells, and long imprisonment terms should be served in the state prisons.[79] As the army did not want to lose control over the soldiers even when they were punished, the army's surveillance scheme influenced the punishment structure. Imprisonment with hard labour exceeding three months had to be undergone in the civil jails which resulted in the soldiers mixing with the civilian prisoners. The army believed that interaction with such characters ruined the soldiers. So, in 1895, the Commander-in-Chief intervened, and ruled that those soldiers who were sentenced to imprisonment with hard labour exceeding three months were to be dismissed.[80]

Some regimental officers were cynical about the way in which punishments became less brutal. This was because the army headquarter took away their power of punishing the soldiers. The commanding officers, as a result, ceased to be paternal despots. Just before the First World War, under the new regulation, soldiers got two months solitary confinement in the regimental cell for desertion. Major G. Casserly, the commandant of a Gurkha battalion argued that this meant that the convicts had a better deal than their more disciplined colleagues, who had to parade daily under the hot sun, while the prisoners relaxed in the cool cells.[81]

Practical difficulties in carrying out sentences influenced the army's response. When the courts martial ordered solitary confinement, the army administration had problems in implementing it. In 1865, when a court martial sentenced a sepoy to solitary confinement, in a regiment stationed in the Dooars in Bhutan, he was sent to the Rangpur jail in the Bengal Presidency. The Bengal government pointed out that the jails in Bengal were unsuitable for such a purpose.[82] Due to inadequate housing facilities, the jails in Bengal could neither provide separate cells for solitary confinement of the soldiers nor could keep the civilian and military prisoners in separation. By the first decade of the twentieth century, as imprisonment became the most common form of punishment, the government started constructing detention barracks for short imprisonments and military prisons for long-term imprisonment. To man the detention barracks and the prisons, an elaborate staff network was also laid down. The Lucknow detention barrack had two drill instructors and four assistants. The military prison-cum-detention barrack at Poona had two drill instructors and eight assistants. This was necessary as short-term imprisonments were occasionally accompanied by extra drills to be performed under the drill inspector's eyes.[83]

The army administration developed bookkeeping and inspecting reports regarding punishment. This was meant to check the abuse of authority by the officers, and also to create written precedents, to educate incoming officers about how to punish certain crimes. As service records shaped the nature of punishments to be inflicted, the army began to keep various forms of documents. Registers were kept by the Adjutants in which the numbers and names of the prisoners, their crimes and periods of sentence, dates of admission and discharge, were recorded. The Adjutants also maintained the prisoners' punishment books which recorded all the offences committed by the prisoners, the punishments given, and sentences they had served previously (if any).[84] Breaches of discipline by the non-commissioned officers and men were entered in the defaulters' sheets. The records of the commissioned Indian officers remained with the Deputy Adjutant General. These records aided the army's disciplinary mechanism in the assessment of the personnel, as these sheets contained records about convictions by courts martial, cases of summary reductions, and cases involving imprisonment and confinements. The army also kept character sheets of the soldiers because, while passing sentences against the convicts, their previous character was taken into account. Each character sheet contained the designation of the unit in which the soldier was employed, his name and rank, the date and the occurrence of crime, and the opinion of the commanding officer.[85]

IV

COMPULSIONS BEHIND INCOMPLETE CENTRALIZATION

The advocates of a personalized regimental command structure demanded that the rights of privates and the Indian officers to challenge their commanding officers should be drastically reduced. But, the army headquarter tried instead to increase the quantum of rights enjoyed by the soldiers within the army's legal framework. This tussle centred around three issues: the share of the Indian officers in running the disciplinary mechanism, how the law was 'perverted' to deny certain legal rights to the soldiers, and the advantages the soldiers derived from the military law.

After the 1857 Mutiny, the army witnessed a debate regarding the role of the Indian officers in manning the disciplinary mechanism. The supporters of the decentralized regimental disciplinary culture, in pursuing their formula of making the regimental officers arbitrary despots, wanted the Indian officers to be mere cyphers. But, the army headquarter supported by Brigadier-General John Jacob obstructed this scheme. The discussions revolved round the question of the professional expertise of the Indian officers, and their loyalty during 1857. In 1858 Jacob claimed:

After many years of experience . . . I assert that one great Resaldar, or a Resaldar Major, is invaluable in a regiment . . . and no number of European officers could supply his place. But the fact is, the value of Indian officer is not properly understood. . . . The squadron and troop commanders of the Sindh Irregular Horse are Indians; yet the greater part of them perform their duties as well, and in all respects as efficiently as the best European officers, whether in quarters, on parade, on the line of march, or in battle.[86]

Even after the questionable role of the Indian officers during the Mutiny, the imperialists vetoed the proposal of replacing them with the non-commissioned British officers. The Punjab lobby like Jacob wanted the Indian officers to continue, as they were seen as a vital link in man-management. European corporals and sergeants could not replace the Indian officers, as the former had no influence over the soldiers. The Punjab lobby concluded that if the Indian officers were selected on the basis of merit, then they could perform better than the European sergeants. Frere commented that the Indian commissioned officers were superior in professional intelligence to the European non-commissioned officers. So, they could not be replaced with European non-commissioned officers.[87]

Christie argued that during the Mutiny the Indian officers failed to show absolute fidelity. They neither gave information in advance about the uprising, nor did they actively aid in quelling it. He calculated that about 50 per cent of the Bengal Army's

Indian officers supported the mutineers. The Punjab lobby, unlike Christie, asserted that most of the Indian officers would remain loyal during a crisis. The Sikh officers had remained loyal and there was no mutiny in the Punjab Frontier Force in 1857. Prior to 1857, the Indian officer corps was more or less loyal, and during the Mutiny the Indian officers were carried away by the storm, rather than leading it. Frere, also emphasized the loyalty of Indian officers during the Mutiny who passed information about the disaffection of their men, and tried to keep them under control. During the emergency, they showed intelligence and fidelity. So, in his view the Indian officers should be given responsibility.[88] In the ultimate analysis, the Indian officers were necessary. The question, then, was how much power should they exercise.

The supporters of the personalized command structure challenged the practice of promotion on the basis of seniority, arguing that it led to dull Indians entering the officer cadre. Interestingly, none of them supported impersonal tests like examinations, to choose the Indians for officer ranks. Rather, they wanted that British regimental commandants exercise discretionary power while appointing Indian officers. This, they believed, would make the personal loyalty bonds between the British officers and the Indian officers stronger, as the latter group would be dependent on the sahib's favour for continuation in their posts and for promotions. A subservient Indian officer corps would pose no challenge to the sahibs. Hence the high command's programme to inculcate professionalism among the Indian officers by conducting written tests for their promotions[89] was obstructed by the self-interest of regimental commanders. For sustaining the patronage network, many officers of the late-nineteenth and early-twentieth-century American Army also opposed promotion to officer rank on the basis of merit.[90]

In the Bengal Irregular Cavalry, promotion was on the basis of a combination of merit (as assessed by the regimental officers), and seniority. There were no tests or examinations required for promotions in the Sepoy Army. Instead of impersonal assessments for assessing the professional expertise of the Indian officers, Christie wanted to continue the personalized sahib-sepoy relationship, in which the sahibs enjoyed the power to promote the privates into officers. So, he declared that there was no need for any examinations to be conducted by the army bureaucracy.[91]

The Punjab lobby argued that as regards promotions in the Bengal Army, preference was given to seniority rather than merit. The privates regarded the officer rank as a reward for long-service, but by the time they reached the rank of a officer, they were too old and had become inefficient. The Punjab lobby concluded that the Indian officers could be intelligent and useful, if only their British officers selected them on the basis of merit.[92] Frere pointed out that promotion by seniority did not occur in the Bombay Army, where the Indian officers remained steadfast in their loyalty. Promotion occurred on the basis of assessment of character of the Indian soldier' by the British officers. This technique allowed the British officers to choose efficient Indians as officers, and Frere wanted this pattern to be followed in the Bengal Army.[93]

For the Punjab School, the Indian officers of the Bengal Army were unfit to sit in courts martial, because the Indian officers had been promoted on the basis of seniority. The Punjab lobby and Frere probably believed that promotion by seniority encouraged the Indian officers to be independent. However, their argument couched in ideological terms claimed that the Indian officers lacked 'moral resolution'. They proposed that if the Indian officers had to sit in the higher courts martial, they needed to be mentally active, and for that their selection had to be on the basis of merit assessed by the regimental officers. If this scheme was accepted, then it would have given the commanding officers total control over the Indian officers, which was the plan of the Punjab School. The Punjab lobby's programme was to disallow the Indian officers from entering even the regimental courts martial.[94] But, the army headquarter turned down this suggestion of the Punjab lobby.[95]

The regimental officers were especially unhappy about sharing power with the Indian officers. In the first decade of the twentieth century, Casserly argued that Indian soldiers disliked to be judged by Indian officers, because the latter were swayed by considerations of race, caste, village and family feuds and they showed favouritism towards some and dislike towards others. Occasionally, personal equations also operated, as most of the Indian officers were promoted from the ranks. When the soldiers committed crimes, they were allowed the option of whether to be judged by courts martial including Indian officers or courts manned by the British officers. Casserly asserted that during his long service, he never saw even one case when a sepoy demanded to be judged by Indian officers.[96]

Another officer of the Gurkhas, Charles Reid in 1876 also tried to prevent any attempt by the high command to raise the power of the Indian officers. Reid in a straightforward manner told the Duke of Cambridge: 'I have no confidence in the Indian officer, and never had.' Reid argued that any further increase in power of the Indian officers was undesirable because they were already disturbing the tenor of discipline within the regiments.[97] He continued:

When from sheer force of character or influence, one or two of them in a regiment acquire ascendancy, then that ascendancy is nearly always, and certainly as a general rule, employed in self-aggrandisement in some shape, and generally to the detriment of regimental discipline. In many corps one or two such Indian officers, unless very carefully watched by their European superiors, became regimental referees in all matters and occurrences in the Lines; the smile of approval or frown of dissent of one of these men probably causes, and as often prevents the report of many offences reaching the ears of the Adjutant or commanding officer. Such Indian officers in many corps wink at, if they do not openly sanction disobedience.[98]

The non-regimental officers were more generous. In 1875, Brigadier-General C.H. Brownlow, a supporter of the Indian officers claimed:

The Indian officers who should constitute the backbone of a Indian corps, and without whom there can be no reliable connecting link between the British officers and the men. . . . The key note of my observation and my belief is, that you cannot have a good Indian regiment without good Indian officers. . . . And its [Indian soldiers] morale, I repeat is dependent upon good Indian officers.[99]

The battle for and against Indian officers acquired a pan-Indian dimension. In 1876, while the Commandant of the Hyderabad Contingent, Brigadier-General T. Wright was for increasing the power of British officers at the expense of the Indian officers, the Resident at Hyderabad supported the cause of the Indian officers.[100]

The army high command turned a deaf ear to the reactionary regimental officers and inducted the Indian officers in all types of courts martial. Indian officers were included in the regimental as well as in the district courts martial by 1877.[101] This was because the Secretary of State Marquis of Salisbury supported the army high command. In 1876, he informed Viceroy Lord Northbrook: 'The Indian officers should be encouraged and supported for getting confidence by the regimental commandants.'[102]

Towards the end of the nineteenth century, General George Chesney pressurized the Raj's politico-military authorities for raising the power of the Indian officers. But, this scheme was obstructed by the all powerful Roberts. In 1884, Roberts the Commander-in-Chief of the Madras Army claimed that devolution of more power in the hands of the Indian officers would result in the British officers losing control over the Sepoy Army.[103] Roberts took the side of the regimental officers and obstructed the policy of inculcating professionalism among the Indian officers by educating them. On 10 July 1889, he wrote to the Viceroy: 'The commanding officers of the regiments are against General Chesney's scheme of increasing the Indian officers' power. Both in 1886 and in 1888, I was against Chesney's policy of educating the Indian officers.'[104]

However, the Commander-in-Chief, General Geo S. White took up the cudgels on behalf of the Indian officers. In 1893, he declared:

I believe the loyalty and value of the Native rank and file will be in proportion to the loyalty and value of the Native officers. I am therefore reluctant to accept any change that could have even the appearance of lowering the status or decreasing the responsibility of the Native officer. . . . Anything that can even be twisted into lowering of the status of the Native officer is also, I venture to say, politically inadvisable.[105]

In 1895, the Adjutant General, alarmed at the commanding officers abusing their authority in the summary courts martial, tried to check it by giving observer status to Indian officers in such courts. He ordered that two commissioned Indian officers should attend each summary court martial. The Indian commissioned officers also occasionally acted as presidents of the general courts martial, the apex body.[106] Though to begin with the Indian officers enjoyed limited power, it increased over time.

The high command kept the petty private affairs of the soldiers outside its domain, as such minor matters did not pose a threat to the war machine. Such autonomy to the soldiers somewhat eroded the regimental officers' authority. An autonomous locus of power for the soldiers was the *panchayat* where they settled their disputes without any interference by the British officers and Western military laws. The *panchayati* system was a unique case of Sepoy Army bowing to indigenous tradition to conciliate the soldiers. Indians were given limited power to sort out matters not directly related to the army. And this reflected the limitations of the army's reach over the private domains of the soldiers. *Panchayats* were held, with the consent of the parties concerned, for the settlement of private disputes. The disputants appointed the arbitrators themselves, and their decision was final. Generally the Subedar was appointed as president of the *panchayat*. The commanding officers had no power to challenge the *panchayat's* verdicts. The British officers merely coordinated the process by recording the names of the arbitrators and the subjects of the disputes. However, the power of the *panchayats* to award punishment was limited. The president (an Indian) of the *panchayat* could only stop the pay and allowances upto six months.[107]

After the Mutiny, the Punjab School demanded the abolition of the *panchayats*, to bring the soldiers within the orbit of direct military legal administration, for closer supervision. But Christie supported the opposite view when he argued that the court martial mechanism did not suit the Indians. He was for its replacement by the *panchayats*.[108] Christie was for 'Orientalizing' the army by introducing the indigenous *panchayati* system in place of the Western disciplinary system. He implied that 'Europeanizing' the Sepoy Army caused the 1857 Mutiny. To some extent, the post-Mutiny army high command accepted Christie's view, as a limited *panchayati* system was introduced.

Along with the *panchayats* the traditional Indian *durbar* also played a vital role in the day-to-day functioning of the regiments' discipline at the regimental level. Field Marshal Birdwood who joined the 11th Bengal Lancers in 1886 pointed out the importance of *durbars* in the following words:

Two or three days a week, instead of 'Orderly Room', the Colonel would hold an open Durbar. All British and Indian officers would sit with him, and all non-commissioned officers and men who wished to do so could attend. Practically all regimental business was discussed and despatched at these Durbars, which served to heighten the 'family' atmosphere of regimental life. Any prisoners were dealt with, though such were really very rare. Men wanting leave or furlough, advances of pay or loans, to take their discharge . . . or to bring up recruits from their villages with a view to enlistment: all came up at Durbar to state their case or needs.[109]

Just after 1857, there was a reaction among the British officers. They wanted to tighten the military judicial system, as they believed that the lax disciplinary system had encouraged the soldiers to rebel. As part of this reaction, the Punjab lobby tried to address the defective technicalities of the court martial mechanism, which allowed the 'guilty' soldiers to escape the law. The Punjab lobby pointed out that errors in procedures or sentences should not be allowed to quash the proceedings, thereby allowing the guilty soldiers to escape punishment. They further argued that when courts wrongly sentenced prisoners to punishment in excess of that prescribed by the articles, the confirming authority, instead of releasing the prisoners, should only reduce the punishment. Again, those prisoners who were erroneously tried and convicted by the lower courts for serious crimes instead of being released, should be remanded for trial by the higher courts.[110]

Just after the 1857 Mutiny, the Punjab lobby, in an attempt to increase the powers of British officers, demanded the revocation of the right of soldiers to appeal against the punishment given by the Brigadiers. Again, in the irregular units, there existed elements of arbitrariness. No attempt was made to stick to the book, and the commanding officers enjoyed wide discretionary power over their men. When the nature of the proofs against the offenders was insufficient to convict them according to the requirements of the articles of war, but where the criminals' 'guilt' was evident to the British officers, then such soldiers were dismissed without trial.[111]

Some articles of war strengthened the power of commanding officers over the soldiers. Article 70 gave them the power to punish soldiers for unspecified offences. To leave no aspect of the soldiers' activities uncovered, the offences included under this article were deliberately left unspecified. To support this, there was Article 25, which gave blanket power to the commanding officers for controlling the soldiers. Under it, the soldiers could be punished for 'unbecoming behaviour' (and the right to define it lay with the sahibs). Another article which reduced the power of soldiers to protest was Article 167. This punished those soldiers who made complaints against officers, which appeared frivolous or groundless to the commanding officers.[112] This certainly discouraged the soldiers from lodging complaints against their officers, as the alien officer cadre always acted as a body against the soldiers. So, even genuine complaints could be interpreted as groundless and frivolous.

Though in many ways the colonial military law curbed the right of troops to challenge British officers, the soldiers enjoyed some protection regarding the quantum of punishment that could be inflicted on them. This was meant to prevent permanent damage to their bodies and minds. It took a lot of time and money to convert peasants into soldiers. The limit on the amount of physical-cum-mental punishment to be inflicted arose out of the necessity to safeguard the army's own combat effectiveness. The army needed the human material back, in a condition of total fitness, after the prescribed period of punishment.

For the mental stability of the soldiers, solitary confinement was limited to fourteen days at a time, and could not exceed eighty-four days in a year,[113] and the soldiers could not be flogged twice in one month.[114] The total amount of hard labour and drill combined, to be exacted from the prisoners daily, was limited to six hours in hot weather and seven hours in cold weather. Extra periods of hard labour and drill were awarded for offences committed by the prisoners subsequent to their initial crimes. But, in no circumstances was drill to exceed two hours a day (one hour at a time) and hard labour to exceed five hours each day. Extra periods of hard labour or drill could be awarded only upto seven days. During hot weather, and at high noon, hard labour was confined to indoor work.[115]

The army high command showed concern to ensure that the punishments were awarded properly and not in an arbitrary manner. In 1893, in the 3rd Madras Lancers, the commanding officer awarded a sepoy fourteen days imprisonment because due to the Soldier's 'slovenly' and 'indifferent' attitude. The Adjutant General's office warned the officer that he had exceeded his power in punishing the sepoy so severely. In response, the commanding officer expressed regrets.[116] The superintending Indian non-commissioned officers were given the responsibility to see that hard labour did not exceed the prescribed limit, and in the hot season it was performed in the shade.[117] When prisoners underwent imprisonment, non-commissioned Indian officers took care of them. It was their duty to see that the prisoners got meals at regular hours. After locking up the prisoners at night, the keys were given to the Indian officers of the guards who were responsible for the safe custody of the prisoners. Their duty also entailed taking prisoners to hospital if they fell ill.[118]

No detention rooms were occupied without the recorded sanction of the general officers. They gave their sanctions after the reports came from the boards, which consisted of Assistant Directors of Medical Service, or the staff officers of the divisions or brigades. The boards had to certify that the rooms were well ventilated, warm and fitted in accordance with the sanitary requirements and standard plans. On the arrival of the prisoners, the commanding officers had to ascertain whether the rooms were fit for their detention.[119] Seniors officers were informed by the army high command that, when the prisoners had to undergo long-term imprisonment at the prisons, over-crowding was to be prevented, as it was injurious to the prisoners' health.[120]

During imprisonment, the prisoners were visited daily by the medical officers or hospital subordinates to ensure that their health was not deteriorating. Even while punishing them, the army took extra care of unfit or sick soldiers. Every morning before the courts sat, medical officers examined the accused awaiting trial. And the commanding officers were responsible for ensuring that if the accused soldiers were declared by the medical officers as unfit to undergo trial, then they should not be brought before the courts.[121] During summary courts martial also, the commanding officers had to attach the medical certificates of the accused to prove that they were healthy.[122] To ensure that the officers were keeping an eye on the health of the soldiers, even when they were undergoing punishment, visitors' books were kept, in which were recorded the date and hour of visits by the medical officers. All these documents were periodically checked by the army high command. The food for the prisoners were supplied by the contractors. For instance, the Yeroda jail at

Poona and the army high command was concerned with the quality of food provided by the contractors. The army regulated prisoners' diets. For misbehaviour, their diet could only be reduced to three meals a day.[123] In 1863, the Commander-in-Chief declared that those prisoners who were on a bread and water diet should not be subjected to hard labour.[124]

The soldiers also enjoyed other legal rights. Article 40 gave the soldiers the right to challenge those commanding officers who physically assaulted or ill treated them.[125] For matters of a purely personal nature, the soldiers could appeal directly to the divisional commanders. So, channels for appealing to the higher authorities existed for the soldiers to convey grievances against their immediate superiors. When accusations were made against British officers, the commanding officer called a court of inquiry. In case of injury to the soldier, the proceedings of the court of inquiry were confirmed, not by the regimental officer, but by the brigade commanders. The army high command was apprehensive that the regimental commandant would act in league with the other British officers of the regiment and victimize the Indian soldier. Hence, the need for outside intervention. If the soldiers were dissatisfied with the court of inquiry, then they could apply to the general courts martial.[126]

The soldiers enjoyed certain legal rights during the summary courts martial proceedings. Though the commanding officers had the final say, the soldiers were given the chance to argue their case during their defence and partly also during the prosecution examination. The prisoners were given the option to cross-examine each witness after the officers examined them, and this cross-examination was recorded for benefit of the army head-quarter. To avoid manipulation by the commanding officers, it was ordered that if the prisoners refused the right of cross-examination, then this also was to be recorded.[127]

However, the higher army administration did not always tolerate the right of soldiers to challenge their commanding officers. This was borne out in the case of Sheikh Torab, a Jemadar who petitioned to the high command in 1861, saying that he had been discharged without any charge being brought against him. The petitioner was subsequently informed that his appeal could not be entertained, as the high command held the commanding officer's decision as final in this regard.[128]

At times, the army headquarter showed more leniency. In the same year, Sheikh Ghulam Husain, a Havildar, appealed to the army headquarter, that he had been dismissed from service and had prayed for readmission, or at least pension for his long and faithful service. In this case, his petition was not rejected. The soldier was informed that the Adjutant General had passed the petition on to the Commander-in-Chief.[129]

From these two cases, we can deduce that at least some soldiers were not satisfied with their commanding officers' high-handed behaviour. They appealed to the high command, but the response of the top echelons of the army varied, because they were confused. On the one hand, they were ready to prevent the commanding officers from becoming too powerful; but on the other, they were afraid that if the soldiers were backed to the full, it would jeopardize the structure of command.

CONCLUSION

In many ways, the disciplinary structure was uniquely colonial. As far as the operative philosophy of the army was concerned, the intellectual paradigm through which the sahibs viewed the sepoys and sowars, and the relation between caste and corporal punishment, were specificities of the colonial scenario. Within the organizational apparatus of the army, the *panchayati* and the *durbar* system along with the courts martial oaths (adapted from religions) were distinctly Indian.

In the second half of the nineteenth century, the regiment-oriented personalized disciplinary fabric partly transformed itself into an impersonal bureaucratic disciplinary system. This transition was an ongoing process which had started long before 1857. While Bentinck the 'liberal' challenged Combermere before 1857, in the post-1859 period, the Adjutant General's department upheld Bentinck's line against the 'reactionaries' who were for increasing the regimental *satraps'* power and favoured harsh discipline. This tussle, as regards centralization versus de-centralization of power for disciplining the sepoys and the sowars continued till 1913. The continuous tension between two lobbies—one trying to make local commanders supreme and another trying to reduce the power of the regimental bosses in order to centralize authority in the hands of the distant military bureaucrats, was the principal feature of this transition. The spokesmen of the regiment-centric command culture wanted total repression of the soldiers, and tried to monopolize the hold over the disciplinary apparatus through the British regimental officers. But the army high command's policy was aimed to thwart the paternal despotism of the regimental sahibs by institutionalizing the disciplinary apparatus.

While most of the contemporary civilian-military elite emphasized the importance of the British regimental officer, the military high command widened the scope of the impersonal institutional disciplinary mechanism. There was a gradual shift from patriarchal despotism towards bureaucratic discipline. The transformation was from the personalized response of the officer to the crimes of his men, towards an impersonal evaluation based on bureaucratic assessment by the Adjutant General's department. One British historian, Ian F.W. Beckett, claims that in the Victorian era, the armies of the British Empire were governed by personalized command structures.[130] This analysis shows that at least in the Indian case, there was a transition from personalized command system towards an impersonal control system. However, this shift was incomplete and occurred in fits and starts. Complete centralization and bureaucratization of the command system was not possible because of the British view of Indian Society tactical-cum-administrative organization of the Sepoy Army and illiteracy among the Indian troops. Incomplete transformation partly explains the low combat performance of the Sepoy Army in the First World War. But, attempts towards an impersonal command system also prevented any large-scale mutiny before 1914.

NOTES

1. The quotation is from Bentinck's minute on military policy, no. 810, 13 March 1835 in Philips, ed., *The Correspondence of Lord William Cavendish Bentinck*, p. 1448.
2. Whittingham to Bentinck, no. 752, 20 July 1834, *Bentinck Correspondence*, p. 1328; MacMunn, *The Armies of India*, pp. 208–20.
3. Mason, *A Matter of Honour*, pp. 164–96.

4. Jagadish Narayan Sarkar, *The Military Despatches of a Seventeenth Century Indian General,* Calcutta: Scientific Book Agency, 1969, pp. 30, 32–3, 105–6; Martin Van Creveld, 'Technology and War to 1945', in Charles Townshend, ed., *The Oxford Illustrated History of Modern War,* Oxford/New York: Oxford University Press, 1997, pp. 176–9; G.D. Sheffield, 'Introduction: Command, Leadership and the Anglo-American Military Experience', in idem., ed., *Leadership and Command: The Anglo-American Military Experience Since 1861,* London: Brassey's, 1997, p. 8.

5. Randolf G.S. Cooper, 'Wellington and the Marathas in 1803', *International History Review,* vol. 11 (1989), pp. 31–8.

6. Irvine, *The Army of the Indian Moghuls,* pp. 9, 14, 182, 234–5, 299; Ravindra Kumar Sharma, 'The Military System of Mewar (Udaipur) State (*ca* 800 to 1947 AD)', *Central Asiatic Journal,* vol. 30 (1986), pp. 117–19.

7. David Killingray, 'Gender Issues and African Colonial Armies', in idem. and David Omissi, ed., *Guardians of Empire: The Armed Forces of the Colonial Powers c. 1700–1964,* Manchester/New York: Manchester University Press, 1999, pp. 225–6.

8. Lowell J. Satre, 'St John Brodrick and Army Reform, 1901–03', *JBS,* vol. 15, no. 2 (1976), pp. 117–39; Geoffrey Parker, 'Dynastic War: 1494-1660', J.A. Lynn, 'States in Conflict: 1661–1763', idem., 'Nations in Arms: 1763–1815', and W.A. Murray, 'The Industrialization of War: 1815–71' and idem., 'Towards World War: 1871–1914', in Parker, ed., *The Cambridge Illustrated History of Warfare: The Triumph of the West,* Cambridge: Cambridge University Press, 1995, pp. 146–265.

9. Charles Chenevix Trench, *The Indian Army and the King's Enemies: 1900–47,* London: Thames & Hudson, 1988, pp. 13–14; K.M.L. Saxena, *The Military System of India: 1900–39,* New Delhi: Sterling, 1999, pp. 96–7.

10. Note by Resident of Hyderabad C.B. Saunders, Footnote to para 83, May 1876, L/MIL/7/14966, OIOC.

11. Menezes, *Fidelity and Honour,* Appendix I, p. 533; No. 802, 16 February 1835, *Bentinck Correspondence,* pp. 14–27.

12. Nos. 802, 810, 16 February 1835, 10 March 1835, *Bentinck Correspondence,* pp. 1427–9, 1431, 1448–9.

13. *Supplementary Report,* pp. 20, 58, 311.

14. Ibid., pp. 33, 61, 65.

15. Ibid., pp. 33, 58.

16. Ibid., p. 311.

17. Ibid., pp. 38–9, 311; Menezes, *Fidelity and Honour,* p. 533.

18. *Supplementary Report,* pp. 33–4.

19. Confidential circular, to officers commanding divisions, districts, brigades and Indian regiments, ADG's office, no. 85/N, 25 August 1863, ADG's circular, vol. 3, NAI.

20. Circular to officers commanding divisions, districts, brigades, regiments of Indian cavalry and infantry, ADG's office, E. Haythorne, no. 26/N, 15 March 1864, ADG's circular, vol. 4.

21. Hugh Rose to John Lawrence, letter no. 3, 9 March 1864, John Lawrence Collection: 1864–7, MSS.EUR.F.90/59, OIOC.

22. Menezes, *Fidelity and Honour*, p. 534; Confidential circular, to officers commanding Indian regiments of cavalry and infantry, 16 May 1865, ADG's circular, vol. 5.

23. Memo by Robert Napier, Commander-in-Chief Bombay, 1866–9, Bombay, 24 January 1866, Notes and Minutes by Napier of Magdala, MSS.EUR.F.114, 1(C), OIOC.

24. From Major-General W. Galbraith, ADG India to the Commander-in-Chief Bombay Army, Enclosure no. 1, 7 July 1893, Annual confidential reports on the regiments, L/MIL/7/17008, OIOC.

25. Rules for summary court martial held under the Indian articles of war, no. 374, 15 April 1895, GO, NAI.

26. Circular to officers commanding divisions, districts and brigades holding warrants for convening district courts martial, ADG's office, no. 27/E, 16 February 1865, ADG's circular, vol. 5.

27. Circular to divisions, districts and stations, ADG's office, Simla, by Haythorne, ADG, no. 80/G, 19 August 1863, ADG's circular, vol. 3.

28. *Army Regulations, India*, p. 1.

29. Circular to divisions, districts and Indian regiments, cavalry and infantry, ADG's office, no. 129/N, 29 September 1864, ADG's circular, vol. 4.

30. G.D. Sheffield, 'Blitzkrieg and Attrition: Land Operations in Europe, 1914–45', in Sheffield and Colin McInnes, ed., *Warfare in the Twentieth Century,* London: Unwin Hyman, 1988, p. 73; Sheffield, 'Introduction', in idem., ed., *Leadership and Command,* p. 4; Joseph G. Dawson III, ' "Zealous for Annexation": Volunteer Soldiering, Military Government, and the Service of Colonel Alexander Doniphan in the Mexican-American War', *JSS,* vol. 19, no. 4 (1996), pp. 10–36; Kaushik Roy, 'Mars Defeated? Conventional Militaries in Unconventional Warfare', *Contemporary India,* vol. 2, no. 2 (2003), pp. 81–3.

31. *Army Regulations,* pp. 1–3; *Supplementary Report,* pp. 31, 33.

32. *Army Regulations,* pp. 2–3, 5; Proceedings of the summary court martial, no. 374, 15 April 1895, GO.

33. *Army Regulations,* pp. 3–4, 6–8.

34. No. 53, 1 September 1896, GO.

35. Arthur N. Gilbert, 'Military and Civilian Justice in Eighteenth Century England: An Assessment', *JBS,* vol. 17, no. 2 (1978), pp. 41–65; G.A. Steppler, 'British Military Law, Discipline, and the Conduct of Regimental Courts Martial in the later Eighteenth Century', *EHR,* vol. 102 (1987), pp. 859–81.

36. Major Gorham, *A Short Course of Military Law as Applicable to Persons*

Subject to Mutiny Act to Which is Added Military Law as Applicable to Persons Subject to the Indian Articles of War, Calcutta: Thacker & Spink, 1887, pp. 10, 14, 16, 167.

37. Ibid., pp. 23, 147, 176, Appendix B; Roberts, *Forty-one Years*, p. 44.
38. No. 374, 15 April 1895, GO.
39. Gorham, *A Short Course*, p. 170, Appendix D.
40. Nos. 118, 469, 628, 9 January 1901, 17 June 1901, 12 August 1901, GO.
41. Gorham, *A Short Course*, pp. 25, 169, 176, 178.
42. Ibid., pp. 169–70; No. 374, 15 April 1895, GO.
43. No. 802, 16 February 1835, *Bentinck Correspondence*, p. 1427.
44. *Supplementary Report*, p. 33.
45. Confidential circular, to officers commanding divisions and districts, ADG's office, 17 February 1865, ADG's circular, vol. 5.
46. *Army Regulations,* pp. 4, 20.
47. Hanson, *Carnage and Culture*, p. 321.
48. Stokes, *The English Utilitarians*, pp. 221, 224–5.
49. *Supplementary Report*, p. 310.
50. Ibid., pp. 21, 34.
51. Ibid., p. 33; No. 802, 16 February 1835, *Bentinck Correspondence*, pp. 1427, 1429, 1432.
52. Betham, *Marathas and Dekhani Musulmans*, pp. 73, 115; Bingley, *Sikhs*, p. 125; *Supplementary Report*, pp. 15, 21, 34; Inspection Reports of the Madras Army for 1874–5, Records of Chief Commands, Napier of Magdala, 1865–6, MSS.EUR.F.114,5(4), OIOC.
53. Circular to officers commanding divisions, districts and regiments, no. 28/E, 16 February 1865, ADG's circular, vol. 5.
54. Notes on the Indian Army of Bengal: Its present material and organization as compared with the past, September 1875, L/MIL/17/2/468, OIOC.
55. Note by C.B. Saunders, para 53, May 1876, L/MIL/7/14966.
56. *Supplementary Report*, p. 309.
57. Ibid., p. 30.
58. The oath is from *Supplementary Report*, p. 30. Longer, *Red Coats to Olive Green*, p. 78.
59. Oaths to be taken, no. 374, 15 April 1895, GO.
60. Nos. 802, 810, 16 February 1835, 13 March 1835, *Bentinck Correspondence*, pp. 1426–8, 1430–2, 1454.
61. E.E. Steiner, 'Separating the Soldier from the Citizen: Ideology and Criticism of Corporal Punishment in the British Armies, 1790-1815', *Social History*, vol. 8, no.1 (1983), p. 25.
62. From the late eighteenth century onwards, imprisonment and fines gradually replaced flogging in the British Army. Reformists like Bentinck faced severe challenges from conservatives like Wellington, who wanted to retain the discipline of the lash. David Gates, 'The

Brown Warriors of the Raj

Transformation of the Army, 1783–1815', and Peter Burroughs, 'An Unreformed Army? 1815–68', in David Chandler and Ian Beckett, ed., *The Oxford Illustrated History of the British Army,* Oxford: Oxford University Press, 1994, pp. 142–6, 171–87; No. 802, 16 February 1835, *Bentinck Correspondence,* p. 1429.

63. No. 802, 16 February 1835, *Bentinck Correspondence,* p. 1430.

64. Whittingham to Bentinck, no. 740, 24 June 1834, *Bentinck Correspondence,* pp. 1310–11. (The quotation is from p. 1311.)

65. No. 802, 16 February 1835, *Bentinck Correspondence,* pp. 1429, 1432.

66. Douglas M. Peers, 'Sepoys, Soldiers and the Lash: Race, Caste and Army Discipline in India, 1820–50', *JICH,* vol. 23, no. 2 (1995), p. 212, Cardew, *Bengal Native Army,* pp. 203–4; *Peel Committee,* pp. 6–7, 9–10.

67. *Supplementary Report,* p. 33.

68. Ibid., p. 58; No. 802, 16 February 1835, *Bentinck Correspondence,* p. 1432.

69. *Army Regulations,* pp. 2–3.

70. Paddy Griffith, *Military Thought in the French Army: 1815–51,* Manchester/New York: Manchester University Press, 1989, p. 99.

71. Allan Ramsay Skelley, *The Victorian Army at Home: The Recruitment and Terms and Conditions of the British Regular, 1859–99,* London: Croom Helm, 1977, p. 129.

72. Military prisons, Minute by Lord Napier of Magdala, Commander-in-Chief Bombay, 1866–9, Poona, 28 April 1869, Notes and Minutes by Napier, MSS.EUR.F.114, 1 (C).

73. Heathcote, *The Military in British India,* p. 62.

74. *Peel Committee,* p. 10.

75. Confidential circular, to officers commanding Indian regiments of cavalry and infantry, 16 May 1865, ADG's circular, vol. 5.

76. Confidential circular to officers commanding divisions and districts, 17 February 1865, ADG's circular, vol. 5.

77. *Army Regulations,* p. 8.

78. No. 374, 15 April 1895, GO.

79. Circular to officers commanding divisions, districts and brigades and holding warrants for convening district courts martial, no. 27/E, ADG's circular, vol. 5.

80. No. 374, 15 April 1895, GO.

81. Major G. Casserly, *Life in an Indian outpost,* London, n.d., p. 198.

82. Circular to officers commanding divisions, districts and Indian regiments, Simla, no. 127/N, 9 September 1865, ADG's circular, vol. 5.

83. *Army Regulations,* p. 7.

84. No. 53, 1 September 1896, GO.

85. *Army Regulations,* p. 130; Adjutant General's office, Simla, 3 February 1896, GO.

86. Extracts of Views and Opinions of Brigadier-General John Jacob of

1858, Appendix A of Resident's letter no. 79, 3 July 1879, L/MIL/7/ 14966.

87. *Supplementary Report*, pp. 23, 26, 35, 56.

88. Ibid., pp. 15, 35, 38, 55, 310.

89. For the view that examinations in the officer corps gave birth to professionalism see William C. Fuller, *Civil-Military Conflict in Imperial Russia: 1881–1914*, Princeton, New Jersey: Princeton University Press, 1985, pp. 4, 8–11.

90. Ronald J. Barr, 'High Command in the United States: The Emergence of a Modern System, 1898–1920', in Sheffield, ed., *Leadership and Command*, p. 65.

91. *Supplementary Report*, pp. 38, 54–5, 309–10.

92. Ibid., pp. 34, 37.

93. Ibid., pp. 54–5.

94. Ibid., pp. 33, 36, 38, 312.

95. Ibid., pp. 56, 58; Gorham, *A Short Course*, p. 171.

96. Casserly, *Life*, pp. 200–1, 241, 257–8.

97. Memorandum on the Indian Army, Inefficient state of the Indian Army laid before the Duke of Cambridge, pp. 1–2, 1 July 1876, Colonel William Merewether Collection, MSS.EUR.D.625/3(C), OIOC.

98. Inefficient state of the Indian Army laid before the Duke of Cambridge, p. 4, Merewether Collection.

99. Notes on the Indian Army of Bengal, Brigadier C.H. Brownlow, September 1875, L/MIL/17/2/468. Robert Napier argued in the same vein for the Indian officers in 1874. Notes on the Bengal Army, 1 May 1874, Records of Chief Commands, 1865–6, Notes and Minutes of Napier, MSS.EUR.F.114, 5(4).

100. Memorandum on proposals relative to the Hyderabad Contingent submitted by Brigadier-General T. Wright, Progs. no. 107, May 1876, para 9, L/MIL/7/14966.

101. Gorham, *A Short Course*, p. 171.

102. *Copy of Recent Correspondence on the Subject of the Organization of the Indian Army*, Salisbury to the Governor General, London, no. 215, 10 August 1876, p. 3, C 1698 in Merewether Collection, MSS.EUR.D.625/4.

103. General Frederick Roberts, *Correspondence with India while Commander-in-Chief in Madras*, p. 151, Part 3, L/MIL/17/5/1615, OIOC.

104. Roberts, *Correspondence with the Viceroy of India (The Marquis of Lansdowne*, pp. 13–14, Part 5, L/MIL/17/5/1615.

105. Memorandum by the Commander-in-Chief, para 7, 8, 21 April 1893, 1Q/4, George White Collection, MSS.EUR.F.108/24, OIOC.

106. Army headquarter, Simla, nos. 94, 374, 3 January 1895, 15 April 1895, GO.

107. *Army Regulations*, p. 6; M.P. Singh, 'Origin of Summary Court Martial', *JUSII*, vol. CII, no. 427 (1972), p. 186.
108. *Supplementary Report*, pp. 33, 309.
109. Birdwood, *Khaki and Gown*, p. 45.
110. *Supplementary Report*, p. 33.
111. Ibid., pp. 33–4.
112. Captain G.F.W. Macmohan, *A Guide to the Correct Framing of Charges under the Indian Articles of War Suitable to All Occasions*, Bombay: Bombay Educational Society Press, 1887, pp. 12, 27–8.
113. Gorham, *A Short Course*, p. 182.
114. *Supplementary Report*, p. 33.
115. No. 53, 1 September 1896, GO.
116. From Brigadier-General H.R. Hope, Secy. to the Madras Govt., MD, to the Secy. to the GoI, MD, 26 October 1893, Ootacamund, Enclosure to General letter no. 6, L/MIL/7/17008.
117. *Army Regulations*, p. 8.
118. No. 53, 1 September 1896, GO.
119. *Army Regulations*, p. 7.
120. Circular to officers commanding divisions, districts and brigadiers holding warrants for convening district courts martial, ADG's office, Calcutta, no. 27/E, 16 February 1865, ADG's Circular, vol. 5.
121. *Army Regulations*, pp. 8, 50.
122. Army headquarter, Simla, no. 374, 15 April 1895, GO.
123. No. 53, 19 September 1896, GO.
124. Prisoners' court martial memo, no. 116/E, 14 Oct. 1863, ADG's circular, vol. 3; Military prisons, Minute by Napier, Commander-in-Chief Bombay, 1866–9, 28 April 1869.
125. No. 357, 1 April 1895, GO.
126. *Army Regulations*, p. 10.
127. Rules for the summary courts martial held under the Indian articles of war, proceedings of the summary courts martial, Simla, no. 374, 15 April 1895, GO.
128. Progs. nos. 27–8, 2 March 1861, MDP, NAI.
129. Progs. nos. 56–7, 4 March 1861, MDP.
130. Ian F.W. Beckett, 'Command in the Late Victorian Army', in Sheffield, ed., *Leadership and Command*, pp. 37–56.

SEVEN

Discipline in Practice

How did the disciplinary system tackle indisciplinary activities of the soldiers till the onset of the First World War? The welfare mechanism of the Raj attracted and retained Indian manpower in the army. The imperial genesis of the soldierly ethos of the 'martial' communities, and their identification with their regiments, enabled the British to condition the peasants into loyal and disciplined soldiers. Finally the courts martial apparatus as part of the bureaucratic disciplinary system promptly nipped indiscipline in the bud, before it could spread among the rank and file. The court martial apparatus was geared towards moderation and enabled the imperialists to maintain discipline in the colonial army. Not over-application of violence, but rather the lack of it, was the characteristic of the disciplinary infrastructure of the army. David Omissi's monograph focuses on the mutinies which occurred, especially from the First World War onwards.[1] This chapter concentrates on the individual crimes of the soldiers till 1913.

The regimental commandants favoured the summary courts martial, as they themselves presided over such bodies. However after 1857, the Adjutant General's department concluded that the regimental officers were abusing their power. The army headquarter's view was that arbitrary despotism of the regimental officers was responsible for the disintegration of loyalty on a large-scale in 1857. Hence, the army headquarter discouraged the regimental colonels from summoning summary courts martial, and favoured the general courts martial. The argument was that since at least five officers sat over each general court martial, the bias and prejudice of the commanding officers would not influence the sentences of these bodies.[2]

As a result, the regimental officers rarely called summary courts martial. The 3rd Brahmin Regiment can be seen as representative of the other infantry regiments. Between 1861 and 1913, this unit experienced no summary court martial.[3] Between 1872 and 1874, the Madras Army experienced 714 trials, out of which only ten were summary trials. For the same period, the Punjab Frontier Force witnessed 245 trials, out of which only eight were summary trials. In these three years, the Bengal Army saw 847 trials, out of which 108 were summary trials. Summary trials were more frequent in this force because the experience of Mutiny haunted the Bengal Army. And, the military hierarchy was unwilling to take any chances.[4] Traditional historiography emphasizes the officer-soldier relationship to explain the functioning of the Sepoy Army's disciplinary infrastructure.[5] But, with the decline in the incidence of the summary courts martial, the crux of maintaining discipline lay with the general courts martial.[6]

Section I charts the imperial policy of making punishments less brutal. This process is illustrated by referring to some cases selected from the vast number of court martial cases documented in the General Orders. The next section brings into focus the various components of the general courts martial, which influenced the moderation of punishment. The final section examines the dialectical relationship between the low quantum of indisciplinary activities by the soldiers and non-coercive disciplinary measures undertaken by the British.[7]

I

MODERATION OF THE DISCIPLINARY SYSTEM

Compared to other multiracial forces like the Austro-Hungarian Army,[8] the Sepoy Army's disciplinary system was less severe. This was partly because, unlike the former force, the Sepoy Army relied on volunteers. In the late Victorian Army punishment became less harsh. Towards the end of the nineteenth century, a shift occurred in the attitude of the British Army towards its personnel. Instead of being viewed as the 'scum of the earth', the British soldiers were perceived as working men with special skills. The nineteenth century witnessed a decline in the scope and frequency of lashing of British soldiers. The reformers attempted to prevent crime through means other than corporal punishment. The emphasis was on bettering the service conditions of the soldiers. The aim was to improve their barracks, diet, pay, pension and to educate them,[9] and the British in India were probably influenced by this trend. The transition towards humane punishment both in the British and in the Indian armies was more or less simultaneous. After 1868, no soldier of the British Army was awarded corporal punishment in peacetime. In the Sepoy Army, after 1877, no soldier could be flogged in peacetime.[10]

The Sepoy Army's disciplinary system was influenced by a 'reformist' philosophy. The underlying assumption was that infliction of excessive violence on the soldiers was inimical to discipline in the long run, because the fear of draconian punishment frequently forced the soldiers towards seditious activities. Thus, the British technique of not awarding harsh sentences kept the soldiers on the right track. In early nineteenth century, 'Liberalism' and Benthamite Utilitarianism influenced the British legal system in India. 'Enlightened' legislation was designed to discourage mutilation and corporal punishment.[11] The principle was to suppress crime with the smallest possible infliction of suffering.[12] The spectacle of physical punishment along with the theatrical representation of pain disappeared. The new penology demanded that the main target was the mind and not the body and the aim was to reform the mind. The prisons came to be recognized as part of the evolving 'humane' penal system of the colonial state.[13] This ideology could be traced back to the Enlightenment idea that punishment is a form of social engineering. The assumption is that crime and deviance are social problems for which there can be technical institutional solution. The moral arguments emphasized that punishment should be correctional rather than punitive. Thus, discipline became a modified form of correction.[14] In fact, the disciplinary system for both the sepoys and white soldiers stationed in India was characterized by a sort of 'humanist' philosophy which was reflected in the moderation of punishment system. Along with this ideology, the imperial understanding of indigenous society, and the British perception of the various roles of communities in the colonial war machine, moderated the imperial response.

So the nineteenth century witnessed a gradual moderation of punishment in the Sepoy Army, even in cases of heinous crimes like combat refusal. Leaving the regimental colours, which represented the unit's pride, was considered a serious crime in the Sepoy Army. Subedar H. Birjee of the 9th Bombay Infantry Regiment was in charge of carrying the regimental flag. During an action fought by this unit on 7 January 1797, the Subedar threw away the colour and abandoned the field of battle. The general court martial sentenced him to death on August 1797.[15]

With the passage of time, punishment for the same type of crime became lenient, as is evident from another case. On 5 March 1836, a detachment of the 14th Madras Infantry Regiment advanced from Oudagerry to Durgepersad pass. When the party was crossing the pass, some Khond tribals attacked. The atmosphere was highly charged. The Khonds rushed forward with hatchets and engaged in close quarter combat, before the sepoys could open fire from their muskets. Two British officers present died on the spot. The Jemadar in charge of the rearguard then lost heart, and his party melted away. For this dismal performance, the Jemadar was sentenced to transportation for life by a general court martial, and the rest of the rearguard, which consisted of five privates, was discharged. Officers were supposed to lead the men in the actions, so the Jemadar's punishment was harsher than the punishment of the privates.[16] It is to be noted that the court martial of 1836, unlike the court assembled in 1797, did not pass any death sentence.

Discharge was a serious enough punishment for the Indians, even if it was not so for the British soldiers. The regulars of the British Army were recruited from the lowest classes of British society and exiled overseas for the bulk of their career. The latter joined the army either to escape the law, family quarrels, or were tricked to join while drunk by the recruiting sergeants. They would have happily accepted dismissal, not as a punishment but as a boon, to escape from the drudgery of military life. But, for the 'martial races', dismissal meant social humiliation. The British officers did not view the Indian soldiers as the 'scum of the earth'. Many Indian recruits came from families who had provided soldiers for generations. Further, army service besides being honourable was also a lucrative job for them and their families depended on the wages. Pension was a great attraction, encouraging the Indians to remain in the army for a long period. Hence, dismissal was an attempt by the army to prevent disintegration of the unit during combat. This had a commensurate effect. In 1840, the same 14th Madras Infantry Regiment volunteered for service in China to wipe out its disgrace.[17]

The 1857 Mutiny had no effect on the trend of increasing leniency in the awards of courts martial. When the 23rd Punjab Infantry Regiment was deployed at the North-West Frontier post of Chubotra in 1867, the unit expected a night attack by the tribals. On 4 March, sepoy Gulab Singh refused to occupy his position on the rampart. A general court martial sentenced him to imprisonment for three months.[18] This sentence appears very lenient when compared with the court martial in 1836, which sentenced the soldiers of the 14th Madras Infantry to discharge, for combat refusal. Discharge was considered harsher than temporary imprisonment in the Indian context. Gulab Singh suffered temporary imprisonment, possibly because the British did not find combat refusal by an individual as menacing as collective combat refusal. If soldiers were discharged, rural society would be full of free-floating armed personnel, who might become a threat to the Raj in the long run. So, imprisonment was favoured rather than discharge.[19]

One dimension of combat refusal was malingering, and the army's response was imprisonment of the malingerers. There were many old serving soldiers in the Bombay and the Madras armies, as they had no incentive to serve beyond fifteen years, because their pension remained same for serving between fifteen to forty years. Hence, many senior soldiers malingered and feigned disability in the hospital at times of active service. This demoralized even the young soldiers, and had an adverse effect on the army's combat capacity. The summary courts martial sentenced such soldiers to imprisonment up to twelve months.[20]

In pre-colonial warfare, large-scale collective desertions were common. This was because the pre-British armies were conglomerates of local leaders and their retainers. Such leaders and their troops often left the service of a prince, and at times were later re-employed by the same prince.[21] But the introduction of a Western style army by the British ended desertions by whole units. Nevertheless, individual desertions and collective desertions by small bands of soldiers continued. During the first half of the nineteenth century branding and flogging for desertion in the British Army units deployed in Canada, were replaced by imprisonment.[22] Similarly, punishment for desertion also became less severe in the Sepoy Army. On 5 January 1880, sepoy Sharin of the 20th Punjab Infantry Regiment deserted when his unit was deployed in the Kurram Valley. He was subsequently caught, and a general court martial at Peshawar sentenced him to transportation for eight years.[23] In 1887, two sepoys were caught while trying to desert from the 8th Bombay Infantry Regiment and were sentenced to imprisonment for a month.[24]

Though collective desertion was more dangerous than individual desertion, the disciplinary apparatus acted leniently. The British accepted that it was impolitic to keep the Indians in the army against their wishes. The demand for manpower in the Sepoy Army was very low compared with the huge populace of the subcontinent. There was no shortage of recruits. Table 7.1 shows that vacancies remained low even when the Sepoy Army was engaged in a colonial campaign like the Third Burma War (1885–6). Hence the Sepoy Army, unlike the British Army, could afford to introduce the scheme of free discharge after three years of service. Nevertheless, voluntary discharge remained rare because, unlike in the British Army, service in the Indian Army was popular. Between 1870 to 1875, only 2.5 per cent of the troops of the Bengal Army and 1.5 per cent of the personnel of the Punjab Frontier Force left of their own accord. Cavalry service was so popular, that till the late 1880s very few sowars took free discharge. Most of the sowars served for about fifteen to twenty years.[25] Instead of taking discharge the Indian soldiers re-enlisted after every three years because of the bounty of Rs. 25.[26] In the case of Sharin the army over-reacted, possibly because the

TABLE 7.1: VACANCIES IN THE SEPOY ARMY IN 1886

Branches	Vacancies at	Various Dates	Remarks
	1 May	1 June	2,000 were recruited in one month
Cavalry	318	214	
Artillery	19 Excess	65	
Infantry	9,295	7,333	
Sappers	59	71	
Total	9,651	7,683	

Source: Roberts, *Correspondence with the Viceroy of India: 1885–88*, p. 56, Part 4.

Second Afghan War (1878–80) was going on and deserters
supplied arms to the frontier tribals.[27]

Till the nineteenth century, the common form of punishment
for being drunk was dismissal. But, in the first decade of the
twentieth century the general courts martial's sentences became
more lenient. On 29 October 1866 Subedar Devi Singh of the 1st
Gurkha Light Infantry Regiment was dismissed from the service
by a general court martial assembled at Buxa in Bhutan. This
was because he was so drunk that he failed to attend the
inspection parade held by the British officers on 2 August 1866.[28]
But when on 3 February 1901, Jemadar Beejia of the Malwa
Bheel Corps was found to be intoxicated during parade, a general
court martial suspended him only for a month.[29]

Abdul Azim Khan, Subedar of the 24th Madras Infantry
Regiment due to the influence of alcohol failed to attend the
commanding officer's inspection parade at Secunderabad on 22
May 1899. The general court martial, instead of dismissing him,
merely ordered him to be demoted.[30] The imperial belief was
that the Madrassis were addicted to drinks by nature.[31] This
probably explains the fact that relaxation of punishment for
drunkenness occurred earlier in the Madras units than in the
Bombay and the Bengal regiments. Thus discipline was lax in
the Madras regiments compared to the Bombay and Bengal
regiments, and this probably contributed to the military ineffectiveness of the Madras forces.

Douglas M. Peers writes that the Indian officers of the early
nineteenth century Madras Army were reduced to cyphers by
British policy. So, to relieve their boredom, they took to drinking.
According to Peers, drunkenness, however, was absent among
the privates.[32] This view holds water for all the regional armies
in the post-Mutiny era. The Subedars were charged with
drunkenness much more often than the privates. For example,
Subedar Boota Singh of the 32nd Punjab Infantry Regiment in
1866 and Subedar Baji Rao of the 28th Bombay Infantry Regiment
in 1905 were both charged with drunkenness.[33] Possibly rabid
drunkenness among the Indian officer corps was an instance of
the 'weapons of the weak'.[34] The Indian officers were frustrated
when after long and faithful service they reached officers' ranks,[35]
the colonial military system denied them adequate power and
status. They realized that if they went for violent rebellion, then

they would lose their jobs and probably their lives also. They, therefore, sabotaged the day to day working of the imperial war machine by not performing their duties properly and getting drunk instead.

Drunkenness was not only inimical to professional efficiency, but was also related to rowdyism. British officers noted that Indian officers were extremely addicted to liquor and frequently got drunk, which then led to trouble with the European troops. The authorities possibly understood that sheer boredom encouraged Indian officers to take to drink. Hence, the high command's response was to station guards at the rum godowns to prevent their looting by the brown officers.[36] The British believed that an idle mind is a devil's workshop. So in order to relieve the boredom of the brown soldiers, the army high command emphasized physical exercise. By 1884, gymnasiums were introduced in every Indian regiment.[37]

The white officers represented the principal mechanism of control for harnessing Indian soldiers. Challenges to the authority of the white officer corps by the brown personnel constituted a serious problem for the imperialists. There were some instances when the Indian privates challenged British officers. In the pre-1857 era, the soldiers were allowed to petition higher authorities if they had trouble with their regimental officers. But after the 1857 catastrophe, the imperialists concluded that the petition system, by weakening the regimental commandants' authority, aided in the disintegration of the command structure, and the petition system was discouraged after 1859.[38]

Ram Singh, a Resaldar of the Awadh Military Police, submitted a petition in February 1860, which started: 'Most respectfully sahib, your poor memorialist submits few lines with the hope that his case may be considered and he begs to be pardoned for interrupting your valuable time and patience'. This sort of language was designed not to offend the British sense of superiority. Ram Singh asserted that he was dismissed from service by the British commandant. He claimed that just before his dismissal when the *Purbiyas* of the 1st Punjab Irregular Cavalry were unwilling to serve in China, he was ready to serve overseas. Ram Singh continued that he was in dire straits, as he had no other means to support himself. Despite Singh challenging the regimental commandant's order of dismissal, the military bureaucrats did not punish him.[39]

At Peshawar in March 1866, a quasi-rebellion occurred. Major-General W.O.G. Haly, commanding the Peshawar Division, received an anonymous petition, which contained serious complaints against the regimental commandant of the 24th Punjab Infantry Regiment. The petition was handed over to Haly by the sepoys Lena Singh and Wazir Singh of the same regiment. When they were interrogated, they confessed that Havildar Natha Singh and Naik Gulab Singh were the masterminds behind this affair. A general court martial was held on August 1866 at Peshawar. The Naik was dismissed from service. Why was the Naik punished, unlike Ram Singh? Ram Singh's petition was clothed in humble language, and it was not generated collectively but centered round personal grievances, so it did not constitute a threat to the military hierarchy. The British, therefore, took no punitive action. Especially, just after 1857, when the imperialists were in the process of re-establishing their rule, the British dared not antagonize the petitioners by punishing them. Again, the British were afraid of antagonizing the Indian officer corps as a body. Hence, Havildar Natha Singh was allowed to go free.[40]

Though the Mutiny receded in time, the image of a crucial linkage between rebellion and religion never dimmed in British memory. The imperialists probably remembered that their evangelical policy had turned the Hindus and the Muslims against them in 1857. In fact after the Mutiny, the British pampered the religiosity of the Muslim sepoys. Each of the regiment with Muslim soldiers employed a *maulvi* at a salary of Rs. 12 anna 8 per month. The *maulvi* provided spiritual comfort to the Muslim personnel.[41] The British refused to punish the soldiers heavily, especially on occasions when religion acted as an adhesive for collective grievances. Instead of applying overt pressure, the regimental officers practiced 'divide and rule' on religious lines allowing communal splits to surface in the regiments, which prevented the possibility of any anti-British combination among the Indian troops. At Hingoli on 4 March 1895 Kote-Dufadar Bachan Singh and Dufadar Harnam Singh of the 4th Lancers Hyderabad Contingent instigated eighteen sowars of their unit for the release of some of their colleagues who were imprisoned on grounds of indiscipline. The Kote-Dufadar and the Dufadar, along with the sowars who had taken an oath to act unitedly were Hindus, while the Muslim personnel* rallied around the

Muslim Resaldar Majid Khan, who sided with the British. Still, the British must have suffered from an acute sense of powerlessness. This was clear from the sentence passed by the general court martial. The eighteen sowars were not punished at all. The two ringleaders got away with light punishment—one year imprisonment with hard labour.[42]

The punishment for attempted murder was transportation for life. But in the last decade of the nineteenth century, the period of transportation was reduced. When sepoy Hira Singh of the 31st Punjab Infantry Regiment tried to shoot sepoy Pakar Singh at Malakand on August 1896, Hira Singh was transported for life. Naik Jalal Khan of the 24th Bombay Infantry Regiment tried to kill private Mohaiden and Muhamad Rafiq on 20 January 1899 at Gwadar. The general court martial sentenced Jalal Khan to suffer transportation, not for life, but only for ten years. Jalal Khan was given a shorter sentence even though his crime was more serious than Hira Singh's for the latter tried to kill only one of his colleagues.[43] Whatever little fighting occurred between the Indian privates and the brown officers was because village, caste and clan rivalries were brought into the regiments. The Pathans in accordance with their *Pukhtunwali* code conducted their blood feuds even within the regiments.[44] Since, these did not pose direct threats to the army, the authorities could afford to relax the punishment system.

II

IMPERIAL MANIPULATION OF THE COURTS MARTIAL MECHANISM

That over-deployment of force, perceived the imperialists, would result in the disintegration of the fragile 'mask of command'.[45] The British drive for the moderation of punishment was accelerated by a mechanism built into the army's disciplinary system. The Indian officers were occasionally members and even presidents of the general courts martial. This was done probably to prevent the notion gaining ground among the Indian soldiers, that the disciplinary apparatus was purely a white man's organization. The British, by allowing the Indian officers to enjoy some power over the Indian privates, tried to drive a wedge between the brown privates and the brown officers. Nevertheless, while manning the court martial mechanism, the Indian officers were sympathetic to their brethren. But, the British held two trump cards. Firstly, in sensitive cases when the Indian officers' sympathies were suspect, British officers were inducted in the courts martial. Secondly, the Commander-in-Chief could order the courts martial to revise their findings, though the Commanders-in-Chief did not always pressurize courts martial for harsher punishments. They occasionally ordered the courts to award lenient punishments, as they themselves were concerned about preventing the 'mask of command' from slipping.

There was a case of combat refusal by private Gulab Singh in March 1867. Subedar Mungul Singh who presided over the general court martial was very lenient with Gulab Singh. The latter was merely imprisoned for three months. As Mungul Singh and Gulab Singh were from different regiments, this indicates that the sympathy of Indian officers for the brown privates cut across regimental boundaries. General W.R. Mansfield, the Commander-in-Chief of the Indian Army from 1865 to 1870 asserted that if such guilty soldiers were not punished severely then combat refusal and decomposition of the command structure would become rampant. He continued by saying that Gulab Singh ought to have been awarded capital punishment for his crime. Yet Mansfield did not reject the court martial sentence passed by an Indian officer,[46] probably to avoid running roughshod over Indian opinion.

Conflict over the issue of leniency of punishment also occurred between the regional and the central army commands. A Subedar of the Bombay Army, with twenty years of service behind him, was dismissed by the Bombay Army headquarter in 1867, for being intoxicated during duty. But considering of his past service, the Subedar was retired from the army and was granted a pension of Rs. 12 per month. The army headquarter was against showing such leniency, and warned regional commands that in future such unnecessary leniency need not be shown to the 'guilty' soldiers.[47]

Occasionally, lack of unanimity within the general court martial allowed the higher authorities to award heavy punishment. One Resaldar Kunhiya Singh of the 17th Bengal Cavalry was drunk at Barrackpore during the evening parade on 6

February 1868. The president of the court, Subedar-Major Munnalal Tiwari, pointed out that the Resaldar deserved pardon, as heavy duty had prevented him from getting any rest the previous three days. The bonhomie between the Indian officers cut across inter-service rivalry. Tiwari, who belonged to the infantry, sympathized with Kunhiya Singh of the cavalry. However, the other members of the court martial did not agree with Tiwari. As no consensus emerged, and the president was unwilling to accept the majority's decision, Tiwari appealed to the Commander-in-Chief, who took the final decision. Because of the split within the members of the court martial, Mansfield could afford to turn down Tiwari's request, and Kunhiya Singh was discharged.[48]

Misbehaviour by Indian officers towards their superior British officers occurred occasionally. Resaldar Rahim Bux Khan of the 19th Bengal Cavalry at Shahdera on 1 February 1870 lost his temper with his British commandant. In front of other Indian officers, Bux Khan continued to shout at his commandant after being repeatedly ordered by his superiors to remain silent. A general court martial presided over by Resaldar-Major Man Singh from the same regiment merely suspended Bux Khan for four months. It is to be noted that Bux Khan and Man Singh belonged to different religions. One wonders if there was a British president, would Bux Khan have been given a more serious punishment? Mansfield caustically commented that Bux Khan's punishment was unnecessarily lenient but he did not ask the court martial to revise the sentence.[49] This was probably because the specter of Hindu–Muslim unity within the regiment haunted the British.

But the top-most military figure did not always tolerate such leniency on the part of the courts martial if the cases involved direct challenges to the British officers by the brown soldiers. British officers in charge of Indian regiments hesitated in acting if religious sentiments of the soldiers were involved. They dilly-dallied, especially when Islam was involved, probably the 'Mutiny mania' worked at the back of the imperial mind. The officers were convinced that Islam provided fuel during the 1857 rising. Even among the Raj's civilian officers, the general belief was that the Muslims at best nurtured passive hostility towards the white man's regime and at worst were actively hostile. This was assumed the British, because of the inherent hostility of Islam towards Christianity. The British were conscious that the growth of their empire in India had displaced Muslims from high government posts which they had occupied in the eighteenth century. Further, the British were nervous because in the second half of the nineteenth century, the Muslims constituted about 45 per cent of the personnel of the Sepoy Army.[50]

A tense situation developed at Buxa near Bhutan on 5 November 1865 when the Indian officers and the privates combined to defy the white man's power, and the incident acquired a religious tinge. On that day, a Muslim private of the 31st Infantry Regiment (which was composed of Punjabi Muslims and Sikhs) while on duty, left his post, in order to pray. Captain T.G. Ross ordered the Subedar-Major Bhuggah Khan to discipline the private. Bhuggah Khan knew well that the men in that regiment were never supposed to leave their posts for religious purposes during duty. But, Bhuggah Khan arrogantly refused to comply with Ross' order. When Ross reported the Subedar Major's behaviour to the regimental commandant Lieutenant-Colonel S. Richards, the latter ordered an enquiry. Events reached a breaking point when, during the investigation, Bhuggah Khan shouted repeatedly and obstructed the proceedings of the investigations. So a general court martial was assembled on 30 January 1866 in which British officers moved with caution. As the Subedar-Major and the private were both Muslims, the imperialists were afraid of antagonizing the religious sensibilities of the regiment's Muslim soldiers. The British officers understood that if the private, who was the real culprit, was punished, then the Muslim soldiers of the unit would interpret the British move as an undue interference in matters of faith. Predisposed to believe the worst, the British officers believed that such a move might snowball into another mutiny. So the private was left alone and the Subedar-Major was brought under the ambit of the 'secular' charge of showing 'disrespect' to his higher officer. Even then, the court's sentence lacked the killer instinct. Instead of dismissal or imprisonment, Bhuggah Khan was merely suspended for six months.[51]

The 'men on the spot' felt immediate pressure, so the general court martial was lenient to the culprits. But, the top echelon of the military bureaucracy which functioned from Calcutta and

Simla, which were far away from the context of local pressure, was unwilling to allow the miscreants to escape so lightly. The president of the court martial, Sibratan Ram, was of the same rank as Bhuggah Khan. Because the president did not outrank the accused, the former probably lacked the moral courage to punish the latter heavily. Mansfield sensed that though Sibratan Ram was from another unit, he was colluding with Bhuggah Khan. Mansfield argued that the court's sentence was not commensurate with the serious nature of the crime committed by Bhuggah Khan, who held the highest rank that could be attained by any Indian. He further commented, that if Khan was not seriously punished, then it would set a fatal example and would send shock waves throughout the army. To bring order out of chaos, Mansfield demanded a far more serious punishment. However, to prevent any reaction from the Muslim privates of the regiment, Mansfield decided to leave the private alone. Mansfield deliberately retained Sibratan Ram as the president of the court martial, and used him as a shield to absorb direct heat from the Indian privates away from the white officer corps. Under pressure from the highest authority, Sibratan Ram complied and passed a revised sentence on 20 February 1866, stating that Bhuggah Khan was to be dismissed. This was a typical example of Indian officers being used as stooges to award heavy punishment to Indian soldiers. Mansfield tried to use this punishment as a deterrent. To deter further defiance by Indians, Mansfield converted this punishment into a public spectacle. In March 1866, he ordered that Bhuggah Khan's sentence should be read publicly to every Indian regiment.[52]

At times, the Indian personnel physically assaulted the British officers. The military policy, in such cases of gross indiscipline within a regiment, was to appoint a British officer from another unit, in the hope that he would be free from the pressure generated by the personnel who were facing charges, and their friends within the unit. The grievances of the soldiers were frequently directed against both the British, and those Indian officers who were considered lackeys of the sahibs. A sepoy, Bichai Singh of the 4th Bengal Infantry Regiment, hit Major John Swinton Melville of his unit with a rifle in Calcutta on 6 March 1899. The Major was seriously wounded. A court martial was assembled at Fort William on 29 May 1899. The army considered the case to be too serious to be left in the hands of Indian officers. Instead of an Indian officer, Lieutenant-Colonel G.G. Monk Mason of the Royal Artillery, was appointed to preside over the court martial, and he sentenced Bichai Singh to suffer transportation for seven years. Monk Mason could afford to award a harsh sentence not only because he was an outsider but also because there was no unified opposition to the white officer corps by the Indians within the unit. In fact Jemadar Ramadin Singh had tried to save Melville during the scuffle.[53]

There were several cases when a private attacked more than one Indian officer of the same regiment. It reflected the anger of privates with those elements of the brown officer's corps, which colluded with the sahibs. At 4 p.m. on 1 April 1864 when Sahib Singh, the Pay Havildar of the 31st Punjab Infantry Regiment (deployed at 24 Pargannas of Bengal Presidency) was passing along the barrack, two sepoys from behind a tree shot at his back. The Subedar-Major heard the shot and came out of his barrack. He called the men but none came out. Then the Jemadar ordered the men to fall in line. The Pay-Havildar said that one of the men who shot him was sepoy Faizullah. At the parade next day, Sahib Singh recognized his other assailant as a sepoy named Sharif. Soon the grievously wounded Sahib Singh died. It was found out that the fatal shot was fired from the musket stolen from another sepoy named Ghasitah. Sahib Singh was a mild mannered man and had no quarrel with any person. The prosecution failed to establish any motive for murder. Probably, Faizullah and Sharif wanted to murder some other Indian officer but mistook Sahib Singh for him in the dark. After committing the murder, Faizullah and Sharif went back to the barrack and pretended to be asleep. The two prisoners were judged by Indian officers who allowed them to go scot free on the 'benefit of doubt'. The Indian jury argued that except for Sahib Singh, there were no other witnesses. But, a British officiating Registrar of the Bengal High Court noted that a dying man never lies. So, the official of the Bengal High Court was for reopening the case. But, the army followed the policy of let sleeping dogs lie.[54] On 22 July 1895, Rifleman Bharajman Rai of the 2nd Battalion 4th Gurkha Rifles at Bakloh shot at Subedar Indarbir Kunwar and Havildar Dalbir Shahi of the same unit with his rifle. The Subedar was seriously wounded and the Havildar died. Then Jhanda

Singh of the 10th Bengal Infantry shot dead Subedar Mehtab Singh of his unit on 27 February 1899. The general courts martial hanged Rai and Singh[55] to prevent the collapse of the imperial auxiliary shield, i.e. the loyalist elements within the Indian officer corps.

The Indian officers frequently misbehaved with the privates. Though such affrays did not reflect direct challenges to the white man's authority, the high command still intervened to prevent the discontent of the privates from taking an anti-establishment colour. In such cases an Indian officer was generally appointed as president of the court martial, to project an image showing that the white men were not over-interested in poking their noses in the internal problems of the Indians. On 29 January 1870, Subedar Shaikh Ali Bux of the Hyderabad Contingent's 5th Infantry Regiment was drunk and assaulted the recruit Peer Bux. Lord Napier of Magdala, the Commander-in-Chief of the Indian Army (1870–6), in order to project the view that whenever possible an Indian should judge another 'guilty' Indian, appointed Subedar-Major Baderuddin as the president of the general court martial. The court martial suspended Ali Bux for six months.[56]

In many cases the Commander-in-Chief played the role of a benevolent angel, especially if the courts martial over-stepped their limits. The bottomline was that, except with those Indians who had challenged the British officers, the military hierarchy was ready to be lenient. The high command went out of its way to reduce the punishment of those Indian officers who were charged with neglect of duty, though it adversely affected the military effectiveness of the force. One Jemadar Jenab Shah of the 2nd Punjab Infantry at Bahadurgarh made a false report to his commander on 15 October 1869. He stated in his report that all the regimental camels, which were used for carrying baggage and munitions, were present. The Jemadar knew very well that two camels were missing. A general court martial, which was presided over by Subedar-Major Habib Khan, suspended Jenab Shah for six months. Though Jenab Shah's crime was less serious than that of Resaldar Rahim Bux, who misbehaved with his British officer in February 1870, Bux got away with lighter punishment. While Bux was served an order of suspension for four months by Resaldar-Major Man Singh's court, Jenab Shah was suspended for six months. This was despite the fact that Jenab Shah's service record was much better than Rahim Bux. Why did this happen? Perhaps either Man Singh shared with his colleague Rahim Bux, a sort of disaffection against the British who had monopolized most of the power and privileges for themselves or Habib Khan had a personal vendetta against Jenab Shah. Anyway, Mansfield noticed this contradiction and he revoked the suspension order.[57]

In certain cases, senior officers acquiesced to the pressure from soldiers even when the army was in the midst of a war. When the Second Afghan War was going on, a Punjabi Muslim sepoy named Sharin of the 20th Punjab Regiment deployed in the Kurram Valley deserted on 5 January 1880. The crime was doubly serious because the soldier deserted with his rifle, when the army was engaged in battle. The man was caught and brought to trial before a general court martial. He was sentenced to suffer transportation for ten years. The Punjabi Muslims constituted a sizeable chunk of the Raj's force. By 1885, they constituted about 6.7 per cent of the Sepoy Army. They numbered about 8,799 men. Major-General C.J. Morsoon commanding the Punjab Frontier Force reduced the term to eight years,[58] probably as a goodwill gesture, so as not to alienate the Punjabi Muslim community.

Even during peace, the Raj's disciplinary apparatus buckled due to pressures from below. The army gave way to the troops' demand for redressal, especially just after 1857, when the British were still suffering from the 'Mutiny shock'. In 1857, when the Bengal Army mutinied, about 100,000 soldiers rebelled. Only a few fought for the Raj. Some soldiers were disarmed and the rest went to their villages and sat tight waiting and watching.[59] Among this group of fence-sitters, a considerable number were dismissed and discharged from various regiments by their commandants, on grounds of their dubious loyalty. After the imperial victory many such characters turned up claiming 'justice'. The Raj lacked the will to turn down everybody as the rebellion was just over. And in such cases, the higher authorities overrode the decisions of the summary courts martial.

One Mohais Singh, an ex-soldier of the 29th Bengal Infantry Regiment, which rebelled in 1857, turned up in 1860 to challenge his dismissal. He claimed that during 1857 he was at Ambala depot, and when ordered by the British commandant to prove his loyalty by firing the greased cartridges, he fired from his Enfield rifle. This news reached his unit, then stationed at Moradabad. When Mohais Singh joined his unit, his *Purbiya* colleagues raised a hue and cry. They claimed that Mohais had become an outcaste as he had handled the impure cartridges, and was hence unacceptable to the regiment. In an attempt to defuse tension, Captain Hoeist of his regiment ordered Mohais Singh to take leave from 20 May till 31 July 1857. As the temper of the *Purbiyas* rose and the Mutiny spread, Hoeist renewed Mohais' leave for another four months. Mohais claimed that when he presented himself at Benares in 1858, the Brigadier in charge there dismissed him. Mohais recounted that he had served the Raj with loyalty for nineteen years but was unduly punished for the guilt of others. He demanded to be reinducted in the army. The soldiers joined with a sense of contract for continuous service. Breach of this contract would have resulted in the loss of faith of thousands of the Raj's soldiers, and the net outcome would have been weakening of their loyalty bonds. This the army could not afford. Moreover, Singh had been thrown out by a summary order. The higher authorities regretted that British officers often behaved as despots, which alienated the soldiers. So, they reopened this case. Captain L. Fraddy acknowledged that, though a Brahmin, he behaved properly at Ambala and he remained in his village when his regiment mutinied in June 1857. Major E. Crompton, who was at Benares, ascertained that Mohais was in his village Moorlichpura in Ballia *parganah* of Ghazipur province during the Mutiny. Satisfied with the enquiry, the Commander-in-Chief ordered the restoration of Mohais Singh in the army without forfeiture of his former period of service.[60]

Occasionally the 'guilty' soldiers enjoyed the benefit of doubt. Naib-Resaldar Sadat Ali Khan of the 18th Irregular Cavalry was on sick leave when the 'devil's wind' blew. He rejoined his unit only on 23 January 1859. What raised the eyebrows of his commandant, Major W.H. Ryves, was that the duration of the Resaldar's sick leave was from 8 April 1857 to 7 November of the same year. What was Khan doing after that date till January 1859? Khan claimed that he was at his home at Rampur and during the Mutiny he had tried to contact the British. Khan demanded his arrears of pay—Rs. 361. Ryves deduced that Khan was at best a passive, and not an active supporter of the Raj. Instead of coming forward and risking life and limb to aid the white men in the time of trouble, Khan spent his time comfortably with his family. At this critical juncture, Ryves' superior, Adjutant General Lieutenant-Colonel W. Mayhew, came to Khan's rescue. Mayhew was afraid that the arbitrary behaviour of the regimental commandants would alienate the Indian personnel. Mayhew asserted that Khan's argument about his several attempts to contact Ryves could not be disproved. Mayhew ultimately restored Khan to his former position in his old unit and released his arrears.[61]

III

LOW LEVEL OF CRIMES AND NON-COERCIVE SURVEILLANCE TECHNIQUES

History shows that very frequently a harsh penal system merely encourages violence on part of the soldiers. One of the reasons for Stalin's soldiers leaning towards crime was because of the inhuman punishment system of the Red Army.[62] The British policy of awarding moderate punishment prevented discontent among the Indian soldiers reaching a breaking point and thus the army had a low crime rate. This becomes evident when one takes a micro as well as macro view of the crime graph. Table 7.2 shows that of the Bengal Army soldiers eligible for Good Conduct Pay, only 1.49 per cent did not receive this because of misconduct.

The 14th Madras Infantry Regiment can be taken as a microcosm of the infantry regiments belonging to the Madras Army. In its long history of more than a century, there was only a single case of desertion which occurred in 1893.[63] From Table 7.3 it is clear that on a macro perspective, desertion remained very low in the Sepoy Army. Compared with other armies, like the American forces during the Civil War,[64] and the Red Army during the Bolshevik takeover,[65] desertions in the Sepoy Army when engaged in campaigns remained very low.

Desertions were miniscule in the Madras infantry regiments, because the privates were allowed to keep their wives with the regiments. The Victorian British Army believed that if the soldiers were allowed to keep their families with the regiments, then

TABLE 7.2: NUMBER OF SOLDIERS RECEIVING GOOD CONDUCT PAY (GCP) IN
THE BENGAL ARMY IN 1875

Number of Soldiers	Sepoys	Sowars	Total	Remarks
Under 6 years of service	14,157	3,308	17,465	Soldiers not in receipt of GCP because it started only after 6 years of service
With 6 years of service and upwards	221	71	292	Forfeited GCP due to misconduct
6-10 years of service	7,782	1,422	9,204	In receipt of First Rate of GCP at Re. 1 per month
10–15 years of service	7,644	976	8,620	In receipt of the Second Rate of GCP at Rs. 2 per month
More than 15 years of Service		1,455		In receipt of the Third Rate of GCP
More than 30 years of service	26	66	92	-Do-
Total on 1 June	29,804	7,232	37,036	

Source: Good Conduct pay in the Bengal Army on 1 June 1875, Records of Chief
Commands, 1865–76, Notes and Minutes by Napier of Magdala,
MSS.EUR.F.114, 5 (4), OIOC.

they would not get drunk and indisciplined. This strand of
thought probably influenced the military of British India. Further,
the families of Indian soldiers in the regimental lines functioned
as imperial hostages; a security for the 'proper' behaviour on
part of the soldiers. The regimental lines became their homes
and they had no other place to go. For instance, in 1893 the 8th
Madras Infantry Regiment's lines had 321 relatives and friends of
the personnel. Many of the family members also functioned as
public followers of the regiment. Moreover, many of the sons of
Madrassi and Gurkha soldiers got jobs in their fathers' units.
Since the Gurkhas had left Nepal along with their families due to
dearth of jobs, there could not be any question of their desertion.
Till the 1880s, the *Ranas* of Nepal were not eager to allow the
Gurkhas to join the Sepoy Army. The *Ranas* believed that British
recruitment of the Gurkhas would result in gradual erosion of
sovereignty of their Kingdom. Many Gurkhas lost their lives in
their attempt to cross into British India. But, regular pay was a
great inducement for them to join the Raj's military service.[66]

TABLE 7.3: DESERTIONS OF THE INDIAN ARMY PERSONNEL STATIONED
WITHIN INDIA (1870–5)

Army	Number of Deserters	Number of Deserters per Regiment per year	% of Strength
Bengal Army		3.5 men (Infantry and Cavalry Regiments taken together); 2 men in Cavalry Regiment; 3 men in Infantry Regiment Bengal Army	.5
Punjab Frontier Force			.25
Madras Army	286	1.3 men (Infantry and Cavalry Regiments taken together)	.5
Bombay Army	532	3 men (Average of the Infantry and the Cavalry Regiments)	.42

Source: Minute on the organization of the army in India, Ch. 2, Bengal Army, general
  conditions, para 60, 63, Ch. 3, Madras Army, para 36–8, Ch. 4, Bombay
  Army, general remarks on the organization, para 19–20, 11 October 1875,
  Norman Minutes, NAI.

Note: Blank spaces denote unavailability of data.

In the Bengal Army and in the Punjab Frontier Force, north
Indians, Punjabis and the North-West Frontier tribes were
inducted. In 1875, these two forces had around 9,000 Gurkhas,
22,000 north Indians, 19,000 Punjabis, and 5,000 frontier tribals.
In the British perception the last two groups were 'wild'. How
was the army able to check desertions? Military service was
considered an honourable profession among Indians. Generally,
small peasant families owning four bullocks and sixty acres of
land supplied personnel to the Raj's military. The small peasants
from Punjab and the Ganga-Jamuna doab generally joined the
army to tide over unfavourable harvests. During harvest, when
the troops' farms needed extra hands, they wanted to go to their
villages. So the army introduced the scheme of furlough. For the
frontier tribes, pay and pension were vital sources of income,
especially in the context of a rising population and dimnishing
economic base. Their population reached 1.6 million by 1911.
Between 1879 and 1915, the number of North-West Frontier
tribals in the Sepoy Army increased from 2,000 to 7,500.[67]

Desertion was minute in the cavalry regiments, because the landed gentry used to join these units along with their retainers and relatives for social prestige. Those who bought their own horses were known as *silladars* and for security, they had to deposit Rs. 500 with the government. If they misbehaved, or were discharged, then they lost their security money.[68] Again many of the retainers joined without horses. They were known as *bargirs* and were provided horses by their chiefs who joined the regiments as officers. These chiefs gave written security for the proper conduct of all the *bargirs* mounted by them.[69] Also peer group pressure on the *bargirs* forced them to behave well. Those Indian officers who had mounted *bargirs* had an additional incentive to ensure proper discipline in the regiment because if they or their *bargirs* misbehaved then not only were they dismissed but they also lost all the money invested in the unit in the form of horses. An account of the capital investment made by the Indian officers can be gleaned from the example of Resaldar-Major Ahmad Baksh Khan. He joined the 3rd Cavalry Regiment of the Hyderabad Contingent in 1836, and remained loyal during the 1857 Mutiny. By 1876, he had mounted 60 *bargirs* and this amounted to an investment of Rs. 75,000. Since it was a sort of family business, Ahmad Baksh Khan's eldest son was also eager to join his father's regiment.[70] Ahmad Baksh Khan was not an exception, for instance, in 1858 there was an Indian officer in Hyderabad Contingent who mounted 500 *bargirs* and another in Gujarat Horse who mounted 300 *bargirs*.[71]

The term fragging means killing or maiming of officers by the privates. It was common in the American Army in Vietnam in the 1960s and early 1970s.[72] This phenomenon was present but minimal in the Sepoy Army. In the 3rd Cavalry Regiment of the Hyderabad Contingent in 1828, a group of soldiers murdered Captain Tucker of that unit during parade. The culprits were never caught. This instance occurred probably because the officer had a personal problem with the men. The murder did not reflect an anti-British attitude on part of the sowars, because during 1857, they fought doggedly against the rebels. No other case of fragging was reported from this unit.[73] In the 125 years of 8th Bombay Infantry Regiment's history, there was only a single case of serious misbehaviour with a British officer, which occurred in 1885.[74] Occasionally the Indian soldiers misbehaved with the sahibs, and some of the cases have been discussed in the previous section. The relationship between the white officers and the brown soldiers represented a crucial interface between the colonizers and the colonized. The above cases should force us to revise at least partly, the picture of a romanticized father-son relationship between the sahibs and the sepoys, as drawn by Philip Mason.[75]

Some discontent was inbuilt between the white officers and the brown privates. But from Table 7.4 it is clear that on the whole, the number of men tried by the courts martial remained marginal compared to the size of the army. How were the British able to prevent the escalation of sahib-sepoy antagonism? The higher level of the military hierarchy understood that, at times, the fault for starting such affrays lay with the British officers. So when any sahib misbehaved with the brown privates, even without the latter complaining about it, the high command took action. One Lieutenant-Colonel Stanley of the Bombay Army in 1867 misbehaved with a soldier during parade. For 'lack of self control', the officer was immediately removed from his position.[76]

Regimental commandants were occasionally allowed to resort to summary courts martial for dismissing Indians who had defied the authority of white officers. However, Table 7.5 shows that the number of soldiers discharged by both the general and summary courts martial, remained small. Moreover, when Indian

TABLE 7.4: TRIALS BY COURTS MARTIAL OF THE INDIAN ARMY
PERSONNEL STATIONED WITHIN INDIA (1870–5)

Army	Number of men tried by Courts* Martial	Number of men tried per Regiment per Year	% of strength	Size
Bengal Army	1,313	4	0.6	44,685
Punjab Frontier Force	318	4.5	0.5	11,500
Madras Army	1,168	5	0.75	30,000
Bombay Army	1,557	8	1.25	22,000

Source: Confidential memorandum on the army, Minute on the organization of the army in India, Ch.2, Bengal Army, Ch. 3, Madras Army, Ch. 4, Bombay Army, Norman Minutes, NAI; Annual army caste return of the troops in Bengal Presidency, 1876, Records of Chief Commands, 1865–76, Notes and Minutes by Napier of Magdala, MSS.EUR.F.114, 5(4), OIOC.

*Includes Summary, Regimental and General Courts Martial.

TABLE 7.5: DISMISSAL OF THE INDIAN ARMY PERSONNEL STATIONED
WITHIN INDIA (1870–5)

Army	Number of men dismissed by General and Summary Courts Martial	Number of Men dismissed/Regiment (Average of infantry and cavalry Regiments)/year	% of Strength
Bengal Army		3.9	
Punjab Frontier Force		3.5	
Madras Army	482	2	
Bombay Army	730	4	.58

Source: Minute on the organization of the Indian Army, Ch. 2, Bengal Army, General
conditions, para 60, 63, Ch. 4, Bombay Army, General remarks, para 19,
Norman Minutes, NAI.
Note: Blank spaces denote unavailability of data.

officers were discharged by the summary courts martial, then other brown officers were promoted, which cooled their discontent. Subedar Moraree Satun of the 8th Bombay Infantry Regiment was dismissed from service for 'misconduct' on 30 January 1885. But, the Indian officers' anger did not coalesce, because their chances of promotion brightened. Few soldiers became Naiks after twenty years of service and very few among them became Havildars after twenty-four years of service if not already invalided. To assuage the feelings of the Indian officers, the commandant immediately promoted Jemadar Parasuram Jadow into Satum's slot and Havildar M. Landay became Jemadar in Jadow's place.[77]

It is observed that the soldiers' respect for their officers increased if the latter happened to be the formers' social superiors.[78] For this reason, the British tried to utilize the clan leaders' natural leadership over their followers, while building the cavalry regiments. This policy probably reduced the quantum of misbehaviour by the sowars towards their Indian officers. The clan leaders were encouraged to join the units with their relatives and followers. When the 1st Punjab Cavalry was raised at Peshawar in 1849, Jai Singh, Nihal Singh and Mehtul Singh from Lahore joined with thirty of their followers. The British, by the technique of commissioning the clan leaders as officers over their retainers, attempted to continue the patron-client relationship between the Indian elite and the indigenous recruits.

This was vital because this was a mixed regiment consisting of 150 Pathans (organized in two troops), 100 Sikhs and 280 Hindustanis. The clan leaders were men of property and influence in their own localities. The imperial assumption was that the retainers would remain disciplined because they already knew their 'natural' leaders and were confident that their chiefs, as officers, would look after their interests within the regiments. So, for controlling the Pathan sowars, the British made five of their clan leaders into commissioned officers, and another six were inducted as non-commissioned officers.[79]

In the Imperial Prussian-German Army of the late nineteenth century, the non-commissioned officers indulged in abusing the privates both physically and emotionally.[80] Affrays between the sepoys and the Indian officers (both commissioned and non-commissioned) were more common than between the sepoys and their British officers. This was due to the imperial attempt to use the Indian officers as a human shield to punish the privates. Further, the British officers, compared with the Indian officers, had more power and status, and could offer the Indian privates far more career incentives and punishment.[81] So, the Indian rank and file had reasons to keep the British officers in good humour. The Indian officers' interaction with the brown privates was also more frequent. Hence, the former got more opportunity to exercise petty power over the privates. In general, the privates flouted the Indian officers' authority frequently, because most of the officers in the infantry regiments were promoted from the ranks. As they were not superior to the common soldier either socially or educationally, the latter failed to show respect to the brown officers.[82] Charles Reid, commandant of the Sirmoor Rifles, probably over-emphasized a bit when in 1876 he asserted: 'Every Adjutant and every commanding officer must be aware that, as a class, Indian officers are not respected by the men'.[83] When the sepoys were in debt to their Indian officers, the latter forced the former to sell their wives. And this heightened the tension between the privates and the Indian officers. One such case occurred in the 11th Punjab Infantry Regiment, when Subedar Pritam Singh bought Rukmini, wife of sepoy Ramdas, in January 1860. To prevent the escalation of tension, Lord Clyde, the Commander-in-Chief of the Indian Army from 1857 to 1860, had the Subedar arrested.[84] Finally, the Indian privates remained a cohesive body due to caste, clan and village ties, hence the absence of negative practices like *dyedovschina* (physical abuse of junior privates by the senior privates) among them.[85] This cohesiveness enabled them to act unitedly against the brown officers.

The British followed a policy that prevention of crimes was better than attempting to cure it through punishment. Charles Reid demanded that to prevent the grievances of the soldiers from crossing the threshold, the British officers must take timely steps. For that it was necessary to get timely information regarding the activities of the privates. The Raj constructed an intelligence system for preempting mutiny. Reid agreed that the sepoys' lines were *terra incognita* for the white officers. In order to get what in modern parlance could be termed as 'real time intelligence', Reid demanded that two European Sergeants should be attached to each Indian regiment. Their duty would be to inform the Adjutant and the commanding officer regarding the activities in the sepoy lines. The Sergeants residing close to the sepoy barracks would be able to procure information through continuous intercourse with the Indian officers and the rank and file.[86]

The Resident of Hyderabad, in charge of political affairs was also responsible for collecting data regarding the state of discipline in the Hyderabad Contingent from the Indian informants. The Resident C.B. Saunders in May 1876 warned the central government in the following words:

I have certain indications from an Indian informant that there is great discontent within the cavalry regiments of the Hyderabad Contingent and a rebellion might occur. The sowars were especially angry because Wright [Brigadier General Wright, Commandant of the Hyderabad Contingent] had reduced their holidays during *Ramzan* and *Muharram* and they were under stoppage due to the Kanpur saddles. . . . The Indians did not like the English saddles prepared at Kanpur. . . . Because of Brigadier-General Wright's unpopular measures, many *bargirs* have sent in their resignations. It is politically dangerous that men who had served us loyally for 20 years are now leaving us and getting scattered to various parts of India with a grievance in his heart.[87]

Thanks to the Resident's timely intelligence, Wright's measures were revoked and probably a mutiny was averted.

From the last decade of the nineteenth century, the army high command started the practice of preparation of annual confidential reports regarding the state of discipline in the regiments. Through warning, forced transfer to the pension establishment, demotion and dismissal of the Indian officers, the Raj attempted to shore up discipline within the units. In 1893, the representative of the Adjutant General of India's office after inspecting the 1st Madras Lancers found that Troop Havildar Major Ibrahim Khan and Havildar Lambaji Rao's conduct as unsatisfactory. The general officer commanding was ordered by the Adjutant General's office to warn these non-commissioned officers that unless their performance improved within the next six months, they would be removed. As regards the 2nd Madras Lancers, the Adjutant General's office informed the general officer commanding, that Subedar Unend Rao must be warned to exert himself. If during the next annual inspection, warned the Adjutant General, the Subedar failed to pull himself together, then he would be removed. The Adjutant General's office also requested the general officer commanding, to forward details regarding the concerned Indian officers and dates of promotion, service records, etc. If many Indian officers of a particular regiment were found to be incompetent, the Raj did not punish all of them as it would alienate the brown officer corps as a body. The army high command punished some of them with the warning that others would also be punished if they did not improve their performance in the near future. The 2nd Lancers' four Indian non-commissioned officers had already got a bad report during the inspection that occurred in 1892. Two Indian non-commissioned officers were pensioned off. Of them one was transferred to the pension list after a service of only fifteen years. Thus he lost the chance of becoming a commissioned officer. This had a shock effect on the other two Indian non-commissioned officers. In 1893, the general officer commanding reported to the Adjutant General that the other two were smartening up. As regards the 3rd Madras Lancers, the Adjutant General's informant in the same year found fault with Subedar Purungswamy of Number 1 Company. Before taking any action, the Adjutant General's office demanded more information on him. The general officer commanding was asked to prepare a special report on that Subedar.[88] In 1893, Jemadars Chet Singh, Akbar Khan and Dewa Singh of the 33rd Madras Infantry

Regiment were unfavourably reported on. Only Chet Singh was transferred to the pension establishment. The other two Jemadars were warned that unless they improve their conduct, in the next year they would also suffer the fate of Chet Singh. In addition, the Adjutant General's office demanded that every regimental commandant should prepare and maintain detailed reports about the recruits' background—the region from they were recruited, and when and by whom.[89] This technique had much in common with the Mughal practice of maintaining *chihran*, which included information regarding the troopers' physical features, social backgrounds and details regarding their families.[90]

Parades were held to ensure discipline. In 1893, the Adjutant General's office heard reports that the sepoys of the 5th Madras Infantry Regiment did not attend parades regularly. The Adjutant General warned the British officers of this regiment that this reflected slackness and want of supervision on part of the white officers. The general officer commanding replied that orders were already issued that every sepoy had to attend the morning parades.[91]

How successful was the disciplinary institution in separating its personnel from society? The British authorities were always concerned about insulating recruits from their social background. Political conditions in Punjab were always a headache for the British because it was the most heavily recruited province. In 1883, a rumour was floating that Dilip Singh (Maharaja Ranjit Singh's successor who was exiled to England after the annexation of the *Khalsa* kingdom in the aftermath of the Second Sikh War) might visit India. Roberts privately warned the Duke of Cambridge that India was boiling due to the controversy regarding the Ilbert Bill and the Indian Vernacular press was further inflaming passions against the white man's rule. Roberts argued that the Sikhs were feudal and clannish in their attitude and Dilip Singh's visit might shake their loyalty by turning their thoughts to the old glory of the *Khalsa*.[92] To Viceroy Northbrook, Roberts was more candid. In 1883, he wrote:

No people in India are more feudal in their instincts, or more clannish in their affection towards their hereditary chieftains than the Sikhs. Many of them are still alive who remember the days when the territory of the great Ranjit Singh stretched from the mouth of the Khyber far away to the southeast, and when the English had to send a representative to the

Court of the 'Lion of the Punjab'. Forty years have passed away since then, but old Sikhs will still tell you of the glories of the Khalsa, before the advancing tide of the invaders wrested their Kingdom from them on the bloody fields of Mudki, Ferozeshah, Sobraon and Chilianwala. It seems quite possible that the presence of the Maharaja Dilip Singh, in the old Sikh capital of Lahore, would raise a wave of loyalty and enthusiasm among the Sikh nation.[93]

When in 1887 Lord Dufferin, the Viceroy enquired whether any disturbance in Punjab might affect the troops, Roberts replied:

I do not believe that there is any general dissatisfaction in the Punjab, but I have always thought that the return or even threatened return of Dilip Singh to India would raise the hopes of a revival of power amongst certain sections of the Sikhs, and that his presence with a Russian force in Afghanistan might cause some trouble with our Sikh soldiers.[94]

In general, the extent of disobedience in the Sepoy Army remained low because of absence of massive battle casualties and mass conscription.[95] Political motives were absent in the 'crimes' committed by the troops. This was because the Congress, the largest political organization in the subcontinent was not interested in spreading sedition among the troops.[96] The soldiers' dissent was shaped by their service considerations, and circumscribed by the regimental institution. Even in the pre-1857 era, the mutinies aimed at the improvement of service conditions. Only in 1857 did the soldiers' grievances snowball into political dissent.[97] So the interpretation of a group of scholars, that the sepoys were peasants in uniform, needs to be revised.[98]

CONCLUSION

Between the pre-colonial and the colonial period, the whole logic of military organization changed. The types of crimes committed by the soldiers, and the punishments meted out to them, were transformed. The princely militaries were clannish and the clan leaders were responsible for the discipline of their followers. Aristocratic families enjoying taxation rights had the responsibility of raising troops and administering them.[99] But, the colonial army was run mostly on an impersonal basis. Military jobbers were eliminated, and the system of chiefs standing as guarantors, was done away with. If the troops were indisciplined, then the army punished them directly. Not the local warlords, but the military bureaucracy, acquired the legitimacy to punish the armed personnel. The impersonal bureaucracy also tended to reduce the arbitrariness of the white officers in punishing the soldiers. Thus, in the British period, the state monopolized its hold over the army's disciplinary system, and the central government's control over the management of violence increased.

If one takes a *long duree* view of South Asian history, then the changes in the nature of crime committed by the soldiers become clear. To realize their arrears of pay, Maratha troops held *dharnas* surrounding their chiefs, and denied them food and drink.[100] In the Sepoy Army, this sort of action was unnecessary, because pay became regular. The British period was not only a break with the pre-colonial period, but also represented a sort of 'modernity'. In the *Khalsa* Army of Ranjit Singh, the punishments were generally amputation of limbs, noses, etc.[101] Then, in the Mughal and the Ahom forces, the punishment for desertion was impalement or beheading.[102] Such barbarism was on its way out in the colonial army, where the common forms of punishment were suspensions, imprisonments and dismissals. This trend was in consonance with Western societies which were moving towards greater leniency in military punishment.[103]

Since the British response towards indisciplinary acts of their colonial soldiers became bureaucratic and moderate, the Sepoy Army can be categorized as a professional institution. The Sepoy Army and the metropolitan armies did not represent two opposite poles. While the Sepoy Army had some colonial specificity (like the use of the Indian officer corps as an imperial shield), it also shared certain similarities with the British Army, especially as regards the gradual moderation of punishment. Many facets of the Sepoy Army's punishment mechanism were more humane than those of the British Army. For example, the practice of branding the deserters was common in the British Army but was absent in the Sepoy Army. Again, some aspects of the Sepoy Army's punishment system was much better than particular metropolitan armies like the Rumanian Army which unlike the former retained lashing till the Second World War.[104] However, all colonial armies cannot be bracketed together. Compared to the other British colonial armies like the African forces,[105] the disciplinary system of the Sepoy Army was much more humane. Corporal punishment in the King's African Rifles was abolished only after the Second World War.[106]

The disciplinary tradition of the Sepoy Army was characterized neither by Foucaltian nor by Wagnerian drama.[107] Rudrangshu Mukherjee's argument, that the sahib-sepoy relationship was characterized by overt violence,[108] applies only for the period between 1857 to 1859. The Mutiny was an aberration. Otherwise crimes were related to mundane, day to day activities, and punishment remained a low-key affair. The Mutiny probably taught the British that the best way to manage the colonial army was not to over-react. Seema Alavi asserts that the tightening of discipline over the Bengal Army resulted in the 1857 uprising.[109] The pendulum swung in the opposite direction in the latter half of the nineteenth century. To conclude, the Sepoy Army functioned on the application of low volume of coercion.

NOTES

1. Omissi, *The Sepoy and the Raj*, pp. 113–52.
2. Minute on the organization of the Indian Army, Ch. 5, pension system, para 21, 38, 11 October 1875, Norman minutes; Confidential circular to officers regarding courts martial, no. 85/N, 25 August 1863, vol. 3, Circular to officers as regards summary trials, no. 26/N, 15 March 1864, Circular as regards discipline, no. 129/N, 29 September 1864, vol. 4, Confidential circulars to officers, 16 May 1865, vol. 5, ADG's circulars, NAI.
3. Digest of services of the 3rd Brahmin, 1861–1914, NAI.
4. Minute on the organization of the Indian Army, Ch. 3, Madras Army, para 37, Norman Minutes.
5. Two representatives are Greenhut's, 'Sahib and Sepoy', *Military Affairs*, vol. XLVIII, no. 1 (1984), pp. 15–18 and S.L. Menezes, 'Race, Caste, Mutiny and Discipline in the Indian Army from Its Origins to 1947', in Alan J. Guy and Peter B. Boyden, eds., *Soldiers of the Raj: The Indian Army, 1600–1947*, London: National Army Museum, 1997, p. 109.
6. Peers in 'Sepoys, Soldiers and the Lash', p. 221 writes that summary courts martial was the most common method of disciplining the sepoys. This was not the case for the post-1859 era.
7. An abridged version of this chapter was published as 'Coercion through Leniency: British Manipulation of the Courts-Martial System in the Post-Mutiny Indian Army, 1859–1913', *JMH*, vol. 65, no. 4 (2001), pp. 937–64.
8. Gunther E. Rothenberg, 'The Austrian Army in the Age of Metternich', *Journal of Modern History*, vol. 40 (1968), pp. 156–61.

9. H.J. Hanham, 'Religion and Nationality in the Mid-Victorian Army', in M.R.D. Foot, ed., *War and Society: Historical Essays in Honour and Memory of J.R. Western, 1928–71,* London: Paul Elek, 1973, pp. 170, 174; Spiers, *The Army and Society,* pp. 62–4, 66–7; Spiers, 'The Late Victorian Army: 1868-1914', in David Chardler and Ian Beckett, ed., *The Oxford Illustrated History of the British Army,* Oxford: Oxford University Press, 1994, p. 192; Skelley, *The Victorian Army at Home,* p. 125; Lawrence James, *Mutiny in the British and Commonwealth Forces: 1797–1956,* London: Buchan & Enright Publishers, 1987, p. 27; Strachan, *Wellington's Legacy,* p. 50.

10. Gorham, *A Short Course,* p. 178; J.R. Dinwiddy, 'The Early Nineteenth Century Campaign against Flogging in the Army', *EHR,* vol. 97 (1982), p. 331.

11. Radhika Singha, '"Providential Circumstances": The Thuggee Campaign of the 1830s and Legal Innovation', *MAS,* vol. 27 (1993), p. 88; Kartik Kalyan Raman, 'Utilitarianism and the Criminal Law in Colonial India: A Study of the Practical Limits of Utilitarian Jurisprudence', *MAS,* vol. 28 (1994), pp. 739–91.

12. Stokes, *The English Utilitarians,* p. 222.

13. David Arnold, 'The Colonial Prison: Power, Knowledge and Penology in Nineteenth-century India', in idem. and David Hardiman, ed., *Subaltern Studies: Essays in Honour of Ranajit Guha,* vol. 8, 1994, reprint, Delhi: Oxford University Press, 1996, pp. 148–9, 161–2, 164.

14. David Garland, *Punishment and Modern Society: A Study in Social Theory,* Oxford: Clarendon Press, 1990, pp. 7–8. Kaushik Roy, 'Spare the Rod, Spoil the Soldier? Crime and Punishment in the Army of India, 1860-1913', *JSAHR,* vol. 84, no. 337 (2006), pp. 9–33.

15. 9th Bombay Regiment, NAI. This document is unpaginated and the information is organized under different years, 1775, 1797.

16. 14th Madras Infantry, NAI, pp. 87–88, 90.

17. Spiers, *The Army and Society,* pp. 42, 44, 49; Hew Strachan, 'Liberalism and Conscription: 1789-1919', in idem., ed., *The British Army, Manpower and Society into the Twenty-first Century,* London: Frank Cass, 2000, p. 3; Philips, ed., *The Correspondence of Lord William Cavendish Bentinck,* no. 802, 16 February 1835, pp. 1431–2; 14th Madras Infantry, pp. 87–8, 90.

18. Simla, 2 July 1867, pp. 251-2, GO, NAI.

19. *Hancock Report,* p. 30.

20. Minute on the organization of the Indian Army, Ch. 5, Pension system, para 21, 38, 11 October 1875, Norman Minutes.

21. See the career of an eighteenth century warlord in William R. Pinch, 'Who was Himmat Bahadur? Gosains, Rajputs and the British in Bundelkhand, *ca.* 1800', *IESHR,* vol. 35, no. 3 (1998), pp. 293–335.

22. Peter Burroughs, 'Tackling Army Desertion in British North America',

Canadian Historical Review, vol. LXI (1980), pp. 28–68. Burroughs seems to imply that rotting in the prisons was as inhuman as being caned.

23. Simla, 25 June 1896, p. 311, GO.

24. 8th Bombay Infantry, NAI (this manuscript is unpaginated and the information is organized under various dates), 2 March 1887.

25. The Marquess of Anglesey, *A History of the British Cavalry: 1872–98*, vol. 3, London: Leo Cooper, 1982, p. 154; Minute on the organization of the Indian Army, Ch. Bengal Army, para 64, 66, 11 October 1875, Norman Minutes.

26. Hartington to the Governor General, para 10, no. 25, 30 June 1880, Colonel William Merewether Collection, MSS.EUR.D.625/5, OIOC.

27. T.R. Moreman, 'The Arms Trade and the Northwest Frontier Pathan Tribes, 1890–1914', *JICH*, vol. 22, no. 2 (1994), pp. 195–7, 201–2.

28. Hathras, 27 November 1866, p. 404, GO.

29. Simla, no. 390, 20 May 1901, GO.

30. Simla, 26 July 1899, pp. 390–1, GO.

31. Captain G.L. Fraser, offfg. Assistant ADG, to the Secy. to the GoI, Simla, Progs. no. 273, 31 July 1862, MDP, August 1862, NAI.

32. Peers, *Mars and Mammon*, p. 85.

33. 28th Bombay Regiment, NAI (this manuscript is unpaginated and the information is organized under various year) August 1905; Simla, 22 May 1866, p. 145, GO.

34. For this concept, I am indebted to James C. Scott's, *Weapons of the Weak: Everyday Forms of Peasant Resistance*, New Haven: Yale University Press, 1985, pp. 29, 31, 33, 36. Scott confines himself to the peasants. But minor workers in any bureaucratic organization could adopt this form of resistance.

35. The average age of the Subedars was 54. From Brigadier R.C. Stewart, ADG, to Colonel A.C. Silver, Secy. to the GoI, MD, Fort Saint George, no. 218, 3 April 1875, in *Copy of Recent Correspondence on the Subject of the Organization of the Indian Army*, London: George Edward Eyre & William Spottswode, 1877, C 1698, in Merewether Collection, MSS.EUR.D.625/4.

36. Fraser to the officer commanding Awadh division, Simla, 6 May 1862, MDP, August 1862.

37. Roberts to Napier, 10 October 1884 in Roberts, *Correspondence with England while Commander-in-Chief in Madras*, p. 216, Part 2, Indian Series, L/MIL/17/5/1615, OIOC.

38. *Supplementary Report*, pp. 30, 61, 65.

39. The memorial of Ram Singh, to Major F.D. Atkinson, offfg. Secy. to GoI, MD, Fort William, Progs. no. 7, February 1860, Office memorandum from Atkinson to Singh, Progs. no. 8, 3 March 1860, MDP, March 1860.

40. Simla, 1 August 1866, pp. 226–7, GO.

41. R.K. Ray, 'Race, Religion and Realm: The Political Theory of "The Reigning Indian Crusade", 1857', in Mushirul Hasan and Narayani Gupta, eds., *India's Colonial Encounter: Essays in Honour of Eric Stokes,* New Delhi: Manohar, 1993, pp. 133–77; From Col. H.K. Burne, Secy. to the GoI, MD, to the Resident at Hyderabad, no. 6C, 1 January 1877, L/MIL/7/14966, OIOC.

42. Simla, para 461, 15 May 1895, pp. 281–2, GO.

43. Simla, para 760, 4 November 1896, pp. 668–9, para 371, 1899, pp. 218–9, GO.

44. Note by General Officer commanding Punjab Frontier District, Confidential reports on the regiments, 1901–2, L/MIL/7/17010, OIOC.

45. I have borrowed this concept from John Keegan's *The Mask of Command,* 1987, reprint, New York: Penguin, 1988. In the context of the late-nineteenth century Sepoy Army, the notion of 'Mask of Command' refers to the symbolic actions on part of the army command to retain legitimacy over the Indian troops.

46. Menezes, *Fidelity and Honour,* p. 534; Simla, 2 July 1867, pp. 251–2, GO.

47. Statement of cases recorded in the proceedings in which there have been differences in opinion between the supreme government and the Bombay government, 15 October 1867, Norman Minutes.

48. Simla, 4 May 1868, pp. 155–6, GO.

49. Calcutta, 22 March 1870, p. 96, GO.

50. Field-Marshal Roberts was a representative of the School, which held the view that the Muslims engineered the Mutiny. Fred Roberts, *Letters Written during the Indian Mutiny,* 1923, reprint, New Delhi: Lal Publishers, 1979, p. 30; W.W. Hunter, *The Indian Musalmans* 1871, reprint, New Delhi: Indological Book House, 1969, pp. 3, 14–16, 21–4, 28–30, 34–5; *Army Committee,* vol. 1-A, *Minority Report,* p. 156.

51. Cardew, Bengal Native Army, p. 331; Calcutta, 14 March 1866, GO.

52. 14 March 1866, GO.

53. Simla, no. 483, 29 June 1899, pp. 318–19, GO.

54. From S.C. Bayley, Junior Secy. to the Bengal Govt. to the offg. Registrar of the High Court, no. 70, 8 May 1864, Proceedings of the Lieut. Governor of Bengal, Judicial, Fort William, no. 69, June 1864, Judicial Proceedings, 1862, WBSA.

55. Simla, 1 November 1895, 15 May 1899, para 363, pp. 718–19, GO.

56. Menezes, *Fidelity and Honour,* p. 534; Simla, 25 May 1870, p. 226, GO.

57. Calcutta, 22 March 1870, 26 March 1870, pp. 96, 115–16, GO.

58. Simla, 25 June 1896, p. 311, GO; *Army Committee,* vol. 1-A, *Minority Report,* p. 156.

59. P.J.O. Taylor, *What Really Happened During the Mutiny: A Day to Day Account of the Major Events of 1857–59 in India,* Delhi: Oxford University Press, 1997, p. 31.

60. This case shows that the feedback apparatus of the Raj reached the lower levels of Indian society. Petition of Mohais Singh, sepoy of the 3rd Company of 29th Bengal Infantry Regiment, to the Commander-in-Chief, Calcutta, Progs. no. 113, 18 November 1859, Major H.K. Burne, offg. Deputy Secy. to the GoI, MD, to the offg. Assistant ADG, Fort William, Progs. no. 114, 3 March 1860, MDP, March 1860.

61. From Lieutenant-Colonel W. Mayhew, ADG, Major F.D. Atkinson, offg. Secy. to the GoI, MD, to the ADG, Fort William, Progs. nos. 252–3, 10 February 1860, 8 March 1860, MDP, March 1860.

62. John E. Jessup, 'The Soviet Armed Forces in the Great Patriotic War, 1941–45', in Alan R. Millet and Williamson Murray, eds., *Military Effectiveness: The Second World War*, vol. 3, Boston: Allen & Unwin, 1988, pp. 263–4.

63. 14th Madras Infantry, p. 36.

64. Brian Holden Reid and John White, ' "A Mob of Stragglers and Cowards": Desertion from the Union and Confederate Armies', *JSS*, vol. 8 (1985), pp. 64–6, 75; Theodore Ayrault Dodge, *Alexander*, 1890, reprint, New York: Da Capo, 1996, pp. 246–8, 680. This analogy is partly true because the Civil War American armies were a sort of militia while the Sepoy Army was composed of long-service volunteers. Further, the American armies suffered from logistical breakdown and high rate of casualties. These two factors encouraged desertion. On the other hand it could be argued that while the Americans were motivated by nationalism, the sepoys and the sowars were quasi-mercenaries.

65. Orlando Figes, 'The Red Army and Mass Mobilization during the Russian Civil War: 1918–20', *Past and Present*, no. 129 (1990), pp. 168–211.

66. Myna Trustram, *Women of the Regiment: Marriage and the Victorian Army,* Cambridge: Cambridge University Press, 1984, pp. 68–9; Vansittart, *Gurkhas* pp. 37–8; idem., *Notes* p. 115; Shakespeare, *Sirmoor Rifles*, pp. 30, 58, 179; 14th Madras Infantry, p. 119; Memorandum on the Gurkha Force, Colonel Charles Reid, 6 August 1861, Merewether Collection, MSS.EUR.D.625/3 (A); Inspection report of the 8th Madras Infantry Regiment, From Brigadier H.R. Hope, Secy. to the Madras Govt. MD, to the Secy. of the GoI, MD, 26 October. 1893, Enclosure to general letter no. 6, Annual confidential reports on the regiments, L/MIL/7/17008, OIOC.

67. R.O. Christensen, 'Tribesmen, Government and Political Economy on the North West Frontier', in Clive Dewey, ed., *Arrested Development in India: The Historical Dimension,* New Delhi: Manohar, 1988, pp. 179–80; *Army Regulations India*, pp. 44–5;. Bingley, *Sikhs*, pp. 120, 138; idem., *Jats and Gujars,* p. 42;. Betham, *Marathas and Dekhani Musulmans,* p. 89; Minute on the organization of army in India, Ch. 2, Bengal Army, composition and organization of the regiments, para 5–6, 9–10, general conditions, para 66, Ch. 3, Madras Army, 11 October 1875, Norman Minutes.

68. Scinde Horse, Brigadier Park's report, Bairseah, 11 October R. 1859, MDP, March 1860; Para 71, May 1876, L/MIL/7/14966.

69. Lumsden's code, para 32–3, May 1876, L/MIL/7/14966.

70. Note by C.B. Saunders, para 71–2, May 1876, Memorandum of proposals by Brigadier-General T. Wright, Correspondence between the Resident at Hyderabad and the Brigadier-General commanding Hyderabad Contingent on the subject of improving the organization, 25 May 1875, Progs. no. 107, L/MIL/7/14966.

71. Extracts of views and opinions of Brigadier-General John Jacob, Appendix A of Resident's letter no. 79, 3 July 1875, L/MIL/7/14966.

72. Guenter Lewy, 'The American Experience in Vietnam', in Sam C. Sarkesian, ed., *Combat Effectiveness: Cohesion, Stress and the Volunteer Military*, Beverly Hills/London: Sage, 1980, pp. 94, 96–8.

73. Digest of Services 3rd Regiment Hyderabad Contingent Cavalry, NAI (this manuscript is unpaginated and the information is organized under the heading of various years), 4 November 1888.

74. 8th Bombay Infantry.

75. Mason, *A Matter of Honour*, pp. 321, 324, 371–92.

76. Statement of cases recorded in the proceedings, case no. 6, 5 October 1867, Norman Minutes.

77. 8th Bombay Infantry, 30 January 1885; Lieutenant-Colonel H.W. Norman, Deputy ADG, to the Secy. to the GoI, MD, Calcutta, Progs. no. 103, 26 July 1861, MDP, October 1861.

78. Paul L. Savage and Richard A. Gabriel, *Crisis in Command: Mismanagement in the United States Army*, 1978, reprint, New Delhi: Himalayan Books, 1986, p. 36.

79. *1st Punjab Cavalry*, pp. 1–3.

80. Showalter, 'Army and Society in Imperial German', Dennies E. Showalter, 'Army and Society in Imperial Germany: The Pains of Modernization', *Journal of Contemporary History*, vol. 18 (1983), p. 601.

81. *Army Regulations, India*, pp. 2–3, 10, 89, 119; *1st Punjab Cavalry*, Appendix no. 3, pp. V, 41.

82. Minute on the organization of the Indian Army, Ch. 3, Madras Army, para 25, 28, 11 October 1875, Norman Minutes.

83. Memorandum on the Indian Army, Inefficient state of the Indian Army laid before the Duke of Cambridge, 1 July 1876, Merewether Collection, MSS.EUR.D.625/3 (C).

84. Menezes, *Fidelity and Honour*, p. 534; From Fraser, Simla, Progs. no. 37, 25 January 1860, MDP, March 1860.

85. *Dyedovschina* is common in the present-day Russian Army. Anatol Lieven, *Chechnya: Tombstone of Russian Power*, New Haven: Yale University Press, 1998, pp. 290, 292.

86. Inefficient state of the Indian Army laid before the Duke of Cambridge, 1 July 1876, Merewether Collection.
87. Note by C.B. Saunders, para 53, 81–3, May 1876, L/MIL/7/14966.
88. Inspection report of the 3rd Madras Lancers, From Brigadier-General H.R. Hope, Secy. to the Madras Govt. MD, to the Secy. to the GoI, MD, Enclosures to general letter no. 6, 26 October 1893, Annual confidential reports on the regiments, L/MIL/7/17008.
89. Inspection report of the 28th and 33rd Madras Infantry Regiments, Hope to the Secy. of the GoI, MD, Enclosures to general letter no. 6, 26 October 1893, Annual confidential reports on the regiments.
90. Singha, 'Settle, Mobilize, Verify' p. 170.
91. Inspection report of the 5th madras infantry regiment, from Hope to the secy. to the GoI, MD, 26 October 1893, Enclosure to general letter no 6, Annual confidential reports on the regiments, L/mil/7/17008.
92. Roberts to the Duke of Cambridge, 25 August 1883, in Roberts, *Correspondence with England while Commander-in-Chief in Madras,* p. 106, Part 2, L/MIL/17/5/1615, OIOC.
93. Roberts to Northbrook, Ootacamund, no. LV, 24 August 1883, in Roberts, *Correspondence with England while Commander-in-Chief in Madras,* p. 106.
94. Roberts to Dufferin, 12 February 1887, in Roberts, *Correspondence with the Viceroy of India,* Part 4, L/MIL/17/5/1615, OIOC.
95. Conscription in Europe created a distaste for military service among the Europeans. As a result the economically marginal groups were forced to join the armies. Nuria Sales De Bohigas, 'Some Opinions on Exemption from Military Service in Nineteenth-century Europe', *CSSH,* vol. 10 (1967–8), pp. 261–89.
96. Both the Russian and the British armies experienced a high level of indiscipline during the First World War due to heavy casualties and political messages spread by the political parties and the newspapers. David Englander and James Osborne, 'Jack, Tommy, and Henry Dubb: The Armed Forces and the Working Class', *Historical Journal,* vol. 21, no. 3 (1978), pp. 593–606; Marc Ferro, 'The Russian Soldier in 1917: Undisciplined, Patriotic, and Revolutionary', *Slavic Review,* vol. 30, no. 3 (1971), pp. 483–511.
97. Heathcote, *The Military in British India,* pp. 77–9.
98. For the sepoy-peasant continuum see Rudrangshu Mukherjee, 'The Sepoy Mutinies Revisited', in Hasan and Gupta, ed., *India's Colonial Encounter,* p. 130. S.P. Rosen states that the British attempt to separate the sepoys from the agrarian society resulted in the 1857 Mutiny. So, in the post-Mutiny period, the imperial attempt was to integrate the army with India's social structure, and this explains absence of mutinies in that period. Idem., *Societies and Military Power.*

99. S. Inayat A. Zaidi, 'Rozindar Troopers under Sawai Jai Singh of Jaipur (AD 1700-43)', *Indian Historical Review*, vol. 10 (1983–4), pp. 45–65; Stewart Gordon, 'The Limited Adoption of European-style Military Forces by Eighteenth-century Rulers in India', *IESHR*, vol. 35, no. 3 (1998) pp. 233–45.

100. Sen, *The Military System of the Marathas* pp. 137–8.

101. Bajwa, *Military System of the Sikhs*, pp. 152–3.

102. Sarkar, *Art of War*, pp. 76, 89.

103. Elihu Rose, 'The Anatomy of Mutiny', *Armed Forces and Society*, vol. 8 (1982), p. 571.

104. Manstein, *Lost Victories*, p. 207; Peter Burroughs, 'Crime and Punishment in the British Army, 1815–70', *EHR*, vol. 100 (1985), p. 570.

105. For the brutal punishments in the African colonial military see, David Killingray, ' "The Rod of Empire": The Debate over Corporal Punishment in the British African Colonial Forces, 1888–1946', *Journal of African History*, vol. 35 (1994), pp. 201–16.

106. Parsons, 'All *askaris* are Family Men', p. 172.

107. For the horrifying disciplinary system of the *Wehrmacht* see Manfred Messerchmidt, 'German Military Law in the Second World War', in Wilhelm Deist, ed., *The German Military in the Age of Total War*, Leamington Spa: Berg, 1985, pp. 323–35.

108. Rudrangshu Mukherjee, ' "Satan Let Loose Upon Earth": The Kanpur Massacres in India in the Revolt of 1857', *Past and Present*, no. 128 (1990), pp. 92–117.

109. Alavi, *The Sepoys and the Company*, pp. 292–302.

Conclusion

If we know how to fight, if we know how to conquer, there is not much
more wanted; to combine successful results is easy, because it is merely
an affair of a well practised judgement. . . . All that is essential in the
few principles which there are, and which depend chiefly on the
constitution of States and Armies. . .
                    Clausewitz's Summary of Instructions to the Crown Prince[1]

Faced with the enormous manpower reserve of South Asia and
its cultural, linguistic and religious heterogeneity, the army had
to chalk out a strategy for selecting groups for enlistment. This
resulted in the birth of the Martial Race theory. The Martial Race
ideology at times appeared like a grand theory, having connections with non-military ideologies operating in the West.
However, ideological opposition and power politics gave birth
to an opposite body of ideas: the Anti-Martial Race theory or
Balanced Recruitment policy. Thus the recruitment policy was
the product of a continuous debate between the two opposing
ideologies.

Besides enlistment, the army was concerned with conditioning
the recruits, so that they would remain in the military machine
and fight for the Raj. A mixture of coercion and welfare, which
included both symbolic elements and material incentives, solved
the problem. Neither the degree of coercion nor the nature of
perquisites had to be overwhelming, because there were no
other potential employers left in the subcontinent, to whom the
sepoys and the sowars could turn to for employment. The Indian
economy was backward and there were no competing civilian
sectors which could attract the recruits away from a long-term
volunteer military force.[2] The imperial techniques which transformed the rural recruits into disciplined and obedient soldiers
were the court martial mechanism, the regimental fabric and the

welfare bureaucracy. The end result was the construction of a bureaucratic standing army.

It was not so much a Military Revolution but a 'Military Synthesis' that took place in India. Military Synthesis stands for a complex amalgam of foreign revolutionary military inputs with indigenous military elements. The Indian context made imported revolutionary institutions inadequate for the military domination of the subcontinent. A balance was required between innovative foreign technologies and managerial techniques with primordial elements in Indian society.[3]

Between 1600 and 1800, north-west Europe experienced a Military Revolution which gave birth to infantry equipped with hand-held firearms, supported by mobile field artillery.[4] The British imported this lethal combination into South Asia. However, the South Asian demography, economy and geography greatly changed this. Instead of the underemployed urban proletariat on which the European infantry forces mainly depended,[5] the British led Sepoy Army had to depend on the peasants. This resulted in the evolution of elaborate recruitment ideologies. Also, the Company was forced to tune its military machine to the demands of an agrarian society. For example furlough was given at harvest time. Traditional Indian institutions like *bazars* were absorbed within the army framework. The old caste, clan and tribal ethos of the subcontinent moulded the imported regimental institution and Western military laws had to coexist side by side with precolonial practices like *durbars* and *panchayats*.

In early modern European warfare, the light cavalry became useless, because of volley firing technique by the infantry. But, in India the lack of light cavalry hampered the Company's warmaking capacity. The heavy European cavalry that the Company brought with it was geared for shock actions. But for reconnaissance, foraging and screening, the British needed light cavalry.[6] Further, the vast theatre of military operations in India made it necessary for the combatants to maintain light cavalry.[7] So the Raj was forced to raise sowars on the Indian model, through the *silladari system*. In the final analysis, the British unlike the Marathas and the Sikhs were able to rule India not merely through an infantry modelled on the West, but because they were able to construct a hybrid military machine, by balancing institutions from the East and the West.[8]

What effect did this process have on the construction of the Raj? In an essay, C. Bayly, influenced by John Brewer's categorization of the early modern British state as a Fiscal-Military State, asserts that Britain's Indian Empire was a Fiscal-Military State. Bayly then goes on to analyse the innovative revenue administration which sustained the British Indian polity.[9] However, he neglects the role of the semi-professional army which maintained this state and was also one of the motors behind its administrative expansion and penetration into Indian society.[10] The other aspect of John Brewer's concept like high taxation for maintaining large armies, if applied to the colonized Indian scenario will not shed much light on the contours of the Raj because this trend was also present in the Mughal polity.[11] In another essay, Bayly asserts that the collection and assessment of information about the 'Orient' aided the British in constructing the Indian Empire.[12] But, he neglects the army's information collection activities. The vast amount of anthropological data, collected by the military officers for aiding in manpower procurement, transformed the colonial polity from a Night Watchman State into a Knowledgeable Military State.[13]

What was so colonial about the Sepoy Army? The Martial Race doctrine was not a peculiar South Asian colonial development. Some of the assumptions of the Martial Race ideology had roots in Western society. Lord Bacon had written: 'It hath seldom or never been seen that the far southern people have invaded the northern, but contrariwise whereby it is manifest that the northern tract of the world is . . . more martial. . . . Cold of northern parts . . . both makes the bodies hardest and . . . courage warmest.[14]

The Martial Race tradition could be traced back to Classical Antiquity. The Caesars preceded Roberts in believing that tall handsome men from cold frontier regions made good soldiers. So, they inducted the Batavi tribe from the Rhine frontier in the *corps de elite* of the Roman Army—the *Germani Custodies Corporis*.[15] Till the eleventh century, the Byzantine Emperors, like the nineteenth century British officials in India, preferred farmers, who were believed to be the best material for soldiering. This preference for small farmers emerged in Classical Greece.[16] The medieval Islamic polities also followed a selective enlistment policy. The Sultans believed that compared to the Greeks, Arabs, Armenians and Kurds, the Turks were much better warriors, due to their 'handsomeness' and 'manliness'. Hence, the Turks were recruited from the Islamic frontier which ran along central Asia.[17]

Back in India, the Mughals preferred the Iranis and the Turanis compared with the Hindustanis and the Afghans in the cavalry, which was the elite branch of their army. *Mansabs* were granted to selected Rajput clans: to the Rajawats and the Shaikhawat clans of the Kachawaha group of Rajputs, but not to the Narooka Rajput clans.[18] The British in India built upon such traditions, and this ideology was then transported to other imperial colonies in the Middle East and Africa.[19]

Even the Anti-Martial Race policy was not unique to colonial India. The balancing strategy had both Western and indigenous roots. The principle of balancing various groups within the military to some extent was present in the eighteenth century Rajput army. The *Maharanas* recruited various clans like the Chauhans, Rathors and the Solankis from different localities of Rajasthan to prevent any one of them becoming very powerful.[20] The Raj, like the Dual Monarchy of the Habsburgs, was an alien regime, which ruled over a polyethnic society. So the Anti-Martial Race lobby, while constructing a multiethnic army, tried to maintain a tripolar balance in the 1880s by absorbing Punjabis, Deccanis and Hindustanis in the following proportion—19.5 per cent, 25 per cent, and 42 per cent respectively. The rest were a motley mixture from various regions.[21] Similarly, the Habsburg Army before 1914 maintained a tripolar balance among the three major ethnic communities: the Germans, Magyars and the Czechs by absorbing them in the following proportion—26.7 per cent, 22.3 per cent, and 13.5 per cents. The rest came from minor groups like the Ruthenians, Poles, etc.[22] The Balanced Recruitment policy was also present in Belgium's African colonial force. Each battalion of the *Force Publique* enlisted members from four different ethnic groups.[23]

The absence of nationalism in the Sepoy Army was not unique. The Habsburg Army also did not depend on nationalism, but depended rather on allegiance to the Emperor. The Habsburg regiments, like the regiments of the Sepoy Army, were composed of three or four nationalities. And the German officers of such units like the British officers of the Sepoy Army had to be specialists in several languages in order to establish working relationship with their soldiers.[24]

The uniqueness of the Sepoy Army lay in the presence of *panchayats, durbars* and excessive emphasis on regimental traditions. The army remained a loose collection of several distinct regiments, rather than a homogeneous, monolithic, unified structure. This proved adequate as long as the Sepoy Army was deployed to check the *'Drang nach Osten'* of the Pathan tribes and the Afghans. But when faced with *der totale krieg* and the Imperial German Army, heavy battle casualties and mass expansion became the order of the day. For the Sepoy Army in France, 1914 brought defeat, death and disaster, a virtual *Gotterdammerung.*

NOTES

1. Colonel F.N. Maude, ed., Von Clausewitz, *On War,* vol. 3, tr. by Col. J.J. Graham, London: Routledge & Keegan Paul, 1968, p. 209.
2. The post-1947 American Army failed to attract satisfactory volunteers in adequate numbers due to the existence of competing civilian occupations. David R. Segal et al., 'The Changing American Soldiers: Work-related Attitudes of US Army Personnel in World War II and the 1970s', *American Journal of Sociology,* vol. 85, no. 1 (1979), pp. 95–108.
3. For Military Synthesis in Indian military history see Kaushik Roy *From Hydaspes to Kargil: A History of Warfare in India from 326 BC to AD 1999* New Delhi: Manohar, 2004.
4. One School challenges the concept of Military Revolution. This School argues that a series of incremental military innovations occurred from 1400 onwards and the slow development of military techniques continued even after 1800. Hence, Jeremy Black argues for using the concept of Military Evolution. Black, *A Military Revolution? Military Change and European Society, 1500–1800,* Basingstoke/London: Macmillan, 1981. Black in *Cambridge Illustrated Atlas of Warfare: Renaissance to Revolution, 1492–1792,* Cambridge: Cambridge University Press, 1996, points out the dynamic growth of non-Western warfare till the eighteenth century. Nicholas Hooper and Matthew Bennett in *Cambridge Illustrated Atlas of Warfare: The Middle Ages, 768–1487,* Cambridge: Cambridge University Press, 1996, p. 153 assert that the process of Military Evolution started in the 'Dark Age'. In response, Clifford J. Rogers has come up with the concept of successive Military Revolutions. The Infantry Revolution occurred between 1420–

40 and then came the Artillery Revolution, etc. To my mind if one takes the long *duree* perspective then the concept of Military Revolution could be maintained especially if we consider the decisive effects that Western arms had on Asia between 1700 and 1900. Rogers, 'The Military Revolutions of the Hundred Years War', and Geoffrey Parker, 'In Defence of *The Military Revolution*', in Rogers, ed., *The Military Revolution Debate: Readings on the Military Transformation of Early Modern Europe*, Colorado/Boulder: Westview Press, 1995, pp. 55–93, 33–65.

5. David Fitzpatrick, 'Militarism in Ireland, 1900–22', in Thomas Bartlett and Keith Jeffrey, eds., *A Military History of Ireland*, Cambridge: Cambridge University Press, 1996, pp. 380–1; V.G. Kiernan, *European Empires, from Conquest to Collapse*, Bungay, Suffolk: Fontana, 1982, p. 15

6. Pradeep Barua, 'Military Developments in India, 1750–1850', *JMH*, vol. 58, no. 4 (1994), pp. 599–616; G.J. Bryant, 'The Cavalry Problem in the Early British Indian Army, 1750–85', *War in History*, vol. 2, no. 1 (1995), pp. 1–21; idem., 'The Military Imperative in Early British Expansion in India, 1750–85', *Indo-British Review*, vol. 21, no. 2 (1996), pp. 18–35. For the military importance of the north-western horse trade and British failure to tap it see Jos Gommans, *The Rise of the Indo-Afghan Empire, c. 1710–80*, Leiden: E.J. Brill, 1995.

7. For the idea that the vast distances resulted in stretching the Asian war machines to the maximum, which in turn made the employment of cavalry necessary, see Jeremy Black, 'War and the World, 1450–2000', *JMH*, vol. 63, no. 3 (1999), p. 677.

8. I am not suggesting that Military Synthesis is an example of European exceptionalism. Ranjit Singh effectively integrated the field artillery of the European armies with the light irregular cavalry of the Sikhs. However, he failed to build a stable political infrastructure. This proved to be the Achilles heel of the *Khalsa* military machine during the Anglo-Sikh Wars. Colonel Mouton, 'The First Anglo-Sikh War (1845–6)', *Panjab Past and Present*, vol. 15 (1981), pp. 116–27; Donald Featherstone, *At Them with the Bayonet: The First Sikh War*, London: Jarrolds, 1968, pp. 3, 6–14, 25, 32–5, 55–9, 72, 80, 165–6; Kaushik Roy, 'Military Synthesis in South Asian Armies, Warfare, and Indian Society, c. 1740–1849', *JMH*, vol. 69 (2005), pp. 651–90.

9. C.A. Bayly, 'The British Military-Fiscal State and the Indigenous Resistance: India 1750–1820', in idem., *Origins of Nationalism in South Asia: Patriotism and Ethical Government in the Making of Modern India*, Delhi: Oxford University Press, 1998, pp. 238–75.

10. The linkage between the attempted expansion of the administrative tentacles of the indigenous states in south India for maintaining the firepower-heavy armies is pointed out by Sanjay Subrahmanyam in

'Warfare and State Finance in Woodeyar Mysore, 1724–25: A Missionary Perspective', *IESHR*, vol. 26, no. 2 (1989), pp. 203–33.

11. K.K. Trivedi, 'The Share of Mansabdars in State Revenue Resources: A Study of the Maintenance of Animals', *IESHR*, vol. 24, no. 4 (1987), pp. 411–22; John Brewer, *The Sinews of Power: War, Money and the English State, 1688–1783*, London: Unwin Hyman, 1989, pp. XI, 29–42, 250–1.

12. C.A. Bayly, 'Knowing the Country: Empire and Information in India', *MAS*, vol. 27, no. 1 (1993), pp. 3–43.

13. I am influenced by Maurice Pearton's *The Knowledgeable State: Diplomacy, War and Technology since 1830*, London: Burnett Books, 1982. However, Pearton develops his concept of 'Knowledgeable State' in the context of industrializing high technology Western societies.

14. Lord Bacon, 'On the Vicissitudes of Things', Essays LVIII, quoted in T. Miller, *Outline of Military Geography*, Cambridge: Cambridge University Press, 1900, p. 324.

15. Michael P. Speidel, *Riding for Caesar: The Roman Emperors' Horse Guard*, London: Batsford, 1994, pp. 77–94.

16. Speros Vyronis Jr., 'Byzantine and Turkish Societies and Their Sources of Manpower', in V.J. Parry and M.E. Yapp, eds., *War, Technology and Society in the Middle East*, London: Oxford University Press, 1975, pp. 127, 151; Hanson, *Carnage and Culture*, p. 445.

17. David Ayalon, 'The Mamluks of the Seljuks: Islam's Military Might at the Crossroads', *JRAS*, vol. 6, no. 3 (1996), pp. 305–33.

18. S. Inayat Ali Zaidi, 'Ordinary Kachawaha Troopers Serving the Mughal Empire: Composition and Structure of the Contingents of the Kachawaha Nobles', *SIH*, vol. 2, no. 1 (1980), pp. 59–80.

19. David Omissi, 'Britain, the Assyrians and the Iraq Levies, 1919-32', *JICH*, vol. 17, no. 3 (1989), pp. 301–22; Anthony A.H.M. Kirk-Greene, ' "Damnosa Hereditas": Ethnic Ranking and the Martial Races Imperative in Africa', *Ethnic and Racial Studies*, vol. 3, no. 4 (1980), pp. 393–414.

20. Saxena, *The Army of the Rajputs*, pp. 8, 12, 54–5.

21. See Table 2.2, p. 105.

22. Herwig, *The First World War*, pp. 13, 38, note 24.

23. Bruce Vandervort, *Wars of Imperial Conquest in Africa: 1830-1914*, Bloomington/Indianapolis: Indiana University Press, 1998, p. 216.

24. Norman Stone, 'Army and Society in the Habsburg Monarchy, 1900–14', *Past and Present*, no. 33 (1966), pp. 95–111.

APPENDIX 1

Class Company Infantry Regiment

GUIDES CORPS INFANTRY REGIMENT

Company	Social Composition	Regions from which Recruited
No. 1	Dogras	Kangra and Jammu
No. 2	Pathans	Trans-Indus
No. 3	Punjabi Muslims	West Punjab
No. 4	Afridis	Trans-Indus
No. 5	Gurkhas	Central Nepal
No. 6	Sikhs	Central Punjab
No. 7	Sikhs	Central Punjab
No. 8	Sikhs	Central Punjab

Total Strength = 600 sepoys, 16 buglers and 96 commissioned and non-commissioned officers.

Source: Memo of the composition of the Corps of Guides, Mardan, 17 January 1862, Lieutenant-Colonel H.B. Lumsden commanding Guides, Correspondence and Memoranda on the Organization of the Indian Army, Records of Chief Commands, 1865–76, Notes and Minutes by Napier of Magdala, MSS.EUR.F.114, 5(2), OIOC.

Class Company Cavalry Regiment

1st HYDERABAD CONTINGENT LANCERS

Squadron	Social Composition	Regions from which Recruited
1st Squadron	Sikhs	Central Punjab
2nd Squadron	Hindustani Muslims	Rohilkhand
3rd Squadron	Deccani Muslims	Hyderabad
4th Squadron	Jats	North-West Province

Total Strength = 510 sowars, 8 trumpeters and 99 commissioned and non-commissioned officers.

Source: No. 236, ADG's office, Simla, 27 March 1903, General Orders by the Commander-in-Chief in India, NAI.

Rank Structure of the Indian Officer Cadre

Cavalry	Infantry	British Equivalents	Remarks
Commissioned Officers			
Resaldar-Major	Subedar-Major		
Resaldar	Subedar		
Resaidar			
Wordie-Major			An Indian Adjutant
Jemadar	Jemadar		
Non-Commissioned Officers			
Dufadar-Major	Havildar-Major	Sergeant-Major	
Dufadar	Havildar	Sergeant	
Lance-Dufadar	Naik	Corporal	
Pay-Dufadar	Lance Naik	Lance-Corporal	
Sowar	Sepoy	Trooper or Private	

Note: Each regular cavalry regiment possessed 4 Resaldars, 4 Resaidars, 8 Jemadars, 48 Dufadars and 280 Sowars. In each regular infantry regiment, there were 8 Subedars, 8 Jemadars, 40 Havildars, 40 Naiks and more than 600 Sepoys. The highest ranking Indian commissioned officer was ranked below the British Second-Lieutenant. The commissioned Indian officers are known as Viceroy's Commissioned Officers.

Source: Birdwood, *Khaki and Gown*, p. 47; *Manual for Bengal and Punjab Cavalry*, p. 30; Progs. no. 112, para 9, May 1876, L/MIL/7/14966; Memo of the composition of the Corps of Guides, Mardan, 17 January 1862, Lieutenant-Colonel H.B. Lumsden, commanding Guides Corps, Correspondence and Memoranda on the Organization of the Indian Army, Records of Chief Commands, 1865–276, Notes and Minutes by Napier of Magdala, MSS.EUR.F.114, 5(2), OIOC.

Glossary

Afridi	An Indus tribe.
Amir	Rulers/Lord of the Muslim Community
Askaris	African equivalent of sepoys.
Atta	Flour.
Badshah	Central Asian Muslim warlords who became rulers in medieval India.
Bania	Hindu businessman.
Banjaras	Grain merchants who used to supply the indigenous armies during campaigns.
Bargir	Irregular sowar mounted by the *silladar*.
Batta	Extra allowance provided to the soldiers during foreign service, or for service in unhealthy regions, and also in regions with high prices within the subcontinent.
Bazar	Market.
Bheels	Tribals who inhabited the jungle clad mountains of central India and Rajputana. They were probably rulers of Rajputana in the pre-Aryan era.
Bhungies	Lowest caste in north India and their hereditary calling was that of sweepers.
Chamar	Low caste.
Chihran	Descriptive roll of the soldiers maintained by the Mughal military bureaucracy.
Chunda fund	The regimental fund in which every sowar of the irregular regiments contributed. This fund aided the sowars in buying a new horse when their mounts died or were wounded in action.
Cummerband	A thin strip of cloth worn around the waist. A type of Indian belt.
Deccanis	Inhabitants of Deccan, i.e. the region south of the river Narmada.
Dharma	Code of conduct as emphasized in Hinduism.
Dharnas	Sitting around the employers by the employees for redressal of grievances. A sort of trade union strike.
Dhoti	Traditional Indian male dress for covering the lower portion of the body.

Doms	A low caste whose hereditary occupation was burning dead bodies.
Durbar	Court of an Indian ruler.
Dyedovschina	Ill treatment of the recruits and the newly enlisted soldiers by the veterans.
Ghee	Clarified butter.
Guru Granth Sahib	Holy book of the Sikhs.
Gwalahs	Middle-caste Hindus engaged in the occupation of selling milk.
Haramzada	A Hindustani abuse meaning bastard.
Hindustan	North India which included North-west Province, Awadh and Bihar.
Hindustanis	Hindu and Muslim inhabitants of Hindustan.
Invalid *Thanahs*	The Sepoys invalided out of the Bengal Army during the first half of the nineteenth century were granted land and settled in colonies in the countryside.
Invalid *Thanahs*	The Sepoys invaded out of the Bengal Army during the post half of the nineteenth century were granted land and settled in colonies in the countryside.
Jagir	Assignment of land revenue by the ruler to a chieftain for raising and maintaining soldiers.
Jagirdar	Holder of *jagir.*
Janeo	Sacred thread which a Brahmin wore as a symbol of ritual supremacy.
Jarwahs	Tribes who resided in the hilly region of Assam. They joined the local corps (like the Assam Rifles) deployed in the eastern frontier of India.
Jawans	Sepoys/Soldiers
Jihad	Holy War conducted by the Muslim against the non-Muslims.
Kabbadi	An Indian form of rugby game.
Kalapani	Literal meaning is 'black water'. Overseas journey which involved crossing an ocean was considered as polluting among the high-caste Hindus. High castes who undertook such journeys lost their caste.
Khalsa	Sikh theocracy.
Khatris	Business community of Punjab.
Khuda	Another word for Allah.
Konkanis	Inhabitants of Konkan or western Maharashtra in the Bombay Presidency.
Kotwal	Mughal term for a police officer.
Kshatra-dharma	Ethics of a Rajput soldier.
Kshatriyas	Warrior caste of traditional India.

Kuccha	Building constructed with mud.
Kukri	Knife used by the tribes of Nepal.
Kunjurs	A low caste of north India.
Lama	Buddhist priest.
Lascar	Coolie employed in the artillery branch.
Madhesias	Men from the plains.
Madrassis	Inhabitants of the Madras Presidency or the south Indians. This category included Tamils, Telugus, Deccani Muslims, etc.
Mahajan	Hindu businessman.
Maharana	Lord of many *Ranas*.
Mansabdar	Holder of a *mansab* or a rank in the *mansabdari* system.
Mansabdari organization	The Mughal military system.
Maugs	Inhabitants of India-Burma border who got the jobs of hangmen in India.
Maulvi	Muslim holy man.
Mazbi	Low-caste Sikhs.
Meenas	A low caste of Rajputana.
Mehters	Sweepers.
Mosulles	Hereditary Muslim sweepers.
Muharram	A day of mourning for the Muslims.
Naukri	Job in the army.
Nawab	Muslim ruler of a province.
Pahariyas	Inhabitants of the hills.
Panchayats	Traditional system of village administration. Five elders known as *panches* were elected by the village assembly.
Pandies	Brahmins from Awadh.
Parganah	Administrative subdivision of a province.
Pasees	Low-caste of north India. Their hereditary occupation was mining.
Peshwa	Hereditary Prime Minister of the Maratha Confederacy.
Pugri	Headdress of the north and north-west Indians. It consisted of a cloth worn around the head. The Indian equivalent of hat.
Puja	Certain set of rituals for worshipping Hindu gods and goddesses.
Pukhtunwali	The Pathans' way of life or code of conduct which involved paying the blood price for murder.
Punjabis	Inhabitants of undivided British Punjab. The communities of this province were Sikhs in central

region, Jats in the eastern region and Muslims in the Salt ranges of western region.

Purab   Homeland of the *Purbiyas,* i.e. eastern part of north India which included Bihar and Awadh.

Purbiyas   Brahmins and Rajputs from Bihar and Awadh.

Raj   British Indian Empire.

Ramzan   Muslim religious festival.

Rana   Rajput ruler. The chieftains of Nepal and Rajputana called themselves *Ranas.* Some Rajput landholders of north India also took the title of *Ranas.*

Risalahs   Troops in the irregular cavalry.

Santhals   Tribes of Dravidian stock who inhabited eastern Bihar.

Sanyasi   A Hindu holy man.

Sardar   Chieftain.

Sarkar   Government.

Scythians   Central Asian tribe of mounted archers who invaded the subcontinent during the early medieval age. The Colonial anthropologists of the Raj believed that the Rajputs had Scythian blood.

Sepoys   Infantry from the Persian word *sipahi* meaning Soldier.

Shudras   The lowest group in the Hindu hierarchy of castes.

Silladar   Sowar of the irregular cavalry who besides owning their own horse also provides horses to the *bargirs.*

Sowar   Trooper.

Taluk   Unit of village administration under the *Talukdar.* This pre-British administrative format was absorbed by the British administration.

Tamils   Inhabitants of the Madras Presidency especially Tamil Nadu.

Tehsil   Pre-colonial unit of village administration under a *Tehsildar.* The British accommodated such units within their administrative fabric.

Telugus   Inhabitants of Andhra Pradesh within the Madras Presidency.

Thakur   High-caste landed elements of north India.

Thanah   Colony, also means a police station.

Varna system   Caste hierarchy of Hinduism. The Brahmins belonged to the highest *varna.* Then came the *Kshatriyas* or warrior class. *Vaisyas* or the business community constituted the third *varna.* Finally, *Shudras* belonged to the lowest *varna.*

Bibliography

PRIMARY SOURCES

Archival Sources

Oriental and India Office Collection, British Library, London

Private Papers

Colonel William Merewether Collection, MSS.EUR.D.625/3, 4,5.
John Lawrence Collection, MSS.EUR.F.90/59.
George White Collection, MSS.EUR.F.108/18, 24.
Notes and Minutes by Lord Napier of Magdala, MSS.EUR.F.114, 1 © 5 (2) (3) (4).
Military Department Files
L/MIL/7/14966
L/MIL/7/17007-8, 17010
L/MIL/17/2/468-69

West Bengal State Archives, Kolkata

Proceedings of the Lieutenant Governor of Bengal, Judicial Department
Judicial Proceedings
National Library, Kolkata
Sanitary Report, Manoeuvers, Mandalay Brigade 1911, GP62375(591)B927

National Archives of India, New Delhi.

Military Department

Adjutant General's Ciculars, 1861-5.
Carter (Adjutant), Lieutenant, Record book of 28th Bombay Infantry Regiment, 1846–1913.
Digest of services of the 14th Regiment of the Madras Infantry, 1775–1913.
Digest of services of the 44th Merwara Infantry, 1818–1916.
Digest of services of the 4th Battalion 9th Jat Regiment.
Digest of services of the 3rd Brahmin, 1861-1914.
Digest of services of the 3rd Regiment Hyderabad Contingent Cavalry.
General Orders by the Commander-in-Chief of India.
Historical records of the 7th Regiment Bombay Infantry.
Historical records of the 8th Bombay Infantry Regiment, 1768–1893.

Historical records of the 9th Bombay Regiment.
Military Department Proceedings.
Military Despatches of the Secretary of State to the Governor-General in Council.
Military Letters from the Resident at Nepal regarding the Gurkha auxiliary expedition at Lucknow, 1857–9.
Military miscellaneous minutes by Major General H.W. Norman, 1863–76.
Proceedings of the Government of India, Burma, 1885–6.
Proceedings of the Government of India, Malakand, 1897–8.

Private Papers, M/F

George Hamilton Papers.
Lord Kitchener Papers.
Bentinck Correspondence.
Copy of Recent Correspondence on the subject of the organization of the Indian Army.

PUBLISHED SOURCES

Oriental and India Office Collection, British Library

L/MIL/17/5/1615
Roberts, General Frederick, *Correspondence with England while Commander-in-Chief in Madras: 1881–85,* Simla: Govt. Central Printing Office, 1890.
———, *Correspondence with India while Commander-in-Chief in Madras: 1881–85,* Simla: Govt. Central Printing Office, 1890.
———, *Correspondence with England while Commander-in-Chief in India: 1888–89,* Calcutta: Superintendent of Govt. Printing, 1890.
———, *Correspondence with the Viceroy of India (The Marquis of Dufferin and Ava): 1885–88,* Calcutta: Superintendent of Govt. Printing, 1890.
———, *Correspondence with the Viceroy of India (The Marquis of Lansdowne): 26 Nov. 1888–2 April 93,* Calcutta: Superintendent of Govt. Printing, 1893.
———, *Short Report on Important Questions Dealt with During the Tenure of Commander of the Army in India: 1885–93,* Simla: Govt. Central Printing Office, 1893, L/MIL/17/5/1613.

NATIONAL LIBRARY, KOLKATA, CENTRAL SECRETARIAT LIBRARY, NATIONAL ARCHIVES LIBRARY AND UNITED SERVICE INSTITUTION LIBRARY, DELHI

Reports

Colebrook, James, *Supplement to the Collection of Regulations,* Calcutta, 1807.

Papers Connected with the Reorganization of the Army in India Supplementary to the Report of the Army Commission, London: HMSO, 1859, Cd, 2541.

Proceedings of the Army in India Committee 1912, vol. 1-A, *Minority Report,* vols. 2–3, Simla: Central Government Press, 1913.

Report of the Commissioners Appointed to Inquire into the Organization of the Indian Army, London: HMSO, 1859, Cd, 2515.

Report of Major General H. Hancock on the Organization of the Indian Army, London: HMSO, 1859, Cd, 2516.

Report of the Sanitary Commission for Bombay 1864, Bombay: Education Society's Press, Byculla, 1865.

Report of the Special Commission Appointed by the Governor General in Council to Inquire into the Organization and Expenditure of the Army in India, Simla: Government Central Printing Office, 1879.

Royal Commission on Agriculture in India: Evidence Taken in Bihar and Orissa, vol. 13, Calcutta, 1928.

Parliamentary Papers

Return East India and native troops, Commons 500 (1867).

ARTICLES AND BOOKS

Anglesey, The Marquess of, ed., *Sergeant Pearman's Memoirs,* London: Jonathan Cape, 1968.

Apthorpe, Captain A., 'The Kachins and Others: A New Recruiting Area', *JUSII,* vol. XLI, no. 186 (1912).

Army Regulations, India: Regulations and Orders for the Army, vol. 2, Calcutta: Superintendent of Govt. Printing, 1913.

Bandopadhyay, Durgadas, *Amar Jivancharit* (Bengali), 1924, reprint, Calcutta: Ananya Prakashan, 1985.

Barrow, Lieutenant E.G., 'Tirah and the Afridi Question', *JUSII,* no. 49 (1881).

Barrow, Major E.G., 'Third Essay', *JUSII,* vol. 20, no. 86 (1891).

Basevi, Captain W.H.F., 'A Proposal to Enlist the Panthyas', *JUSII,* vol. 31, no. 147 (1902).

Beatson, Brigadier-General Stuart, *A History of the Imperial Service Troops of Native States,* Calcutta: Superintendent of Govt. Printing, 1903.

Bellew, H.W., *The Races of Afghanistan: Being a Brief Account of the Principal Nations Inhabiting that Country,* 1880, reprint, New Delhi: Asian Educational Services, 2004.

———, 'A New Afghan Question', *JUSII,* no. 47 (1881).

Betham, Major R.M., *Handbook for the Indian Army: Marathas and Dekhani Musulmans,* Calcutta: Superintendent of Govt. Printing, 1908.

Bingley, Major A.H., *Class Handbook for the Indian Army: Dogras*, Simla: Govt. Central Printing Office, 1899.

———, *Handbook for the Indian Army: Sikhs*, 1899, reprint, Chandigarh: Department of Languages, 1970.

———, *History, Caste and Culture of the Jats and Gujars*, 1899, reprint, New Delhi: ESS Publications, 1978.

———, *Handbook on Rajputs*, 1899, reprint, New Delhi: Asian Educational Services, 1986.

———, *Caste Handbook for the Indian Army: Jats, Gujars and Ahirs*, Calcutta: Superintendent of Govt. Printing, 1904.

Bingley, Captain A.H. and Nicholls, A., *Caste Handbook for the Indian Army: Brahmins*, Simla: Govt. Central Printing Office, 1897.

Birdwood, Field-Marshal, *Khaki and Gown: An Autobiography*, London: Ward, Lock & Co., Ltd., 1941.

Bonarjee, P.D., *A Handbook of the Fighting Races of India*, Calcutta: Thacker Spink & Co., 1899.

Candler, Edmund, *The Sepoy*, London: John Murray, 1919.

Cardew, Lieutenant F.G., 'Our Recruiting Grounds of the Future for the Indian Army', *JUSII*, vol. 20, no. 86 (1891).

———, *A Sketch of the Services of the Bengal Native Army to the Year 1895*, 1903, reprint, New Delhi: Today and Tomorrow's Printers and Publishers, 1971.

Casserly, Major G., *Life in an Indian Outpost*, London, n.d.

Chaudhuri, Nirad C., 'The Martial Races of India', *Modern Review*, vol. XLVIII, nos. 1&3 (1930), vol. XLIX, nos. 1-2 (1931).

———, 'India and Imperial Defence', *Modern Review*, vol. XLIX, no. 4 (1931).

Chesney, General George, *Indian Polity: A View of the System of Administration in India*, 1894, reprint, New Delhi: Metropolitan Books, 1976.

Compton, Herbert, *A Particular Account of the European Military Adventurers of Hindustan from 1784 to 1803*, 1892, reprint, Karachi: Oxford University Press, 1976.

Dodwell, H.H., *Sepoy Recruitment in the Old Madras Army*, Calcutta: Superintendent of Govt. Printing, 1922.

Falcon, Captain R.W., *Handbook on Sikhs for the Use of Regimental Officers*, Allahabad: Pioneer Press, 1896.

Garrett, H.L.O., ed., C. Grey, *European Adventurers of Northern India, 1785–1849*, 1929, reprint, Madras: Asian Educational Services, 1993.

Goodenough, Lieutenant-General W.H. and Dalton, Lieutenant-Colonel J.C., *The Army Book of the British Empire: A Record of the Development and Present Composition of the Military Forces and Their Duties during Peace and War*, London: HMSO, 1893.

Gorham, Major, *A Short Course of Military Law as Applicable to Persons Subject to the Mutiny Act to Which is Added Military Law as Applicable to Persons Subject to the Indian Articles of War*, Calcutta: Thacker & Spink, 1877.

Hamilton, Colonel W.G., 'Ochterlony's Campaign in the Simla Hills', *JUSII*, no. 187 (1912).

————, 'Ochterlony's Campaign in the Simla Hills—Some Further Notes on', *JUSII*, vol. XLI, no. 189 (1912).

History of the 1st Punjab Cavalry, Lahore: Civil Military Gazette Press, 1887.

Hunter, W.W., *The Indian Musalmans*, 1871, reprint, New Delhi: Indological Book House, 1969.

Keene, H.G., *Hindustan under Free Lances: 1770–1820, Sketches of Military Adventure in Hindustan during the Period Immediately Preceding British Occupation*, London: 1907.

King-Harman, Lieutenant Colonel M.J., 'Second Essay', *JUSII*, vol. 20, no. 86 (1891).

Lunt, James, ed., *From Sepoy to Subedar: Being the Life and Adventures of Sita Ram, a Native Officer of the Bengal Army*, 1873, tr. by Colonel Norgate, 1970, reprint, London: Macmillan, 1988.

Macmohan, Captain G.F.W., *A Guide to the Correct Framing of Charges under the Indian Articles of War Suitable to All Occasions*, Bombay: Bombay Educational Society Press, 1887.

MacMunn, Major G.F., *Vignettes from Indian War*, 1901, reprint, New Delhi: Low Price Publications, 1993.

————, *The Armies of India*, 1911, reprint, New Delhi: Heritage Publishers, 1991.

————, 'The Martial Races of India', *Army Review*, vol. 1, no. 2 (1911), reprinted in *Panjab Past and Present*, vol. 4, no. 1 (1970).

Malcolm, Lieutenant Colonel, *Sketch of the Sikhs*, 1812, reprint, New Delhi: Asian Educational Services, 1986.

Malcolm, Major General John, *A Memoir of Central India including Malwa and Adjoining Provinces with the History and Copious Illustration of the Country*, vol. 1, 1880, reprint, New Delhi: Sagar Publications, 1970.

Manual for Bengal and Punjab Cavalry, 1893, reprint, Delhi: Mayur Publications, 1985.

McGregor, W.L., *The History of the Sikhs*, vols. 1 & 2, 1846, reprint, Allahabad: R.S. Publishing House, 1979.

Molesworth, Captain E.K., 'Indian Army Castes: Madrassis', *JUSII*, vol. XLII, no. 190 (1913).

Mouton, Colonel, 'The First Anglo-Sikh War (1845–6)', *Panjab Past and Present*, vol. 15 (1981).

Philips, C.H., ed., *The Correspondence of Lord William Cavendish Bentinck, Governor General of India: 1832–5*, vol. 2, Oxford: Oxford University Press, 1977.

Pryor, Major P. Holland, *Class Handbook on the Indian Army: Mappillas or Moplahs*, Calcutta: Superintendent of Govt. Printing, 1904.

Rainey, Lieutenant R.M., 'The Madras Army', *JUSII*, vol. 20, no. 85 (1891).

Roberts, Field Marshal Frederick, *Forty-one Years in India: From Subaltern to Commander-in-Chief*, 1897, reprint, London: Richard Bentley & Son, 1898.

Roberts, Frederick, *Letters Written during the Indian Mutiny*, 1923, reprint, New Delhi: Lal Publishers, 1979.

Robson, Brian, ed., *Roberts in India: The Military Papers of Field-Marshal Lord Roberts, 1876–93*, Stroud, Gloucestershire: Alan Sutton, 1993.

Shakespear, Colonel L.W., *History of the 2nd King Edward's Own Goorkha Rifles (The Sirmoor Rifles)*, vol. 1, Aldershot: Gale and Polden, 1912.

———, 'The War with Nepal: Operations in Sirmoor', *JUSII*, vol. XLII, no. 193 (1913).

———, *History of the Assam Rifles*, 1929, reprint, Gauhati: United Publishers, 1980.

Showers, Lieutenant H.L., 'The Meywar Bhil Corps', *JUSII*, vol. 20, no. 85 (1891).

Simcox, A.H.M., *Memoir of Khandesh Bhil Corps, 1825–91*, Calcutta: Thacker & Spink, 1912.

Sinclair, Lieutenant-Colonel H.M., ' The First Sikh War: 1845–6', *JUSII*, vol. 28, no. 134 (1899).

Smith, Lewis Ferdinand, *A Sketch of the Rise, Progress and Termination of the Regular Corps Formed and Commanded by the Europeans in the Service of the Native Princes of India with Details of the Principal Events and Actions of the late Maratha War*, Calcutta: J. Greenway Harkaru Press, 1805.

Steinbach, Henry, *The Country of the Sikhs*, 1845, reprint, New Delhi: KLM Book House, 1977.

Stockley, Captain, J.P., 'Local Corps in India and Their Military Value', *JUSII*, vol. XLII, no. 191 (1913).

Sundaram, Lanka, *India's Armies and Their Costs: A Century of Unequal Imposts for an Army of Occupation and a Mercenary Army*, Bombay: Avanti Prakashan, 1946.

The Armies of the Native States of India, reprinted from *The Times*, London, 1884.

The Army in India and Its Evolution, 1924, reprint, New Delhi: Anmol Publications, 1985.

Tyrrell, Lieutenant-Colonel F.W., 'The Races of the Madras Army', *JUSII*, no. 48 (1881).

Vansittart, Captain Eden, *The Gurkhas*, 1890, reprint, New Delhi: Ariana, 1980.

———, *Notes on Nepal*, 1896, reprint, New Delhi: Asian Educational Services, 1992.

————, *Handbook for the Indian Army: The Gurkhas*, 1906, reprint, New Delhi: Asian Educational Services, 1992.

Wikeley, J.M., *Punjabi Musalmans*, 1915, reprint, New Delhi: Manohar, 1991.

Wilson, Lieutenant-Colonel W.J., *Historical Records of the Fourth Prince of Wales' Own Regiment Madras Light Cavalry*, Madras: Govt. Press, 1877.

————, *History of the Madras Army*, vols. 1 & 3, Madras: Govt. Press, 1882, 1883.

SECONDARY SOURCES

ARTICLES AND BOOKS

Aberg, Alf, 'The Swedish Army from Lutzen to Narva', in Michael Roberts, ed., *Sweden's Age of Greatness 1632–1718*, London: Macmillan, 1973.

Alavi, Seema, *The Sepoys and the Company: Tradition and Transition in Northern India, 1770–1830*, Delhi: Oxford University Press, 1995.

Allen, Charles, *Soldier Sahibs: The Men who Made the Northwest Frontier*, London: John Murray, 2000.

Anderson, Benedict, *Imagined Communities: Reflections on the Origin and Spread of Nationalism*, 1983, reprint, London, New York: Verso, 1987.

Anderson, J.K., *Xenophon*, London: Duckworth, 1974.

Anderson, Warwick, 'Disease, Race and Empire', *Bull. Hist. Med.*, vol. 70, no. 1 (1996).

————, 'Immunities of Empire: Race, Disease, and the New Tropical Medicine, 1900–20', *Bull. Hist. Med.*, vol. 70, no. 1 (1996).

Andreski, Stanislav, *Military Organization and Society*, 1954, reprint, Berkeley/California: University of California Press, 1968.

Anglesey, The Marquess of, *A History of the British Cavalry: 1872–98*, vol. 3, London: Leo Cooper, 1982.

Archer, Christon, I., 'Combating the Invisible Enemy: Health and Hospital Care in the Army of New Spain, 1760–1810', in Douglas M. Peers, ed., *Warfare and Empires: Contact and Conflict between European and Non-European Military and Maritime Forces and Cultures*, Aldershot, Hampshire: Variorum, 1997.

Arnold, David, *Colonizing the Body: State Medicine and Epidemic Disease in Nineteenth-century India*, Delhi: Oxford University Press, 1993.

————, 'The Colonial Prison: Power, Knowledge and Penology in Nineteenth-century India', in idem., and David Hardiman, eds., *Subaltern Studies: Essays in Honour of Ranajit Guha*, vol. 8, 1994, reprint, Delhi: Oxford University Press, 1996.

Ayalon, David, 'The Mamluks of the Seljuks: Islam's Military Might at the Crossroads', *JRAS*, vol. 6, no. 3 (1996).

Bajwa, Fauja Singh, *Military System of the Sikhs during the Period 1799–1849*, Delhi: Motilal Banarssidas, 1964.

Banskota, Purushottam, *The Gurkha Connection: A History of the Gurkha Recruitment in the British Indian Army*, New Delhi: Nirala, 1994.

Barat, Amiya, *The Bengal Native Infantry: Its Organization and Discipline, 1796–1852*, Calcutta: Firma KLM, 1962.

Barnett, Correlli, *Britain and Her Army: A Military, Political and Social Survey*, London: Penguin, 1970.

Barr, Ronald J., 'High Command in the United States: The Emergence of a Modern System, 1898–1920', in G.D. Sheffield, ed., *Leadership and Command: The Anglo-American Military Experience Since 1861*, London: Brassey's, 1997.

Bartov, Omer, 'Indoctrination and Motivation in the *Wehrmacht*: The Importance of the Unquantifiable', *JSS*, vol. 9, no. 1 (1986).

———, 'Daily Life and Motivation in War: The *Wehrmacht* in the Soviet Union', *JSS*, vol. 12, no. 2 (1989).

Barua, Pradeep, 'Military Developments in India, 1750–1850', *JMH*, vol. 58, no. 4 (1994).

———, 'Inventing Race: The British and India's Martial Races', *Historian*, vol. 58, no. 1 (1995).

———, 'Strategies and Doctrines of Imperial Defence: Britain and India', *JICH*, vol. 25, no. 3 (1997).

Bates, Crispin, 'Race, Caste and Tribe in Central India: The Early Origins of Indian Anthropometry', in Peter Robb, ed., *The Concept of Race in South Asia,* Delhi: Oxford University Press, 1995.

Bayly, C.A., ed., Eric Stokes, *The Peasant Armed: The Indian Revolt of 1857,* Oxford: Oxford University Press, 1986.

———, 'Knowing the Country: Empire and Information in India', *MAS*, vol. 27, no. 1 (1993).

———, 'The British Military-Fiscal State and the Indigenous Resistance: India 1750–1820', in idem., *Origins of Nationalism in South Asia: Patriotism and Ethical Government in the Making of Modern India,* Delhi: Oxford University Press, 1998.

Bayly, Susan, 'Caste and "Race" in the Colonial Ethnography of India', in Peter Robb, ed., *The Concept of Race in South Asia,* Delhi: Oxford University Press, 1995.

Beckett, Ian F.W., 'Command in the Late Victorian Army', in G.D. Sheffield, ed., *Leadership and Command: The Anglo-American Military Experience Since 1861*, London: Brassey's, 1997.

Black, Jeremy, *A Military Revolution? Military Change and European Society, 1500–1800*, Basingstoke/London: Macmillan, 1991.

———, 'A Military Revolution? A 1660–1792 Perspective', in Clifford J. Rogers, ed., *The Military Revolution Debate: Readings on the Military Transformation of Early Modern Europe,* Colorado/Boulder: Westview Press, 1995.

——, *Cambridge Illustrated Atlas of Warfare: Renaissance to Revolution, 1492–1792*, Cambridge: Cambridge University Press, 1996.

——, 'War and the World: 1450–2000', *JMH*, vol. 63, no. 3 (1999).

Blumenson, Martin, 'The Development of Modern Military', *Armed Forces and Society*, vol. 6, no. 4 (1980).

Bohigas, Nuria Sales De, 'Some Opinions on Exemption from Military Service in Nineteenth-century Europe', *CSSH*, vol. 10 (1967–8).

Bopegamage, A., 'Caste, Class and the Indian Military: A Study of the Social Origins of Indian Army Personnel', in Jacques Van Doorn, ed., *Military Profession and Military Regimes: Commitments and Conflicts*, The Hague/ Paris: Mouton, 1969.

Bossenbroeck, Martin, 'The Living Tools of Empire: Recruitment of European Soldiers for the Dutch Colonial Army, 1814–1909', *JICH*, vol. 23, no. 1 (1995).

Brewer, John, *The Sinews of Power: War, Money and the English State, 1688–1783*, London: Unwin Hyman, 1989.

Bruce, George, *The Burma Wars: 1824–86*, London: Hart-Davis, MacGibbon, 1973.

Bryant, G.J., 'Officers of the East India Company's Army in the Days of Clive and Hastings', *JICH*, vol. 6, no. 2 (1978).

——, 'Pacification in the Early British Raj, 1755–85', *JICH*, vol. 14, no. 1 (1985).

——, 'The Cavalry Problem in the Early British Indian Army, 1750–85', *War in History*, vol. 2, no. 1 (1995).

——, 'The Military Imperative in Early British Expansion in India, 1750–85', *Indo-British Review*, vol. 21, no. 2 (1996).

Burroughs, Peter, 'Tackling Army Desertion in British North America', *Canadian Historical Review*, vol. LXI (1980).

——, 'Crime and Punishment in the British Army, 1815–70', *EHR*, vol. 100 (1985).

——, 'An Unreformed Army? 1815–68', in David Chandler and Ian Beckett, ed., *The Oxford Illustrated History of the British Army*, Oxford: Oxford University Press, 1994.

Butalia, R.C., *The Evolution of the Artillery in India: From the Battle of Plassey to the Revolt of 1857*, New Delhi: Allied, 1998.

Callahan, Raymond, *The East India Company and Army Reform: 1783–98*, Cambridge/Massachusetts: Harvard University Press, 1972.

Caplan, Lionel, ' "Bravest of the Brave": Representations of "The Gurkha" in British Military Writings', *MAS*, vol. 25, no. 3 (1991).

——, *Warrior Gentlemen: 'Gurkhas' in the Western Imagination*, Providence/Oxford: Berghahn Books, 1995.

——, 'Martial Gurkhas: The Persistence of a British Military Discourse on "Race"', in Peter Robb, ed., *The Concept of Race in South Asia*, Delhi: Oxford University Press, 1995.

Carr, E.H., *What is History?*, 1961, reprint, Harmondsworth: Penguin, 1986.

Chene, Mary Des, 'Soldiers, Sovereignty and Silences: Gurkhas as Diplomatic Currency', *South Asia Bulletin*, vol. 13, nos. 1–2 (1993).

———, 'Military Ethnology in British India', *South Asia Research*, vol. 19, no. 2 (1999).

Childs, John, 'The Restoration Army, 1660–1702', in David Chandler and Ian Beckett, eds., *The Oxford Illustrated History of the British Army*, Oxford: Oxford University Press, 1994.

Chodof, Elliot P., 'Ideology and Primary Groups', *Armed Forces and Society*, vol. 9, no. 4 (1983).

Christensen, R.O., 'Tribesmen, Government and Political Economy on the Northwest Frontier', in Clive Dewey, ed., *Arrested Development in India: The Historical Dimension*, New Delhi: Manohar, 1988.

Cohen, Stephen P., 'The Untouchable Soldier: Caste, Politics and the Indian Army', *JAS*, vol. 28, no. 3 (1969).

———, *The Indian Army: Its Contribution to the Development of a Nation*, 1971, reprint, Delhi: Oxford University Press, 1991.

Cohn, Bernard S., 'Cloth, Clothes, and Colonialism: India in the Nineteenth Century', in idem., *Colonialism and Its Forms of Knowledge: The British in India*, Delhi: Oxford University Press, 1997.

Constable, Philip, 'The Marginalization of a Dalit Martial Race in Late Nineteenth and Early Twentieth Century Western India', *JAS*, vol. 60, no. 2 (2001).

Cook, Hugh, *The Sikh Wars: The British Army in Punjab, 1845–49*, New Delhi: Thomson Press, 1975.

Cooper, Randolf G.S., 'Wellington and the Marathas in 1803', *International History Review*, vol. 11 (1989).

———, *The Anglo-Maratha Campaigns and the Contest for India: The Struggle for Control of the South Asian Military Economy*, New Delhi: Foundation Books in association with Cambridge University Press, 2005.

Corrigan, Gordon, *Sepoys in the Trenches: The Indian Corps on the Western Front, 1914–15*, Staplehurst: Spellmount, 1999.

Creveld, Martin van, *Command in War*, Cambridge/Massachusetts: Harvard University Press, 1985.

———, 'Technology and War to 1945', in Charles Townshend, ed., *The Oxford Illustrated History of Modern War*, Oxford/New York: Oxford University Press, 1997.

Crowell, Lorenzo M., 'Military Professionalism in a Colonial Context: The Madras Army circa 1832', *MAS*, vol. 24, no. 2 (1990).

———, 'Logistics in the Madras Army circa 1830', *War & Society*, vol. 10, no. 2 (1992).

David, Saul, *The Indian Mutiny: 1857*, London: Viking, 2002.

Dawson III, Joseph G., ' "Zealous for Annexation": Volunteer Soldiering,

Military Government, and the Service of Colonel Alexander Doniphan in the Mexican-American War', *JSS*, vol. 19, no. 4 (1996).

Delgoda, Sinharaja Tammita, ' "Nabob, Historian and Orientalist", Robert Orme: The Life and Career of an East India Company Servant (1728–1801)', *JRAS*, vol. 2 (1992).

Desai, Z.A. and Begley, W.E. eds., *The Shah Jahan Nama of Inayat Khan*, tr. by A.R. Fuller, Delhi: Oxford University Press, 1990.

Dewey, Clive, 'Some Consequences of Military Expenditure in British India: The Case of Upper Sind Sagar Doab, 1849–1947', in idem., ed., *Arrested Development in India: The Historical Dimension*, New Delhi: Manohar, 1988.

Dinwiddy, J.R., 'The Early Nineteenth Century Campaign against Flogging in the Army', *EHR*, vol. 97 (1982).

Dodge, Theodore Ayrault, *Alexander*, 1890, reprint, New York: Da Capo Press, 1996.

Doorn, Jacques, van, 'Political Change and the Control of the Military: Some General Remarks', in idem., ed., *Military Profession and Military Regimes: Commitments and Conflicts*, The Hague/Paris: Mouton, 1969.

Ellinwood, DeWitt C., 'The Indian Soldier: The Indian Army and Change, 1914–18', in idem. and S.D. Pradhan, ed., *India and World War I*, New Delhi: Manohar, 1978.

———, 'Ethnicity in a Colonial Asian Army: British Policy, War, and the Indian Army, 1914–18', in idem. and Cynthia H. Enloe, eds., *Ethnicity and the Military in Asia*, New Brunswick/London: Transaction Books, 1981.

———, 'The Indian soldier: Ellinwood, DeWitt, C. Jr., *Between Two Worlds: A Rajput officer in the Indian Army, 1905-21: Based on the Diary of Amar Singh*, Boulder: Hamilton Books, 2005.

Englander, David and Osborne, James, 'Jack Tommy and Henry Dobb: The Armed Forces and the Working Class', *Historical Journal*, vol. 21, no. 3 (1978).

Englander, David, 'Mutinies and Military Morale', in Hew Strachan, ed., *The Oxford Illustrated History of the First World War*, Oxford: Oxford University Press, 1998.

Enloe, Cynthia H., *Ethnic Soldiers: State Security in Divided Societies*, Harmondsworth, Middlesex: Penguin, 1980.

———, 'Ethnicity in the Evolution of Asia's Armed Bureaucracies', in idem. and DeWitt C. Ellinwood, eds., *Ethnicity and the Military in Asia*, New Brunswick/London: Transaction Books, 1981.

Farrell, Theo, 'Figuring out Fighting Organizations: The New Organizational Analysis in Strategic Studies', *JSS*, vol. 19, no. 1 (1996).

Farwell, Byron, *Queen Victoria's Little Wars*, 1973, reprint, Hertfordshire: Wordsworth, 1999.

———, *Armies of the Raj: From the Great Indian Mutiny to Independence, 1858–1947*, 1989, reprint, London: Viking, 1990.

Featherstone, Donald, *At Them with the Bayonet: The First Sikh War*, London: Jarrolds, 1968.

Ferro, Marc, 'The Russian Soldier in 1917: Undisciplined, Patriotic, and Revolutionary', *Slavic Review*, vol. 30, no. 3 (1971).

Fields, Lanny Bruce, 'Ethnicity in Tso Tsung-Tang's Armies: The Campaign in North-west China, 1867–80', in Cynthia H. Enloe and DeWitt C. Ellinwood, eds., *Ethnicity and the Military in Asia*, New Brunswick/London: Transaction Book, 1981.

Figes, Orlando, 'The Red Army and Mass Mobilization during the Russian Civil War: 1918–20', *Past and Present*, no. 129 (1990).

Finlay, Mark, 'Quackery and Cookery: Justus von Liebeg's Extract of Meat and the Theory of Nutrition in the Victorian Age', *Bull. Hist. Med.*, vol. 66 (1992).

Fitzpatrick, David, 'Militarism in Ireland, 1900–22', in Thomas Bartlett and Keith Jeffrey, ed., *A Military History of Ireland*, Cambridge: Cambridge University Press, 1996.

Fox, Richard G., *Lions of the Punjab: Culture in the Making*, New Delhi: Low Price Publications, 1990.

Fredericks, Pierce G., *The Sepoy and the Cossack*, London: W.H. Allen, 1972.

Freedman, Lawrence, ed., *Oxford Readers: War*, Oxford: Oxford University Press, 1994.

French, Craig, F., 'The Fashioning of Esprit de Corps in the 51st Highland Division from St Valery to El Alamein', *JSAHR*, vol. 77, no. 312 (1999).

Fuller, William C., *Civil-Military Conflict in Imperial Russia, 1881–1914*, Princeton/New Jersey: Princeton University Press, 1985.

Garland, David, *Punishment and Modern Society: A Study in Social Theory*, Oxford: Clarendon Press, 1990.

Gates, David, 'The Transformation of the Army, 1783–1815', in David Chandler and Ian Beckett, eds., *The Oxford Illustrated History of the British Army*, Oxford: Oxford University Press, 1994.

Gaylor, John, *Sons of John Company: The Indian and Pakistan Armies, 1903–91*, 1992, reprint, New Delhi: Lancer International, 1993.

Gilbert, Arthur N., 'Military and Civilian Justice in Eighteenth-century England: An Assessment', *JBS*, vol. 17, no. 2 (1978).

Gommans, Jos, 'Indian Warfare and Afghan Innovation during the Eighteenth Century', *SIH*, vol. 11, no. 2 (1995).

———, *The Rise of the Indo-Afghan Empire, c. 1710–80*, Leiden: E.J. Brill, 1995.

Gordon, Stewart, 'The Limited Adoption of European-style Military Forces by Eighteenth-century Rulers in India', *IESHR*, vol. 35, no. 3 (1998).

Greenhut, Jeffrey, 'The Imperial Reserve: The Indian Corps on the Western Front, 1914–15', *JICH*, vol. 12, no. 1 (1983).

————, 'Sahib and Sepoy: An Inquiry into the Relationship between the British Officers and the Native Soldiers of the British Indian Army', *Military Affairs*, vol. XLVIII, no. 1 (1984).

Gregory Jr., Stanford W., 'Towards a Situated Description of Cohesion and Disintegration in the American Army', *Armed Forces and Society*, vol. 3, no. 3 (1977).

Griffith, Paddy, *Military Thought in the French Army: 1815–51*, Manchester/New York: Manchester University Press, 1989.

Haas, Jonathan and Winifred Creamer, 'Warfare among the Pueblos: Myth, History, and Ethnography', *Ethnohistory*, vol. 44, no. 2 (1997).

Hackett, General John, *The Profession of Arms*, 1983, reprint, London: Sidgwick & Jackson, 1984.

Hall, Edith, 'Asia Unmanned: Images of Victory in Classical Athens', in John Rich and Graham Shipley, ed., *War and Society in the Greek World*, 1993, reprint, London/New York: Routledge, 1995.

Handley, Matthew, ' "Help Us to Secure a Strong, Healthy, Prosperous and Peaceful Britain": The Social Arguments of the Campaign for Compulsory Military Service in Britain, 1899–1914', *CJH*, vol. 25, no. 2 (1995).

Hanham, H.J., 'Religion and Nationality in the Mid-Victorian Army', in M.R.D. Foot, ed., *War and Society: Historical Essays in Honour and Memory of J.R. Western, 1928–71*, London: Paul Elek, 1973.

Hanson, Victor Davis, *Warfare and Agriculture in Classical Greece*, 1983, reprint, Berkeley/Los Angeles: University of California Press, 1999.

————, 'The Ideology of Hoplite Battle, Ancient and Modern', in idem., ed., *Hoplites: The Classical Greek Battle Experience*, 1991, reprint, London: Routledge, 1993.

————, *Carnage and Culture: Landmark Battles in the Rise of Western Power*, New York: Doubleday, 2001.

Harrison, Mark, *Public Health in British India: Anglo-Indian Preventive Medicine, 1859–1914*, Cambridge: Cambridge University Press, 1994.

————, ' "The Tender Frame of Man": Disease, Climate, and Racial Difference in India and the West Indies, 1760–1860', *Bull. Hist. Med.*, vol. 70, no. 1 (1996).

————, 'Medicine and the Management of Modern Warfare', *History of Science*, vol. 30, no. 106 (1996).

————, 'Disease, Discipline and Dissent: The Indian Army in France and England, 1914–15', in idem., Roger Cooter and Steve Sturdy, eds., *Medicine and Modern Warfare*, Amsterdam-Atlanta, GA: Rodopi, 1999.

Hauser, William, 'The Will to Fight', in Sam C. Sarkesian, ed., *Combat Effectiveness: Cohesion, Stress and the Volunteer Military*, Beverly Hills/London: Sage, 1980.

Hayter, Tony, 'The Army and the First British Empire, 1714–83', in David

Chandler and Ian Beckett, eds., *The Oxford Illustrated History of the British Army*, Oxford: Oxford University Press, 1994.

Headrick, Daniel R., *The Tools of Empire: Technology and European Imperialism in the Nineteenth Century*, New York/Oxford: Oxford University Press, 1981.

Heathcote, T.A., *The Indian Army: The Garrison of British Imperial India, 1822–1922*, Newton Abbot/London: David & Charles, 1974.

———, *The Military in British India: The Development of British Land Forces in South Asia: 1600–1947*, Manchester/New York: Manchester University Press, 1995.

Herodotus, *The Persian Wars*, tr. by George Rawlinson, New York: The Modern Library, 1942.

Herwig, Holger H., *The First World War: Germany and Austria-Hungary, 1914–18*, London: Arnold, 1997.

Hoiberg, Anne, 'Military Staying Power', in Sam C. Sarkesian, ed., *Combat Effectiveness: Cohesion, Stress and the Volunteer Military*, Beverly Hills/London: Sage, 1980.

Holmes, Richard, 'Battle: The Experience of Modern Combat', in Charles Townshend, ed., *The Oxford Illustrated History of Modern War*, Oxford/New York: Oxford University Press, 1997.

Hooper, Nicholas and Matthew Bennett, *Cambridge Illustrated Atlas of Warfare: The Middle Ages, 768–1487*, Cambridge: Cambridge University Press, 1996.

Hoover, James W., 'The Recruitment of the Bengal Army: Beyond the Myth of Zamindar's Son', *Indo-British Review*, vol. 21, no. 2 (1996).

Howard, Michael, *The Franco-Prussian War: The German Invasion of France, 1870–71*, 1961, reprint, London/New York: Methuen, 1979.

———, 'Colonial Wars and European Wars', in J.A. de Moor and H.L. Wesseling, ed., *Imperialism and War: Essays on Colonial Wars in Asia and Africa*, Leiden: E.J. Brill, 1989.

———, 'Leadership in the British Army in the Second World War: Some Personal Observations', in G.D. Sheffield, ed., *Leadership and Command: The Anglo-American Military Experience Since 1861*, London: Brassey's, 1997.

Hutt, Michael, 'A Hero or Traitor? Representations of the Gurkha Soldier in Modern Nepali Literature', *South Asia Research*, vol. 9 (1989).

Irvine, William, *The Army of the Indian Moghuls: Its Organization and Administration*, 1903, reprint, Delhi: Low Price Publications, 1994.

James, Lawrence, *Mutiny in the British and Commonwealth Forces: 1797–1956*, London: Buchan & Enright Publishers, 1987.

Jessup, John E., 'The Soviet Armed Forces in the Great Patriotic War, 1941–45', in Alan R. Millet and Williamson Murray, eds., *Military Effectiveness: The Second World War*, vol. 3, Boston: Allen & Unwin, 1988.

Jones, Colin, 'The Welfare of the French Foot Soldiers', *History*, vol. LXV (1980).

————, 'The Military Revolution and the Professionalization of the French Army under the *Ancien Regime*', in Clifford J. Rogers, ed., *The Military Revolution Debate: Readings on the Military Transformation of Early Modern Europe*, Colorado/Boulder: Westview Press, 1995.

Jones, Ellen, *Red Army and Society: A Sociology of the Soviet Military*, Boston: Allen & Unwin, 1985.

Kantak, M.R., *The First Anglo-Maratha War, 1774–83: A Military Study of Major Battles*, Bombay: Popular Prakashan, 1993.

Kanya-Forstner, A.S., 'The French Marines and the Conquest of the Western Sudan: 1880–99', in J.A. de Moor and H.L. Wesseling, eds., *Imperialism and War: Essays on Colonial Wars in Asia and Africa*, Leiden: E.J. Brill, 1989.

Kaul, Vivien Ashima, 'Sepoys' Links with Society: A Study of the Bengal Army, 1858–95', in P.S. Gupta and Anirudh Deshpande, eds., *The British Raj and Its Indian Armed Forces: 1857–1939*, New Delhi: Oxford University Press, 2002.

Keegan, John, 'Regimental Ideology', in Geoffrey Best and Andrew Wheatcroft, eds., *War, Economy and the Military Mind*, London: Croom Helm, 1976. *The Face of Battle: A Study of Agincourt, Waterloo and the Somme*, 1976, reprint, Harmondsworth, Middlesex: Penguin, 1978.

————, 'Inventing Military Traditions', in Chris Wrigley, ed., *Warfare, Diplomacy and Politics: Essays in Honour of A.J.P. Taylor*, London: Hamish Hamilton, 1986.

————, *The Mask of Command*, 1987, reprint, New York: Penguin, 1988.

————, *The Price of Admiralty: The Evolution of Naval Warfare*, 1988, reprint, New York: Penguin, 1989.

————, *A History of Warfare*, 1993, reprint, New York: Vintage, 1994.

————, *War and Our World: The Reith Lectures 1998*, 1998, reprint, London: Pimlico, 1999.

Kiernan, V.G., 'Conscription and Society in Europe before the War of 1914–18', in M.R.D. Foot, ed., *War and Society: Historical Essays in Honour and Memory of J.R. Western, 1928–71*, London: Paul Elek, 1973.

————, 'Colonial Africa and Its Armies', in Brian Bond and Ian Roy, eds., *War and Society: A Yearbook of Military History*, vol. 2, London: Croom Helm, 1977.

————, *European Empires from Conquest to Collapse, 1815–1960*, Bungay, Suffolk: Fontana, 1982.

Killingray, David, 'Colonial Warfare in West Africa: 1870–1914', in J.A de Moor and H.L. Wesseling, eds., *Imperialism and War: Essays on Colonial Wars in Asia and Africa*, Leiden: E.J. Brill, 1989.

————, 'The Rod of Empire: The Debate over Corporal Punishment in the British African Colonial Forces, 1888–1946', *Journal of African History*, vol. 35 (1994).

————, 'Gender Issues and African Colonial Armies', in idem., and David Omissi, eds., *Guardians of Empire: The Armed Forces of the Colonial*

Powers c. 1700–1964, Manchester/New York: Manchester University Press, 1999.

Kirk-Greene, Anthony A.H.M., ' "Damnosa Hereditas": Ethnic Ranking and the Martial Races Imperative in Africa', *Ethnic and Racial Studies,* vol. 3, no. 4 (1980).

Kolff, Dirk H.A., 'The End of an *Ancien Regime*: Colonial War in India, 1798–1818', in J.A. de Moor and H.L. Wesseling, eds., *Imperialism and War: Essays on Colonial Wars in Asia and Africa,* Leiden: E.J. Brill, 1989.

———, *Naukar, Rajput and Sepoy: The Ethnohistory of the Military Labour Market in Hindustan, 1450–1850,* Cambridge: Cambridge University Press, 1990.

Lal, K.S., 'The Striking Power of the Army of the Sultanate', *Journal of Indian History,* vol. LV (1977).

Latter, Edwin, 'The Indian Army in Mesopotamia, 1914–18', *JSAHR,* vol. LXXII, no. 291 (1994).

Lewy, Guenter, 'The American Experience in Vietnam', in Sam C. Sarkesian, ed., *Combat Effectiveness: Cohesion, Stress and the Volunteer Military,* Beverly Hills/ London: Sage, 1980.

Lieven, Anatol, *Chechnya: Tombstone of Russian Power,* New Haven: Yale University Press, 1998.

Lindner, R.P., 'Nomadism, Horses and Huns', *Past and Present,* no. 92 (1981).

Little, Roger W., 'Buddy Relations and Combat Performance', in Morris Janowitz, ed., *The New Military: Changing Patterns of Organization,* 1964, reprint, New York: W.W. Norton & Company, 1969.

Longer, V., *Red Coats to Olive Green: A History of the Indian Army, 1600–1974,* Bombay: Allied, 1974.

Lynn, John A., 'The History of Logistics and Supplying War', in idem., ed., *Feeding Mars: Logistics in Western Warfare from the Middle Ages to the Present,* Colorado /Boulder: Westview Press, 1993.

———, 'States in Conflict: 1661-73', in Geoffrey Parker, ed., *The Cambridge Illustrated History of Warfare: The Triumph of the West,* Cambridge: Cambridge University Press, 1995.

———, 'Nations in Arms: 1763–1815', in Geoffrey Parker, ed., *The Cambridge Illustrated History of Warfare: The Triumph of the West,* Cambridge: Cambridge University Press, 1995.

Macdonell, A.G., *Napoleon and His Marshalls,* 1934, reprint, London: Prion, 1996.

Machiavelli, Niccolo, *The Art of War,* 1965, reprint, tr. by Ellis Farneworth with an Introduction by Neal Wood, New York: Da Capo Press, 1990.

Mazumder, Rajit K., *The Indian Army and the Making of Punjab,* Delhi: Permanent Black, 2003.

Manstein, Field-Marshal Erich Von, *Lost Victories*, tr. by Anthony G. Powell, 1958, reprint, Dehradun: Natraj, n.d.

Mason, Philip, *A Matter of Honour: An Account of the Indian Army, Its Officers and Men*, 1974, reprint, Dehradun: EBD Publishers, 1988.

Maude, Colonel, F.N., Von Clausewitz, eds., *On War*, tr. by Col. J.J. Graham, London: Routledge & Keegan Paul, 1968.

McAlpin, Michelle, 'Price Movements and Fluctuations in Economic Activity (1860–1947)', in Dharma Kumar, ed., *The Cambridge Economic History of India, c.1757–c. 1970*, vol. 2, 1982, reprint, New Delhi: Orient Longman in association with Cambridge University Press, 1991.

Mehra, P.L., 'The Panipat Campaign', in Hari Ram Gupta, ed., *Marathas and Panipat*, Chandigarh: Punjab University Press, 1961.

Menezes, Lieutenant-General S.L., *Fidelity and Honour: The Indian Army from the Seventeenth to the Twenty-first Century*, New Delhi: Viking, 1993.

———, 'Race, Caste, Mutiny and Discipline in the Indian Army from its Origins to 1947', in Alan J. Guy and Peter B. Boyden, eds., *Soldiers of the Raj: The Indian Army, 1600–1947*, London: National Army Museum, 1997.

Messerchmidt, Manfred, 'German Military Law in the Second World War', in Wilhelm Deist, ed., *The German Military in the Age of Total War*, Leamington Spa: Berg, 1985.

Miege, J.L., 'The French Conquest of Morocco: The Early Period, 1901–11', in J.A. de Moor and H.L. Wesseling, eds., *Imperialism and War: Essays on Colonial Wars in Asia and Africa*, Leiden: E.J. Brill, 1989.

Miller, T., *Outline of Military Geography*, Cambridge: Cambridge University Press, 1900.

Mollo, Boris, *The Indian Army*, Poole/Dorset: Blandford Press, 1981.

Moor, J.A. de, 'Warmakers in the Archipelago: Dutch Expeditions in Nineteenth century Indonesia', in idem. and H.L. Wesseling, eds., *Imperialism and War: Essays on Colonial Wars in Asia and Africa*, Leiden: E.J. Brill 1989.

———, 'The Recruitment of Indonesian Soldiers for the Dutch Colonial Army, c. 1700–1950', in David Killingray and David Omissi, eds., *Guardians of Empire: The Armed Forces of the Colonial Powers c. 1700–1964*, Manchester/New York: Manchester University Press, 1999.

Moreman, T.R., 'The Arms Trade and the Northwest Frontier Pathan Tribes: 1890–1914', *JICH*, vol. 22, no. 2 (1994).

———, *The Army in India and the Development of Frontier Warfare: 1849–1947*, Basingstoke/London: Macmillan, 1998.

Mukherjee, Rudrangshu, *Awadh in Revolt, 1857–58: A Study of Popular Resistance*, Delhi: Oxford University Press, 1984.

———, ' "Satan let Loose Upon Earth": The Kanpur Massacres in India in the Revolt of 1857', *Past and Present*, no. 128 (1990).

————, 'The Sepoy Mutinies Revisited', in Mushirul Hasan and Narayani Gupta, eds., *India's Colonial Encounter: Essays in Memory of Eric Stokes*, New Delhi: Manohar, 1993.

Murray, W.A., 'The Industrialization of War: 1815–71', in G. Parker, ed., *The Cambridge Illustrated History of Warfare: The Triumph of the West*, Combridge: Cambridge University Press, 1995.

————, 'Towards World War: 1871–1914', in Parker, ed., *The Cambridge Illustrated History of Warfare: The Triumph of the West*, Cambridge: Cambridge University Press, 1995.

Omissi, David, 'Britain, the Assyrians and the Iraq Levies: 1919–32', *JICH*, vol. 17, no. 3 (1989).

————, ' "Martial Races": Ethnicity and Security in Colonial India, 1858–1939', *War & Society*, vol. 9, no. 1 (1991).

————, *The Sepoy and the Raj: The Indian Army, 1860–1940*, Basingstoke/London: Macmillan, 1994.

Overy, Richard, *Russia's War*, 1997, reprint, London: Penguin, 1998.

Pant, Rashmi, 'The Cognitive Status of Caste in Colonial Ethnography: A Review of Some Literature on the North-west Provinces and Oudh', *IESHR*, vol. 24, no. 2 (1987).

Parker, Geoffrey, *The Army of Flanders and the Spanish Road: 1567-1659, The Logistics of Spanish Victory and Defeat in the Low Countries' Wars*, 1972, reprint, Cambridge: Cambridge University Press, 1995.

————, *The Military Revolution: Military Innovation and the Rise of the West, 1500–1800*, Cambridge: Cambridge University Press, 1988.

————, 'Dynastic War: 1494–1660', in idem, ed., *The Cambridge Illustrated History of Warfare: The Triumph of the West*, Cambridge: Cambridge University Press, 1995.

————, 'The "Military Revolution, 1560–1660"—A Myth', in Clifford J. Rogers, ed., *The Military Revolution Debate: Readings on the Military Transformation of Early Modern Europe*, Colorado/Boulder: Westview Press, 1995.

————, 'In Defence of The Military Revolution', in Clifford J. Rogers, ed., *The Military Revolution Debate: Readings on the Military Transformation of Early Modern Europe*, Colorado/Boulder: Westview Press, 1995.

Parsons, Timothy, 'All *Askaris* are Family Men: Sex, Domesticity and Discipline in the King's African Rifles, 1902–64', in David Killingray and David Omissi, eds., *Guardians of Empire: The Armed Forces of the Colonial Powers c. 1700–1964*, Manchester/New York: Manchester University Press, 1999.

Pearton, Maurice, *The Knowledgeable State: Diplomacy, War and Technology since 1830*, London: Burnett Books, 1982.

Peers, Douglas M., ' "The Habitual Nobility of Being": British Officers and the Social Composition of the Bengal Army in the Early Nineteenth Century', *MAS*, vol. 25, no. 3 (1991).

————,'Contours of the Garrison State: The Army and the Historiography of Early Nineteenth-century India', in Nancy G. Cassels, ed., *Orientalism, Evangelicalism and the Military Cantonment in Early Nineteenth-century India*, Lewiston/Queenstown: The Edwin Mellen Press, 1991.

————, 'Sepoys, Soldiers and the Lash: Race, Caste and Army Discipline in India, 1802–50', *JICH*, vol. 23, no. 2 (1995).

————, *Between Mars and Mammon: Colonial Armies and the Garrison State in India, 1819–35*, London: I.B. Tauris, 1995.

————, 'Imperial Vice: Sex, Drink and the Health of British Troops in North-Indian Cantonments, 1800–58', in David Killingray and David Omissi, eds., *Guardians of Empire: The Armed Forces of the Colonial Powers c. 1700–1964*, Manchester/New York: Manchester University Press, 1999.

Pemble, John, *The Invasion of Nepal: John Company at War*, Oxford: Clarendon Press, 1971.

————, 'Resources and Techniques in the Second Maratha War', *Historical Journal,* vol. 19, no. 2 (1976).

Perry, F.W., *The Commonwealth Armies: Manpower and Organization in Two World Wars*, Manchester: Manchester University Press, 1988.

Philips, C.H., ed., *The Correspondence of Lord William Cavendish Bentinck, Governor General of India: 1832–35*, vol. 2, Oxford: Oxford University Press, 1977.

Pinch, William R., 'Who was Himmat Bahadur? Gosains, Rajputs and the British in Bundelkhand, *ca.* 1800', *IESHR*, vol. 35, no. 3 (1998).

Porch, Douglas, *The French Foreign Legion: A Complete History of the Legendary Fighting Force*, 1991, reprint, New York: Harper Perennial, 1992.

Posen, Barry, R., *The Sources of Military Doctrine: France, Britain and Germany between the World Wars*, Ithaca/London: Cornell University Press, 1984.

Pradhan, Kumar, *The Gorkha Conquests: The Process and Consequences of the Unification of Nepal with Particular References to Eastern Nepal*, Calcutta: Oxford University Press, 1991.

Prebble, John, *Mutiny: Highland Regiments in Revolt, 1743–1804*, 1975, reprint, Harmondsworth, Middlesex: Penguin, 1977.

Preston, Adrian, 'Wolseley, The Khartoum Relief Expedition and the Defence of India', *JICH*, vol. 6, no. 3 (1978).

Qaisar, A. Jan, 'Horsehoeing in Mughal India', *Indian Journal of History of Science*, vol. 27, no. 2 (1992).

Raman, Kartik Kalyan, 'Utilitarianism and the Criminal Law in Colonial

India: A Study of the Practical Limits of Utilitarian Jurisprudence', *MAS*, vol. 28 (1994).

Ranger, Terence, 'The Invention of Tradition in Colonial Africa', in idem., and Eric Hobsbawm, eds., *The Invention of Tradition*, 1983, reprint, Cambridge: Canto 1985.

Rapoport, Anatol, Carl Von Clausewitz, eds., *On War*, tr. by J.J. Graham, 1908, reprint, London: Penguin, 1982.

Ray, R.K., 'Race, Religion and Realm: The Political Theory of "The Reigning Indian Crusade", 1857', in Mushirul Hasan and Narayani Gupta, eds., *India's Colonial Encounter: Essays in Honour of Eric Stokes*, New Delhi: Manohar, 1993.

Razzell, P.E., 'Social Origins of Officers in the Indian and British Home Army: 1758–1962', *The British Journal of Sociology*, vol. 14 (1963).

Reid, Brian Holden and John White, ' "A Mob of Stragglers and Cowards": Desertion from the Union and Confederate Armies', *JSS*, vol. 8 (1985).

Robb, Peter, 'Introduction: South Asia and the Concept of Race', in idem., ed., *The Concept of Race in South Asia*, Delhi: Oxford University Press, 1995.

Roberts, Michael, 'The Military Revolution: 1560–1660', in Clifford J. Rogers, ed., *The Military Revolution Debate: Readings on the Military Transformation of Early Modern Europe*, Colorado/Boulder: Westview Press, 1995.

Robson, Brian, 'The Eden Commission and the Reform of the Indian Army, 1879–95', *JSAHR*, vol. LX, no. 241 (1982).

Rogers, Clifford J., 'The Military Revolutions of the Hundred Years War', in idem, ed., *The Military Revolution Debate: Readings on the Military Transformation of Early Modern Europe*, Colorado/Boulder: Westview Press, 1995.

Rose, Elihu, 'The Anatomy of Mutiny', *Armed Forces and Society*, vol. 8 (1982).

Rosen, Stephen Peter, *Societies and Military Power: India and Its Armies*, Delhi: Oxford University Press, 1996.

Rothenberg, Gunther E., 'The Austrian Army in the Age of Metternich', *Journal of Modern History*, vol. 40 (1968).

Roy, Ian, 'Towards the Standing Army, 1485–1660', in David Chandler and Ian Beckett, eds., *The Oxford Illustrated History of the British Army*, Oxford: Oxford University Press, 1994.

Roy, Kaushik, 'The Historiography of the Colonial Indian Army', *SIH*, vol. 12, no. 2 (1996).

———, 'Recruitment Doctrines of the Colonial Indian Army: 1859–1913', *IESHR*, vol. 34, no. 3 (1997).

———, 'Beyond the Martial Race Theory: A Historiographical Assessment of Recruitment in the British Indian Army', *CHJ*, vol. 21 & 22 (1999–2000).

————, 'Mars in Indian History', *SIH*, vol. 16, no. 2 (2000).

————, 'The Construction of Regiments in the Indian Army: 1859–1913', *War in History*, vol. 8, no. 2 (2001).

————, 'Coercion through Leniency: British Manipulation of the Courts-Martial System in the Post-Mutiny Indian Army, 1859–1913', *JMH*, vol. 65, no. 4 (2001).

————, 'Feeding the Leviathan: Supplying the British-Indian Army, 1859–1913', *JSAHR*, vol. 80, no. 322 (2002).

————, 'Logistics and the Construction of Loyalty: The Welfare Mechanism in the Indian Army, 1859–1913', in P.S. Gupta and Anirudh Deshpande, eds., *The British Raj and Its Indian Armed Forces: 1857-1939*, New Delhi: Oxford University Press, 2002.

————, 'Mars Defeated? Conventional Militaries in Unconventional Warfare', *Contemporary India*, vol. 2, no. 2 (2003)

————, *From Hydaspes to Kargil: A History of Warfare in India from 326 BC to AD 1999*, New Delhi: Manohar, 2004.

————, 'Military Synthesis in South Asia: Armies, Warfare, and Indian Society, *c.* 1740–1849', *JMH*, vol. 69 (2005).

————, *India's Historic Battles: From Alexander the Great to Kargil*, New Delhi: Permanent Black, 2004.

————, 'Space the Rod, spoil the Soldier? Crime and Punishment in the Army of India', *JSAHR*, vol. 84, no. 337 (2006).

Roy, Tapti, *The Politics of a Popular Uprising: Bundelkhand in 1857*, Delhi: Oxford University Press, 1994.

Said, Edward, W., *Orientalism: Western Conceptions of the Orient*, 1978, reprint, New Delhi: Penguin, 2001.

Sarkar, Jadunath, *Fall of the Mughal Empire, 1771–88*, vol. 3, 1938, reprint, New Delhi: Orient Longman, 1991.

————, *Military History of India*, 1960, reprint, Bombay/New Delhi: Orient Longman, 1970.

Sarkar, Jagadish Narayan, *The Military Despatches of a Seventeenth-century Indian General*, Calcutta: Scientific Book Agency, 1969.

————, *The Art of War in Medieval India*, New Delhi: Munshiram Manoharlal, 1984.

Satre, Lowell J., 'St John Brodrick and Army Reform, 1901–03', *JBS*, vol. 15, no. 2 (1976).

Savage, Paul L. and Richard A. Gabriel, *Crisis in Command: Mismanagement in the United States Army*, 1978, reprint, New Delhi: Himalayan Books, 1986.

Saxena, K.M.L., *The Military System of India, 1850-1900*, New Delhi: Sterling, 1974.

————, *The Military System of India: 1900-39*, New Delhi: Sterling, 1999.

Saxena, R.K., *The Army of the Rajputs: A Study of Eighteenth-century Rajputana*, Udaipur: Saroj Prakashan, 1989.

Scott, James C., *Weapons of the Weak: Everyday Forms of Peasant Resistance*, New Haven: Yale University Press, 1985.

Scott, William F., and Harriet Scott, *The Armed Forces of the Soviet Union*, 1979, reprint, Boulder: Westview Press, 1984.

Segal, David R. et al., 'The Changing American Soldier: Work-related Attitudes of US Army Personnel in World War II and the 1970s', *American Journal of Sociology*, vol. 85, no. 1 (1979).

Sen, S.N., *The Military System of the Marathas*, 1928, reprint, Calcutta: K.P. Bagchi, 1979.

Sharma, Lieutenant-Colonel Gautam, *Indian Army Through the Ages*, Bombay: Allied, 1979.

Sharma, Ravindra Kumar, 'The Military System of the Mewar (Udaipur) State (*ca.* 800 to 1947)', *Central Asiatic Journal*, vol. 30 (1986).

Sheffield, G.D., '*Blitzkrieg* and Attrition: Land Operations in Europe, 1914–45', in idem. and Colin McInnes, eds., *Warfare in the Twentieth Century*, London: Unwin Hyman, 1988.

Sheffield, G.D., 'Introduction: Command, Leadership and the Anglo-American Military Experience', in idem, ed., *Leadership and Command: The Anglo-American Military Experience Since 1861*, London: Brassey's, 1997.

Showalter, Dennis, E., 'Army and Society in Imperial Germany: The Pains of Modernization', *Journal of Contemporary History*, vol. 18 (1983).

———, 'Caste, Skill, and Training: The Evolution of Cohesion in European Armies from the Middle Ages to the Sixteenth Century', *JMH*, vol. 57, no. 3 (1993).

Singh, M.P., 'Origin of Summary Court Martial', *JUSII*, vol. CII, no. 427 (1972).

Singha, Radhika, ' "Providential Circumstances": The Thuggee Campaign of the 1830s and Legal Innovation', *MAS*, vol. 27 (1993).

———, 'Settle, Mobilize, Verify: Identification Practices in Colonial India' *SIH*, vol. 16, New Series, no. 2 (2000).

Sinha, B.K., *The Pindaris: 1798–1818*, Calcutta: Bookland, 1971.

Skelley, Allan Ramsay, *The Victorian Army at Home: The Recruitment and Terms and Conditions of the British Regular, 1859–99*, London: Croom Helm, 1977.

Speidel, Michael, P., *Riding for Caesar: The Roman Emperors' Horse Guard*, London: Batsford, 1994.

Spiers, Edward M., *The Army and Society: 1815–1914*, Harlow/London: Longman, 1980.

———, 'The Late Victorian Army, 1868–1914', in David Chandler and Ian Beckett, eds., *The Oxford Illustrated History of the British Army*, Oxford: Oxford University Press, 1994.

Steiner, E.E., 'Separating the Soldier from the Citizen: Ideology and Criticism of Corporal Punishment in the British Armies, 1790–1815', *Social History*, vol. 8, no. 1 (1983).

Steppler, G.A., 'British Military Law, Discipline, and the Conduct of Regimental Courts Martial in the Later Eighteenth Century', *EHR*, vol. 102 (1987).

Stokes, Eric, *The English Utilitarians and India*, 1959, reprint, Delhi: Oxford University Press, 1982.

Stolfi, Russel H.S., 'Chance in History: The Russian Winter of 1941–42', *History*, vol. LXV. 1980.

Stone, Norman, 'Army and Society in the Habsburg Monarchy, 1900–14', *Past and Present*, no. 33 (1966).

Strachan, Hew, *European Armies and the Conduct of War*, 1983, reprint, London: Routledge, 1993.

———, *Wellington's Legacy: The Reform of the British Army, 1830–54*, Manchester: Manchester University Press, 1984.

———, 'Liberalism and Conscription: 1789–1919', in idem, ed., *The British Army, Manpower and Society into the Twenty-first Century*, London: Frank Cass, 2000.

Streets, Heather, *Martial Races*, Manchester: Manchester University Press, 2004.

Streusand, Douglas, *The Formation of the Mughal Empire*, Delhi: Oxford University Press, 1989.

Subrahmanyam, Sanjay, 'Warfare and State Finance in Woodeyar Mysore, 1724–25: A Missionary Perspective', *IESHR*, vol. 26, no. 2 (1989).

Sundaram, Chandar S., 'Preventing "Idleness": The Maharajah of Cooch Behar's Proposal for Officer Commissions in the British Army for the Sons of Indian Princes and Gentlemen, 1897–98', *South Asia*, vol. 18, no. 1 (1995).

———, ' "Martial" Indian Aristocrats and the Military System of the Raj: The Imperial Cadet Corps, 1900–14', *JICH*, vol. 25, no. 3 (1997).

———, 'Reviving a "Dead Letter": Military Indianization and the Ideology of Anglo-India, 1885–91', in P.S. Gupta and Anirudh Deshpande, eds., *The British Raj and Its Indian Armed Forces: 1857–1939*, New Delhi: Oxford University Press, 2002.

Talbot, Ian, 'British Rule in Punjab, 1849–1947', *JICH*, vol. 20, no. 2 (1991).

Tallett, Frank, *War and Society in Early Modern Europe, 1495–1715*, 1992, reprint, London: Routledge, 1997.

Taylor, P.J.O. (General Editor), *A Companion to the Indian Mutiny of 1857*, Delhi: Oxford University Press, 1996.

———, *What Really Happened During the Mutiny: A Day to Day Account of the Major Events of 1857–59 in India*, Delhi: Oxford University Press, 1997.

Teltscher, Kate, *India Inscribed: European and British Writing on India, 1600–1800*, Delhi: Oxford University Press, 1995.

Tolen, Rachel J., 'Colonizing and Transforming the Criminal Tribesmen; The Salvation Army in India', *American Ethnologist*, vol. 18, no. 1 (1991).

342   *Bibliography*

Tomes, Nancy, 'The Private Side of Public Health: Sanitary Science, Domestic Hygiene, and the Germ Theory, 1870–1900', *Bull. Hist. Med.*, vol. 64, no. 4 (1990).

Treadgold, Warren, *Byzantium and Its Army: 284–1081*, Stanford/California: Stanford University Press, 1995.

Trench, Charles Chenevix, *The Indian Army and the King's Enemies: 1900–47*, London: Thames & Hudson, 1988.

Trevor-Roper, Hugh, 'The Invention of Tradition: The Highland Tradition of Scotland', in Eric Hobsbawm and Terence Ranger, eds., *The Invention of Tradition*, 1983, reprint, Cambridge: Canto, 1985.

Trivedi, K.K., 'The Share of Mansabdars in State Revenue Resources: A Study of the Maintenance of Animals', *IESHR*, vol. 24, no. 4 (1987).

Trustram, Myna, *Women of the Regiment: Marriage and the Victorian Army*, Cambridge: Cambridge University Press, 1984.

Tzu, Sun, *The Art of War*, tr. by Yuan Shibing, 1990, reprint, Hertfordshire: Penguin, 1993.

Tzu II, Sun, *The Lost Art of War*, tr. with a Commentary by Thomas Cleary, New York: Harper Collins, 1996.

Vandervort, Bruce, *Wars of Imperial Conquest in Africa: 1830–1914*, Bloomington/Indianapolis: Indiana University Press, 1998.

Visaria, Leela and Pravin Visaria, 'Population: 1757–1947', in D. Kumar, ed., *The Cambridge Economic History of India: c. 1757–1970*, vol. 2, 1982, reprint, New Delhi: Orient Longman in association with the Cambridge University Press, 1991.

Vyronis Jr., Speros, 'Byzantine and Turkish Societies and Their Sources of Manpower', in V.J. Parry and M.E. Yapp, eds., *War, Technology and Society in the Middle East*, London: Oxford University Press, 1975.

Warren, Alan, *Waziristan, The Faqir of Ipi and the Indian Army: The North West Frontier Revolt of 1936–37*, Karachi: Oxford University Press, 2000.

Weller, Jac, *Wellington in India*, London: Longman, 1972.

Wesseling, H.L., 'Colonial Wars: An Introduction', in idem., and J.A. de Moor, ed., *Imperialism and War: Essays on Colonial Wars in Asia and Africa*, Leiden: E.J. Brill, 1989.

Wickremesekera, Channa, *'Best Black Troops in the World': British Perception and the Making of the Sepoy, 1746–1805*, New Delhi: Manohar, 2002.

Wilson, Constance M., 'Burmese-Karen Warfare, 1840–50: A Thai View', in DeWitt C. Ellinwood and Cynthia H. Enloe, eds., *Ethnicity and the Military in Asia*, New Brunswick/London: Transaction Books, 1981.

Yadava, B.N.S., 'Chivalry and Warfare', in Jos J.L. Gommans and Dirk H.A. Kolff, eds., *Warfare and Weaponry in South Asia: 1000–1800*, New Delhi: Oxford University Press, 2001.

Yang, Anand A., *The Limited Raj: Agrarian Relations in Colonial India, Saran District, 1793–1920*, Delhi: Oxford University Press, 1989.

Yapp, M.E., 'British Perceptions of the Russian Threat to India', *MAS*, vol. 21, no. 4 (1987).

Yong, Tan Tai, 'Maintaining the Military Districts: Civil-Military Integration and the District Soldiers' Boards in the Punjab, 1919–30', *MAS*, vol. 28, no. 4 (1994).

————, 'Sepoys and the Colonial State: Punjab and the Military Base of the Indian Army, 1849–1900', in P.S. Gupta and Anirudh Deshpande, eds., *The British Raj and Its Indian Armed Forces: 1857–1939*, New Delhi: Oxford University Press, 2002.

————, *The Garrison State: The Military Government and Society in Colonial Punjab, 1849–1947*, New Delhi, Sage, 2005.

Zaidi, S. Inayat Ali, 'Ordinary Kachawaha Troopers Serving the Mughal Empire: Composition and Structure of the Contingents of the Kachawaha Nobles', *SIH*, vol. 2, no. 1 (1980).

————, 'Rozindar Troopers under Sawai Jai Singh of Jaipur (AD 1700–43)', *Indian Historical Review*, vol. 10, 1983–4.

UNPUBLISHED PAPERS

Arnold, David, ' "Criminal Tribes" and "Martial Races": Crime and Social Control in Colonial India', Postgraduate seminar paper, CCSH/ 84/5, Institute of Commonwealth Studies, University of London.

Dewey, Clive, 'Racism and Realism: The Theory of the Martial Castes', University of Leicester.

Index